TRAGEDY AND ARCHAIC GREEK THOUGHT

Tragedy and Archaic Greek Thought

Editor

Douglas Cairns

Contributors

William Allan, Douglas Cairns, P. E. Easterling,
Fritz-Gregor Herrmann, Vayos Liapis, Michael Lloyd,
Richard Seaford, Alan H. Sommerstein

The Classical Press of Wales

First published in 2013 by
The Classical Press of Wales
15 Rosehill Terrace, Swansea SA1 6JN
Tel: +44 (0)1792 458397
www.classicalpressofwales.co.uk

Distributor
Oxbow Books,
10 Hythe Bridge Street,
Oxford OX1 2EW
Tel: +44 (0)1865 241249
Fax: +44 (0)1865 794449

Distributor in the United States of America
The David Brown Book Co.
PO Box 511, Oakville, CT 06779
Tel: +1 (860) 945–9329
Fax: +1 (860) 945–9468

© 2013 The authors

All rights reserved. No part of this publication may be reproduced, stored in a retrieval system, or transmitted, in any form or by any means, electronic, mechanical, photocopying, recording or otherwise, without the prior permission of the publisher.

ISBN 978-1-905125-57-9

A catalogue record for this book is available from the British Library.

Typeset, printed and bound in the UK by Gomer Press, Llandysul, Ceredigion, Wales

---

The Classical Press of Wales, an independent venture, was founded in 1993, initially to support the work of classicists and ancient historians in Wales and their collaborators from further afield. More recently it has published work initiated by scholars internationally. While retaining a special loyalty to Wales and the Celtic countries, the Press welcomes scholarly contributions from all parts of the world.

The symbol of the Press is the Red Kite. This bird, once widespread in Britain, was reduced by 1905 to some five individuals confined to a small area known as 'The Desert of Wales' – the upper Tywi valley. Geneticists report that the stock was saved from terminal inbreeding by the arrival of one stray female bird from Germany. After much careful protection, the Red Kite now thrives – in Wales and beyond.

CONTENTS

		Page
Preface		vii
Introduction: Archaic Thought and Tragic Interpretation *Douglas Cairns* (University of Edinburgh)		ix
1	*Atē* in Aeschylus *Alan H. Sommerstein* (University of Nottingham)	1
2	Aeschylus, Herakleitos, and Pythagoreanism *Richard Seaford* (University of Exeter)	17
3	Eteocles' Decision in Aeschylus' *Seven against Thebes* *Fritz-Gregor Herrmann* (Swansea University)	39
4	Creon the Labdacid: Political Confrontation and the Doomed *Oikos* in Sophocles' *Antigone* *Vayos Liapis* (Open University of Cyprus)	81
5	Divine and Human Action in the *Oedipus Tyrannus* *Douglas Cairns*	119
6	'Archaic' Guilt in Sophocles' *Oedipus Tyrannus* and *Oedipus at Colonus* *William Allan* (University of Oxford)	173
7	Sophocles and the Wisdom of Silenus: A Reading of *Oedipus at Colonus* 1211–48 *P. E. Easterling* (University of Cambridge)	193
8	The Mutability of Fortune in Euripides *Michael Lloyd* (University College Dublin)	205
Bibliography		227
Indices		253

PREFACE

This volume has its genesis in a conference held in Edinburgh in June 2008 and organized by myself and Michael Lurje. I am grateful to Michael for his role in making the conference a success and to the School of History, Classics, and Archaeology (Edinburgh), the Classical Association, and the Society for the Promotion of Hellenic Studies for financial support. Several of the papers delivered at the conference could, for various reasons, not be published here, but the conference itself was greatly enriched by the participation of Alex Garvie, Lutz Käppel, Michael Lurje, Scott Scullion, Simon Trépanier, and Robert Zaborowski. Alex Garvie's paper was incorporated into the introduction to his edition of Aeschylus' *Persae* (Garvie 2009), and Simon Trépanier's appeared as part of a larger study in J. N. Bremmer and A. Erskine (eds), *The Gods of Ancient Greece: Identities and transformations* (Edinburgh Leventis Studies 5, Edinburgh 2010) 273–317. These discussions are a valuable complement to the papers collected here, all of which have been thoroughly revised for publication together in their current form.

Contributors have been allowed their preferences in the spelling of Greek names and transliteration of Greek words, and so there is variation between chapters in that regard (e.g. Tiresias in one chapter, Teiresias in another; *hybris*, but also *hubris*). References to ancient authors and works are for the most part those given in LSJ, with occasional (but wholly familiar) deviations and expansions in the interests of intelligibility.

For their assistance in the production and editing of this volume I am greatly indebted to Anton Powell, to Louise Jones of Gomer Press, typesetter, to John Holton for his help with the Index Locorum, and to my Research Assistant during my stay at Florida State University in Spring 2012, Travis King. My thoughts on the *Antigone*, some of which are reflected in the Introduction to this work, were greatly inspired by the FSU graduate class of which Travis was a member. To read Sophocles' play with that lively and industrious group of committed young scholars was one of the great pleasures of my career. I am most grateful to them for their work and their welcome, and to my colleagues in Classics at FSU for inviting me and for making my stay such a rewarding experience.

DLC
Edinburgh
June 2012

INTRODUCTION: ARCHAIC THOUGHT AND TRAGIC INTERPRETATION

Douglas Cairns

1. General

The impetus behind this volume is the claim that the understanding of archaic Greek thought is an indispensable aspect of the interpretation of Greek tragedy to which researchers must now return. Since the 1980s, the focus of much scholarly discussion of Greek tragedy has been on the plays' contemporary civic, political, ritual, and performative contexts.[1] This shift was essential and has proved salutary, yielding many enduring insights not only into tragedy's contexts, but also into its content. Behind this movement lay a clear sense that the traditional emphasis on the interpretation of the primary intellectual, religious, and ethical aspects of tragedy had, for the meantime, run its course. This sense seems to persist. A recent and valuable collection of essays on Sophocles edited by Simon Goldhill and Edith Hall (published in honour of one of the present volume's most distinguished contributors) has an introductory chapter entitled 'Sophocles: the state of play'.[2] Yet the approaches that the authors regard as current and topical (concentrating on politics, performance, linguistic ambiguity, and reception, pp. 19–20) have now been current for more than 30 years, firmly in the tradition of what Thomas Rosenmeyer already in 1993 referred to as 'the new orthodoxy'.[3] Goldhill and Hall themselves trace the shift in focus to the seminal works of intellectual history *cum* structuralism collected in the volumes of Vernant and Vidal-Naquet; but these date to the 1960s and 1970s.[4] For Goldhill and Hall (and, as they rightly imagine, p. 12, most scholars of their generation) the classics of interpretative scholarship on Sophocles remain, as they were in the 1980s, the works of Reinhardt, Bowra, Kitto, Knox, Whitman, and Winnington-Ingram.[5]

The gulf that is here identified – by two scholars whose own work has been influential in shifting the focus of research on tragedy – is in many respects a real one. But it is a gulf that cannot be left unbridged. The sense that there are classic interpretations of Sophocles in particular or of tragedy in general does not merely reflect the naivety and reactionary conservatism of those classicists who are uncomfortable with exciting new theories and methods, but involves a recognition that there is abiding worth in approaches from which those who wish to position themselves at the cutting edge of scholarship have largely turned away. Yet whatever the insights of classic scholarship may be, they ossify if they are not subjected to repeated questioning and criticism. Not much of this is happening. Abandoned as the focus of primary research, the discussion of tragedy's roots in the popular and philosophical thought of archaic Greece, if it occurs at all, has been left largely to undergraduate textbooks and companions (many of which are in their own terms of very high quality). These again, for such issues, rely on the classic works of the past. The great interpretative scholarship of the nineteenth and earlier twentieth centuries, scholarship that grappled intensively with tragedy's place in the development of Greek thought, is no longer part of the toolkit with which the scholar seeks to come to terms with the meaning of tragic texts, but instead has become the focus of reception studies, of the history of interpretation, and of the sociology of knowledge.[6] There are many reasons for this: chief among them is no doubt the anthropological turn taken by classical scholarship in the period under discussion, but (at least in the United Kingdom) the premium placed on novelty in an environment of increasingly intense competition for PhD scholarships and external research grants has also played a substantial role, as has the rise of non-linguistic Classical Civilization degree programmes, encouraging a shift from textual to broader cultural questions, as well as factors such as the declining knowledge of German among Anglophone students and scholars.

This volume does not advocate a return to some lost golden age of classic scholarship. But its contributors do maintain that classic scholarship on tragedy focuses on questions that are essential for any interpretative approach to the genre, questions rooted in tragedy's origins in and responses to its traditional background in archaic Greek thought – questions of the role of the gods and fate in human action; of the justice or otherwise of the gods and of the world over which they preside; of the causes of human suffering and of the stability, indeed of the nature and possibility of human happiness. We cannot simply regard such issues as settled: old answers will no longer suffice, but old questions remain live and need to be answered in our own contemporary terms. If there is one thing that unites us in our profession as scholars and teachers it is surely that all orthodoxies, old and new, need to be subjected to continuing examination and scrutiny.

Classic, especially German, scholarship may have focused on aspects of intellectual history that are fundamental to the interpretation of tragedy, but with its rootedness in the post-Enlightenment philosophical tradition, it often did so in progressivist and teleological terms, assuming linear intellectual and spiritual development both within Greek culture itself and over the centuries that separate Greeks and moderns. To take just one example: the best extended discussion of the archaic notion of *atē*, the subject of Alan Sommerstein's chapter in this volume, is a 1950 Göttingen dissertation (not published until 1968) by Josef Stallmach.[7] This is a work of great insight and skill in its careful analysis of individual passages. It is sensitive to all the questions that anyone who seeks to understand the phenomenon in question will need to consider – in what circumstances *atē* is mentioned, with what scenarios it is associated, what its supposed origins are, how it affects human responsibility for action, how its presentation changes over time and from one genre to another, and so on. But its great demerit is an *a priori* assumption, widely shared by studies of its type and period, that there is inevitably a progression, both from earlier to later Greek authors and from antiquity to modernity, from primitive, irrational, and supernatural explanations to naturalistic, rational, and sophisticated ones. The general validity of such approaches has been decisively undermined by scholars such as Bernard Williams and Christopher Gill;[8] but if one looks for the direct influence of these newer approaches to intellectual history in substantive works of tragic interpretation, one will search largely in vain.[9] There are, of course, more recent discussions of *atē* that take a different approach;[10] but the point is that these questions are typically pursued in works of intellectual history, no longer in interpretative studies of tragedy itself. And thus Sommerstein's chapter is needed.

Sommerstein himself argues for a degree of development in the conceptualization of *atē* between Homer and Aeschylus, at least in so far as he suggests that in the latter 'the ultimate cause of *atē* has arguably been secularized' (p. 12 below),[11] but this is for him no simple linear progression from more to less primitive, first because he is perfectly aware that neither Homer's conception nor Aeschylus' is primitive, but more importantly because his own account of *atē*'s semantic history is not a straightforward one of progressive secularization – the notion of *atē*, Sommerstein argues, was not originally a religious one, but rather an everyday term meaning not 'delusion' (divinely inspired or otherwise), but 'harm', 'damage', or 'loss'. Since this is the predominant meaning also in later tragedy (especially Euripides: see Sommerstein below, pp. 11–12), the simple developmental schemes of older scholarship are untenable.[12] Sommerstein's interpretation argues for development in the semantics of *atē*, but that development is not simple, and certainly not teleological.

2. *Atē* and archaic thought in Sophocles' *Antigone*: a test case

If we apply Sommerstein's approach to the analysis of *atē* in Sophocles' *Antigone* (a topic that arises in Liapis' chapter), we can gauge something of the importance of the central concepts of archaic Greek thought that are explored by the contributors to this volume.

First, there are ten instances of the noun, *atē*, in the play (one, unfortunately, in a corrupt passage at *Ant.* 4), two of the verb ἀτάω or ἀτάομαι, and one of the adverb ἀνατεί (485). In all of its occurrences, the noun means 'harm' or 'ruin'; in each of the two uses of the verb, the present participle middle or passive means 'harmed' or 'ruined'; and the adverb means 'with impunity'.[13] This fits very well with Sommerstein's account of the term's semantic history. But it would be wrong to conclude from this that there is therefore no trace of *atē* in its prototypical Homeric sense, of the mental impairment that leads human beings to their ruin.

Four of the play's ten uses of the noun, *atē*, occur in the second stasimon (583–625), a central exhibit in Liapis' demonstration that the archaic notion of cycles of suffering in successive generations of a single family is an important element in the play's meaning. In each of these cases, the immediate reference of the term is to ruin or disaster: 'Blessed are those whose life has not tasted evils', sing the Chorus at the beginning of their song (583–5), 'for when a house is shaken by the gods, there is no element of disaster (*atē*) that does not advance towards the family's members, in all their numbers.' Though the text is uncertain, it is clear that the end of the first stanza of the second strophic pair answers this sentiment: either 'great wealth does not come to mortals without *atē*' or 'nothing that is great comes to the life of mortals without *atē*'.[14] The song then concludes with an endorsement of the wisdom of the 'famous saying' (620–1), that 'bad seems good to a man whose mind a god is leading towards *atē*; he fares but the shortest time without *atē*' (622–5). In all four cases *atē* is the calamity, whatever it is, that impairs mortal *eudaimonia* (or, in the worst cases, destroys it utterly). But such disaster affects one's mind as well as one's fortunes (ὅτῳ φρένας | θεὸς ἄγει πρὸς ἄταν, 623–4).[15] Accordingly, the cause of disaster is traced to the mind: the last scion of the House of Oedipus is threatened by 'folly of *logos* and an Erinys of the mind' (603),[16] both expressions clear periphrases for *atē* in its subjective sense.[17] In the final stanza of their song, the Chorus conclude: hope may be beneficial in some circumstances (616), but it is 'much-wandering' and thus prone to delusion (πολύπλαγκτος, 615);[18] for many it amounts to no more that the 'deception of empty-headed passions' (πολλοῖς δ' ἀπάτα κουφονόων ἐρώτων, 617). Thus, by a popular etymology already familiar in Homer, *atē* (delusion or disaster) is brought into relation with *apatē*, deception.[19] The victim of deception (the singers go on) knows nothing until it is too late (618–19),[20] because (as we have seen) bad seems good to those whose minds the gods are leading to disaster (620–5). Where, as here, there is a divine agent behind the delusion or misapprehension that constitutes *atē*, *atē* and *apatē* coalesce. We might compare not only Theognis 402–6 and trag. adesp. 455,[21] as cited

Introduction: Archaic Thought and Tragic Interpretation

by Jebb and Griffith, but also Aeschylus' *Persians* 93–100, lines which are worth quoting here in full:[22]

δολόμητιν δ' ἀπάταν θεοῦ τίς ἀνὴρ θνατὸς ἀλύξει;
τίς ὁ κραιπνῷ ποδὶ πηδήματος εὐπετέος ἀνάσσων;   95
φιλόφρων γὰρ <ποτι>σαίνουσα τὸ πρῶτον παράγει
βροτὸν εἰς ἄρκυστ<ατ'> Ἄτα·
τόθεν οὐκ ἔστιν ὑπὲρ θνατὸν ἀλύξαντα φυγεῖν.   100

What mortal man can escape the god's treacherous deceit? Who is the lord of an easy jump with nimble foot? For fawning on him at first with friendly intent Ate leads a man astray into her nets. From there no mortal can free himself; there is no escape.

The Aeschylean passage encompasses the entire *atē*-sequence from delusion (or deception) to disaster and makes the same association between *atē* and *apatē* as does our Sophoclean ode. If not the source for Sophocles' version, it at least presents a closely similar conception. The thought that the gods lead on those who are headed for ruin recurs later in Aeschylus' play. To Darius' incredulous question about Xerxes' closing of the Bosporos, the Queen replies, 'Yes, I suppose that some *daimōn* took hold of his judgement' (ὧδ' ἔχει, γνώμης δέ πού τις δαιμόνων ξυνήψατο, 724), and Darius agrees: 'Alas, great indeed was the *daimōn* whose arrival ruined his judgement' (φεῦ μέγας τις ἦλθε δαίμων ὥστε μὴ φρονεῖν καλῶς, 725). That the intervention of the malign and deceptive *daimōn* does not relieve the human agent of responsibility emerges from Darius' realization, at 739–42, that Xerxes' invasion and its consequences signify the fulfilment of an old oracle:[23]

φεῦ ταχεῖά γ' ἦλθε χρησμῶν πρᾶξις, ἐς δὲ παῖδ' ἐμὸν
Ζεὺς ἀπέσκηψεν τελευτὴν θεσφάτων· ἐγὼ δέ που   740
διὰ μακροῦ χρόνου τάδ' ηὔχουν ἐκτελευτήσειν θεούς·
ἀλλ', ὅταν σπεύδῃ τις αὐτός, χὠ θεὸς συνάπτεται.

Alas, the achievement of oracles came swiftly, and Zeus has hurled the fulfilment of prophecies down upon my son. I had prayed that the gods would somehow take a long time to bring them to pass. But when a man himself is eager, the god also joins in.

Hence Xerxes bears full responsibility for his youthful impetuosity (744, 782), his folly and derangement (749–51), his impiety (808–12), and the arrogant *hybris* that leads one to despise one's current fortune, destroy one's prosperity, and bring forth a crop of *atē* (808, 818–31).

As in the *Persians*, *atē* in the second stasimon of the *Antigone* brings with it a whole set of wider associations (the gap between aims and outcomes, the instability of wealth and prosperity, and the notion that this instability has causes both in humans' own errors, delusions, and transgressions and in the plans of the gods), and it is evident that the full Homeric or Aeschylean scope of the concept is crucial to this central, but difficult ode.[24] The extent to which *atē* and with it other salient notions of archaic Greek thought pervade and shape the entire play, however, is often overlooked or underestimated. The immediate application of the Chorus' words in the second stasimon is to Antigone's family, the Labdacids: theirs is the house which is currently being shaken (583), theirs the ancient sorrows, the interminable and divinely inspired generations of suffering, that have now manifested themselves in the disaster which has overtaken Antigone (594–603). If we follow the apparent direction of the Chorus' argument, so too Antigone must, at least in their minds, have contributed to her plight by her own *anoia*[25] and under the influence of an 'Erinys of the mind' which may or may not be imagined as a fully personified demonic agent.[26] The application of the second strophic pair (604–25) to Antigone is more of a challenge, but *atē* is still the theme – explicitly, and with reference to objective misfortune, at 613–14 and 624–5; implicitly (and encompassing the term's subjective aspect) in the deceptive and foolish variety of hope that brings one to unexpected disaster (615–19) and in the divine deception that makes bad seem good to one whom a god is leading to ruin (622–4). But if Antigone can, in the first antistrophe, be said to be under the influence of an Erinys of the mind that is adding to the generations of suffering in the House of Labdacus, then these statements, at least on the explicit level, can be applied to her or her family too. This must also be the case, at least at the surface level, in the presentation of the view that no great wealth (or nothing great) comes to mortals without *atē* as an eternally valid and vigilant law of Zeus that withstands men's transgression (ἀνδρῶν ὑπερβασία, 604–5).[27]

As an explanation of Antigone's situation, the ode is thoroughly Aeschylean: we have a lineage that is 'welded to *atē*' (the Chorus' description of the Atreidae at *Ag.* 1566), but though the family's tribulations recur across the generations, each generation appears to contribute to its own suffering, through folly and transgression (even if one of the explanations for both of these is a divine determination to bring the individual to ruin). The deluded, deceived, and transgressive individual may be marked out for suffering by membership of a doomed family, and the family's prosperity may in itself be a source of danger, but the sense that the individual nonetheless bears some responsibility for his or her misfortune persists.

This is not out of step with other evaluations elsewhere in the play. The issue of *atē* in Antigone's family is almost certainly (despite the textual corruption) raised in her very first lines in the play (4), and Ismene confirms the theme at 17;[28] Ismene's elaboration of this point at 49–60 uses no *atē*-word, but in effect prefigures the Chorus' point in the second stasimon (594–603): she and Antigone are the last of the family, and Antigone's plan to bury the body of Polynices, in defiance of Creon's edict, constitutes a further instalment in the ills that this family has inflicted upon itself. Creon, for his part, uses the adverb ἀνατεί at 485: Antigone will not defy him 'with impunity', i.e. without *atē*.[29] The point that *atē* runs in her family is then rehearsed by Antigone herself at 863–5, where (reiterating Ismene's arguments on the sufferings of their parents and their brothers) she laments the *atai* of her parents' incest.[30] The consequences of Antigone's actions in burying her brother can be regarded, at least by Creon and the Chorus, as *atē*, and the Chorus, Ismene, and Antigone herself are as one in their opinion that *atē* has bedevilled their family in the past. The Chorus' view that there are hereditary reasons for her behaviour and its consequences is one that they put forward more than once elsewhere, both before and after the second stasimon. At 379–80 she is the 'unhappy child of an unhappy father', and at 471–2 she has inherited her father's 'raw' or 'savage' temperament.[31] At 856 they wonder whether her ordeal may be payment for some debt that Oedipus incurred. This touches a nerve (857–8, ἔψαυσας ἀλγεινοτάτας ἐμοὶ μερίμνας), and she refers to her father's travails, those of the entire Labdacid clan, the *atai* of her parents' incest, and the wretchedness of her own state as a reflection of theirs (859–66).[32] Now, she continues, she goes to join them, 'accursed and unwed' (ἀραῖος ἄγαμος, 867). This use of the adjective ἀραῖος is the only positive indication in the play that the sufferings of Antigone may have an origin in an actual curse. With the exception of direct references to Oedipus, his wife, and their sons, the play's allusions to the mythological background of the Labdacid family are so sparse and unspecific that one could never be sure that it assumes familiarity with a version in which a curse doomed not only Eteocles and Polynices,[33] but the entire *genos*; yet the basic notion that Antigone's actions and their consequences fall into a pattern that is repeated in the history of her family is well established in the text.[34] Any interpretation that chooses to minimize or reject this notion as an explanation for what happens to Antigone must still recognize that it is not a localized or isolated one.

For the Chorus in the second stasimon, *atē* in the sense of 'disaster' has among its causes 'folly of *logos* and an Erinys of the mind' (603), transgression (*hyperbasia*, 605), the 'deception of light-minded passions' (ἀπάτα κουφονόων ἐρώτων, 617), failure to foresee the harm that one's actions will cause (618–20), and the confusion of good and bad that afflicts those whose mind a god is leading to disaster (622–4). This language of mental disturbance, misjudgement, and transgression is also widely applied to Antigone, both before and after this ode. Her proposal to defy Creon's edict exhibits no *nous*, according to Ismene at 67–8 (cf. *anous*, 99); she is 'in love with the impossible' (90, cf. 'hunting the impossible', 92);³⁵ even Antigone herself refers ironically to the inevitable construal of her actions as a crime (74) and as *dysboulia* (95). Accordingly, when the Chorus see her, the 'unhappy child of an unhappy father' (379–80; cf. above), being led in as the one who has disobeyed 'the king's laws' (τοῖς βασιλείοις...νόμοις, 382), they describe the act for which she has been arrested as one of *aphrosynē* (383). The theme is taken up by Creon. Ismene's intervention in her sister's support is for him confirmation that she has begun to manifest the lack of reason that Antigone has shown from birth (561–2: τὼ παῖδέ φημι τώδε τὴν μὲν ἀρτίως | ἄνουν πεφάνθαι, τὴν δ' ἀφ' οὗ τὰ πρῶτ' ἔφυ), his use of the adjective *anous* echoing Ismene's own at 99 and prefiguring the Chorus's λόγου...ἄνοια at 603. In the immediately preceding scene, Creon charges Antigone with 'transgressing the laws' (ὑπερβαίνειν, 449; cf. 605). Antigone counters with her famously defiant reply (450–70), which (as we saw) the Coryphaeus sees as a reflexion of the character that she has inherited from her father (471–2). For Creon, her behaviour in defiantly justifying her position is a form of *hybris* that compounds the *hybris* that she has already shown in 'transgressing the laws that had been laid down' (νόμους ὑπερβαίνουσα τοὺς προκειμένους, 480–3); but this *hybris*, he is determined to show, will lead to *atē* (she will not challenge his power ἀνατεί, 485).³⁶ The link between *hyperbasia*, *hybris*, and *atē* at 480–5 points to the presence of the same set of associations in the ensuing second stasimon (604–14), where the second strophe opens with *hyperbasia* (605) and ends with a reference to the wealth or success that results in *atē* (613–14). *Hybris* is not mentioned, but *hybris* and *koros* are the missing links in the familiar 'archaic chain' that links *atē*, the result, to its causes in the inability to deal appropriately with wealth and success.³⁷ The chain is equally apparent in the stasimon's preceding stanza: the 'bloody dust of the nether gods', i.e. Antigone's actions in burying her brother, has its cause in 'folly of *logos* and an Erinys of the mind' (601–3) – mental impairment, in other words, is leading to further disasters in the House of Labdacus. This is *atē* in both its subjective and objective aspects. We note, then, that the dust, i.e. Antigone's action and the derangement from which it derives, results in the disastrous 'harvesting' of the last of her family. This is a harvest of *atē*, a notion that occurs in the speech of Darius' Ghost in *Persae*, where it is part of the complex of vegetation imagery that accompanies the 'archaic chain'.³⁸ The activation of these associations of *atē* in the second stasimon, and especially the clear association with too much of a good thing in 613–14, thus imply a second popular etymology, namely the derivation of *atē* from ἄω, 'satiate', to stand alongside the one already noted, which links *atē* and *apatē*.³⁹ The presentation of Antigone's actions in terms of *atē* is not only prominent in the scene that precedes the second stasimon, but also involves a wider nexus of characteristically 'archaic' notions with which *atē* is traditionally associated.

The representation of Antigone's actions as irrational and transgressive continues after the second stasimon. It is her behaviour that prompts Creon, in his opening speech to Haemon, to reflect in general terms on the dangers of transgression and the importance of obedience (663–5):

ὅστις δ' ὑπερβὰς ἢ νόμους βιάζεται,
ἢ τοὐπιτάσσειν τοῖς κρατύνουσιν νοεῖ,
οὐκ ἔστ' ἐπαίνου τοῦτον ἐξ ἐμοῦ τυχεῖν. 665

No one who transgresses by violating the law or by presuming to give orders to his rulers will get any praise from me.

Equally, in the final scene before Antigone is led away to her death, both she and the Chorus return, in language that repeatedly recalls that of the second stasimon, to Antigone's transgression, its causes, and its results. The Chorus' lyric iambics at 853–6 link her 'advance to the limit of daring' (προβᾶσ' ἐπ' ἔσχατον θράσους, 853) with her 'fall before the pedestal of Justice' (854–5) and seek a cause for her suffering in her 'repayment' of a debt incurred by her father (πατρῷον δ' ἐκτίνεις τιν' ἆθλον, 856). Antigone, as we have seen, immediately responds with a reference to the sufferings of the Labdacidae, including the *atai* of her parents' incest.[40] The latest instalment of those sufferings is Antigone's own death, brought about by her actions in burying Polynices (869–71); but for the Chorus, though this act manifests *eusebeia* of a sort (872), it remains a transgression (873–4) rooted in Antigone's passionate and self-willed nature; it is this that has destroyed her.[41] This is an interpretation that Antigone disputes in her final words in the play: what divine law has she transgressed (παρεξελθοῦσα, 921)? Yet she is apparently abandoned by the gods, and has been branded with *dyssebeia* in spite of her piety (τὴν δυσσέβειαν εὐσεβοῦσ' ἐκτησάμην, 924). As she is led away to her tomb she calls once more on the Chorus, as leading men of Thebes, to witness the injustice of her treatment, τὴν εὐσεβίαν σεβίσασα ('for revering reverence', 943).

There is thus plenty of purchase in the text of the play for the view enunciated by the Chorus in the second stasimon that Antigone comes to disaster and ruin (that is, to *atē*) as a result of a transgression that is at once a product of irrational elements in her own character and a reflexion of a recurrent sequence of trials, transgressions, and sufferings in her family. Both of these factors answer to aspects of *atē* as it had become familiar in Sophocles' day through its prominence (especially) in Homer, Solon, and Aeschylus. As an account of Antigone's situation the second stasimon's recourse to the archaic notion of *atē* is by no means a localized or isolated perspective; it is a construction that pervades both others' perceptions of Antigone and the self-representation that seeks to contest those perceptions. But this does not necessarily mean that this construction is correct.

Antigone's complaint that, despite her piety, she has apparently been abandoned by the gods is immediately qualified, in words that bear crucially on the issue of her *atē* (925–8):

> ἀλλ' εἰ μὲν οὖν τάδ' ἐστὶν ἐν θεοῖς καλά, 925
> παθόντες ἂν ξυγγνοῖμεν ἡμαρτηκότες·
> εἰ δ' οἵδ' ἁμαρτάνουσι, μὴ πλείω κακὰ
> πάθοιεν ἢ καὶ δρῶσιν ἐκδίκως ἐμέ.

> However that may be, if this is fitting in the eyes of the gods, we shall learn through our suffering that we have erred. But if it is *they* [i.e. Creon] who are in error, may they suffer evils no greater than those that they are actually inflicting, without justice, upon me.

In Homer and (as Sommerstein shows) also in Aeschylus, *atē* is regularly a name for a process in which an error leads to disaster and regret.[42] The association between *atē* and *hamartia*, moreover, is as old as the *Iliad*'s allegory of the Litai, which is presented as an amplification of the *a fortiori* argument that even the gods accept entreaty from an offender who wishes to make amends for *hyperbasia* and *hamartia* (ὅτε κέν τις ὑπερβήῃ καὶ ἁμάρτῃ, *Il.* 9. 501); the closeness of the association, in archaic poetry and in tragedy, is demonstrated in a seminal study by Roger Dawe.[43] But in spite of all that she has said, in 806–923, about the horror, pathos, and injustice of her fate, Antigone does not think she is in error and never regrets her deed;[44] her words in lines 925–6 represent, in her mind at least, a rejected hypothesis that serves as a foil for the eventuality for which she prays, which she regards as more likely, and which does in fact come to pass.[45] Antigone here highlights the crucial role of results in the determination of *atē* – a mistake that does not lead to disastrous results is not *atē*. By definition, an agent who is subject to *atē* does not foresee the disaster to come; an observer might, but only results will prove that person correct.[46] Antigone *is* suffering, and she certainly regards her lot, typical of her family history as it is, as a calamity. There is material here for others to draw conclusions in terms of *atē* on Antigone's part, as indeed the Chorus have done.[47] But as Antigone herself represents the situation, the results of her action are not yet in; they will be clear only when we learn what in fact happens to Creon.

This takes us back to the second stasimon. We saw that the Chorus' language of transgression (605) could, given parallels elsewhere in the play, be taken as a reference to Antigone (possibly also including an allusion to

Introduction: Archaic Thought and Tragic Interpretation

further but unspecified transgressions in the history of her family). Similarly, on one level, at least, the notion that nothing great (or no great wealth) comes to mortals without *atē* could be taken as a lesson drawn from the sufferings of the Labdacidae. But the eternal laws of Zeus whose transgression brings disaster (604–15) sound more like the principles that Antigone claimed to uphold at 450–7. If Antigone is right about the import of these laws (and Creon's conclusion at 1113–14 – that 'it may be best to end one's life in preservation of the established laws' – suggests that she is),[48] then Creon and not she is their violator. We note that it is the transgression of *men* (ἀνδρῶν) that is said to be insufficient to check the power of Zeus (604–5): the phrase is one of several in the play in which the use of marked gender terms is ironic in its force.[49] In the previous act, in which Creon charged Antigone with *hyperbasia* and *hybris*, he also expressed the view that if Antigone were to be allowed to act with impunity (i.e. without *atē*, ἀνατεί), then she, not he, would be the ἀνήρ (484–5).[50] Where Creon's words raise the issue of who is to be regarded, normatively, as the man, those of the Chorus on men's *hyperbasia* invite us also to consider whose is the transgression, whose the *hybris*, whose the *atē*.[51]

The association of Creon with the theme of *atē* is even more pervasive and explicit than it is in the case of Antigone. His first reference to the concept comes in that crucial first speech in which he sets out the principles behind his prohibition of Polynices' burial (184–6):

ἐγὼ γάρ, ἴστω Ζεὺς ὁ πάνθ' ὁρῶν ἀεί,
οὔτ' ἂν σιωπήσαιμι τὴν ἄτην ὁρῶν   185
στείχουσαν ἀστοῖς ἀντὶ τῆς σωτηρίας...

As Zeus who sees all at all times is my witness, I could not keep silent if I saw *atē* advancing upon the citizens in place of *sōtēria*...

Creon has just begun his speech by emphasizing that his accession to the throne is a recent event, a consequence of the deaths of Oedipus' sons in the battle which ended only the previous evening. He then expresses his conviction that only time will reveal a man's – especially a ruler's – character and judgement (175–7):

ἀμήχανον δὲ παντὸς ἀνδρὸς ἐκμαθεῖν   175
ψυχήν τε καὶ φρόνημα καὶ γνώμην, πρὶν ἂν
ἀρχαῖς τε καὶ νόμοισιν ἐντριβὴς φανῇ.

It is impossible thoroughly to learn any man's mind, thought, or judgement until he is tried and tested in office and laws.

Both this opening statement of principle and his observations on *atē* encourage an audience to focus on the consequences of the action that

Creon is currently justifying. Having emphasized that he is a new ruler and that the judgement of someone in his position can be evaluated only in the light of experience, he sets his present decisions and conduct firmly under the shadow of the future. And this is where *atē* comes in, for in its traditional guise as a cornerstone of archaic Greek thought, *atē* rests fundamentally upon the relation between intention, action, and result: *atē* (at least as it is exploited in the *Iliad* and in the plays of Aeschylus) is not simply any calamity, but one that arises from a catastrophic failure to foresee that disaster is a potential outcome of one's choices.[52] Creon is determined to speak up should he see *atē* advancing on his fellow citizens; but *atē,* at least when it results from one's own error, is not something that one sees coming; Zeus sees everything (ὁ πάνθ' ὁρῶν ἀεί) and Zeus is the one who knows (ἴστω), but Creon does not.[53] Lines 184–6 establish *atē* as a potential opponent that may come upon Creon despite his attempts to guard against it;[54] just so, in the second stasimon, *atē* is something that 'moves towards' the generations of a family whose house is shaken by god (οἷς γὰρ ἂν σεισθῇ θεόθεν δόμος, ἄτας | οὐδὲν ἐλλείπει γενεᾶς ἐπὶ πλῆθος ἕρπον, 584–5), no great wealth (or nothing great) 'comes to' mortals without *atē* (οὐδέν' ἕρπει | θνατῶν βίοτος πάμπολυς ἐκτὸς ἄτας, in the text of Lloyd-Jones and Wilson, 613–14), and the negative consequences of the harmful *elpis* that is really a deception (with the play on *atē/apatē* that we have already noted) 'come upon' a person unawares (εἰδότι δ' οὐδὲν ἕρπει, πρὶν πυρὶ θερμῷ πόδα τις προσαύσῃ, 618–19).[55] Lines 184–6 thus place *atē* firmly in a thematic nexus that unites the play's abundant references to good and bad judgement and their good and bad outcomes. As Liapis rightly cautions, we do not at this stage of the play necessarily reach a firm conclusion that Creon is doomed and his precepts misguided, much less that he is a villain or a tyrant, but we do notice the substantial hostage to fortune created by his emphasis on his inexperience, on the proof of character and judgement that only experience can provide,[56] and on the *atē* that may be advancing upon Thebes as a result of his actions.

In their personification of *atē*, the link that they suggest between the quality of Creon's judgement and its potential effects upon the citizens of Thebes, and their antithesis between *atē* and *sōtēria*, Creon's words introduce themes that pervade the rest of the play. The association with *sōtēria* immediately recurs in Creon's concluding remarks to the Guard at 304–14. In another gnomically charged passage, Creon again raises the issue of the relation between Zeus' purposes and his own (εἴπερ ἴσχει Ζεὺς ἔτ' ἐξ ἐμοῦ σέβας, 304 – *is* he still showing respect for Zeus?), before concluding his threat to punish the guards if they do not find 'the perpetrator of this burial' (τὸν αὐτόχειρα τοῦδε τοῦ τάφου) with a statement of the lesson that he believes such punishment would impart (310–14):

> ἵν' εἰδότες τὸ κέρδος ἔνθεν οἰστέον   310
> τὸ λοιπὸν ἁρπάζητε, καὶ μάθηθ' ὅτι
> οὐκ ἐξ ἅπαντος δεῖ τὸ κερδαίνειν φιλεῖν.
> ἐκ τῶν γὰρ αἰσχρῶν λημμάτων τοὺς πλείονας
> ἀτωμένους ἴδοις ἂν ἢ σεσωμένους.
>
> ...in order that you should in future conduct your depredations knowing whence profit (*kerdos*) is to be won, and learn that it is not right to love profiting from any source. For you would see that more are ruined (ἀτωμένους) as a result of shameful profits than are saved (σεσωμένους).

The initial opposition between *atē* and safety now blends into one between *atē* and *kerdos*, a frequent antithesis that is indicative of the term's core sense of 'loss' as opposed to 'profit'.[57] And since *kerdos* is one of the play's key themes, this is further attestation of *atē*'s deep roots in the conceptual structure of the play.

The theme recurs with another reminder of *atē*'s core sense of 'harm', 'damage', or 'loss' at 484–5 (already discussed): Creon is not the man, but rather Antigone is, if she is to get away with challenging Creon's power ἀνατεί. 'Harm' is what Creon intends for Antigone; this will prove that he is the ἀνήρ. But, as we noted, it is the transgression of ἄνδρες that is pronounced to be no match for the power of Zeus in the second stasimon at 604–5, and the god's inevitable victory manifests an eternal law that enshrines the principle that no great wealth (or nothing great) comes to mortals without *atē*. The contest between Creon and Antigone will similarly end in *atē*; the ironic implication of line 485 is that this *atē* may be his, not (or not only) hers.

The role of *atē* as a link between the two is suggested by Creon's description of Antigone and Ismene as 'two Atai' in the scene immediately preceding the second stasimon at 532–3: οὐδ' ἐμάνθανον | τρέφων δύ' ἄτα κἀπαναστάσεις θρόνων ('I did not realize that I was nurturing two Ruins, to overthrow my throne').[58] Creon imagines that he has diagnosed a source of ruin and nipped it in the bud; but in the end he is ruined, and his royal power is destroyed; he has not yet learned the extent to which Antigone instantiates his *atē*. The suggestion made by Antigone herself at 925–8, that her own suffering will be answered by equal suffering on Creon's part, is here foreshadowed in the notion that Antigone will be the embodiment of Creon's ruin. If the suffering in Antigone's family is caused by 'folly of *logos* and an Erinys of the mind' (603), Antigone herself becomes a kind of quasi-demonic agent of Creon's downfall.

one of the most salient and emblematic passages of the ancient world's most authoritative poetic archetype, comes at the point at which the balance between the sufferings that await Creon and those that he has imposed upon Antigone begins to become apparent. This balance represents the fulfilment not only of Antigone's wish (at 925–8) that Creon's *hamartia* should involve him in suffering no less painful than the suffering she endures as a result of her own alleged *hamartia*, but also of Tiresias' prophecy (at 1064–86) that Creon will be caught in the same evils as he inflicted upon Antigone and Polynices. These evils come upon him after he has rejected Tiresias' earlier advice that, though it is human to err (τοὐξαμαρτάνειν), it is nonetheless sensible (and apparently possible) to heal one's error by changing one's mind (1023–7), where the words ὅστις ἐς κακὸν | πεσὼν ἀκεῖται μηδ' ἀκίνητος πέλει in all likelihood constitute another allusion to the allegory of the Litai, in which one who 'transgresses and errs' (*Il.* 9. 501) can make amends by means of Prayers, which 'come after to heal the damage' (αἳ δ' ἐξακέονται ὀπίσσω, 507). It may be not be precisely correct to claim that Antigone's *atē* passes to Creon in the way that Agamemnon's is transferred to Achilles when he rejects the warning that Phoenix's allegory represents (for Antigone's *atē* may, in the end, be a red herring), but it is undeniable that *atē*-terms are first applied to Antigone's actions and their outcomes, before it becomes clear that the *atē*-sequence of delusion and disaster is exemplified in a more canonical and traditional form in the case of Creon.[70] The importance of *atē* in linking the fates of Antigone and Creon is underlined by the evocation of a passage that establishes the thematic links between the errors of Agamemnon and Achilles in the *Iliad,* and the *Antigone* thus advertises the extent to which it shares a central theme with that most exemplary of poems.

At the centre of this nexus of links between the putative *atē* of Antigone and the demonstrable *atē* of Creon stands the second stasimon. This song introduces the notion of *atē* in explanation of the generations of suffering in Antigone's family, but at another level of meaning accurately diagnoses the causes of Creon's downfall. We noted above many of the verbal and thematic echoes that link that ode to evaluations of the conduct of both Antigone and Creon elsewhere in the play. Among the most significant of these are the recurrent references to the personified, daemonic agents that bring ruin to mortals. The Blabai (= Atai) that the Coryphaeus fears will overtake Creon if he does not remedy his folly in time (1103–4) are prefigured in the Erinyes who, according to Tiresias, lie in wait for him (1074–6):[71]

τούτων σε λωβητῆρες ὑστεροφθόροι
λοχῶσιν Ἅιδου καὶ θεῶν Ἐρινύες, 1075
ἐν τοῖσιν αὐτοῖς τοῖσδε ληφθῆναι κακοῖς.

As a result of this, Erinyes of Hades and the gods lie in wait for you, agents of ruin who wreak their destruction after the fact, so that you will be caught up in these very same evils.

The words λωβητῆρες and ὑστεροφθόροι emphasize the harm that these Erinyes cause.[72] The former occurs in three passages of the *Iliad*,[73] none especially salient or significant for our purposes; but ὑστεροφθόρος occurs only here in classical Greek. Sophocles' phrase, however, is quoted by Eustathius on *Il.* 9. 506–7, where he notes that, in so far as they are ὑστεροφθόροι, the Erinyes of the *Antigone* resemble the Litai in Phoenix's allegory, who see to it that Ate attends anyone who rejects them, ἵνα βλαφθεὶς ἀποτείσῃ ('that he be harmed and pay the penalty', *Il.* 9. 512). Thus, as Eustathius further observes, Ate herself is ὑστεροφθόρος.[74] Eustathius has clearly seen the link between this passage of the *Antigone* and the allegory of *Iliad* 9. That link is confirmed by the similarity between Tiresias' words at 1074–6 and the Coryphaeus' at 1103–4, where the *Iliad* 9 passage is plainly evoked, and it is further substantiated by the way that Sophocles' ὑστεροφθόρος so clearly recalls Aeschylus' ὑστερόποινος, used of Erinys at *Ag.* 58–9, but (in a similarly-worded passage) of Ate at *Cho.* 382–3.[75] The signs of a virtual equivalence between Ate and Erinys are therefore strong; and thus both 1074–6 (with Erinyes) and 1103–4 (with Blabai, i.q. Atai), referring to Creon, recall the words of the Chorus in the second stasimon, where they see λόγου τ' ἄνοια καὶ φρενῶν Ἐρινύς as the cause of the disaster that is extinguishing the surviving light of the House of Oedipus (599–603). Whether or not there is any sense in which this is to be regarded as an accurate assessment of Antigone's plight, the later reflexions of the same theme exploit the latent application of this notion, and indeed of the entire ode, to Creon. The way in which the *atē*-theme, as applied to Antigone, becomes a foil for and mutates into the application of the same theme to Creon is aptly summed up in Creon's observation, more accurate than he knows, that in giving a home to Antigone and Ismene he has been nurturing 'two Atai' in his house (533).

Again, it is clear that *atē* is operative in the *Antigone* in its fullest Iliadic or Aeschylean guise: though in most of the actual occurrences of *atē*-words themselves the primary reference is to the concept's objective aspect (harm, damage, or loss – apparent in the play's frequent opposition between *atē* and *kerdos*), the way in which it is brought into relation with *hamartia* (explicitly at 1259–62, implicitly at 914–15, 925–8, 1023–7; cf. 588, 743–4) illustrates what is in any case apparent at 623–4 (ὅτῳ φρένας | θεὸς ἄγει πρὸς ἄταν) and in the second stasimon in general, that *atē* in the *Antigone* is still, as in Homer and Aeschylus, the name of a process in which a harmful state of mind is the cause of a harmful state of affairs.

Douglas Cairns

This impression is confirmed by the way in which the *Antigone* activates a large number of *atē*'s traditional associations and connotations. We have already noted the etymological play on *atē* and *apatē* at 615–25 and the implicit presence of the 'archaic chain' (which again has an etymological aspect) of *olbos, koros, hybris*, and *atē* at 604–14 (taken with 473–85). Another potential etymological (or quasi-etymological) link is with the verb *aēmi*, to blow (of winds). This association appears to be activated in Agamemnon's statement that 'the gusts of *atē* are still alive' (ἄτης θύελλαι ζῶσι) at Aeschylus, *Ag.* 819.[76] Thus there may be a folk-etymological aspect to the pervasive use of wind-imagery, with persistently negative connotations of disaster and destruction, in the Oresteian trilogy as a whole.[77] The same association (even if it does not in fact entail a popular etymology) seems to me to be clearly active in the Chorus' words in the second stasimon (583–92):

> εὐδαίμονες οἷσι κακῶν ἄγευστος αἰών.
> οἷς γὰρ ἂν σεισθῇ θεόθεν δόμος, ἄτας
> οὐδὲν ἐλλείπει γενεᾶς ἐπὶ πλῆθος ἕρπον· 585
> ὥστε ποντίας ἁλὸς
> οἶδμα δυσπνόοις ὅταν
> Θρῄσσησιν ἔρεβος ὕφαλον ἐπιδράμῃ πνοαῖς,
> κυλίνδει βυσσόθεν 590
> κελαινὰν θῖνα καὶ δυσάνεμοι
> στόνῳ βρέμουσιν ἀντιπλῆγες ἀκταί.

> Blessed are those whose life has not tasted evils. For when a house is shaken by the gods, there is no element of *atē* that does not advance towards the family's members, in all their numbers, as when the swell of the open sea, driven by ill-blowing Thracian blasts, runs over the submarine darkness and rolls the black sand from the depths, and struck by ill winds the headlands groan and roar in response.

The gods' shaking of the house need not specifically suggest a storm, and the description of *atē* as 'advancing' shows that there are more metaphors than one in play here, but 'shaking' has already been used in a nautical metaphor by Creon at 162–3 (after tossing the *polis* on heavy seas, the gods have set her upright again: τὰ μὲν δὴ πόλεος ἀσφαλῶς θεοὶ | πολλῷ σάλῳ σείσαντες ὤρθωσαν πάλιν), and if σεισθῇ in 584 is a general environmental metaphor, the sense is soon specified by the storm imagery of 586–92.[78] The storm is a recurrent image of disruption in the play,[79] and if, ultimately, Creon's career is one of error resulting in disaster, then the image of winds and storms has a role to play in its presentation.[80] In the second stasimon, the point of this imagery is to emphasize the force of divinely-inspired disaster; but the cause of that disaster is soon revealed as psychological (603, 615–25).[81] Just so, Tiresias affirms that the cause of the sickness that

Introduction: Archaic Thought and Tragic Interpretation

afflicts the city is to be located in the mind of Creon (1015). Accordingly, the imagery of storms and winds is also used of psychological disturbance. As we saw, the Coryphaeus' view that Antigone, in refusing to give in to evils, has inherited her father's temper (471–2) is one of the passages that foreshadows the Chorus' meditations on recurrent cycles of *atē* in the second stasimon. That being so, we might notice the similarity of the diagnosis at 929–30, immediately after the speech in which she has defended her actions, lamented the injustice of her treatment, and expressed the wish that suffering as painful as her own might attend Creon should he, and not she, prove to have erred:

ἔτι τῶν αὐτῶν ἀνέμων αὐταὶ
ψυχῆς ῥιπαὶ τήνδε γ' ἔχουσιν. 930

Still the same blasts of the same winds of the soul possess her.

The notion of psychological winds (a natural image in a language in which the terms for psychological phenomena such as *psychē*, *pneuma*, and *thymos* all rest on ontological metaphors of breathing and blowing)[82] has already appeared in the parodos in connexion with the impious Argive invader, Capaneus (134–7):

ἀντιτύπᾳ δ' ἐπὶ γᾷ πέσε τανταλωθεὶς
πυρφόρος ὃς τότε μαινομένᾳ ξὺν ὁρμᾷ 135
βακχεύων ἐπέπνει
ῥιπαῖς ἐχθίστων ἀνέμων.

Swung in the balance, he fell and struck the hard earth, the fire-bearer who till then had been breathing over us with blasts of hostile winds, raging in his mad onrush.

With these winds of unreason we might compare and contrast the 'windy thought' (ἀνεμόεν φρόνημα) of 354–5. Though these words occur in the first stasimon's ostensible praise of human rationality, they are as ambiguous as the immediately following ἀστυνόμους ὀργάς of 355–6: *phronēma* and *orgē* are inherently ambivalent terms ('thought', but also 'arrogance'; 'temperament', but also 'anger') and their negative senses soon assert themselves.[83] Tellingly, perhaps, the ode's first example of the forces that human rationality seeks to control is the sea (334–7), where the language clearly prefigures the opening lines of the second stasimon, quoted above (esp. οἰδμάσιν, 337, with οἶδμα, 587).[84] The winds of *atē* blow through the play, before finally sinking Creon, captain of the ship of state; like *atē* itself, these winds can represent both states of affairs and states of mind.

Blows of another sort may also be relevant. Though Wilhelm Havers' hypothesis that *atē* actually derives from a root meaning 'strike' does not carry conviction,[85] it is undeniable that *atē* can be spoken of as if it were the result of a physical blow. In Aeschylus' *Choephori*, for example, the Chorus sing of 'the inborn trouble and the discordant, bloody blow of *atē*' (466–8):[86]

ὦ πόνος ἐγγενής,
καὶ παράμουσος ἄτας
αἱματόεσσα πλαγά.

One might compare the 'shameful-minded, wretched *parakopa*, the beginning of pain' (αἰσχρόμητις | τάλαινα παρακοπὰ πρωτοπήμων) that knocks Agamemnon sideways at *Ag.* 222–3, as a result of which, constrained by the destructive winds from the Strymon that 'came...and carded the flower of the Argives' (192–8) and 'breathing in concert with the fortunes that struck him' (ἐμπαίοις τύχαισι συμπνέων, 187), he 'breathes an impious, impure, unholy change of mind' (φρενὸς πνέων δυσσεβῆ τροπαίαν | ἄναγνον ἀνίερον, 219–20).[87] The term *atē* does not occur in these lines, but they nevertheless contain imagery that is associated with *atē* in *Antigone* and elsewhere. Accordingly, when Creon fears 'striking [his] *thymos* on Ate's net' (if that is the right text) at 1097, the association between *atē* and a physical blow may be enough, in a play in which the blows of *atē* do occur and in which that concept is so pervasive, for us to detect *atē* also in the supernatural blow to the head that Creon suffers at 1272–4 or the 'great blows' that punish his 'great words' and demonstrate that good sense is the first part of happiness (1347–53).[88]

However that may be, there is more than enough to show that the central role of *atē* in the play encompasses the entire range of the traditional *atē* sequence, in which ruin and psychological impairment are linked as effect and cause. As a major theme in the play, *atē* cannot be dissociated from an even more prevalent concatenation of terms which present the characters' motives and their actions in terms of good and bad judgement and its good and bad consequences.[89] This pervasive theme, in turn, encompasses a wider dialectic between the powers of human reason and the irrational forces that limit and undermine it,[90] a dialectic that is exemplified most of all in the antithesis between the first stasimon, with its enumeration of the achievements of human ingenuity, and the subsequent choral odes – the second stasimon tracing ruin to its source in 'folly of reason and an Erinys of the mind' (603); the third on the power of Eros to drive people mad (790) and to warp their minds to their ruin (791–2); the fourth showcasing, *inter alia*, the madness of Lycurgus in seeking to restrain the frenzy of the female worshippers of Dionysus (the ἔνθεοι γυναῖκες of 963–4); and the fifth on the power of Dionysus himself, invoked to help cleanse the city of Thebes of its sickness, but already present, perhaps, in the destruction of the royal house brought about by a woman's rejection of restraint.[91] 'Madness' or irrationality is predicated variously of Antigone, Creon, Haemon, and Eurydice.[92] The first stasimon, famously, draws on the confidence of contemporary Sophists, especially Protagoras, in the potential of human reason and the possibility of progress; the subsequent odes, especially the second stasimon, and indeed the dénouement of the play in general, confront such attitudes with the limitations upon human rationality and the much more pessimistic assessments of the human capacity for progress that are characteristic of archaic thought. Such a confrontation is, in this play, an aspect of the tension between the world of contemporary society and politics and the values inherited from traditional poetry and myth that Vernant saw as definitive of the 'tragic moment'.[93]

The *Antigone*'s engagement with such ideas does not amount to a simple advocacy of piety over intelligence, but rather specifies the ethical and religious content of 'true wisdom'. A number of the play's reflexions on the nature of human intelligence therefore intersect with the theme of *atē* and *kerdos* in another sense, in so far as they contribute to an overall presentation of wisdom as the greatest and folly as the worst of human qualities. Pronouncements of what is best and what is worst for a person or for a community recur throughout the play; as Easterling shows in her chapter, this is a debate that is characteristic of archaic thought and thus of tragedy's debt to archaic thought.[94] Haemon opens and closes his long speech in the *agōn* with his father with reflexions on this subject: the *phrenes* (mind, sense) that the gods implant in human beings are the greatest of possessions (683–4);[95] hence (720–3) the best thing is for a man to be born full of knowledge (*epistēmē*), but if that proves not to be the case (as it often does), to learn from those who speak well is also good. Such a willingness to learn will in this case secure Creon's good fortune, for a father's success is a 'possession' which no other source of pride can surpass in value (701–11):[96] the son's joy in his father's flourishing (and vice versa) is, on the face of it, an alternative candidate for the best thing in life, but Haemon makes it clear that such an end can be secured only by the wisdom whose paramount value he emphasizes at the beginning and end of his speech.[97] The point recurs in the Tiresias scene: Tiresias reflects that *euboulia* is the best of possessions (1050) and Creon agrees that, by the same token, lack of sense (μὴ φρονεῖν) is the greatest harm (*blabē*, 1051).[98] Once the seriousness of Tiresias' prophecy has struck home, the Coryphaeus reiterates the value of *euboulia* in the present circumstances (1098) and (as we have seen) warns Creon of the Blabai, the Harms, that overtake the imprudent (1103–4); the allusion to the role of Ate in the allegory of the Litai thus brings the rhetoric of the best and worst for human beings into the ambit of the *atē*-theme.

Once the consequences of Creon's folly have become clear, the general lesson is repeated, first by the Messenger at 1242–3 (Haemon's death reveals to all mankind the extent to which *aboulia* is the greatest evil for a man), and then by the Chorus in the anapaests that close the play (1347–53):

πολλῷ τὸ φρονεῖν εὐδαιμονίας
πρῶτον ὑπάρχει· χρὴ δὲ τά γ' ἐς θεοὺς
μηδὲν ἀσεπτεῖν· μεγάλοι δὲ λόγοι   1350
μεγάλας πληγὰς τῶν ὑπεραύχων
ἀποτείσαντες
γήρᾳ τὸ φρονεῖν ἐδίδαξαν.

Good sense is by far the first part of *eudaimonia*: one must not disrespect the gods in any way. Mighty words of the boastful have paid their debt in mighty blows and taught good sense in old age.

'Good sense', it is clear, is not value-neutral: what it secures is a form of prosperity that depends on the right relationship with the gods. It may bring the greatest of advantages, for those who understand what is truly advantageous, but its goal is not simply the maximization of advantage. Hence Creon's suspicion, once he has been shaken by Tiresias' prophecy, that it may be best to complete one's life in preservation (σῴζοντα) of the established laws (1113–14) presents not another candidate for the title of 'best thing', but an understanding of what the best thing, i.e. good sense, consists in. From the entrance of Haemon onwards, i.e. from the point at which Creon's judgement begins to be questioned even by those who wish him well,[99] opinions are unanimous that good judgement is the best and bad judgement the worst thing. Earlier in the play, however, Creon had expressed different views: in line with his profession at 184–90 that his priority is the city's safety (as opposed to ruin, *atē*, 185), for it is the city that ensures the safety of her citizens (189–90), so at 295–303 he regards money as the worst thing in the world, for money sacks cities and turns citizens out of their homes, while at 672–7 he describes disobedience to authority in very similar terms.[100] Where at 189–90 it is the successful sailing of the ship of state that brings *sōtēria* to its citizens (ἥδ' ἐστὶν ἡ σῴζουσα καὶ ταύτης ἔπι | πλέοντες ὀρθῆς τοὺς φίλους ποιούμεθα), so at 675–6 it is the citizens' obedience that secures the same end (τῶν δ' ὀρθουμένων | σῴζει τὰ πολλὰ σώμαθ' ἡ πειθαρχία). These views on what saves and ruins a city are, at least implicitly, views about what constitutes *atē*, 'disaster'; they are replaced, in the final analysis, by the view that harm as a state of affairs has its cause in impaired and harmful states of mind that take insufficient account of divine law.

Introduction: Archaic Thought and Tragic Interpretation

As we have seen, much of the play's debate about what is valuable in human existence is conducted in terms of the nature of *kerdos*, 'profit'. *Kerdos* is a regular antonym of *atē*; accordingly, the antithesis of *kerdos* and *atē* is drawn into the play's reflexions on good and bad forms of wealth and prosperity and on the nature of happiness. Creon himself does not believe that material prosperity is the goal of existence; for him, money is the root of all evil (295–6). He is rather one of 'those who care about power' (ὅτῳ κράτος μέλει), as the Chorus put it at 873. But Creon's evaluations of others' motives do not rise above the material: even before the Guard has entered with his report of the first burial of Polynices, Creon betrays his suspicion that, if anyone should, on pain of death, defy his edict, profit would be their motive (221–2):

καὶ μὴν ὁ μισθός γ' οὗτος. ἀλλ' ὑπ' ἐλπίδων
ἄνδρας τὸ κέρδος πολλάκις διώλεσεν.

Aye, that [sc. death] is the reward [sc. for disobeying the edict]. But profit accompanied by hope often ruins men.

Here is a form of profit-seeking that entails loss and ruin; there is a link between 'hope' here and the deceptive hope that leads to disaster (*atē*) in the second stasimon (615–25). The antithesis between *kerdos* and *atē* that is implicit in this passage is explicit, and subsumed in the related opposition between *atē* and *sōtēria*, in Creon's presentation of the Guards' motivation at 308–14:[101]

οὐχ ὑμὶν Ἅιδης μοῦνος ἀρκέσει, πρὶν ἂν
ζῶντες κρεμαστοὶ τήνδε δηλώσηθ' ὕβριν,
ἵν' εἰδότες τὸ κέρδος ἔνθεν οἰστέον   310
τὸ λοιπὸν ἁρπάζητε, καὶ μάθηθ' ὅτι
οὐκ ἐξ ἅπαντος δεῖ τὸ κερδαίνειν φιλεῖν.
ἐκ τῶν γὰρ αἰσχρῶν λημμάτων τοὺς πλείονας
ἀτωμένους ἴδοις ἂν ἢ σεσωμένους.

Death alone will not suffice for you, until you are hanged alive and reveal this *hybris*, in order that in future you may conduct your depredations in full knowledge of the proper sources of *kerdos* and learn that it is not right to love to take *kerdos* from just any source. For you will see that more men are ruined than saved as a result of shameful profits.

The appearance of *hybris* in 309 brings in that characteristically 'archaic' sequence, the 'archaic chain' of wealth, *hybris*, and *atē* – a sequence that is latent in the second stasimon's assertion that no great wealth (or nothing great) comes to human beings without *atē*.[102]

Creon's suspicions of others' mercenary motives resurface in his confrontation with Tiresias. Tiresias, like all seers, is allegedly motivated only by money and profit (1033–47, 1055, 1061, 1077–8); Creon himself is one of the commodities to be bought and sold (1035–6, 1063). By focusing so single-mindedly (and, of course, erroneously) on the material *kerdē* that, in his view, motivate others, but not himself, Creon reveals the limitations of his own outlook.[103] In the end, that outlook brings him to a point at which he is 'rich' only in misfortune (ὡς ἔχων τε καὶ κεκτημένος, 1278) and the only *kerdos* in the midst of his ruin is to be hidden from sight as quickly as possible (1320–7, especially 1326, κέρδη παραινεῖς, εἴ τι κέρδος ἐν κακοῖς).

Both Tiresias and Antigone offer Creon alternative conceptions of *kerdos*, but he is blind to them. Creon's denunciation of the profit-seeking of seers is itself prompted by Tiresias' suggestion that *kerdos* (1032) can be secured if only he recognizes his *hamartia* (1023–7), remedies the damage (1026–7), and is prepared to learn from one who speaks wisely and with good intent (1031–2). This is the most pleasant thing (1032), since *euboulia* is the greatest of possessions (*ktēmata*, 1050). Antigone, for her part, seeks a *kerdos* that is beyond the ken of men like Creon and the Chorus. For Creon, death is the ultimate sanction (35–6, 221, 308, 488–9, 498, 577, 750, 760–1, 768–80, 936–7) – a sanction that he characteristically speaks of in monetary terms (as the *misthos* for defying his edict, 221). For the Coryphaeus no one is so stupid as to desire death (220). But Antigone's desire, her *erōs*, for actions that will bring her death, has already been deprecated by Ismene (90; cf. 95–7); and at 460–70 she justifies that desire:

> θανουμένη γὰρ ἐξῄδη, τί δ' οὔ;   460
> κεἰ μὴ σὺ προὐκήρυξας. εἰ δὲ τοῦ χρόνου
> πρόσθεν θανοῦμαι, κέρδος αὔτ' ἐγὼ λέγω.
> ὅστις γὰρ ἐν πολλοῖσιν ὡς ἐγὼ κακοῖς
> ζῇ, πῶς ὅδ' οὐχὶ κατθανὼν κέρδος φέρει;
> οὕτως ἔμοιγε τοῦδε τοῦ μόρου τυχεῖν   465
> παρ' οὐδὲν ἄλγος· ἀλλ' ἄν, εἰ τὸν ἐξ ἐμῆς
> μητρὸς θανόντ' ἄθαπτον <ὄντ'> ἠνεσχόμην,
> κείνοις ἂν ἤλγουν· τοῖσδε δ' οὐκ ἀλγύνομαι.
> σοὶ δ' εἰ δοκῶ νῦν μῶρα δρῶσα τυγχάνειν,
> σχεδόν τι μώρῳ μωρίαν ὀφλισκάνω.   470

I knew that I should die – of course I did. Even if you hadn't proclaimed it, I'd have known. But if I am going to die before my time, I call that *kerdos*. For when you live, as I do, in the midst of many evils, how is it not *kerdos* to die? So for me to meet with this fate is a trivial source of pain. But if I had countenanced my mother's dead son being unburied, *that* would have caused me pain; at *this* I feel none. And if you now think that my actions are foolish, one might almost say that I am charged with folly by a fool.

Antigone's willingness to die rather than compromise her obligations to her brother presents a notion of 'profit' that is utterly different from those envisaged by Creon (while at the same time ironically confirming his suspicion that, at least in some sense, *kerdos* is the motive of those who oppose him).[104] But it also represents a variation on the theme that is discussed at length in Easterling's contribution to this volume: given that Antigone has already been born, and into a family such as her own at that, an early death is the next best thing to not being born at all.

In presenting the issues in such terms Sophocles draws on a long tradition of archaic moralizing on good and bad ways to acquire material wealth and on material *versus* non-material forms of prosperity.[105] In the end, the play's manifold dialectic on the best and worst things, profit and loss, benefit and harm, safety and ruin – i.e. on *kerdos*, *atē*, and their various counterparts – represents a sustained reflexion on the nature of *olbos* or *eudaimonia*. Accordingly, *eudaimonia* is the topic which, in the form of a traditional *makarismos*, introduces the second stasimon's thoughts on *atē* (582–5):

εὐδαίμονες οἷσι κακῶν ἄγευστος αἰών.
οἷς γὰρ ἂν σεισθῇ θεόθεν δόμος, ἄτας
οὐδὲν ἐλλείπει γενεᾶς ἐπὶ πλῆθος ἕρπον.   585

Blessed are those whose life has not tasted evils. For when a house is shaken by the gods, there is no element of *atē* that does not advance towards the family's members, in all their numbers.

Here, *atē* seems simply to be *eudaimonia*'s negation, ruin or catastrophe. In the first antistrophe, however, its origin (in the case of the Labdacidae) is traced to its traditional source in the aberrations of the human mind (593–603). In the second strophe, mental disturbance is replaced by transgression of Zeus' law as the source of *atē* (604–14), but the cause of transgression is then again specified, in the second antistrophe, as delusion (god-inspired). As we have seen, the second stasimon's presentation of the human propensity to error and destruction proves to be an accurate account of the actions of Creon. When the consequences of those actions are known, both the wider pattern (in which error and its consequences exemplify the instability of human fortunes) and the narrower one (which highlights humans' responsibility for their own suffering, whether directly or through the intervention of the gods to punish transgressors) are emphasized.

The former construction is the one put forward by the Messenger at 1155–71:

Κάδμου πάροικοι καὶ δόμων Ἀμφίονος   1155
οὐκ ἔσθ' ὁποῖον στάντ' ἂν ἀνθρώπου βίον
οὔτ' αἰνέσαιμ' ἂν οὔτε μεμψαίμην ποτέ.
τύχη γὰρ ὀρθοῖ καὶ τύχη καταρρέπει

> τὸν εὐτυχοῦντα τόν τε δυστυχοῦντ' ἀεί·
> καὶ μάντις οὐδεὶς τῶν καθεστώτων βροτοῖς.　　　　　1160
> Κρέων γὰρ ἦν ζηλωτός, ὡς ἐμοί, ποτέ,
> σώσας μὲν ἐχθρῶν τήνδε Καδμείαν χθόνα,
> λαβών τε χώρας παντελῆ μοναρχίαν
> ηὔθυνε, θάλλων εὐγενεῖ τέκνων σπορᾷ·
> καὶ νῦν ἀφεῖται πάντα. καὶ γὰρ ἡδοναὶ　　　　　　　1165
> ὅταν προδῶσιν ἀνδρός, οὐ τίθημ' ἐγὼ
> ζῆν τοῦτον, ἀλλ' ἔμψυχον ἡγοῦμαι νεκρόν.
> πλούτει τε γὰρ κατ' οἶκον, εἰ βούλῃ, μέγα,
> καὶ ζῆ τύραννον σχῆμ' ἔχων, ἐὰν δ' ἀπῇ
> τούτων τὸ χαίρειν, τἄλλ' ἐγὼ καπνοῦ σκιᾶς　　　　1170
> οὐκ ἂν πριαίμην ἀνδρὶ πρὸς τὴν ἡδονήν.

> Neighbours of the house of Cadmus and of Amphion, there is no human life of any kind that I should ever praise or blame as a stable entity. For *tychē* raises up and *tychē* causes to sink both the fortunate and the unfortunate at any given time; and there is no prophet of what is established for mortals. For Creon was enviable once, as it seems to me: he saved this Cadmeian land from its enemies, he assumed complete and sole command over the country, and he ruled, flourishing with noble offspring. And now all is lost. When a man's pleasures desert him, I do not reckon him to be alive, but consider him a living corpse. So amass great riches at home, if you will, and live in the manner of a tyrant; but if the joy of these things should leave, I should not buy the rest from a man for a shadow of smoke, in comparison to pleasure.

This evaluation does not diminish Creon's responsibility or deny that he has perpetrated acts that warrant divine punishment: these aspects of his plight are emphasized once Creon himself has returned at 1257.[106] But there, too, considerable emphasis is placed upon his status as an example of the mutability of fortune, the fragility of happiness, and the inevitability of suffering (1265, 1276, 1296, 1337–8). The two strands are maintained in the Chorus' closing anapaests (1347–53, quoted above), with their reference to the role of good sense in *eudaimonia*, but also the dangers of pride and impiety as aspects of human folly.

The Messenger's summary account of Creon's downfall is full of traditional ideas – the impossibility of passing judgement on the quality of a person's life (at least until it is over),[107] the alternation of good and bad fortune,[108] the shadowy, insubstantial nature of human existence[109] – but this is not just trite, all-purpose moralizing, for the moral is fully integrated into the thematic structure of the play as a whole. There is, for example, irony in the Messenger's statement that there is no *mantis* of what is established for mortals (1160): Creon was certainly no *mantis* (despite his confidence, in the ironic formulation of line 631, that he would soon know the future 'better than *manteis*'), and by the time he recognized that it may be better to 'preserve the established laws' (τοὺς καθεστῶτας νόμους... σῴζοντα, 1113–14; cf. τῶν καθεστώτων, 1160), it was too late. In truth, it needed no *manteia* for Creon to conjecture that the ominous sounds he hears on entering Antigone's 'unhallowed bridal chamber' portend disaster (1206–14, esp. 'Am I a *mantis*?' at 1212); but *manteia* does exist and is, as practised by Tiresias, veridical. Equally, the notions of τὸ ὀρθόν (1158) and *sōtēria* (1162) have been important in the text ever since Creon enunciated his belief that 'the city is our salvation and only if she remains upright as we sail on her do we choose our friends' (189–90).[110] Creon has steered his ship (cf. ηὔθυνε, 1164), and that of the city whose salvation he sought, not into safety, but into disaster – into a harbour of Death (1284). Similarly, the Messenger's pronouncement that Creon is now 'a living corpse' (1165–7) shows that the parallelism between her fate and Creon's for which Antigone prayed (925–8) and which Tiresias predicted (1065–76) is now coming to pass. The balance between the fates of Polynices, Antigone, and Creon that these words establish is subsumed in a larger pattern of imagery which presents the shifting balance of human fortunes as an example of a universal pattern. For while the use of the verb ὀρθόω in 1158 recalls the earlier use of words from the same root with reference to the successful sailing of the ship of state, in this particular context it is part of an image of weighing objects in the balance (see especially καταρρέπει in 1158), an image that is reinforced by the precise balance of antithetical terms in each of the lines 1157–9 (οὔτ' αἰνέσαιμ' ἂν οὔτε μεμψαίμην ποτέ, | τύχη γὰρ ὀρθοῖ καὶ τύχῃ καταρρέπει | τὸν εὐτυχοῦντα τόν τε δυστυχοῦντ' ἀεί).[111] This is an image which presents the abstract concept of human happiness as if it were a commodity which could be weighed in the pans of the scales, precisely in order to demonstrate that human happiness does *not* in fact reside in things that one can weigh or count. This is the burden of all the language of *kerdos* in the play, which in the end emphasizes that what is of true value in life cannot be bought and sold. Just so, the Messenger dismisses mere wealth and power (πλούτει τε γὰρ ..., 1168–9), all of which is worth nothing in comparison with pleasure – and again non-material value is expressed in language of monetary exchange (οὐκ ἂν πριαίμην, 1171).[112]

Here, the language of money and material exchange is being used as a way of thinking about non-material notions of value in terms of a universal pattern of equilibrium and exchange. The mutability of fortune, a recurrent pattern that is a facet of the social, moral, and existential conditions under which humans live, can also be seen in terms of yet more abstract, universal patterns. These can be understood in terms of the affinity between the ethical, political, and socioeconomic thought of archaic Greece and the more abstract concepts of presocratic philosophy that is explored, in this volume and elsewhere, by Richard Seaford.[113] As Seaford argues, to trace such affinities is less a matter of drawing lines of influence between this or that fragment of a presocratic thinker and its alleged echoes in tragedy, or of allegorizing tragic myth in presocratic terms, but rather of the way that archaic social, ethical, and political notions have shaped the thought of both tragedians and philosophers, to the extent that the embedding of such principles in presocratic cosmology often has analogues in the dialectical structure of tragic texts. In constructing a model of the cosmos on the basis of human ethical and social concepts, tragedy reflects archaic thought at both the popular and the philosophical level.[114]

Creon initially creates an imbalance by keeping a corpse in the world of the living, but that is followed by a further and complementary disequilibrium when he condemns Antigone to a living death; the opposites 'up' and 'down' have, as Tiresias sees it, been confounded; as a result, Creon is condemned to redress the balance by giving a corpse in exchange for a corpse, a 'child of his own entrails' (1064–73); and if the loss of Haemon demonstrates the importance of the ties of kinship that Creon sought to deny in the case of Antigone and Polynices, so the subsequent loss of his wife emphasizes the conjugal bond that he denied in the case of Antigone and Haemon.[115] This notion of equilibrium is emphasized in the Messenger's speech, especially via the image of the scales. His is a conception of balance in human affairs, but Tiresias' speech reveals a corresponding cosmic and natural notion of equilibrium.[116] The 'cosmological confusion' (as Seaford calls it, 2012, 330, 331) created by Creon's actions is mirrored in the disruption of the natural world. This represents the breakdown of the sacrificial order that reflects the hierarchy of god, man, and beast. The social, the religious, and the natural environment form part of a single, interconnected system in which disruption in one part affects the others in what can be seen both as a natural sequence of cause and effect and a reflexion of divine displeasure. Perhaps inevitably, one thinks of the presocratic Anaximander's system of cosmic reciprocity (A 9 DK, subsuming B 1 DK).[117] In general terms, one might compare the Hymn to Eros that forms the play's third stasimon (781–800). Here, Eros is both a divinity and a psychosocial phenomenon, but also a force of nature that 'roams over the sea and in pastoral steadings' (785–6). Sophocles' contemporary, Empedocles, similarly thought of Love (Philotes) as a cosmic principle, but one that could still be called by the name of the traditional Olympian divinity, Aphrodite (B 17. 24 DK).[118] For Empedocles, the universe was subject to a constant cycle of separation and recombination governed by Philotes and Neikos (Strife).[119] It *may* be mere coincidence that in the *Antigone*'s third stasimon Eros is a source of *neikos* (793–4), but this is a play and a myth in which the categories of *philia, erōs,* and *neikos* have repeatedly been confounded. Strife is an important principle also for Heraclitus, whose emphasis on the unity of opposites Seaford brings into relation with Aeschylus both in this volume and elsewhere. Though *Antigone* ostensibly portrays the working of a universe ruled by anthropomorphic divinities, its cosmos can also be seen as exhibiting patterns analogous to those found in the impersonal systems of certain presocratic thinkers. Sophoclean tragedy in general, and *Antigone* in particular, share with Aeschylus and the presocratics a sense of the interaction of natural and universal laws on the one hand and human ethical and social norms on the other. Yet, though its universe is pervasively patterned upon human social institutions, the world of the *Antigone* is most certainly not, despite the first stasimon's reflexion of contemporary theories of human progress, one in which man is the measure of all things, but a more pessimistic and 'archaic' one whose rhythms are substantially resistant to human control.

The *Antigone* is a play that emphasizes the role of states of mind and character in choice and in the outcomes of choice, yet the choices that it dramatizes are also presented as depending on factors that lie beyond the agent's control. For the Chorus, Antigone's own 'self-willed temper' (αὐτόγνωτος ... ὀργά, 875) has destroyed her; yet they also believe that she is paying for a debt incurred by her father (856, cf. 471–2) and that her actions instantiate a recurrent pattern of suffering in her family (594–8). The Chorus charge Creon with responsibility for his sufferings (1258–60), and he accepts the charge (1261–9), yet he also attributes his *dysbouliai* to a god who struck him on the head and overturned his happiness (1272–6), and sees his troubles as 'fated' (*potmos*, 1296, 1345–6). The Chorus concur: 'there is no release for mortals from a disaster that is fated' (ὡς πεπρωμένης | οὐκ ἔστι θνητοῖς συμφορᾶς ἀπαλλαγή, 1337–8).[120] What was true of the Labdacids, according to the second stasimon (οὐδ' ἀπαλλάσσει γενεὰν γένος, ἀλλ' ἐρείπει | θεῶν τις, οὐδ' ἔχει λύσιν, 596–8), is apparently true of Creon.[121] Well may we ask (with Winnington-Ingram, loc. cit.), what kind of fate this is. The premise of Tiresias' intervention is that Creon can be dissuaded from his error, that disaster can be averted (1023–32); yet Antigone's suffering is apparently part of an inherited pattern from which her family cannot break free; and Creon seems to believe that he himself exemplifies 'the famous dictum that bad seems good to a man whose mind a god is leading towards *atē*' (621–4). The very different plot-structures of *Antigone* and *OT* appear to demand, on one level, different audience perspectives on the ability of human beings to shape their lives. In the *OT*, the plot

Athenian theatre-goer; but in *Antigone, OT*, and elsewhere, there are patterns that ordinary Athenians, by virtue of their familiarity with a shared cultural model that is prominent in some of the most authoritative works of their poetic tradition, can recognize in their own lives.

From the principle of alternation, the cornerstone of the archaic Greek world view, flow many of archaic thought's other most typical observations: of the ambivalence of hope, of man's ephemeral nature, of the need to call no man happy until he is dead, and so on.[129] Alternation is not the only motif from which tragic plots are fashioned, but it is a central aspect of several, especially in Sophocles, and the norms with which it belongs are reflected more peripherally in many more.[130] It does not dictate a single plot-structure, but is nonetheless a crucial factor in the presentation of the *mythos* in plays such as *Antigone, Ajax, Trachiniae*, and the *OT*. This, moreover, is a salient enough feature of tragic plots to find its way into Aristotle's *Poetics*. The details are well known. In one of Aristotle's preferred types of plot, the audience is emotionally affected by a character's change from good fortune to bad. This emotional reaction relies on the ability to refer what happens to the character to what might happen to oneself. The character should contribute to his own misfortune but not entirely deserve it. And while the character should therefore be in some respects like us, the typical examples are provided by a few familiar (heroic) figures.[131] Aristotle's approval of this classic plot type in the *Poetics* is matched by the serious consideration that he gives its archaic ethical underpinnings in the *Ethics*.[132] It is true, at least in a sense, that one should count no man happy until he is dead;[133] *eudaimonia* is a quality of a whole life, and lives as wholes are vulnerable to the kinds of vicissitude that feature in the representations of the downfall of exemplary figures from the heroic past in epic and tragedy. In conceding something to traditional wisdom, Aristotle tellingly makes his point by means of the traditional *exemplum* of Priam (*EN* 1100a 4–9, 1101a6–13) – Priam who is both the recipient of Achilles' exemplary consolation in *Iliad* 24 and himself an embodiment of that speech's exemplary force. Aristotle's model in *Poetics* 13 fits only a few tragedies; but this is in itself interesting. In eschewing a purely descriptive model, Aristotle has his own agenda, but this is an agenda that in both the *Ethics* and the *Poetics* makes room for central concepts of archaic Greek thought. The plot-type that he finds instantiated in the *OT* is not typical, but it may be, in his mind and in those of many of his contemporaries and predecessors, prototypical.[134] Aristotle's focus on plots that involve the fallibility of human choice, a resulting change in fortune, and the arousal of sympathetic but self-referential emotions in an audience instantiates a salient and influential cultural model that goes back to the ancient world's most authoritative poetic archetype, the *Iliad*.

3. Conclusion

In his own way and from his own individual philosophical perspective, Aristotle takes archaic Greek thought seriously both in his exploration of tragic poetry and by accommodating and developing in his ethical thought archaic concerns with the nature and possibility of *eudaimonia*. The relation between tragedy and archaic Greek thought, therefore, is not something that contemporary students of tragedy can afford to ignore. But if that relation is to form part of the modern reader's interpretative response, then the issues raised need to be presented to students not as the fruits of a survey of a limited range of older views on allegedly settled questions, but through lively and first-hand engagement with the evidence and arguments, both those on which previous generations built their hypotheses and such new arguments as we ourselves can bring to bear. Interpretation should not be a matter of affiliating oneself to movements, tendencies, or schools of thought, but of working through the subject-matter for oneself at first hand; this is a task that each reader, each scholar, each generation of scholars needs to perform, building on what has gone before but not taking the answers of previous generations on trust. Interpretation of Greek tragedy can be presented as – and sometimes is – a dismal rehearsal of tired old views. But it must not be. If the exploration of tragedy's relation to archaic thought is central to the interpretation of tragedy more generally, it cannot simply be left to works of synthesis and pedagogy. And if an understanding of archaic Greek thought is essential to tragic interpretation, then research on the relevant topics needs to reclaim its place alongside the dominant trends of contemporary research that focus on tragedy's contexts, performance, and reception. For these are sub-disciplines that presuppose the main business, of seeking to enjoy and to understand the plays themselves. To be sure, to do this one must know as much as one can about tragedy's contexts in Athenian culture, about its performance history, and about its reception, but one must also come to grips with the traditional intellectual fabric of the plays themselves.

Hence this volume reflects its contributors' firm belief that the intellectual content of tragedy and its roots in archaic Greek thought, both popular and elite, still matter and require discussion in our terms. The volume's approach is historicist, but not naively so. It is not a vain attempt to attain unmediated access to the issues 'as they really were'; inevitably, even the identification of the issues themselves reflects our own contemporary concerns, with their own intellectual history. This is why the enterprise is worth undertaking. The volume assumes not only that archaic thought is a context as significant for tragic scholarship as the civic, the ritual, and the performative, but also that tragedy's engagement with its legacy from archaic thought has profoundly shaped the intellectual content of the plays themselves. We hope that an understanding of tragedy's engagement with archaic thought might enhance approaches that concentrate on alternative contexts, civic, ritual, performative, or poetic, just as those approaches have enhanced our own. We do not attempt to close down interpretation, to advocate a single approach, or simply to return to 'traditional scholarship'. Rather, the volume reflects our sense that there are new and interesting ways to investigate archaic Greek thought as an element in tragedy's conceptual fabric; it takes its inspiration from the seriousness accorded archaic thought by the very different approaches of scholars such as Williams, Theunissen, and Seaford.[135] Of the many different ways in which this might be done, most inevitably remain untouched in a volume as slim as this one. But however we may effect it, the return to a focus on archaic thought is surely overdue.

Notes

[1] This shift, in turn, has been followed by an increased focus on reception, modern performance, and the history of scholarship.

[2] Goldhill and Hall 2009, 1–24.

[3] Rosenmeyer 1993, 563, referring to works of the 1970s and 80s.

[4] See esp. Vernant and Vidal-Naquet 1990; on their influence, cf. Goldhill and Hall 2009, 14–17. The notion of a decisive change of direction can be exaggerated: the influence of Winnington-Ingram's 'Tragedy and Greek archaic thought' (Winnington-Ingram 1965, developed especially in Winnington-Ingram 1980; cf. Winnington-Ingram 1983) on Vernant is substantial, though acknowledged only sporadically (e.g. Vernant 1990a, 71, 77).

[5] Cf. Goldhill 2012, 3–4.

[6] See Goldhill 2012, esp. Part II.

[7] Stallmach 1968. Stallmach is heavily influenced by the work of Kurt Latte, especially his 'Schuld und Sünde in der griechischen Religion', first published in 1921 and reprinted in his *Kleine Schriften* (Latte 1968, 3–35).

[8] Williams 1993; Gill 1996.

[9] See, however, the recent studies of Sewell-Rutter 2007 and (to an extent) Apfel 2011. The latter's application of Isaiah Berlin's doctrine of value pluralism to such quintessentially 'archaic' authors as Herodotus and Sophocles is valuable, but the author retains a progressivist approach which presents the Homeric poems as the less sophisticated ethical soil from which more developed conceptualizations spring.

[10] See e.g. Padel 1995.

[11] This claim is indeed arguable. For a different view, see Cairns 2012a, 13–16, against Dodds 1951, 5.

[12] See e.g. Seiler 1954 (repeated in Seiler 1955) or G. Müller 1956, 5–7, on the development, allegedly traceable even within the *Iliad* itself, from *atē*'s 'original' core meaning of *Verblendung* (what Müller calls 'die echte alte ἄτη') to that of *Schaden*.

[13] Cf. Sommerstein below, p. 13 n. 10.

Introduction: Archaic Thought and Tragic Interpretation

[14] The first translates the OCT's οὐδέν' ἕρπει θνατῶν βίοτος πάμπολυς ἐκτὸς ἄτας (Lloyd-Jones, following the Aldine's οὐδέν' and Musgrave's πάμπολυς), the second Heath's emendation (πάμπολύ γ') of MSS' οὐδὲν ἕρπει θνατῶν βιότῳ πάμπολις ἐκτὸς ἄτας, as printed by Jebb 1900b and Dawe 1985. Either would be a traditional thought, which (as the content of the eternal law) is what seems to be what is required here. This makes οὐδ' ἐφέρπει ... πάμπολυς (sc. νόμος, as proposed by Brown 1987, 175) less likely. For the general notion that unalloyed happiness is impossible, see e.g. *Il.* 24. 525–33; Archil. fr. 130 W; Sem. 1. 20–2; Mimn. 2. 15–16 W; Sol. fr. 14 W; Thgn. 167–8, 441–6; Sim. 520–3, 526–7 *PMG* (= 21, 244, 258, 245, 259/348, 349 Poltera, the last two regarded as *spuria*); B. 5. 50–5; Pi. *N.* 7. 54–6; this is the basis of the 'principle of alternation' that will occupy us later in this Introduction.

[15] Cf. Brown 1987, 176, on 624: 'For a mind there is little difference between *ātē* in the sense "ruin" and in the sense "infatuation", so the two senses are bridged here.' Cf. n. 24 below.

[16] I see these as the alleged causes of Antigone's action in burying the body of Polynices, and thus in apposition to MSS' κόνις, dust, not Jortin's κοπίς, cleaver, in 602, a position I hope to defend at appropriate length and in full detail elsewhere; for the opposing view, see Liapis, this volume, 94.

[17] Cf. Havers 1910, 235; Dawe 1968, 100–1, 108–9; Easterling 1978, 149; Kitzinger 2008, 38–9. Personified Ate and the Erinys are famously associated in Agamemnon's Apology at *Il.* 19. 87–8. On the importance of *atē* and Erinyes in A. *Th.* see the chapters by Sommerstein and Herrmann in this volume, with further references.

[18] The ambivalence of hope is proverbial: see Hes. *Op.* 498–501; Sem. fr. 1. 6–10 W (cf. 23, where hope is equated with κακῶν ἐρᾶν); Thgn. 637–8; Sol. fr. 13. 33–6 W; Pi. *O.* 12. 5–6, 13. 83, *P.* 3. 21–3, *N.* 8. 45, 11. 45–6, *I.* 2. 43; B. 3. 75–6; E. *Supp.* 479–80; Antiph. B 58 DK; Thuc. 5. 103; cf. Wehrli 1931, 6–14; Easterling 1978, 153; Theunissen 2002, 341–95. For πολύπλαγκτος in a negative sense and a psychological application, cf. B. 11. 35, with Cairns 2010, ad loc.

[19] See esp. *Il.* 2. 111–15, 9. 18–22, 10. 391–9, 19. 95–7; A. *Pers.* 93–100, *Supp.* 110–11 (also *Ag.* 385, with Sommerstein, this vol. 7–8, and Dawe 1968, 101); S. *Tr.* 849–50. At Hes. *Th.* 224–30 Ate is the daughter of Apate's sister, Eris. Cf. Havers 1910, 236; Dawe 1968, 100–1; Cairns 2012a, 15 n. 27.

[20] So Easterling 1978, 152; unnecessarily complicated by Brown 1987, 175–6.

[21] Thgn. 402–6:

πολλάκι δ' εἰς ἀρετήν
σπεύδει ἀνὴρ κέρδος διζήμενος, ὅντινα δαίμων
πρόφρων εἰς μεγάλην ἀμπλακίην παράγει,
καί οἱ ἔθηκε δοκεῖν, ἃ μὲν ᾖ κακά, ταῦτ' ἀγάθ' εἶναι   405
εὐμαρέως, ἃ δ' ἂν ᾖ χρήσιμα, ταῦτα κακά.

Often a man, in pursuit of *kerdos*, is eager for excellence, but a *daimōn* deliberately leads him astray into great error, and easily makes what is bad seem good to him, and what is good, bad.

Tr. adesp. 455:

ὅταν δ' ὁ δαίμων ἀνδρὶ πορσύνῃ κακά,
τὸν νοῦν ἔβλαψε πρῶτον ᾧ βουλεύεται.

Whenever the *daimōn* gives a man evils, he first harms the mind with which he plans.

See Jebb 1900b, 119–20 on 622 ff. (also citing Lyc. *Leocr*. 92); M. Griffith 1999, 230 on 622–4.

[22] The text is that printed by Garvie 2009 (which is in all essentials that of M. L. West 1990a). For the question of the location of this stanza in the *parodos* and the implications of transposition *versus* the MS order, see Garvie 2009, 46–9. Here it is only the association between Ate and divine deceit that concerns us.

[23] On this motif, see Hose 2006, esp. 95–6 on this passage.

[24] Cf. Brown 1987, 170–1: 'The archaic word *ātē* resounds ominously through [the ode] ... Here, though the idea of infatuation is very much present, the word *ātē* itself bears the sense "disaster", as it usually does in tragedy...'

[25] If the Chorus mean λόγου ἄνοια to apply to Antigone, then there is no need to be categorical about whether λόγου means 'speech' or 'reason' (see Liapis, this volume, 114 n. 50). The singular λόγου may favour the latter, but then the phrase λόγου ἄνοια is pleonastic, which might be thought to favour the former. But (again, if the primary reference in the minds of the Chorus, at least as we are to infer it, is to Antigone) Antigone has contributed to what the Chorus regard as a calamity both by what they see as the folly of her actions and by the words she used when brought to account for those actions (a point made by Creon in the preceding episode, 480–3). Equally, if we eventually conclude (see below) that the words bear an ironic reference to Creon, he too has both failed in his reasoning and implemented that failure in speech.

[26] I do not share Winnington-Ingram's worries (1979, 7–8; 1980, 168, 211) about the ontological status of the Erinys and so do not share the doubts about the authenticity of the phrase φρενῶν Ἐρινύς to which those concerns give rise. As Kitzinger (2008, 37 n. 54) observes, the use of the phrase to adumbrate the subjective, psychological aspect of *atē* does not preclude personification: 'it merely allows the source of the destruction to be understood as both the self and the divine'; see further below.

[27] On this phrase, see further below (at n. 49).

[28] Using the participle ἀτώμενος, which recurs at 314; also *Aj*. 269, 384; E. *Supp*. 182. Otherwise, ἀτάω/ἀτάομαι is restricted in classical sources to Cretan legal inscriptions, where it refers to the harm suffered by the injured party, the loss of a suit, or the penalty imposed: see *Leg. Gort*. col. 4. 29, 6. 23, 43, 10. 21; *IG* 5(1). 1155 (Gythium).

[29] On the adverb, cf. Sommerstein, this volume, 13 n. 10.

[30] The essential point for our purposes remains the same whether we read ματρῷαι (with most MSS) or πατρῷαι (with L and R) in 863.

[31] Cf. Liapis, below, p. 91. Again, the point is clear despite the doubts about the text. M. Griffith 1999 prints the text as found in the majority of MSS, but his translation ('The savage breeding of the daughter, from her savage father, is making itself plain') founders on the fact that γέννημα means (concrete) 'offspring' not (abstract) 'breeding' (as in 627, *Tr*. 315). With any text that retains γέννημα we need to take τῆς παιδός as explanatory ('the offspring, namely the child'), which even Jebb (who supports it) concedes is problematic (1900b ad loc). Without much conviction, Brown (1987 ad loc., after Nauck and Blaydes) suggests δῆλόν γέ τοι λῆμ' *exempli gratia* for what seems to be the required sense.

[32] Cf. Easterling 1978, 156. Her family's woes, of which hers are worst, are restated in iambic summary at 892–6.

[33] As in A. *Th*. 69–70, 655, 695–7, 766–7, 785–7, 832–3, 893, 945–6, 953–5; see Herrmann, this volume.

[34] For the issues here, with bibliography, see Liapis in Chapter 4 below, 90–5 and nn. 38, 52–6, and cf. Herrmann's Chapter 3 on the Aeschylean background.

[35] With ἀμηχάνων ἐρᾷς (90) cf. the hope that, for many, represents ἀπάτα κουφονόων ἐρώτων in the second stasimon at 617 (as well as the ironic application to Antigone of the Coryphaeus' statement at 220 that no one is so foolish as to be in love with death (οὐκ ἔστιν οὕτω μῶρος ὃς θανεῖν ἐρᾷ); and of course the Hymn to Eros at 781–800.

[36] The notion of *hybris* is latent in the whole of 473–83, even before it is explicitly enunciated at 480 and 482. The 'too hard *phronēmata*' of 473 activate the ambiguity of *phronēma* that recurs at various points in the play (176, 207, 353, 459; the nature of Creon's *phronēma* is a central issue, raised by his own observation at 175–7 that it is impossible to judge a man's *phronēma* until he has been tested in office). Similarly, the reference to 'high-spirited horses' (τοὺς θυμουμένους | ἵππους, 477–8) supplies a typical and recurrent exemplar of *hybris* (Fisher 1992, 119–21, 232–3, 353–4). And finally φρονεῖν μέγ' ('thinking big') in 479 uses a familiar periphrasis (which Creon uses again at 768 of Haemon) to express what is then conveyed by the two uses of *hybris*-words in 480 and 482. The 'archaic chain' is also implicit in the second stasimon of the *OT* (873–9; cf. Cairns below, 151–2, 156).

[37] On the 'archaic chain' see esp. Sol. 4. 34–5 W, with Fisher 1992, 72 (cf. 206, 213, 221, 236 ff.; also Seaford, this volume, 28–30); cf. Helm 1993, 2004. Its presence in the second stasimon is denied by Kitzinger 2008, 41; this depends largely on an adverbial reading of Heath's emendation πάμπολύ γε in 614 that is widely regarded as implausible (Easterling 1978, 15; M. Griffith 1999, 228). For me, the link between 480–5 and 604–14 proves the point.

[38] See *Pers.* 821–2:

ὕβρις γὰρ ἐξανθοῦσ' ἐκάρπωσε στάχυν
ἄτης, ὅθεν πάγκλαυτον ἐξαμᾷ θέρος.

For *hybris* burst into bloom and bore fruit in a crop of *atē*, whence it reaped a harvest of lamentation.

See Fisher 1992, 260. For Easterling (1978, 147), *Ant.* 601–2 does not presuppose the notion of a 'crop of evils' (for which she cites Sol. 4. 35 W, A. *Th.* 601, and *Ag.* 1655, as well as *Pers.* 821–2); but since the context is one in which mental impairment is said to lead to disaster, i.e. of the *atē* that is explicitly prominent in the ode, this is unlikely.

[39] See esp. Pi. *O.* 1. 55–8, with Wyatt 1982, 265–7. On both these folk etymologies, cf. Dawe 1968, 100–1, and see also below, xxvi.

[40] Antigone takes the Chorus' words not as a reference to Oedipus' *guilt*, but to the unfortunate destiny (*potmos*, 861) of the Labdacids; but that destiny includes her parents' incest, a horrific transgression – the passage preserves the ambivalence of the second stasimon between inherited suffering and inherited guilt.

[41] 872–5:

σέβειν μὲν εὐσέβειά τις,
κράτος δ', ὅτῳ κράτος μέλει,
παραβατὸν οὐδαμᾷ πέλει,
σὲ δ' αὐτόγνωτος ὤλεσ' ὀργά.   875

[42] See Cairns 2012a; Sommerstein, this volume.

[43] Dawe 1968; cf. Bremer 1969, 99–134.

[44] Cf. Foley 2001, 31–3.

[45] On the symmetry between the fate that Creon inflicts on Antigone (which itself recalls his treatment of Polynices' corpse) and his own, see 1064–76, 1166–7, 1288 (answering 1029–30), 1324–5.

[46] See e.g. Achilles' prediction that Agamemnon 'will recognize his *atē* in failing to pay honour to the best of the Achaeans' (*Il.* 1. 412, a sentiment repeated by Patroclus at 16. 274). This means simply that Agamemnon will regret his action once its consequences have become obvious (as he does: 2. 375–8, 9. 115–20; cf. and contrast 19. 85–144). Definitive recognition of *atē* must be retrospective; cf. Cairns 2012a, 19–20.

[47] Cf. Antigone at 914: Κρέοντι ταῦτ' ἔδοξ' ἁμαρτάνειν.

[48] δέδοικα γὰρ μὴ τοὺς καθεστῶτας νόμους
ἄριστον ᾖ σῴζοντα τὸν βίον τελεῖν.

The words are an ironic but nonetheless clear vindication of Antigone's position. It is Antigone's view of what is best that prevails; this is a theme to which I return below.

[49] Cf. 248, 289–90, 348, 661. Elsewhere in the second stasimon (at 615–17) the ambivalent hope that both benefits and deceives is likewise attributed specifically to *men* (ἀνδρῶν).

[50] Cf. 677–80. Antigone, for her part, will not compromise her principles for fear of any man's *phronēma* (ἀνδρὸς οὐδενὸς φρόνημα δείσασ', 458–9). Her words (a) echo Creon's own statement of principle at 175–7, (b) bring out the ambiguity of his term, *phronēma*, and (c) activate the antithesis not only between man and woman, but also between man and god. For Creon's normative conception of manhood, cf. 661–2, 668–9. Haemon (710–11, 720–1) and Tiresias (1023–7) enunciate other ideals of how a man (ἀνήρ) should behave, ideals that Creon cannot meet, so that, by the end of the play, he is a dead man (ὀλωλότ' ἄνδρ', 1288), a foolish man (μάταιον ἄνδρ', 1339), the one who has demonstrated in people's eyes (ἐν ἀνθρώποισι, 1242) that *aboulia* is the greatest evil for a man (ἀνδρί, 1243).

[51] On the way that the language of this and the other choral odes implicitly foregrounds the dangers and dubieties of Creon's conduct, see e.g. G. Müller 1961; Dawe 1968, 112; Easterling 1978, 157–8; Winnington-Ingram 1980, 91–116 *passim*, 118, 172; Brown 1987, 172, 187, 202–4; M. Griffith 1990, 220, 255, 284–5.

[52] On *atē* and agency in Homer, cf. Cairns 2012a, 9–17, esp. 16–17.

[53] On *atē*'s relation to results, cf. above (with n. 46 on *Il.* 1. 412). See also Solon 13. 65–70 W (~ Thgn. 585–90):

πᾶσι δέ τοι κίνδυνος ἐπ' ἔργμασιν, οὐδέ τις οἶδεν   65
  πῇ μέλλει σχήσειν χρήματος ἀρχομένου·
ἀλλ' ὁ μὲν εὖ ἔρδειν πειρώμενος οὐ προνοήσας
  ἐς μεγάλην ἄτην καὶ χαλεπὴν ἔπεσεν,
τῷ δὲ κακῶς ἔρδοντι θεὸς περὶ πάντα δίδωσιν
  συντυχίην ἀγαθήν, ἔκλυσιν ἀφροσύνης.   70

Risk attends all actions, and no one knows at the beginning how a thing is going to turn out. One who tries to do well falls into great and difficult *atē* without foreseeing it, while to the one who does badly a god gives a good outcome in every respect, an escape from folly.

[54] Antigone has already used the same verb and the same image (of the advance of a hostile opponent) at 9–10; the war against the Argives may be over, but both Antigone and Creon have further battles to fight.

⁵⁵ The personified *atē* here perhaps brings to mind the similarly personified δημόσιον κακόν against which Solon warns his fellow Athenians at fr. 4. 17–29 W; Creon's moralizing, both here and elsewhere, has a strongly Solonian colouring; cf. n. 105 below.

⁵⁶ Creon's metaphor of the touchstone at 177 implies a comparison between the value of gold and that of men that is common in the Theognid corpus: see Thgn. 119–28 (and cf. n. 57 below), 415–18, 447–52, 963–70, 1105–6, 1164g–h. The language and thought of *Ant.* 175–7 and Thgn. 963–70 in particular are close enough for Creon's words to remind an audience of Theognis' warning, that we should not praise a man until we know his character, i.e. his ὀργὴν καὶ ῥυθμὸν καὶ τρόπον (964), because many are counterfeit, not what they seem at first sight. We shall return below to the play's pervasive confrontation of material with non-material value; on the touchstone metaphor, cf. Seaford 1998, 135–6.

⁵⁷ See Sommerstein, this volume, 2 and Cairns 2012a, 1 n. 2, both with further references. For a clear play on *atē* as both 'loss' (as opposed to profit) and 'disaster', see Thgn. 119 (and cf. 133, 205–6).

⁵⁸ The conceit of the sisters as 'two Atai' is repeated, in a different context, at *OC* 531.

⁵⁹ Cf. 1050–1: as *euboulia* is the best of possessions, so μὴ φρονεῖν is the greatest harm (βλάβη), as Creon himself admits. On 'the best/worst thing' as an important theme in the play, see below.

⁶⁰ *Ant.* 1023–4. For the thought, cf. Thgn. 327–8; E. *Hipp.* 615, 916, 1434, *Supp.* 250–1; *Rhet. Alex.* 36. 35; and the further passages cited by Pearson 1917 on S. fr. 665 Radt. As Pearson observes, the thought is commonplace, but by no means trivial.

⁶¹ Creon himself was once able to secure the city's *sōtēria* (1162), but only with Tiresias' help (1058; cf. 995).

⁶² On the language of exchange here, see Seaford 2004, 160 and cf. below xxxv–xxxvi and n. 112.

⁶³ See Dawe 1978, 113–14; Brown 1987, 212; Lloyd-Jones and Wilson 1990b, 142.

⁶⁴ That being so, Tiresias' remark that Creon should learn τρέφειν τὴν γλῶσσαν ἡσυχαιτέραν | τὸν νοῦν τ' ἀμείνω τῶν φρενῶν ὧν νῦν φέρει ('to nurture a quieter tongue and a better mind than the one he has now') might well evoke 603's λόγου τ' ἄνοια καὶ φρενῶν Ἐρινύς.

⁶⁵ Lloyd-Jones's and Wilson's text, with Lloyd-Jones's own Ἄτης ... λίνῳ for MSS' Ἄτῃ ... δεινῷ in 1097 (Lloyd-Jones 1964). Lloyd-Jones himself (1964, 129) translates 'by offering resistance my anger may strike against the net of Ate', but taking ἀντιστάντα as referring to Creon, the subject, and θυμόν as object of πατάξαι ('accusative of the thing set in motion', LSJ s.v. πατάσσω, II) gives the verb its regular sense. As for the paradosis, repetition of the adjective δεινός in both halves of the antithesis is unlikely without a modifier in the second half, such as καί, and 'it is a terrible prospect to strike one's *thymos* with *atē*' is anyhow weak. The notion of Ate's net, on the other hand, has good Aeschylean pedigree (*Pers.* 97–9, *Ag.* 355–61; cf. *Pr.* 1071–9), on which cf. Sommerstein, this volume, 6–7, 15 n. 6. If this is plausible, then we might note that the image of Ate as a hunter or fisherman is (a) a further example of Sophocles' application of *atē*'s traditional imagery, (b) suggestive of the link between *atē* and *apatē*, and (c) an image that encompasses *atē*'s subjective aspect (the error that leads to one's capture) as well as its objective one (the disaster that results). For an

alternative emendation, given the unsatisfactory nature of the paradosis, see Dawe 1968, 113–14 n. 40.

[66] I take ἄτην as cognate accusative with ἁμαρτών, so that it suggests both the objective and the subjective senses, both 'ruin' and 'error'.

[67] Nothing in the commentaries of Jebb, Müller, Kamerbeek, Brown, or Griffith.

[68] On Ate's swiftness of foot, see Yamagata 2005, 22–3, with Cairns 2012a, 27.

[69] For a full defence of this position, see Cairns 2012a, 8, 15–16, 22–3, and (esp.) 26–33.

[70] Cf. R. M. Torrance 1965, 299–300; Winnington-Ingram 1980, 117, 147.

[71] Cf. (once more) Dawe 1968, 113–14 n. 49.

[72] For ὑστεροφθόροι cf. Σ ad loc.: αἱ ὕστερον μέλλουσαι βλάψαι. If λωβητῆρες is also being used here to suggest *atē*, then compare the Chorus' apostrophe of Eros at 791–2:

σὺ καὶ δικαίων ἀδίκους

φρένας παρασπᾷς ἐπὶ λώβᾳ.

You seize the minds even of the just and pervert them to injustice, to their ruin. Eros is another form of mental aberration that leads, according to the Chorus, to disaster; cf. below.

[73] 2. 275, 11. 385, and 24. 239.

[74] See Eust. 2. 777–8 Van der Valk. He has already cited the Sophoclean phrase at 2. 760 on *Il*. 9. 454, στυγερὰς δ' ἐπεκέκλετ' Ἐρινῦς.

[75] In the former, Apollo, or Pan, or Zeus sends a ὑστερόποινος Ἐρινύς against transgressors; in the latter, the Chorus pray to Zeus, who sends down ὑστερόποινος Ἄτη on reckless criminals. The adjective occurs elsewhere only at Nonnus, *Dion*. 9. 135.

[76] Cf. the storm which represents Zeus' punishment, and thus the *atē* which follows *hybris*, in Sol. 13. 11–25.

[77] See Scott 1966. Scott does not himself see the potential for folk-etymology, but for poetic reflexions of the *atē*/*aēmi* etymology, see Francis 1983. Cf. perhaps A. *Eum*. 938 (the Erinyes pray, 'may tree-vexing *blabē* not blow', δενδροπήμων δὲ μὴ πνέοι βλάβα); also S. *OC* 1239–48, with Easterling, this volume, pp. 199–200. The possible etymological link was, as far as I can tell, originally suggested by Goebel 1877, 32–55.

[78] Cf. Easterling 1978, 144.

[79] Cf. 391, 417–21, 670, 712–17.

[80] NB the recurrence of σείω at 1274, of a divine 'shaking' that echoes both the second stasimon at 584 and the 'shaking' of the ship of state in Creon's opening words at 162–3.

[81] Cf. Kitzinger 2008, 35 n. 46.

[82] See e.g. Padel 1992, 89–95, Clarke 1999.

[83] For *phronēma*, cf. nn. 36, 50, and for *orgē* and synonyms n. 92.

[84] With a pun on the name of Antigone's father?

[85] Havers 1910. On the weakness of this hypothesis, cf. Seiler 1954, 409–10; Dawe 1968, 96–7; Francis 1983, 87. Nor do there appear to be any clear examples of popular etymologies linking *atē* with words for 'striking a blow' (unlike those which link it with ἄω, 'satiate', ἄημι, and ἀπατάω).

[86] Cf. Havers 1910, 231.

[87] Cf. Dawe 1968, 96–7, 110–11. Dawe argues for a transposition of *Ag*. 160–91 *post* 217 that is immaterial to my argument.

[88] ἐν δ' ἐμῷ κάρᾳ | θεὸς τότ' ἄρα τότε με μέγα βάρος ἔχων | ἔπαισεν (1272–4); πολλῷ τὸ

φρονεῖν εὐδαιμονίας | πρῶτον ὑπάρχει· ... | ... μεγάλοι δὲ λόγοι | μεγάλας πληγὰς τῶν ὑπεραύχων | ἀποτείσαντες | γήρᾳ τὸ φρονεῖν ἐδίδαξαν (1347–53). Cf. Havers 1910, 234.

[89] See 67–8, 95, 99, 175–6, 179, 207, 220, 281, 310–14 (with the antithesis of *atē* and *sōtēria* in 314), 323, 342–67, 389, 469–70, 473–4, 557, 561–5, 603, 614–25 (hope, delusion, and *atē*), 637–8, 648–9, 681–4, 707–11, 719–27, 754–5, 791–2, 960–1, 1015, 1023–8, 1031–2, 1048–52, 1090, 1098, 1103–4 (the Blabai cut off the imprudent), 1228–9 (where the conjunction of 'mind' or 'intention' [τίνα νοῦν ἔσχες;] with 'disaster' [ἐν τῷ συμφορᾶς διεφθάρη;] suggests the *atē*-sequence), 1242–3, 1250, 1261–2 (φρενῶν δυσφρόνων ἁμαρτήματα, picking up *atē* and *hamartia*, in 1259–60), 1265, 1269, 1271, 1339–40, 1347–53, with Cropp 1997, 143–7; cf. Winnington-Ingram 1980, 121; Liapis, this volume, 114 n. 50.

[90] See Winnington-Ingram 1980, 91–116.

[91] Cf. Seaford 1990, 87–9; 2012, 331–2; cf. Seaford 1993. Arguably, Dionysus has been present and at work throughout the play: he is invoked as chorus-leader not only in the fifth stasimon at 1146–54 but already in the Parodos at 153–4, as 'the god who makes Thebes shake' (on the 'choral projection' that this involves, see Henrichs 1995; cf. Seaford 2012, 109). Earlier in the same song, the threat to the city posed by the Seven is presented in Dionysiac terms – Capaneus ὃς τότε μαινομένᾳ ξὺν ὁρμᾷ | βακχεύων ἐπέπνει | ῥιπαῖς ἐχθίστων ἀνέμων ('who, raging in his mad onrush, breathed on us with blasts of most hostile winds'); the winds of madness continue to buffet Thebes throughout the play. On the wind and storm imagery, see above, pp. xxvi–xxvii.

[92] Antigone: esp. 603 (cf. also above, xv–xvi); Creon: 765 (cf. 755); Haemon: 633 (hypothetically; cf. 648–9), 754; cf. 790 (of the one who has Eros – clearly Haemon, in the Chorus' mind, but NB ἐρᾶν used of Antigone at 90 and, indirectly, at 220), 1231; Eurydice: 1254. Cf. Creon of Ismene, 491–2. Mental disturbance on the human level is also mirrored in the frenzy (*oistros*) of the birds whose unintelligible cries Tiresias reports at 1001–2. Cf. also various references to the destructive power of forces such as *orgē* and *thymos* (718, 766–7, 875, 955–6) and note the ambivalence of both *phronēma* and *orgai* at 355–6 in the first stasimon's praise of human rationality.

[93] In Vernant and Vidal-Naquet 1990, 23–8. On the first stasimon's relation to the subsequent choral odes, to the rest of the play, and to contemporary thought, see esp. the exhaustive study by Utzinger 2003.

[94] For 'what is best' in gnomic contexts in archaic poetry, cf. such classic formulations as Tyrt. 12. 13–16 W, Thgn. 255–6 (cited by Arist. *EN* 1099a27, *EE* 1214a5), Pi. *O.* 1. 1, and the *skolion PMG* 890; for cases in which the answer is 'not to be born', see Easterling, this volume, 193–6. For Seaford 1998, 121–2, such rankings are facilitated by monetization.

[95] The *gnōmē* is traditional: see e.g. Thgn. 1171–6 (where 1172 echoes Sol. 16. 2 W).

[96] Within this passage note especially 707–9 (people who think that they alone are wise, when opened up, are found to be empty), on which M. Griffith 1999 is right to compare Thgn. 221–6, where the one who thinks that he alone is clever, while his neighbour knows nothing, is 'impaired in his good sense' (νόου βεβλαμμένος ἐσθλοῦ, 223); all are capable of cleverness, but some eschew *kakokerdeiai* (225). The source context in Theognis has the 'harm' *versus* 'profit' antithesis that is so prominent in the target context in the *Antigone*.

[97] The juxtaposition of innate capacity and learning as sources of wisdom in 710–13 and 720–3 sounds a Pindaric note: the Pindaric primacy of the former is maintained,

but with greater respect for the latter. Cf. especially 710–11 (ἀλλ' ἄνδρα, κεἴ τις ᾖ σοφός, τὸ μανθάνειν | πόλλ' αἰσχρὸν οὐδέν) and 720–3 (φήμ' ἔγωγε πρεσβεύειν πολὺ | φῦναι τὸν ἄνδρα πάντ' ἐπιστήμης πλέων· | εἰ δ' οὖν ... | καὶ τῶν λεγόντων εὖ καλὸν τὸ μανθάνειν) with e.g. Pi. *O.* 2. 86–8 (σοφὸς ὁ πολλὰ εἰδὼς φυᾷ· μαθόντες δὲ λάβροι | παγγλωσσίᾳ κόρακες ὣς ἄκραντα γαρυέτων | Διὸς πρὸς ὄρνιχα θεῖον). Cf. M. Griffith 1999 on 721. At the same time, Haemon's model in 720–3 is an even more canonical passage of archaic poetry, namely Hes. *Op.* 293–7:

οὗτος μὲν πανάριστος, ὃς αὐτῷ πάντα νοήσει
φρασσάμενος τά κ' ἔπειτα καὶ ἐς τέλος ᾖσιν ἀμείνω·
ἐσθλὸς δ' αὖ κἀκεῖνος ὃς εὖ εἰπόντι πίθηται·   295
ὃς δέ κε μήτ' αὐτῷ νοέῃ μήτ' ἄλλου ἀκούων
ἐν θυμῷ βάλληται, ὃ δ' αὖτ' ἀχρήιος ἀνήρ.

That man is best of all who notices everything by himself, devising whatever is better for the immediate future and in its final outcome. But he too is also good who listens to good advice. But one who neither notices by himself nor takes to heart what he hears from another is, for his part, a useless man.

[98] Since Creon's words at 1049 highlight the proverbial nature of what Tiresias is about to say, cf. *Ant.* 1050–1 with Thgn. 895–6 ('a man has nothing better in him than judgement nor anything more painful than its opposite'); cf. also Thgn. 1171–6.

[99] As opposed to Antigone, who at 469–70 observes that she is being accused of foolishness by a fool.

[100] i.e. *anarchia*: cf. Seaford, this volume, 27–30.

[101] Cf. 324–6: 'If you do not reveal the culprits to me, you will declare that base *kerdē* produce pains'.

[102] Cf. nn. 36–7 above. By the time the second stasimon has introduced this sequence, in the context of the Chorus' confidence in the power of Zeus' law to resist all human transgression, Creon has charged Antigone with *hybris* at 473–83 (where the reference to 'high-spirited horses', 477–8, and to 'thinking big', 478–9, activate traditional connotations of *hybris* before the term itself is introduced in 480–3), but the question of Creon's own potential *hybris* has also been raised by the repeated references to his *phronēma* at 176, 207, 459; cf. 353 (the first stasimon), 473–4 (an ironic foreshadowing of what will in fact happen to Creon).

[103] See Seaford 1998, 132–7; cf. 2012, 328–31.

[104] Equally, the utterly different notion of *kerdos* put forward by the woman, Antigone, adds point to Creon's observations on the *kerdos* that motivates *andres*, men, at 221–2. Cf. above, p. xix and n. 49. In 221–2 Creon saw death as the *misthos* for defying his edict and *kerdos* as the inducement that might lead *men* to take the risk; Antigone collapses both *misthos* and *kerdos* into one, in a conception that is utterly different from Creon's.

[105] See e.g. Sol. 13 W, distinguishing first between *olbos*, which depends on more than money, and material wealth, and then between just and unjust ways of acquiring wealth, and NB esp. (a) the association between unjust wealth, *hybris*, and *atē* at 11 ff. and (b) the antithesis between *kerdos* and *atē* at 74–5; on the pursuit of wealth in Solon cf. Seaford, this volume. The two substantial examples of Solon's elegiac poetry, frr. 4 and 13 W, are major intertexts for the *Antigone*. A full examination of their influence would need in particular to include a discussion of the ways in which the first and second stasima of the play draw on fr. 13, the *Musenelegie*. The first stasimon exhibits

close similarities with Solon's priamel of human skills at 13. 43–64, while the second exploits his emphasis on *atē* (13. 3–42, 63–76; cf. nn. 18, 53, 76 above, 127–8 below; also nn. 37–8, 55 on Sol. 4 W), with the result that intertextuality with Solon's poem encourages us to read the second stasimon against the first and both against the *Musenelegie*. But this is a project I hope to pursue elsewhere. For similar notions, cf. Thgn. 197–208 (in which the pursuit of mistaken forms of *kerdos* depends on deception, *apatē*) and 227–32 (*ploutos* leads to *aphrosynē* and thence to *atē*). For the distinction between real prosperity and mere wealth, cf. also B. 3, esp. 22–3 (θεὸν θ[εό]ν τις ἀγλαϊζέθω γὰρ ἄριστος [ὄ]λβων, 'The god! The god! Let a man glorify the god! For that is the best prosperity') and 83–4 (ὅσια δρῶν εὔφραινε θυμόν· τοῦτο γὰρ κερδέων ὑπέρτατον, 'cheer your heart by doing holy things; for that is highest profit'), with Cairns 2010, 70–4. With the *Antigone*'s use of the language of material wealth (*kerdos, ktēma*, etc.) to emphasize the superiority of non-material prosperity (n. 112 below), cf. passages such as 'we shall not exchange wealth for virtue' (οὐ διαμειψόμεθα τῆς ἀρετῆς τὸν πλοῦτον) at Sol. 15. 2–3 W (roughly = Thgn. 316–17), 'you will lay down no better treasure for your children than *aidōs*' (οὐδένα θησαυρὸν παισὶν καταθήσει ἀμείνω | αἰδοῦς), Thgn. 409–10 (cf. 1161–2); also Sol. 24 W/Thgn. 719–28. For monetary exchange as a model for thinking about other domains, cf. e.g. Hclt. B 90 DK with Seaford 2004, 11–12, 232; and on anxieties over the improper pursuit of wealth in archaic poetry and tragedy, cf. Seaford 1998; 2004, 149–72 *passim*; 2012, 170–1, 196–205, 221–2.

[106] Creon's responsibility: 1259–60 (Ch.), 1261–9 (Cr.), 1270 (Ch.), 1302–5, 1312–13 (the Mess., citing Eurydice), 1317–19 (Cr.), 1339–40 (Cr., albeit οὐχ ἑκών); divine intervention: 1272–5 (Cr.), 1345–6 (Cr.). For wider discussion of issues of responsibility in Aeschylean and Sophoclean tragedy, cf. the chapters in this volume by Herrmann and Allan.

[107] Cf. esp. the closely similar passage at *OT* 1186–96, with my discussion in Chapter 5 below. For 'count no man happy' cf. Sim. 521 *PMG* = 244 Poltera; A. *Ag.* 928–9 (with Fraenkel 1950, ii. 420 ad loc.); E. *Andr.* 100–2, *Hcld.* 865–6 (with Fränkel 1946, 135), *Tro.* 509–10; Hdt. 1. 32. 7; Arist. *EN* 1. 9–10, 1100a4–1101b9.

[108] Cf. above all *Il.* 24. 525–48, with the discussions by Cairns and Lloyd in this volume; further examples in Krause 1976; cf. Versnel 2011, 152–60.

[109] For parallels, see *Aj.* 125–6 (with Garvie 1998 ad loc.), *Phil.* 946, frr. 13, 659. 6, 945 R; cf. Mastronarde 2002 on *Med.* 1224. Among earlier examples cf. esp. A. *Ag.* 839, frr. 154a.9, 399. 2 R, and (above all) Pi. *P.* 8. 95–6. See further Cairns 2006, 102–3.

[110] For uses of *orthotēs* in the same or similar connexions, cf. 163 (explicitly of the ship of state), 635–6, 675–6, 994 (again, explicitly of the ship of state); for the ship of state/seafaring/storm at sea image-complex in general see also 136–7, 334–7 (literal seafaring, symbolic of humans' attempts to master the environment), 391, 586–92, 715–17, 929–30, 951–4 (ships not immune to power of fate), 1000, 1284. Behind the application of this theme to Creon lie passages such as Thgn. 671–82, where the ship of state is buffeted in a political storm caused by those who pursue material wealth by illegitimate means; cf. esp. Thgn. 674–5 (ἣ μάλα τις χαλεπῶς | σῴζεται) with *Ant.* 313–14 (ἐκ τῶν γὰρ αἰσχρῶν λημμάτων τοὺς πλείονας | ἀτωμένους ἴδοις ἂν ἢ σεσωμένους). On seafaring as an image of rational control over the forces of nature in the first stasimon and beyond, see C. P. Segal 1964, 63; cf. Oudemans and Lardinois 1987, 125–6, 133–4, 160; on the history of the image of the ship of state in Greek political thought, see Brock (forthcoming) ch. 5.

[111] For the scales as an image of alternation, cf. Thgn. 157–8 (and cf. 159–68, 355–60, 441–6, 591–4, 657–66 on the rhythm of alternation in general); in S., cf. *Aj.* 131–2, fr. 576, with Krause 1976, 183–4, 197; also E. *Hec.* 55–8, with Krause 237. Cf. Seaford, this volume, 35 n. 24 and 37 n. 87, Herrmann, this volume 60–1, on the image of the scales in Aeschylus. See also Seaford 2012, 236–9, 242, 253–4, and cf. 225–39 on 'form-parallelism' of the sort that we see in 1158–9 (τύχη γὰρ ὀρθοῖ καὶ τύχη καταρρέπει | τὸν εὐτυχοῦντα τόν τε δυστυχοῦντ' ἀεί).

[112] Accordingly, when Creon returns, the Messenger ironically addresses him as a man of wealth (ὡς ἔχων τε καὶ κεκτημένος, 1227), though his 'possessions' now consist in the corpses of his son and his wife; just so, Haemon is the object of the exchange predicted by Tiresias at 1064–7. For the use of *ktēmata* etc. of non-material goods, cf. 684, 702, 924, 1050. Cf. n. 105 above, and on the language of exchange in *Ant.* cf. Seaford 2004, 158–60.

[113] Cf. Seaford 2003, 2004, 2012, as well as Ch. 2 below.

[114] This is not, of course, a purely Greek phenomenon. The construction of the natural and supernatural worlds on the basis of models drawn from human society is a function of the fundamentally social nature of the evolved human mind: on the role of the social mind in fashioning (esp.) religious conceptions of how the world works, see Boyer 2001. Similarly, the projection of the social onto the cosmic is, on one level, simply one of many ways in which metaphor manifests itself as a basic mechanism of concept-formation: see above all Lakoff and Johnson 1980. Thus, while I greatly admire Seaford's stimulating and innovative work on the social character of philosophical and religious cosmology in archaic Greece, I retain doubts, first about his reluctance to see this in terms of the ubiquitous mechanism of cognitive metaphor, and more generally about his insistence that money and coinage are in a class of their own as key factors in the development of abstract thought in archaic Greece. Phrases such as 'merely metaphor' (2012, 244), 'not so much metaphors...not so much metaphorical...not a metaphor...what we call metaphor' (2012, 245), and 'more than mere metaphor' (2012, 247) seem to work with a trivializing, purely ornamental notion of metaphor that denies that metaphor could ever have conceptual, epistemic, or theory-constitutive force (cf. the explicit discussion at 2012, 248–9). The phenomena in question clearly do involve thinking about one domain in terms which are proper to another: e.g. the idea that the sky and the earth feel sexual desire (A. fr. 44. 1–2 Radt; 'not a metaphor', according to Seaford 2012, 245; cf. ibid. 305–8) must derive from the observed phenomenon of such desire in creatures that are in fact capable of it. And so the metaphorical nature of the process cannot be denied: thinking of one domain in terms of another, and even in some cases creating a domain on the basis of another, is what metaphor *does*. Metaphor in general does for abstract thought what Seaford attributes to monetary metaphors in particular.

[115] See esp. 569, 575, 653–4, 750. Creon's perspective on the fungibility of the spouse's role (569) is of course shared by Antigone (906–12); cf. Neuburg 1990.

[116] Cf. e.g. S. *Aj.* 666–77; E. *Pho.* 541–7.

[117] On which see Seaford 2004, 190–1, 201–4; 2012, 53–5, 57–8, 60. For the presentation of cosmic equilibrium in terms of human society and politics, cf. Hclt. B 94 DK; Emped. B 17. 27–9, B 135 DK. Alcmaeon B 4 DK similarly uses political language with reference to the internal harmony of the body. Cf. Brock forthcoming, ch. 1 at nn. 62–4, ch. 7 at nn. 87–9, ch. 8 at nn. 60–1, ch. 9 at nn. 50–3.

Introduction: Archaic Thought and Tragic Interpretation

[118] Cf. Seaford 2004, 226–7; 2012, 308. For 'Empedoclean' presentations of Eros or Aphrodite as natural force and cosmic principle, cf. A. *Danaides* fr. 44 Radt (with Seaford 2012, 305–10); S. fr. 941. 7–12 Radt; E. *Hipp.* 447–50. This is, however, a conception of divinity that goes back before Empedocles: e.g. Thgn. 1275–8; cf. Hes. *Th.* 194–5, with *Il.* 14. 347–51 and Janko 1992, 206 on *Il.* 14. 346–53.

[119] See esp. B 17, B 20–2, B 26, B 30, B 35 DK.

[120] See Winnington-Ingram 1980, 164.

[121] See Liapis, this volume.

[122] See further my Chapter 5 below.

[123] See Winnington-Ingram 1965, 37, 47 (where he comments on the phrase's syntactic reversibility); cf. 1980, 177.

[124] For extensive discussion, see Versnel 2011, 151–237. Versnel insists on the separateness and incompatibility of these and other explanations, and argues that Greek thought tends to present them paratactically, rather than subordinating one to the other. This is a valuable corrective to the tendency to reduce all such explanations to a single, consistent (and often moralistic) pattern, but it risks obscuring the fact that the most general explanation, in terms of mutability, (a) is clearly capable of subsuming other, more specific explanations and (b) tends (as in the *Iliad*, the *Antigone*, and the *OT*) to be presented in contexts of a summative and exemplary nature. Archaic poetry and tragedy seem to me repeatedly to regard humans' capacity to ruin their lives by their own errors and transgressions as a subset of the limitations upon their ability to secure their own happiness that are imposed by their place in the nature of things. This does not make those positions interchangeable: that we bring some of our misfortunes upon ourselves by error or transgression can illustrate the wider phenomenon of the inevitability of suffering without providing its sole explanation, and it still makes an important difference whether one's suffering results from (culpable or non-culpable) error, (major or minor) transgression, or just the way the world is; my point is simply that on one level and from one perspective (normally a sympathetic one) error and transgression also reflect the way the world is. See also n. 127 below.

[125] Again, see *Iliad* 24. 525–48, with Cairns 2012a, 26–49 on the Iliadic pattern.

[126] See esp. *Od.* 1. 32–4, with Dodds 1951, 32–3.

[127] Μοῖρα δέ τοι θνητοῖσι κακὸν φέρει ἠδὲ καὶ ἐσθλόν,
   δῶρα δ' ἄφυκτα θεῶν γίγνεται ἀθανάτων.

Fate brings mortals both bad and good and the gifts of the immortal gods are inescapable.

On 'the poem's two inconsonant themes', see most recently Versnel 2011, 201–12 (quotation p. 207). My concern here is not to effect the kind of reconciliation between the mutability of fortune and theodicy that Versnel deprecates, but I do, to a greater extent than does Versnel himself, want to describe what he describes as the 'peaceful coexistence' of these explanations (2011, 212) in terms of a tendency to see error and transgression as reflections of a more general human vulnerability.

[128] For her vindication, see again 1113–14 with n. 48 above. For her abandonment by the gods, see her complaints at 921–4, 943. For archaic complaints that the righteous are not rewarded, see e.g. Thgn. 373–85, 731–52 (esp. 743–6); the observation that the principle of alternation allows the bad (or at least the foolish) to prosper is also made Sol. 13. 63–70 W (65–70 = Thgn. 585–90); cf. Hesiod's wish

that neither he nor his son be just, unless the just get more *dikē* than the unjust (*Op.* 270–3). Hence the sense that Antigone has suffered for her piety is not necessarily a modern moralistic imposition. Those (both ancient and modern) for whom this question arises have several (not mutually exclusive) considerations at their disposal: first, that the universe is not ordered in such a way that piety is rewarded (perhaps because an entire lineage may be doomed to disaster, but also for other reasons); second, that Antigone's alternatives at 925–8, immediately following her complaint at 921–4, indicate that she is not after all abandoned by the gods, at least to the extent that the complementary sufferings she wishes on Creon do indeed befall him; and third that (as Antigone herself observed at an earlier stage, 460–8) there can be greater *kerdos* in death than in survival; cf. the story of Cleobis and Biton at Hdt. 1. 31. 3–5. Part of the point here, I think, is that whatever story we tell ourselves about the extent to which Creon brought his sufferings upon himself, the fate of Antigone reminds us not to see that story – whether we regard it as comforting or unsettling – as the only possible pattern. Yet there remains a level of generality at which the specific and different patterns illustrated by the fates of Antigone and Creon are in some respects comparable.

[129] See Easterling, Chapter 7, init.

[130] Cf. e.g. A. *Ag.* 1327–9; S. *Tr.* 1–3, 29–30, 126–31, 129–31, 296–302, 943–6; *OC* 394, 607–20; fr. 871 R; E. *Med.* 1224–30; *Hipp.* 1105–10; *Supp.* 331; *Oedipus* frr. 92, 97 Austin = 549, 554 Kannicht. On Euripides, see further Lloyd, this volume. For the motif in the Histories of Hdt., see 1. 5. 4, 1. 207. 1, 7. 50. 2.

[131] See Arist. *Po.* 13, 1452b28–1453a23. The issue of the apparent inconsistency between chapters 13 and 14 of the *Poetics* is too complex to be discussed here; see rather Heath (forthcoming), with further references. For our purposes here, it does not matter that the 'best' plot of chapter 13 is either a subset of or one of two candidates for the best type of plot overall; it is enough that the plot type is both salient and commended. As far as the relation between that plot type and archaic Greek thought is concerned, Aristotle omits the theological dimension that is prominent in archaic and tragic applications of the principle of alternation; he also insists (at least in ch. 13, *via* the endlessly debated notion of *hamartia*) on the individual's contribution to his or her own undeserved suffering, a prominent and recurrent aspect of the traditional complex (especially in the *Iliad* and in tragedy), but not an essential one. It is worth noting that change of fortune is a more general requirement for tragedy in *Poetics* (1452a 14–18); *hamartia* helps specify one of the better forms that such a change might take.

[132] See esp. *EN* 1100a4–11, 1101a6–13.

[133] See n. 107 above.

[134] In classic formulations of prototypicality as a central feature of category formation (e.g. Lakoff 1987) Aristotle is often saddled with the role of inventor of 'classical' approaches to definition (by identification of necessary and sufficient conditions for membership of a particular class). The influence of prototypicality in his own thought would repay further study. For a start, see e.g. W. V. Harris 2001, 58–9 and Fortenbaugh 2008, 29–47, each making the important point that the *Rhetoric*'s definitions of the *pathē* are prototypes and not 'classical' definitions. A further step would be to consider Aristotle's notion of ὁμονυμία πρὸς ἕν (*Met.* Γ, 1003a33 ff.) in the light of prototype theory, before establishing the importance of prototypical thinking elsewhere in the *corpus Aristotelicum*.

[135] Williams 1993; Theunissen 2002; Seaford 2012.

1

ATĒ IN AESCHYLUS

Alan H. Sommerstein

The overwhelming impression one gets after exposure to the recent literature on *atē*[1] is that, firstly, it is an extremely hard concept for the modern mind to understand and, secondly, no two scholars agree on what it meant. I strongly suspect that this is because the problem has usually been attacked from the wrong end. *Atē*, in fact, may well have suffered the same fate that once befell another concept often textually linked to it, *hybris*. Because *hybris* tended to be used, in serious poetry, in reference to people who thought (or acted as if they thought) that the limitations of the human condition did not apply to them, thereby gravely offending the gods, it came to be supposed that the word *hybris* actually denoted this state of mind, despite the existence of perfectly well-known evidence that the word was a familiar term in everyday Attic, with no particular religious associations at all, referring to degrading and contemptuous treatment of fellow human beings.[2] This error – for such it was – was encouraged by three factors that tended to focus the attention of interpreters on epic and tragedy at the expense of texts of less exalted types. Firstly, ever since the classical period itself, epic and tragedy have had enormous prestige as the supreme forms of ancient Greek literature; this is as evident in Plato, where they are the almost exclusive targets of his iconoclastic assault,[3] as in Aristotle's *Poetics* where they are the only two genres thought worthy of serious discussion. Secondly, and partly for this reason, they are a major staple of study in every Greek literature course, with the result that every researcher working on Greek conceptual patterns is familiar with epic and tragedy, whereas I doubt whether most of them could say offhand where one can find the text of the Athenian law on *hybris*.[4] And thirdly, there is the tempting but fallacious assumption (quite often made without realizing it is being made) that the oldest discoverable stage of a linguistic or social or cultural development must be that which is evidenced in the oldest surviving source – which for most language-related features of Greek culture (other than those attested in Mycenaean documents) means the Homeric epics.

It is even easier to fall into these traps in the case of *atē* than in the case of *hybris*, because *atē*, at least in the forms of Greek with which most of us are most familiar, is much the more poetic word of the two; in Attic, indeed, at least by the fifth century, it did not even exist outside the higher genres of poetry. At any rate, a great many studies of *atē* have proceeded by first trying to define the term as it is used in Homer (or just in the *Iliad*) and then treating all other recorded usages as imitations, modifications, or degenerate developments of this.[5] This seems to me to be standing things on their heads. The word *atē* was certainly not invented by the poet of the *Iliad* or by any of the many nameless and highly gifted singers who must have gone before him. One or another of them *took it over* from the ordinary language of his day, and by constant use in the highly specialized contexts of heroic song it developed a special meaning. Meanwhile, in some dialects though not all, it went on being used in ordinary language as before, and it is to these, not to Homer, that we should look for the earliest traceable stages of the word's semantic history.

And we will not look in vain. The basic meaning of *atē* (or rather ἀϝάτα) turns out to be 'harm, damage, loss', a semantic range corresponding roughly to that of two classical Attic words, βλάβη and ζημία. In Cretan legal texts[6] it is the regular word for a sum to be paid as a penalty or as compensation. A series of glosses in Hesychius demonstrate the existence of a verb ἀ(ϝ)άσκειν or ἀ(ϝ)άσσειν meaning 'to harm'.[7] The proverb ἐγγύα, πάρα δ' ἄτα[8] – which, as its dialect shows, cannot possibly have been the creation of Thales of Miletus, to whom it was often ascribed – can be roughly rendered as 'go surety today, lose your shirt tomorrow'. Even in poetry the traces of this early sense of *atē* are clear to see. In Hesiod, in Theognis, in Solon, even in Aeschylus and Sophocles, *atē* and *kerdos* 'gain, advantage' (or their derivatives) can be treated as antonyms;[9] and the privative adjective ἄνατος, despite being almost exclusively poetic, never means 'undeluded', 'unruined', or anything portentous like that, but just 'unharmed'.[10]

In the Ionic dialect, however, the noun *atē* itself seems early to have become specialized; our actual evidence in prose texts for this specialization dates only from the fifth century, but it must in fact be much older, because the Homeric usage is built on it and presupposes it. When we find *atē* in Herodotus (1.32 *bis*) and in Democritus (fr. 213 DK) it means not just 'harm' but 'great harm, disaster' – though still with no theological overtones. The Herodotean Solon, explaining to Croesus why he holds that no man should be called happy till he is dead, compares a rich but unfortunate man to a relatively poor but fortunate one; the rich man's sole advantage, in Solon's eyes, is that he is better able to satisfy his desires and to cope with 'a great *atē* falling upon him'. Since part of the point Solon is trying to make is that wealth is no protection against what may be called 'human' disasters – illness, injury, bereavement, etc. – the *atai* of which he is speaking must be *material* disasters (such as shipwreck or crop failure) which may be terminally catastrophic for someone who was previously making only a modest living, but against which a rich man will probably have a cushion of reserves. And when Democritus says ἀνδρεία τὰς ἄτας μικρὰς ἔρδει 'courage makes *atai* smaller', we are again a long way from the world of Homer or Aeschylus: he is merely saying that if you face up to disaster with courage, it will benefit you both psychologically (by making the disaster seem smaller and easier to cope with) and practically (since if you undauntedly strive to find a way out of your difficulties, that gives you a far better chance of success).

Presumably this was the sense that *atē* already bore in Ionic Greek when it was adopted into the poetic *Kunstsprache* of heroic epic. To reach the Homeric position, all that is now necessary is to apply two principles which we know to have been widespread in early Greek thought, and to exploit an ambiguity in the application (rather than the meaning) of *atē* and of the verb ἀάειν from which it was derived. The first of the two principles is that *nothing of any importance happens by accident* – or more accurately, perhaps, that the very concept of an event happening by accident did not exist; if a significant event occurred, and was clearly not due to wilful human action, then it must have been due to wilful divine action. The second is that *human suffering is the outcome of human folly* – though not necessarily the folly of the sufferers themselves.

Now the characters of myth and epic who act in foolish ways, with disastrous consequences, are not as a rule foolish by nature and character; they are persons of high birth, of power, and usually of considerable achievement. So they must have acted *out* of character; some force outside themselves must have made them do what they did – and what could that force be, if not a divine agent?

Thus we have the picture, familiar to students of *atē* in Homer, of a divinity deceiving a mortal, or disrupting his mental processes, so that he commits some act of folly which then has disastrous consequences. By a not uncommon semantic transition – which later affected both βλάβη and ζημία[11] – the word that means 'harm' came to mean also 'that which causes harm', in this case either the delusion or infatuation itself or the act of folly that springs from it. A process has now been identified, starting with a divine initiative and finishing with a human catastrophe, whose beginning, middle and end can all be called *atē*: it is then a very small step to thinking of the whole process as a single instance of *atē*, and this step Homer takes. Not that he is likely to have been the first to do so, since he never feels it necessary to explain the meaning of the concept, even though familiarity with it is essential to the understanding of, for example, Phoenix's famous allegory of Ate and the Litai in *Iliad* 9;[12] we must presume that the concept, in all its complexity, was as familiar to Homer's audience as any other concept common in heroic poetry. Homer tends to focus attention (predominantly in the *Odyssey*, almost invariably in the *Iliad*) on the beginning of the process,[13] but the end is always kept in mind: a mental aberration which does not have catastrophic consequences is not called *atē*.

In later archaic poetry there is something of a tug of war between the start and end points of the *atē* process, between damage to mind and damage to fortune – some poets laying more emphasis on the former, others on the latter – and between both and the simpler, untheological sense of *atē* that survived in ordinary speech in some dialects. On the whole, 'disaster' gets decidedly the better of 'folly', except in one corpus, the *Homeric Hymns*[14] – an exception that is hardly surprising if, as is likely, the composers of these poems were also professional reciters of the Homeric epics themselves. In other poetic texts from Hesiod to Pindar and Bacchylides (but not including Aeschylus), I find at most ten instances of *atē* (or its cognates) denoting folly, delusion, or the like, compared with eighteen in which it denotes ruin or disaster.[15] I say 'at most' because in several cases it is not entirely clear which of the two ideas is uppermost in the poet's mind, or would have been uppermost in the minds of his audience; indeed there are only two passages in which I think it is beyond reasonable doubt that the primary reference is to a mental aberration. Both are Pindaric, both are in odes written for the same honorand (Hieron of Syracuse), and they describe the follies and sufferings of a brother and sister, Ixion and Coronis. In the third Pythian ode we hear how Coronis was misguided enough to sleep with her father's house-guest Ischys when already pregnant by Apollo, for which the god had his sister Artemis shoot her. Many people, the poet comments, are foolish in this kind of way, longing for what they cannot get (20–3); 'this is the great ἀυάτα that the mind of fair-robed Coronis had; for she went to bed with the stranger who came from Arcadia' (24–7). Here the ἀυάτα is explicitly associated with Coronis' 'mind' and presented as an instance of human folly. The second Pythian (21–41) describes how Ixion, having been admitted to Olympus, conceived a passion for Hera, 'but *hybris* aroused him to arrogant *ata*, and soon he got a unique and appropriate punishment' (28–30).

No archaic poet, however, when thinking of *atē*, can quite escape from the spell of the Homeric tradition; it continues to be the case that whether one is thinking of *atē* as cause or as consequence, the thought of its other aspect is nearly always latent – whether it is Hesiod affirming (*Works* 230–1) that 'neither famine nor *atē* is a companion to men of upright justice', or Alcaeus (fr. 70.10–13) speaking of the civil war 'which one of the Olympians has stirred up among us, leading the community into αὐάτα but giving Pittacus the glory that men long for' (it is certain here that Alcaeus and his hearers will have Pittacus' criminality in mind – because when thinking of Mytilenean politics, they can never forget it), or Ibycus (*PMG* 282a.8–9) saying that '*atē* scaled the citadel of Troy because of golden-haired Aphrodite', or Theognis (631–2) warning Cyrnus that 'a person whose reason (νόος) is not stronger than his passions (θυμός) will always lie in *atai* and in great helplessness', or Pindar (*O.* 1.55–63) telling how Tantalus 'could not digest his great prosperity, and through surfeit got himself an almighty *ata*, such a great stone did the Father suspend over him' because of his theft of the gods' nectar and ambrosia. Throughout this period, *atē* in poetry remains, either a folly that causes disaster, or a disaster that is caused by folly. Sometimes the folly is seen as being of divine origin, but by no means always; there is no hint of it, for example, in the Ixion and Coronis passages in Pindar.

And so to Aeschylus, who is fonder of the word *atē* than any other author.[16] As we have seen, it is likely that for him and his audience, *atē* was a word that existed only in poetry, and both he and they will have understood it against the background of its uses by earlier poets. And it appears that the practice of lyric and elegy was more influential, in this instance, than that of epic. In Aeschylus *atē* normally denotes a deadly or disastrous event, and only rarely does it refer to the mental aberration that ultimately caused that event.

I cannot in the space available go through all Aeschylus' fifty or so uses of *atē* and its cognates and derivatives[17] to justify this statement; instead, after briefly illustrating a few typical passages, and then drawing attention to the small number of clear cases where *atē* does denote a mental aberration, I shall concentrate on passages where one might well be tempted to understand the word thus but where it seems to me more likely that *atē* denotes the *outcome* of what I have called the *atē* process and corresponds to such English words as 'disaster', 'ruin', or 'destruction'. I leave aside *Prometheus Bound*, which I regard as not the work of Aeschylus[18] (a view that can be supported, as we shall see later, by the treatment of *atē* in the play), and also *Seven against Thebes* 601 (ἄτης ἄρουρα θάνατον ἐκκαρπίζεται 'the soil of *atē* produces a crop of death') which was clearly not written for the context in which it now stands (see Hutchinson 1985, 138).

To begin with, we may note that the distribution of *atē*-words among Aeschylus' plays is very uneven. *Persians* has them five times, *Seven against Thebes* four, *Suppliants* probably seven;[19] in the *Oresteia*, there are seventeen instances in *Agamemnon*, thirteen in the much shorter *Choephoroi*, but only four in *Eumenides* (two of which are prayers, by the Erinyes and Athena respectively, that *atē* should *not* affect Athens). The words tend to be found in chanted or sung rather than spoken verse: 30 per cent of their occurrences are in iambic trimeters, 12 per cent in anapaests, and no less than 58 per cent in lyrics.

First, then, the typical Aeschylean usage of *atē* to mean 'disaster, ruin, destruction'. I will take four or five instances from *Agamemnon*.

(1) On learning from Clytaemestra that Troy has been captured, the Chorus sing to Zeus and Night, and say that the latter has cast a net over Troy such that no one, old or young, can escape the meshes of '*atē* and total subjugation' (ἄτης παναλώτου, lit. '*atē* that captures all') (355–61).

(2/3) Telling the parable of the lion-cub reared in a human family, the Chorus sing of how, on growing up, the lion revealed its true inherited nature by 'making, with the *atai* of slaughtered sheep (μηλοφόνοισι σὺν ἄταις), a feast unbidden' (730–1); shortly afterwards the lion is described as a 'priest of Ate' (ἱερεύς τις Ἄτας, 735–6).

(4) The returning Agamemnon, boasting of his achievements, says that the ruins of Troy are still smoking: 'the gusts of *atē* are still alive and blowing' (ἄτης θύελλαι ζῶσι, 819).

(5) Cassandra, tearing off and trampling upon her prophetic insignia, tells them to 'make some other woman rich with *atē*,[20] instead of me' (ἄλλην τιν' ἄτης ἀντ' ἐμοῦ πλουτίζετε, 1268).

Now to the clear Aeschylean cases of *atē* as mental aberration. These number just five. Three of them appear in *Seven against Thebes*. In the first stasimon (312–16) the Chorus pray to the gods to cast upon the besieging enemy 'the cowardice that destroys men, the *atē* that makes them throw away their arms' (ἀνδρολέτειραν κάκαν, ῥίψοπλον ἄταν); since these two phrases are apparently in apposition, the *atē*, like the cowardice, must be a mental phenomenon, and 'panic' would be a very reasonable translation. At 686–8, with Eteocles seemingly set on fighting his brother, the Chorus beg him not to let himself be carried away by the 'spear-mad *atē* (δορίμαργος ἄτα) that fills your heart' but to cast away his evil desire; and at 1001 the two brothers, now dead, are described retrospectively as 'possessed by *atē*' (δαιμονῶντες ἄτᾳ). The fourth, partly obscured by textual corruption, is at *Suppliants* 104–11. The Danaids are here asking Zeus to look upon the rampant *hybris* of their cousins, the sons of Aegyptus, whose 'frenzied thoughts...goad [them] on implacably', and, according to the one manuscript, they describe the Aegyptiad family as ἄται δ' ἀπάται μεταγνούς. This last expression makes no sense as it stands and must be corrupt, but there is no particular reason to doubt that the line always included the lexical item ἄτα, and if so – describing as it does the *present* behaviour of the Aegyptiads, which Zeus is being invited to punish – it must refer to their evil disposition, not to a catastrophe which has not yet occurred (much though the Danaids wish it would).[21]

There is probably only one such instance in the *Oresteia*, but it is a very important one; this is the πρώταρχον ἄτην 'the *atē* that first began it all'[22] about which Cassandra hears the choir of the Erinyes sing in *Agamemnon* 1192, presently identified as (or associated with) the adultery of Thyestes with Aërope, the wife of Atreus. This was, no doubt, a disaster for Atreus when he discovered it, but it was trivial in comparison to its consequences, beginning with Atreus tricking Thyestes into eating the flesh of his children. And to call an event πρώταρχος is to treat it as a cause of other events (cf. Doyle 1983, 59), including the one which at that moment is uppermost in every spectator's mind – the impending murder of Agamemnon. We can thus safely assume that the *atē* of which the Erinyes sing here is the folly that possessed the mind of Thyestes and Aërope and led them into the guilty relationship from which so many evils flowed.

I turn thirdly to some passages where this interpretation of *atē* may at first sight be tempting but cannot, in my view, be sustained.[23] In several of these, the issue is complicated by the personification of Ate as a goddess. In *Persians* 97–101 we hear how this goddess first fawns on mortals and then leads them astray into a net from which they cannot escape. Ate is certainly here a causative agent, but the net into which her victims blunder is *her* net, the net of Ate, and that net is ruin. The whole process, both its beginning and its end, is her action, and as the passage ends we are left thinking of what she has achieved – of the impossibility of escaping from her snares (101) – more than of the manner in which she has achieved it. Certainly on the only other occasion when Ate is personified in the play (1007) the immediate context is entirely concerned not with Xerxes' folly but with Persia's ruin.

Ate the goddess reappears in *Agamemnon* 386. The Chorus are singing of Paris, who 'kicked the great altar of Justice into oblivion' (383–4) when he abducted Helen: a man who does that, they say, has 'no defence against surfeit of wealth' (381–2), and 'miserable Temptation (Peitho) forces her way in, the unendurable child of scheming Ate; every remedy is in vain'. One might well be inclined to suppose that by making Ate the *mother* of Peitho the poet is saying that *atē* was the cause, not the result, of Paris being tempted, or induced, to act as he did; and accordingly Fraenkel (1950, ii. 201; cf. Doyle 1983, 43) identified *atē* here as 'the blind infatuation...which leads to crime and ruin'. That certainly seems logical, but symbolic parenthood and literal causality do not always go hand in hand. Consider another divine personification, Eros. He is given a wide range of genealogies (and sometimes none at all), but already in the sixth century (Sappho fr. 198, Simonides *PMG* 575), and frequently thereafter, he is the child of Aphrodite – a pedigree which those who created it clearly meant to imply, contrary to what the logic of the affiliation might suggest, that sexual *desire* (Eros) was the precursor and cause of sexual *activity* (Aphrodite), not vice versa. There is more than one way, after all, to see the parent-child relationship. Children could be seen as coming after, and being produced by, their parents; but they could also be seen as those who have a duty to honour and serve their parents (and remember too that the son of a craftsman would more often than not become an apprentice in his father's workshop). Eros serves Aphrodite by providing her with lovers to unite; Peitho might be envisaged as serving Ate by providing her with victims to ruin. In the context, moreover, little or nothing is said about Paris' mental state, and a great deal about the inevitability of his doom: he has no defence (381), every remedy is in vain (388), no god hears his prayers (396), he is brought to justice (393) which destroys him (398), and he inflicts unendurable harm on his community (395). I conclude that the goddess Ate here, even more than in the *Persians* passage, is primarily the goddess of Ruin.

After the murder of Agamemnon, a defiant Clytaemestra swears (1431–6) 'by the fulfilled Justice that was due for my child, by Ate and by the Erinys, through whose [plural] aid I slew this man' (or perhaps 'to whom I sacrificed this man') that she has no fear while Aegisthus is her protector. Justice (for Iphigeneia), Ate, and the Erinys, then, she claims, all contributed to Agamemnon's death. The Erinys, or avenging spirit, must certainly be that of Iphigeneia (Clytaemestra has not yet claimed to be avenging the children of Thyestes),[24] so Doyle (1983, 76–7) is right to look for a way to associate Ate here with Iphigeneia too; his own suggestion that it means the destruction of Iphigeneia herself is hardly convincing, and more likely Clytaemestra means that Ate, acting through her, has brought destruction on Agamemnon for what he did to Iphigeneia. At the same time we may well recognize other, ironic significances: Clytaemestra, we already know, will herself become a victim of the Erinyes of Agamemnon and the Justice that is due for him, the Chorus have already said more than once (1407–11, 1426–30) that she must have been mentally deranged to commit such an act, and her open avowal of adultery (not to mention her near-obscene denunciation of Cassandra)[25] is something that could never have come from the lips of any normal, sane Greek woman. Once again, however, the immediate and direct meaning of the goddess's name in this passage is Ruin or Destruction.

In one or two other passages, where personification is not involved, the 'mental aberration' interpretation is nevertheless for various reasons tempting. In *Choephoroi* 594–8, following a *Priamel* that ranged over the many fearsome and destructive things in the world, the Chorus home in on the minds of men, and especially the desires of women, as being the most fearsome and destructive things of all, and they describe the desires of women as ἄταισι συννόμους βροτῶν 'partners in humans' *atai*'. Garvie (1986, 207–8) is uncertain here whether *atē* means 'infatuation' (cf. Doyle 1983, 61) or 'ruin', but in fact only the latter makes sense. The *atai* referred to are not, or not primarily, those of the women themselves, as βροτῶν 'of humans' shows; and all the mythological *exempla* the Chorus proceed to give – Althaea and Meleager (602–12), Scylla and Nisus (613–22), the women of Lemnos (631–8), and of course Clytaemestra herself (623–30) – relate to women who brought about, not the infatuation, but the destruction, of their near ones.

Choephoroi 829–30 and 835–6 are closely linked; in successive stanzas (though they are not a strophic pair) Orestes is twice urged to bring about an *atē*. That is decidedly unusual, since normally *atē* is treated as something very much to be avoided, and one does not ordinarily describe one's own actions, or those of one's friends or allies, as *atai* (though, it will be remembered, Clytaemestra in effect did this when she said that she killed Agamemnon by means of, or in the name of, Ate). What is more, the *atē* is at least once described as one 'that carries no blame' (ἀνεπίμομφον ἄταν).[26] The *atē* in question is clearly, each time, the killing of Clytaemestra (presented in 829 as a mother, in 835 as a Gorgon); but are we to take it as an 'act of destruction' or an 'act of folly' that will recoil disastrously on its perpetrator? It is in fact, of course, both, but which is supposed to be uppermost in the minds of the singers? That cannot be doubted. Throughout this ode the Chorus are supporting Orestes (who is not on stage) and urging him on to action; and they have just said (824–5) that '*atē* [here contrasted with *kerdos*] stands far from my friends' – of whom Orestes is certainly the most important. So they must mean 'act of destruction' – the destruction of Clytaemestra;[27] hence there is no intentional oxymoron in 830, and no intentional paradox in 836. But once again, and even more than in Clytaemestra's oath of *Ag.* 1431–6, the very use of the word *atē* inevitably makes us think of the consequences that Orestes can expect to suffer afterwards, consequences which will have been familiar from earlier poetry[28] and which have been foreshadowed by the frequent references to the Erinyes in the trilogy so far.[29]

In Aeschylus, then, the trend already noticeable in earlier post-Homeric poetry is accentuated: *atē* normally means 'disaster, ruin, destruction'. This applies, however, more strongly in some plays than in others; indeed in *Seven against Thebes* three of the four occurrences of the word denote a mental state (and with a neat symmetry the first (315) refers to the attacking forces, the second (688) to the leader of the defenders, and the third (1001) to the two rival brothers together). This is not a matter of early versus late plays: in the two other pre-*Oresteia* plays combined, *Persians* and *Suppliants*, there is just one instance of *atē* in the mental sense (*Supp.* 110–11), against eleven where it means 'ruin' or the like. More likely *atē* as mental aberration was thematically important in the Theban trilogy; and the retrospective choral ode in *Seven* (720–91) strongly suggests that this was so, as the Chorus sing of the 'mindless madness' that brought together a bridal couple who are probably Laius and Iocasta (756–7) and of the 'warped mind' and 'maddened heart' of Oedipus (725–6, 781) who put out his own eyes and cursed his own sons. Not that mental aberration, under various names, is unimportant in Aeschylus' other plays: it just is not generally called *atē*.

Having said this, the Homeric and archaic duality of the word retains much of its power. *Atē* means disaster, yes; but nearly always it is a disaster that the victim has, at least in part, brought on himself, or herself, through wicked or foolish action – an instantiation, in fact, of the principle δράσαντι παθεῖν 'for him who does, suffering' (*Cho.* 313). There are certainly plenty of disasters of that kind in Aeschylus. Indeed there are hardly any disasters that are *not* of that kind; I have claimed elsewhere (Sommerstein 2010a, 267) that in Aeschylus 'there are...few if any [sufferers] who cannot with good reason blame a mortal as well as a god for their suffering'. In his genuine plays, with three possible exceptions, when *atē* means 'disaster' it always refers to a disaster caused by a wicked or foolish action of the sufferer, or one of the sufferers (as when Xerxes brings destruction on all Persia, or Paris on all Troy), or an ancestor of the sufferers. One of the exceptions, *Suppliants* 444, is textually dubious, and even if it is correct, the 'disaster' is not, by tragic standards, much of a disaster (it seems to be something like a robbery)[30] and moreover it proves to be remediable; *atē* here probably bears its older and weaker meaning of 'material loss'. The other two are both in *Agamemnon*. In the first the Herald is elaborately describing what it is like when news is brought to a city of the destruction of its army, causing both public and private grief 'in a two-pronged *atē*, in gory double harness' (643); in the second, the Chorus, reacting to Cassandra's sinister visions, say they feel like dying soldiers on a battlefield for whom '*atē* comes swiftly' (1124). It may be significant that all these passages relate to hypothetical situations affecting unidentified persons or communities. Whenever in Aeschylus *atē*-disaster strikes an identifiable individual or group, it is always the consequence of *atē*-folly. And vice versa.

Even Cassandra (*Ag.* 1268) should have known that in saying no to Apollo, after having accepted his gift of prophecy, she was asking for trouble; the Elders, not always the most stellar of intellects, perceive this as soon as they hear her story, asking how she could possibly have remained unharmed (ἄνατος) by Apollo's anger (1211).

Does Aeschylus still think of *atē*-folly as being the result of a divine visitation? At first sight, he certainly seems to, at least in the play in which the concept is most prominent, *Seven against Thebes*: in one of the three relevant passages (312–17) the Chorus actually pray to the gods to afflict their enemies with *atē*, in another (1001) the victims of *atē* are described as divinely possessed (δαιμονῶντες), and in the third Eteocles' *atē* (687) seems to be closely linked with Apollo's hatred of the house of Laius (691). That hatred, however, arose (so far as we are told) from Laius' defiance of Apollo's thrice-repeated oracle (742–57), which is treated, one might say, as the πρώταρχος ἄτη, and which, like the πρώταρχος ἄτη of Thyestes and Aërope in *Agamemnon*, is not traced to any origin except the desires and weaknesses of the human agents – their 'ill counsel' (δυσβουλία *vel sim.*), as it is repeatedly called in reference to Laius (750, 802, 842). Thus the study of *atē* confirms what I have argued on other grounds about divine action in Aeschylus (Sommerstein 2010a, 257–8): 'the Aeschylean gods...impose no arbitrary dooms[; r]ather, they hold humans rigidly to the consequences of their own or their rulers' or their community's actions and decisions'.

In Sophocles, and even more in Euripides, divine justice is often, to say the least, much more inscrutable, and it is therefore not surprising to find that in their works *atē* often means merely 'disaster, ill-fortune' with no particular reference to its cause, not even an ironic one. In *Ajax* (1185–90) the Chorus wonder when will come the end of the years that have brought them 'an endless *atē* of toil in battle' before Troy; of course there had long been a tendency to think of the Trojan war as a stupid and unnecessary waste of Greek life, but this never becomes an issue in *Ajax*, even though the main Greek authors of the war, Menelaus and Agamemnon, are prominent and disagreeable characters in the play. In *Oedipus Tyrannus*, the Messenger sums up the catastrophe by saying that Oedipus and Iocasta now have, between them, 'lamentation, *atē*, death, shame, and every kind of evil' (1283–5); this when Sophocles has so crafted the story that neither of them, nor indeed anyone else,[31] has done anything that can reasonably be seen as an act of mad folly, nor are they held morally blameworthy by themselves or by others. In *Electra*, again, when Chrysothemis, who thought she was bringing Electra the joyful tidings of Orestes' return, learns the devastating news that he is dead, she comments 'I didn't know, then, where we were in *atē*' (935–6); and later on, after he has revealed

315, 688, 958, 1001; *Supp.* 110–11, 356, 359, 410, 444, 470, 530; *Ag.* 361, 386, 643, 730, 735, 771, 819, 1124, 1192, 1211, 1230, 1268, 1283, 1433, 1483–4, 1523, 1566; *Cho.* 68, 271–2, 339, 383, 403, 404, 467, 598, 824–5, 830, 836, 968, 1076; *Eum.* 59, 376, 982–3, 1007–8. All citations and translations of Aeschylus are from Sommerstein 2008, except that I have left *atē* untranslated (which has occasionally necessitated modifying renderings in the immediate context).

[18] See M. Griffith 1977; M. L. West 1979; M. L. West 1990b, 51–72; Bees 1993.

[19] At 850 the one manuscript has ἄταν, and at 886 the scholiast, and Eustathius on *Od.* 1.346 (or his source), evidently read ἄτα or ἀτᾷ, but in both passages corruption is likely; see M. L. West 1990b, 157–60 and 164.

[20] Given the past semantic history of *atē*, and its opposition to *kerdos* (see above) which was still very much alive in Aeschylus' time, this is likely to have been perceived as a very sharp oxymoron; see Dawe 1988, 105–6.

[21] M. L. West 1990a and Sommerstein 2008 both obelize the phrase quoted (except for μεταγνούς). The latter commends, and translates, the former's conjecture (M. L. West 1990b, 134) ἄταν δ' ἀγαπᾶν μεταγνούς 'having had its mind transformed to love *atē*'.

[22] Began, that is, the long chain of evils in the house of Atreus.

[23] Doyle 1983 sees the sense 'folly, infatuation' in a number of other passages too, but unconvincingly. To take one of his better efforts, at *Pers.* 821–2 he argues (Doyle 1983, 38–9) that *atē* must mean 'infatuation' because it is presented as being the *cause* of ruin – of the 'harvest of universal sorrow' (πάγκλαυτον...θέρος) which is being reaped – and can hardly therefore be identified with that ruin itself. But it is *hybris*, not *atē*, that is 'reaping' (ἐξαμᾷ) this harvest, after having 'blossomed and produced a crop' (ἐξανθοῦσ' ἐκάρπωσεν στάχυν) of *atē*. Thus we are given two successive results of *hybris*: first *atē* (the disaster that has befallen Xerxes and his army), then the 'universal sorrow' which this disaster has produced throughout Persia and Asia.

[24] She presented herself as the avenger of Iphigeneia in 1414–21 (and will do so again in 1523–9 and 1555–9); she mentions the children of Thyestes only in 1500–4. Even Cassandra, though she says a great deal about the Thyestean feast, mentions no other event as a cause of Agamemnon's murder, and overwhelmingly emphasizes Clytaemestra's role in the killing, never actually says that Clytaemestra is avenging the crime of Atreus, but rather that Aegisthus is (1223–5).

[25] On which see Sommerstein 2002, 154–7.

[26] '*At least* once', because M. L. West (1990b, 256–7) caused the idea to appear twice by restoring 836–7 as φόνιον ἄταν τιθείς, ἀναίτιον δ' ἐξ Ἀπόλλωνος μόρον 'wreaking bloody *atē*, but a death exempt from blame by Apollo'. It is doubtful, however, whether the phrase could bear the meaning that West wants to give it (he cites no parallel to show that ἀναίτιος ἐκ could mean 'not held guilty by'); and, more importantly, neither the Chorus nor the audience have yet been told (nor will they be until 1029–33) that Apollo has undertaken to treat Orestes as 'exempt from blame' if he kills his mother, only (a very different thing) that Apollo has told Orestes he will undergo terrible suffering if he does *not* do so (269–96) – see Sommerstein 1980, 65–6 and 2010b, 191–2.

[27] So rightly Doyle 1983, 78–80.

[28] The pursuit of Orestes by the Erinyes was certainly already a familiar part of the story, since it must have been to ward them off that Apollo in Stesichorus' *Oresteia*

(*PMG* 217, cf. schol. E. *Or.* 268) gave Orestes a bow made by his own hands. We may also grant to Bremer (1969, 128–30) that the double use of the word *atē* may well stimulate the thought that a man who must steel himself to kill his mother can hardly be in a fully normal state of mind, any more than was Agamemnon when, for reasons that seemed to him compelling, he sacrificed his daughter (*Ag.* 218–25).

[29] Up to this point the Erinyes have been named thirteen times, most recently at *Cho.* 652 (the last word of a choral song, immediately after which Orestes' murder-plot is set in motion as he enters in disguise and knocks at the door of his own house).

[30] The two lines that make clear sense in a corrupt context (in which one line appears to have been lost and one or more others displaced) speak of 'goods from a ransacked house' (χρήμασιν ... ἐκ δόμων πορθουμένων, 443) and of the acquisition 'by the grace of Zeus god of possessions' of 'other goods' to replace them (γένοιτ' ἂν ἄλλα κτησίου Διὸς χάριν, 445). If 444 is rightly placed after 445 (as most recent editors have done, correctly I believe [*contra*, Sandin 2003, 201–2], following a proposal by an unknown early modern scholar [not Casaubon; see Dawe 2001a]), these newly acquired goods are said to be 'in excess of what was lost' (ἄτης...μείζω).

[31] Unless it be Laius, who made a wanton and potentially murderous assault on an unknown traveller; see Sommerstein (2011a, 111–13).

[32] Cf. also *Ant.* 17, 185, 863; *OT* 1205; *El.* 1002; *Phil.* 706; *OC* 526, 1244.

[33] 'A fossil of tragic and epic language' (Doyle 1983, 139).

[34] Compared with an average of eight occurrences per play in Aeschylus and six or seven in Sophocles, who is still using the word in spoken verse even at the end of his life (*OC* 93, cf. 786).

[35] Other Euripidean instances of *atē* referring to suffering *not* presented as being caused by the sufferer's folly include *Med.* 129, 279; *Hcld.* 607; *Hec.* 688; *Tro.* 121, 163, 1314; *IT* 148; *Or.* 962.

[36] The other two occurrences of the term in *Prometheus* (1072, 1078) are much more 'traditional'; they appear in Hermes' final warning to the Chorus not to stay with Prometheus, where he tells them that 'when *atē* hunts you down...you will have brought it on yourselves, for knowingly...you will have been caught up in the inescapable net of *atē* [imitated from *Ag.* 358–61?] through your own folly'.

2

AESCHYLUS, HERAKLEITOS, AND PYTHAGOREANISM

Richard Seaford

1. Introductory

In the cosmos of Herakleitos opposites are identical with each other, or ceaselessly transformed into each other. But in the cosmos constructed by fifth-century Pythagoreanism we can detect the idea that opposites retain their identities in being combined into a stable whole. I argued in 2003 that in Aeschylus' *Oresteia* the action moves from the Herakleitean unity of opposites to their Pythagorean reconciliation.[1] I will now take this case further, in particular by exploring the significance of the number three in early Pythagoreanism and in Aeschylus.

The philosophers most often used to illuminate Greek tragedy are Plato, Aristotle, and – for Euripides – the sophists. But Aeschylus is a contemporary of *presocratic* philosophy. Surprisingly, there has been very little research on the relations between tragedy and presocratic philosophy. And almost all the research so far is based on the wrong question, namely 'is the tragedian here alluding to (or influenced by) this fragment of presocratic philosophy?' Even an unequivocal 'yes' to this question, which in fact is never possible, would not take us very far.[2]

Much clearer and more interesting is that certain basic structures are shared by tragedy and presocratic cosmology. The point is not that the tragedian has read a particular philosopher, possible though that is. Cosmological ideas may travel from one city-state to another, whether in 'philosophical' or mythical form, whether in written texts (mostly now lost) or orally. Or similar cosmological ideas may be produced independently in various city-states. Such receptivity and such independent production are both possible because the city-states are at the same stage of economic and political development. This correlation between social process and 'philosophical' cosmology I will not explore here, as I have done so in other publications.[3] I note instead merely that the correlation is in fact confirmed by my argument here, for in Aeschylus, with his concern with revenge and accumulation of wealth as well as with (in the broad sense) cosmology, we

17

can observe in detail an instance of the very link between social process and cosmology that my earlier argument implies.

We must distinguish between three senses in which ideas may be 'Pythagorean': (a) as held by people as adherents of a sect or movement with allegiance to Pythagoras (I call this adherence 'Pythagorean[ism]'); (b) as directly or indirectly influenced by Pythagoreanism but held by non-adherents;[4] (c) as identical or similar to Pythagorean ideas, but uninfluenced by Pythagoreanism.

Although the Pythagoreans were of more historical importance than the Herakleiteans (Ἡρακλείτειοι: Pl. *Tht.* 179d), the previous paragraph could be written with Herakleitean(ism) substituted for Pythagorean(ism).

To which category should we assign Aeschylus' *Oresteia*? My main concern is to show, on the basis of *internal* evidence, that (c) is true of the *Oresteia* with respect to both Pythagorean and Herakleitean ideas. But I start with (b), by setting out all the *external* evidence for the likelihood of Pythagorean influence on Aeschylus, because to the best of my knowledge this has never been done.

Firstly, there was an ancient tradition – preserved by Cicero – that Aeschylus was a Pythagorean.[5]

Secondly, Pythagoras is mentioned by three Ionian contemporaries of Aeschylus – Herakleitos, Ion of Chios, and Herodotos.[6] Ion wrote a work of Pythagorean content (§4 below) and spent much time in Athens,[7] where he produced drama, and so we might well have inferred – without having to rely on the ancient reports[8] to that effect – that he knew Aeschylus personally. Even if he encountered Pythagoreanism after the death of Aeschylus, he embodies a connection between tragedy in fifth-century Athens and Pythagoreanism.[9]

Thirdly, Aeschylus himself, on his voyages to Sicily, could not have avoided southern Italy, at the very time when – according to Aristoxenos and others – Pythagoreanism was powerful and successful there.[10] If Aeschylus encountered Pythagorean ideas on those journeys, undertaken late in his life, this might explain why it was his last extant work, the *Oresteia*, that seems influenced by Pythagoreanism.

Fourthly, Aeschylus' lost *Lykourgeia* (of unknown date) may well have dramatized reconciliation between Dionysiac and Pythagorean mystery-cults.[11] It is perhaps worth adding the likelihood of a Pythagorean provenance for the influence of mystic ideas on the anonymous Prometheian trilogy.[12]

As for Aeschylus being influenced by the ideas of Herakleitos, the only external evidence is that Herakleitos was probably born about fifteen years before Aeschylus, and that his influence in fifth-century Athens is attested by both Plato and Aristotle.[13]

2. Aeschylus and the unity of opposites

In *Agamemnon* a relay of beacons brings to Argos the news of the fall of Troy. Klutaimestra (312–14) describes it in terms of the Athenian torch-races (*lampadēphoriai* or *lampadēdromiai*):

> Such are my laws of torch-bearers (λαμπαδηφόρων), one filled from another in succession, and the winner is the one who ran first and last (νικᾷ δ' ὁ πρῶτος καὶ τελευταῖος δραμών).

The much discussed[14] third line means that the winner is – as indeed was the case in Athens – the winning *team*, which includes the runners of the first and last legs.[15] Indeed the phrase used here for 'the one running first' ὁ πρῶτος δραμών) is used by Herodotus to describe the first leg of the Persian relay system, which he compares to the Greek *lampadēphoria*.[16] But this metaphor, taken by itself, is pointless, as well as inappropriate – there is only one team of beacons, and so no 'victory'. Some scholars have accordingly rejected this interpretation of 314. But we should instead look for secondary meaning to give it point.

In 314 'first' and 'last' surely form an opposition, but the runners of the first and last legs are not in opposition – they are rather two members of the same team. What then is the opposition? The words 'victory goes to the first...runner' suggest the first to *finish*, and that is what πρῶτος δραμών normally meant.[17] And indeed the *lampadēphoria* itself is described by an ancient notice[18] thus: 'the first to light (the altar with the torch) was the victor and so was his tribe': ὁ πρῶτος ἅψας ἐνίκα καὶ ἡ τούτου φυλή.

Line 314 may then suggest the mild paradox that the first runner to finish (the victor) is the last of the team to run.[19] But the paradox acquires substance, and interest in the context, only if 'last' also connotes the opposite of 'first' meaning 'victor', i.e. only if 'last' connotes *finishing* last (i.e. *losing*). This is surely the riddling, secondary meaning implied here. The *formulation* of the innocent but irrelevant idea of the whole team winning implies (by virtue of 'first' and 'last' being taken as opposed terms) the sinister paradox that defeat is somehow the same as victory. The paradox resembles such Herakleitean ones as 'the way up and down is one and the same', and 'immortals are mortal and mortals immortal'.[20] The victory transmitted by the fire is both Agamemnon's over Troy and Klutaimestra's over Agamemnon,[21] who is therefore both winner and loser. The seemliness of the victor being defeated is even made explicit by a charming Klutaimestra (941). His desire 'let victory, since it attended me, remain fixed' (854) is precisely what cannot be fulfilled.

We may add a further point of similarity with Herakleitos. With what is each of the torch-bearers successively (as if) 'filled' (πληρούμενοι)? It cannot be anything other than the fire. The structure of thought is like that of Herakleitos, for whom change in the cosmos is a process of the transformation of opposites into each other, and through this transformation fire persists as the single underlying substance. It is fire that persists throughout the relay, and 'fills' (a strong word) each runner, so that there is no difference between the opposites of first and last. I do not mean that Aeschylus was influenced here specifically by Herakleitos. And it may be insignificant that the underlying substance is common to both (fire). But I insist on the structural similarity with the Herakleitean notion of a single substance persisting through a process of transformation in which opposites are unified.

This is merely one instance of the unity of opposites in *Agamemnon* and *Libation Bearers*, to be added to the many others that I have discussed elsewhere,[22] and from which I select for mention here only the aforementioned scene in which Klutaimestra urges the seemliness of defeat on the victor of Troy, in *stichomuthia* in which Agamemnon allows himself to be treated like a woman, a barbarian, and a god, thereby confusing within himself the opposites – male-female, Greek-barbarian, mortal-immortal – by which a Greek male was primarily defined.

The cosmology of Aeschylus in these two plays, pervaded as they are by instances of the unity of opposites, may be said to be Herakleitean, in sense (c) above. What is not of course found in Herakleitos is the effect of anxiety and tension that such pervasion creates in *drama*. A substantial instance of such anxiety is provided by the identity of offence with counter-offence:

ὄνειδος ἥκει τόδ᾽ ἀντ᾽ ὀνείδους,
δύσμαχα δ᾽ ἐστὶ κρῖναι.   1560
φέρει φέροντ᾽, ἐκτίνει δ᾽ ὁ καίνων.

This insult has come in exchange for insult, and they are hard to separate/judge. He plunders the plunderer. The killer pays (*Ag.* 1559–62).

Similarly,

ἀντὶ μὲν ἐχθρᾶς γλώσσης ἐχθρὰ
γλῶσσα τελείσθω· τοὐφειλόμενον   310
πράσσουσα Δίκη μέγ᾽ ἀυτεῖ·
ἀντὶ δὲ πληγῆς φονίας φονίαν
πληγὴν τινέτω...

'In exchange for hostile speech let hostile speech be paid'
In exacting what is owed Justice shouts aloud,
'In exchange for bloody blow let (someone) pay bloody blow' (*Cho.* 309–13).

Counter-violence, if identical with the violence that elicits it, will elicit more violence, and the cycle of violence is 'hard to put a stop to' (*Cho.* 470; cf. 1075–6). A seemingly unceasing cycle, cosmic in Herakleitos, in the *Oresteia* excludes peace.

We should, finally, note two further features shared by Herakleitos and *Oresteia*. The first is that the unity of opposites is – as in the passages just quoted – frequently expressed in the same *style*, which I dub form-parallelism, and which is frequent in the ritual contexts of lamentation and mystic initiation.[23]

The second feature shared by Herakleitos and *Oresteia* is that the principle of the unity of opposites is expressed by an instrument formed by a simple internal tension. 'They do not understand' writes Herakleitos 'how being at variance (brought apart) it agrees (is brought together) with itself: there is a back-stretching *harmoniē* (fitting together), as of bow and of lyre'. In the *Oresteia* the instrument is the balance (scales), which is frequent there (and elsewhere in Aeschylus) as a metaphor.[24]

Of special interest here is the parodos of the *Agamemnon*.[25] The narrative of the sacrifice of Iphigeneia at Aulis is structured to emphasize the impasse produced by *opposition between equal forces*. The omen that appeared to the Atreidai as they set out for Troy, of eagles 'sacrificing' a hare, is interpreted by the seer Kalchas as 'favourable on the one hand, inauspicious on the other' (145 δέξια μὲν κατάμομφα δέ). For it prefigures the fall of Troy, but may demand 'the other[26] sacrifice' (of Iphigeneia), which will create future conflict. 'Such things', conclude the Chorus, 'did Kalchas cry out with blessings as fated from the birds on the way for the royal house. In consonance therewith say woe, woe, but may the good prevail' (156–9...αἴλινον αἴλινον εἰπέ, τὸ δ' εὖ νικάτω).

It is at this very moment, in which the emphasized ambivalence of the omen itself as well as of Kalchas' utterance ('with blessings') is reproduced ('in consonance') in the liturgical syntax of the refrain,[27] that the Chorus breaks off the narrative to invoke Zeus:

οὐκ ἔχω προσεικάσαι
πάντ' ἐπισταθμώμενος
πλὴν Διός, εἰ τὸ μάταν ἀπὸ φροντίδος ἄχθος   165
χρὴ βαλεῖν ἐτητύμως.

I am unable to liken him (i.e. Zeus) to anything as an equivalent,[28] putting everything on the balance, except Zeus, if from my mind I am to throw off genuinely the vain weight.

The commentators have noted, but failed to explain, the seeming abruptness of this transition, and failed to see the allusion to the balance in the *Iliad* that is operated by Zeus and determines victory in battle.[29] It was adopted by Aeschylus as a central theme in his (lost) *Psychostasia*, and is invoked at critical moments in his *Suppliants* (403, 405, 823). Having just referred to Aeschylus' use of the *metaphor* of the balance, we now find that it is imagined as a (divine) *reality* – albeit a reality created by metaphorical thinking.[30]

The human crisis of equally opposed forces (equilibrium) requires one side of the divine balance to fall. A balance, unlike bow and lyre, resolves (ends) the unity of opposites – if one side outweighs the other, which is how the battle is decided in Homer. In the Aulis narrative, as elsewhere, a crisis of the unity of opposites is resolved at the divine level. Only Zeus can outweigh the Chorus' mental 'weight'.

This brings us to the overall necessity, in the *Oresteia* though not Herakleitos, for the unity of opposites to be resolved so that one opposite may prevail permanently over the other. For the cycle of violence to end, the acts of violence have to be differentiated, as indeed occurs in the *Eumenides*: killing the mother was not the same as killing the husband (625, etc.). Along with this differentiation of formerly united opposites go several other such differentiations. For instance, the unity of male and female within the warrior Athena is – at the crucial point of judicial decision – differentiated in favour of the male: she favours the male because she has no mother (736–40). Another instance: the unity of victory and defeat, and the transformation of victory and defeat into each other, are both permanently ended by the 'victory' of Orestes (741) that is explicitly declared *not* to be a 'defeat' for the Furies (795). Victory (for all) prevails permanently (974–5) over defeat.

This transition, of which I can give only a brief indication here, represents the transition from Herakleitean to Pythagorean cosmology. In the former, opposites are identical with each other, or are transformed into each other in an unceasing cycle. In the latter, on the other hand, within each opposition one opposite prevails over the other in a stable structure. In *Agamemnon* and *Choephoroi* there is a pervasive unity of opposites, and opposites are transformed into each other in a seemingly unceasing cycle. Then in *Eumenides* permanent well-being is achieved by differentiation of the opposites with one prevailing over the other.

In our best evidence for fifth-century Pythagoreanism, Aristotle gives a table of ten pairs of opposites that he says are held by some Pythagoreans to be the fundamental constituents of the world (*Met.* 986a). This probably goes back to the time of Aeschylus if not before.[31] Implicit or explicit in *Eumenides* are six of these pairs: male prevails over female, limit over the unlimited, light over darkness, one over many, still over moving, good over bad.[32] But how, in contrast to Herakleitos, may the Pythagorean opposites be combined into a stable whole? To answer this question I will make a detour to (§3) an abstract problem, that will lead us to (§4) a metaphysical feature found in early Pythagoreanism and (§5) in the *Oresteia*.

3. Limit, odd, and even

For fifth-century Pythagoreanism Guthrie[33] demonstrates that

> there are in a sense only two opposites, of which the ten listed by Aristotle are no more than different aspects or manifestations...the ultimate principles are the two contraries limited and unlimited. With these are equated numerical oddness and evenness respectively, and they thus form the principle of the number series which in turn is to provide the elements of all existing things... The general principle applied by the Pythagoreans to the construction of a kosmos is that of the imposition of limit (*peras*) on the unlimited (*apeiron*) to make the limited (*to peperasmenon*).

But *why* is limited numerically odd and the unlimited even? A clue is preserved by Simplicius:[34] 'an odd number added (to an even number) limits it, for it prevents its division into equals.' Odd numbers are divided into unequals and so, as Aristoxenos (fr. 23 Wehrli) put it, 'have a middle (*meson*)' (i.e. a number left over in the middle). But when an even number is divided, then 'an empty space is left that is without a master (*adespotos*) and without number (*anarithmos*),' and so it (the even number) is lacking and incomplete (*atelēs*).[35]

What an even number lacks is an *internal* limit that makes it one complete number, prevents it disintegrating into two identical numbers. The assumption is that doubleness is inconsistent with unity. The 'empty space' that separates the two identical numbers is (in contrast to the *meson*) *anarithmos* (there is no number there) and *adespotos* (there is no master there, no control). All this taken together implies that what makes the odd number complete (in contrast to the 'incomplete' even number) is the control exercised by its *meson*, which – we have seen – prevents disintegration by *limiting*.

In a doctrine preserved in Plutarch (*Mor.* 388ab) this control acquires the dimension of gender. 'Complete separation' of an even number leaves a 'receptive space' that resembles the female, whereas the *meson* left by an odd number divided resembles the male (penis). The odd number, continues Plutarch, 'in combination always dominates and is never dominated'. Of this combination of odd with even he has in fact just given an example: the first (female) even number (two) combined with the first (male) odd number (three) makes five, which has been called 'marriage'. This is Pythagorean doctrine, alluded to already by Aristotle.[36] Such reasoning would produce the alignment of three sets of opposites in Aristotle's table: odd, limited, and male set against even, unlimited, and female. Moreover, the latter group is associated with what is lacking, incomplete, and uncontrolled, and is accordingly in Aristotle aligned with bad.[37]

These abstractions may seem remote from Aeschylus. But they illustrate the ideological determination of Pythagorean metaphysics. Even the most abstract reasoning, the mathematical basis of the metaphysics, is determined not by mathematics but by ideology.

Fundamental is, I suggest, the need to resolve conflict, to integrate opposites into a whole, both within the polis generally and specifically between male and female. Equality between opposed parties provides no limit, no means of resolving the conflict, and so makes possible a Herakleitean cosmology of opposites identical with – or ceaselessly transformed into – each other. Limit may be provided in principle by (a) the domination of one opposite by the other, or (b) the mediating effect of a third party. In this problem projected onto what the Pythagoreans regarded as the constituents of the world, numbers, we find both of these ways: (a) an odd number combined with an even number dominates it in the sense of creating an odd total number (as Plutarch notes); (b) an odd number is complete because it contains a limiting *meson*, i.e. a third party between two equals.[38]

There is in principle no reason why (a) and (b) should not combine, why mediation should not produce the domination of one opposite by the other, as we shall soon see is indeed the case with the domination of the unlimited by limit (limiting the unlimited) through the mediation of *harmonia* in the earliest extant fragments of Pythagoreanism (Philolaos). Indeed, at the political level domination without mediation may be considered unsatisfactory and unstable.

4. The triad in early Pythagoreanism

The late Pythagorean texts discussed above imply that completeness is composed of *three* elements (two plus a mediating *meson*). We find the same idea in *early* Pythagoreanism. In the words of Aristotle (*De Caelo* 268a10):

> As the Pythagoreans say, the universe and all things are defined by the number three; for end, the middle (*meson*), and beginning have the number of the whole, and their number is the triad.

The *meson* is required for creating completeness out of difference or opposition, and *meson* plus the opposites of beginning and end makes three. Accordingly, threeness is required for the world to come into being. In the Pythagorean cosmogony of the *Timaios* Plato states, on the original combination of fire and earth to make the universe, that (31bc) it is not possible for two things alone to combine well without a third, for it is necessary for there to be some bond in the middle (*meson*) to bring them together. And the fairest bond is the one that most unites itself and the things bound together.[39]

And in his Pythagoreanizing ontology[40] in the *Philebos* Plato states the view that limit (*peras*) should control the unlimited (*apeiron*). The mixture of the finite with infinite produces offspring, a 'third thing', that 'puts an end to the conflict of opposites'. By introducing limit 'this goddess' brings salvation (ἀποσῶσαι) in countless (μυρία) spheres, notably in health and music (25d–26c).

A similar cosmic structure is found even earlier, among the very few fifth-century texts that are certainly Pythagorean in our senses (a) or (b) (§1). Philolaos lived from circa 470 to circa 390 BC, but probably derives ideas from an earlier period.[41] Among his very few genuine fragments[42] are the following:

> Nature in the *kosmos* (world-order) was fitted together (or 'harmonized', ἁρμόχθη) from unlimiteds and limiters, both the whole *kosmos* and all the things in it (B1).

> ...since these beginnings (the unlimiteds and limiters) pre-existed and were neither alike each other nor even related, they could not have been ordered if *harmonia* (fitting-together, harmony) had not come upon them (ἐπεγένετο)... (B6).

One basic opposite (limiters) prevails over the other (unlimiteds)[43] by their being fitted together by a third element, *harmonia*.[44] If taken together with another genuine fragment:

> all things that are known have number; for nothing can be known or understood without this (B4),

this implies cosmogonical importance for the number three.

Ion of Chios, Aeschylus' contemporary, wrote a work entitled *Triagmoi*.[45] Of the four surviving fragments two refer by name to Pythagoras, and a third is as follows:

> (This is the) beginning of my account. All things are three, and there is nothing more or less than this three. Of each one thing the virtue (*aretē*) is a triad (*trias*): understanding (*sunesis*) and power (*kratos*) and chance (*tuchē*).[46]

Ion also maintained (B3) that cleverness (*sophia*) and chance (*tuchē*) are very unlike each other and yet have very similar results.

This is puzzling. How can understanding, which only animate beings have, be in each and every thing? And what does it mean to say that cleverness and chance have very similar results? These questions have never been answered.[47]

For presocratic cosmology understanding need not be confined to human action but may, like *nous* in Anaxagoras, order everything in the cosmos. Philolaos implies that knowing involves limiting,[48] and limiting – Pythagoreanism maintains – creates the cosmos. The Pythagorean way of life is based, it seems, on understanding the universe (§6). Understanding aims at control, but the human mind cannot create a perfect world. It is in its activity itself limited, by the power of chance, which is by definition uncontrolled. Understanding and chance may be regarded as – in the sphere of action or virtue – aligned with the basic Pythagorean opposition between limit and unlimited. If understanding and chance 'have very similar results', it can only be because in action they must combine. In the Pythagorean cosmogony in Plato's *Timaios* (48a) the *kosmos* was created by the combination (*sustasis*) of mind and necessity, with mind ruling necessity by persuasion (*peithō*). In Ion the opposites of understanding and chance are integrated – by *kratos*, the middle term – into the triad that is the virtue of each one thing. *Kratos* plays a role analogous to that played by *peithō* in the *Timaios* passage, and in the cosmogony of Philolaos by *harmonia*, which as the middle term combines limiters and the unlimited.

The idea that the cosmos is three is not of course a product of mere logic or mere observation but rooted in preconception. I have indicated, as relevant preconceptions, the need for political stability and for male domination of the female. But this is not to deny that there are others, for instance whatever it is that gives the number three its wide appeal in religious belief and ritual.[49]

Finally, before returning to the *Oresteia*, it is worth emphasizing the opposition between Pythagoreanism and Herakleitos. Philolaos' insistence in B6 that 'they could not have been ordered if *harmonia* (fitting-together, harmony) had not *come upon them* (ἐπεγένετο)' seems polemical. In the *kosmos* of Herakleitos, *harmonia* inheres in opposition or results from opposition.[50] Herakleitean opposites are 'one', 'the same',[51] or identified with the same thing or with each other,[52] and so do not need a third entity to unite them. But Philolaos insists that *harmonia* must have come into being *in addition to* (ἐπεγένετο) the opposites to combine them.[53] For Herakleitos the *logos* is a formula according to which 'all things happen'. It is not a third entity that brings opposites into combination. For Herakleitos the universe is not three: rather 'all things are one' (B50, B10).

Further, whereas Pythagoreanism privileges the limited, Herakleitos privileges the unlimited. For Herakleitos the *kosmos* has neither beginning nor end; the conflicting opposites are ceaselessly transformed into each other; the soul has no limits.[54] Early Pythagoreanism and Herakleitos seem to agree that opposites by themselves cannot enter stable combinations, but differ in that whereas Herakleitos accepts limitless conflict between them as the reality of the cosmos, the early Pythagoreans emphasize the existence of a third entity to mediate between the opposites. Whereas in the Pythagorean oppositions reported by Aristotle 'still' is aligned with limit and good ('moving' with unlimit and bad), for Herakleitos everything is in constant motion,[55] and even the opposites of justice and injustice are one and the same.[56] Small wonder that Herakleitos expressed hostility to Pythagoras.[57]

5. The *meson* in the *Oresteia*

The unity of opposites, and their transformation into each other, is ended by the verdict of the law court. Fundamental is – as in Aristotle's account of Pythagoreanism – limiting the unlimited, for the verdict ends the potentially unlimited conflict. Fundamental also is the opposition male-female, for the acquittal of Orestes depends on the principle that it also establishes – that the male rather than the female is the parent of the child.

The transformation is brought about by a third party. But who or what exactly is the third party? Is it the newly founded law court? Or its founder, Athena? We will soon see that another candidate is Zeus. And yet another candidate is *peithō* (persuasion), which is used by Athena and praised as a deity.[58] Indeed, *peithō* may be regarded as the political correlate of the cosmological mediating power of *harmonia* in Philolaos, and in the Pythagorean cosmogony in Plato's *Timaios* it is itself the third element through which mind prevails over necessity (§4).

However, in *Eumenides* a specific identification of the third element is impossible, because whereas Pythagoreanism produces abstraction from the life of the polis, Aeschylus dramatizes that life in the concrete multiplicity of (mythical) narrative. In early Pythagoreanism the fundamental opposition limit-unlimited is metaphysical and abstract, and the importance of mediating opposites gives rise to the abstract idea of a middle entity (*meson*) with universal power. But in the political dramatization of myth ultimate power belongs to personal deity, and the *Oresteia* is no exception. This is not to deny that the Aeschylean Zeus is sometimes represented in abstract terms.[59] But here in *Eumenides* the contradiction between Pythagorean abstraction and dramatic myth is resolved by the Chorus stating that power is *passed by deity to an abstraction*, the middle (*meson*):

> There is a place where the *deinon* (awesome) is good and fear watching over the mind... Who without nourishing his heart at all with innate fear[60] would revere Justice? Approve neither an anarchic life nor one ruled by a despot.

Aristotle, having said that the whole world is defined by the number three (§4), adds 'hence we have taken this number from nature, as it were one of her laws, and made use of it even for the worship of the gods.' An instance of threeness in the worship of the gods is in a fragment of Aeschylus (55): a first libation was poured for Zeus and Hera, the second for the heroes, and the third for Zeus Saviour (*Sōtēr*). This series of three libations – for Olympians, (chthonic) Heroes, Zeus Saviour – was a general practice.[88] Hence the association of 'third' with '(Zeus) Saviour'.[89] Aeschylus has the Danaids pray to 'the gods above and the honoured chthonic ones occupying tombs and Zeus saviour third' (*Su.* 24–6). According to Iamblichus[90] Pythagoras recommended a tripartite pre-meal libation, for Zeus Saviour, Herakles, and the Dioskouroi. And according to Philochoros of Athens 'the third krater was for Zeus *Teleios*[91] *Sōtēr* because three is the first *teleios* (complete) number, having beginning and end (*telos*) and middle (*mesa*)'.[92] Might this connection between the ritual and the Pythagorean privileging of the number three[93] have been already known at Athens two centuries earlier, in the time of Aeschylus? The frequent evocation of this ritual is a striking feature of the *Oresteia*.[94]

For instance, Klutaimestra's third blow to Agamemnon is given for 'Zeus beneath the earth, Saviour of the dead' (*Ag.* 1387). Threeness may express a vain desire for *completion*, for instance when Klutaimestra then calls the *daimōn* of the clan, whom she desires to leave the house (1572), *tripachuntos*, 'thrice-gorged' (1476): this may express her hope that now, after the third killing, he will want no more blood. We have seen that in the lament in *Choephoroi* disastrous delusion (*atē*) is *atriaktos* (339, another *hapax*), meaning that there is no prospect of the kind of victorious completeness that comes with the third throw in wrestling (as *triaktēr*). Orestes appeals to Power and Justice 'with the third, greatest of all, Zeus' (*Cho.* 244–5), and his description of his proposed killing of Aigisthos as the Fury drinking 'unmixed blood, a third drink' (578) implies the hope of completion.[95] Each perpetrator of a violent act sees it as the final one in a series of three.[96] But in the final words of the play (1065–76) the Chorus mention the killings first of Thyestes' children, then of Agamemnon, and continue

> but now there came from somewhere a third saviour (*sōtēr*) – or should I say a doom (*moron*)? Whither indeed will there be completion, whither will the power of *atē* be brought to rest and cease?[97]

The completion desired in evoking the third libation to Zeus *Sōtēr* turns out to be merely the third killing in the seemingly unstoppable cycle of violence in a world of the Herakleitean unity of opposites (salvation may be doom). In the last words of the final play, by contrast, Zeus and *Moira* are harmoniously conjoined.

The idea of the completing third libation to Zeus is in *Agamemnon* and *Choephoroi* perverted by the horrors of violent revenge, as a third blow, a third drink of blood, a third killing. But in *Eumenides* it is transferred to a wider sphere that has been prefigured in the role of Zeus *triaktēr* in the parodos of *Agamemnon*. Orestes, once acquitted, refers to his salvation as 'by the will of Pallas and of Loxias and of the third Saviour who completes all things' (τοῦ πάντα κραίνοντος τρίτου Σωτῆρος).[98] The completing function of Zeus *Sōtēr* is perhaps why there were sacrifices to him on the last day of the Athenian year.[99]

'Third' here combines ritual propriety (Zeus Saviour is third in the list) with his power to 'complete all things' – here through the polis institutions (law court and cult) that integrate the opposed positions expressed in the trial. And this is the conclusion of the third play in a trilogy in which the first and second plays focus on – respectively – the violence and counter-violence of the opposed positions. This 'third' Zeus is similar in effect to the Zeus who in the three stanzas of the Hymn ended the crisis of equilibrium, emerged victor in wrestling against Ouranos and Kronos,[100] and put men on the road to understanding. Just as the conclusion of this cosmogony is that Zeus, *triaktēr* and third ruler, rules permanently and everywhere, so too the three libations have a cosmological dimension: they move – we have seen – from the Olympian to the chthonic, and then to the 'third' Zeus who is 'Saviour', even 'Saviour of the dead'.[101]

Such a third Zeus unites Olympian with chthonic, the upper with the lower world,[102] as does also in its way the introduction of festive light into the Furies' cave 'beneath the earth' (1006, 1023). In the figure of Zeus political unity is expressed cosmologically.[103] His power to mediate between opposites (in cosmological space) and to transform equilibrium into transition (in cosmological time) qualifies him to preside as all-seeing and all-completing 'third Saviour' over the final resolution of the trilogy. Ritual utterance, dramatic form, narrative, polis, and cosmology finally cohere in the Saviour who, I suggest, personifies the universality of the completing function of three in early Pythagoreanism.

Notes

1 Seaford 2003.

2 The most recent case for Pythagorean influence on Aeschylus was made as long ago as 1966 by George Thomson, who in his commentary on the *Oresteia* adduces Pythagorean texts in thirteen places (*Ag.* 36–7, 76–82, 179–80, 1001–4, 1232–4, 1663; *Cho.* 315–22, 583–5; *Eum.* 269–72, 307, 526–31, 650–1, 1045–6). Although this may perhaps have some cumulative persuasiveness, there is no single instance in which it is persuasive. Rösler (1970) criticizes Thomson, and concludes (36–7) that there was no Pythagorean influence on Aeschylus.

3 Seaford 2004, 2012.

4 Plato is generally regarded as much influenced by Pythagoreanism, but he does not explicitly acknowledge it, and mentions Pythagoras only once and the Pythagoreans only once (*Rep.* 600b, 530d: here he expresses agreement only). We should therefore assign his Pythagorean ideas to category (b).

5 Cic. *Tusc.* 3. 23. Cicero had access to Greek philosophical traditions, and studied in Athens.

6 DK 22B40, B129; 36B2, B4 (= Leurini 2000, frr. 116, 92); Hdt. 4.95–6.

7 Ion's date of birth is unknown, but was probably in the 480s. He was dead by 421 (Ar. *Peace* 834–7). For Ion see most recently Jennings and Katsaros 2007; material: Leurini 2000.

8 fr. 108 Leurini (=*FGrHist* 392F22) (at Isthmian games).

9 For the later influence of Pythagorean mathematics on the design of the theatre at Epidauros see Käppel 1989.

10 Aristox. fr. 11–25 Wehrli; Iambl. *Vit. Pyth.*129–30, 249–51; Minar 1942, 73–5 calls it 'a golden age', which he dates from the expulsion of the tyrant Kleinias (c. 494 BC) to the catastrophic defeat about fifty years later (perhaps 454 BC: Minar 1942, 77–8). Aristoxenos was a fourth century BC scholar from southern Italy who consorted with Pythagoreans.

11 Seaford 2005, developing M. L. West 1990b, 26–50. Such a reconciliation would be welcome to one who was both inspired by Dionysos (Lada-Richards 1999, 234–47) and impressed by the political effectiveness of the Pythagorean group constituted by mystic initiation (Burkert 1972, 115, 119; Minar 1942, 15–35).

12 Seaford 1986.

13 Pl. *Tht.* 179–80; Arist. *Met.* 987a, 1010a.

14 To the report of various views in Fraenkel's commentary (1950, ad loc.) add Kaimio 1985 and Judet de la Combe 2001, ad loc.

15 For the syntax cf. 324.

16 Hdt. 8.98. The fact that he writes ὁ πρῶτος δραμών of a team of *horsemen* suggests (even though δραμών might be metaphorical) that it was already in his mind as the term used of the *lampadēphoria*.

17 Despite Hdt. 8.98; cf. e.g. Thuc. 4.111.2; Xen. *Anab.* 4.7.11; Eupolis fr. 129K-A; Pi. *O.* 6.75.

18 Schol. Patm. Dem. 57.43.

19 So Foucart 1899.

20 B60, 62.

21 1378, where victory should not be emended away: Thomson 1966, ad loc.; cf. Judet de la Combe 2001, ad loc.

[22] See Seaford 2003.
[23] Seaford 2003.
[24] *Pers.* 346, 437, 440, *Su.* 403, 405, 605, 823, 982, *Th.* 21, *Ag.* 251, 349, 574, 707, 1042, 1272, *Cho.* 61, 240, *Eum.* 888; Seaford 2003, 154.
[25] See further Seaford 2012.
[26] 150 ἑτέραν, always mistranslated as 'an other'.
[27] Repeated from 121 and 139.
[28] For this translation cf. *Cho.* 518–20; Seaford 2003, 151.
[29] At *Il.* 8. 69–72 and 22. 209–19 the fall of one side of the divine scales is caused by the (respective weights of) the two fates put on the scales by Zeus. At 19. 223–4 it is caused by Zeus himself (κλίνῃσι). Cf. 14. 99; 16. 658.
[30] On metaphorical thinking as imagining the divine see Cairns in this volume, and on the lack of a clear boundary between cosmology (in the broad sense) and metaphor see Seaford 2012, 245–9.
[31] According to Aristotle the table influenced – or was influenced by – Alkmaion of Kroton, who probably lived in the early to middle part of the fifth century: W. K. C. Guthrie 1962, 341–4, 357–9. For differing opinions on its date see Raven 1948, 11; Burkert 1972, 52, 294–5.
[32] Seaford 2012, 293–6.
[33] W. K. C. Guthrie 1962, 246–8; Burkert 1972, 32–3. NB Arist. *Met.* 986a17; 987a14 ff. (with Guthrie 240–4); 990a8; *EN* 1106b29.
[34] In Arist. *Phys.*, 455. 20.
[35] Pythagorean doctrine preserved in Stobaeus I p. 22. 19 Wachsmuth. Imagining even and odd numbers as occupying space also underlies Aristotle's obscure 'illustration' involving gnomons at *Phys.* 203b.
[36] Aristotle fr. 203 (=Alex. Aphr. *Comm. Met.* 39.8); fr. 199; 1078b23; Burkert 1972, 34 n. 31, 467 n. 8.
[37] Arist. *EN* 1106b29: 'Bad is of the unlimited, as the Pythagoreans surmised, and good is of the limited'. Cf. Burkert 1972, 51. That may help to explain the absence of hot-cold, wet-dry.
[38] Cf. Arist. *Met.* 1083b28: for the Platonists the one is middle (*meson*) in odd numbers.
[39] The Pythagoreanizing ontology of Pl. *Phlb.* is fourfold: (a) unlimited, (b) limit, (c) what is mixed out of unlimited and limit, (d) the cause of the mixture (27b). But (d) is easily seen as derivative.
[40] Huffman 1993, 106.
[41] Recent scholarship favours this view: Kahn 2001, 34–8; Riedweg 2005, 79.
[42] Burkert 1972; Huffman 1993.
[43] notably in the cosmogonic limiting of the unlimited (fire) to produce a central 'hearth': B17; Huffman 1993, 42–3.
[44] In Philolaos *harmonia* means 'harmonious fitting together,' 'both because it is specifically tied to a musical attunement in F6a, and because it is explicitly used not just to explain any old combination of dissimilar elements but a combination of elements into an order (*kosmos*)': Huffman 1993, 139. Pythagorean also no doubt is the idea 'that the soul is a kind of harmony, for harmony is a blend or composition of contraries, and the body is composed out of contraries' (Arist. *De Anima* 407b27): W. K. C. Guthrie 1962, 307–8.
[45] Another title transmitted from antiquity is the singular *Triagmos* (A1: Harpokration).

Such titles may have been invented (on the basis of the opening words) in the Hellenistic age. Discussion: Baltussen 2007, 311–15. Another title attributed to Ion is *Kosmologikos*, which was perhaps of the same work.

[46] Cf. also A6; Pl. *Soph*.242cd.

[47] The best existing account is by Dover 1988.

[48] B3: Huffman 1993, 118–20.

[49] Burkert 1972, 469, 474–6. A detailed study of the number three in Greek religion (though not in Pythagoreanism) is Usener 1903. Cf. e.g. Pl. *Parm*. 145a.

[50] B51 'in being at variance it agrees with itself; backward-stretching *harmonia*, as of bow and lyre'; B8 'from things at variance the finest *harmonia*'.

[51] B10, 60, 88, 103.

[52] B8, 10, 48, 61, 62, 67, 84a.

[53] For Philolaos 'limiters' set boundaries within a continuum, but to produce an order the combining of opposites by *harmonia* is also required. For instance, 'in itself hot is an unlimited and can cause disease, but heat that is limited in accordance with *harmonia* produces health': Huffman 1993, 48, 89, 140, 145.

[54] B12, B30, B31, B36, B62, B67, B77, B88, B91, B126; B45; cf. B115.

[55] B12, 91, A6 rest and the static are for the dead. Cf. also Pl. *Tht*. 179–80 on the followers of Herakleitos.

[56] This is the implication of B102: 'For god all things are fine and good and just, but humans assume some things as just and others as unjust'.

[57] B40, 81, 129; cf. 35. The criticism of P. for his *polumathiē*, 'much learning', may impute failure to understand that things happen according to a single principle (B1, 41).

[58] *Eum*. 829, 885, 970.

[59] Notably when invoked to resolve opposition between equal forces, as at *Ag*. 160–7: Seaford 2012.

[60] I read ἐμφυεῖ...φόβῳ τρέφων (Thomson) for MS ἐν φάει...ἀνατρέφων. But this problem does not affect my argument.

[61] 'Every' (παντί) is in emphatic position.

[62] The aristocratic Cylon and democrat Ninon both spoke against the Pythagoreans in the same assembly: Iamblichos *VP* 258, derived from Apollonios of Tyana, who may have derived it from Timaios: Minar 1942, 54–65, and bibl. in Burkert 1972, 104 n. 37.

[63] 13.71–3. The unlimited accumulation of individual wealth, an idea not found in the premonetary world of Homer, becomes a preoccupation of the monetized polis (e.g. Ar. *Wealth* 189–97; Arist. *Pol*. 1256b26–57a4; Seaford 2004, 165–9). It is not just that there was no point in accumulating millions of e.g. tripods. Rather, the old ideology of reciprocity created a limit that is eroded by the individualistic self-sufficiency fostered by money: Seaford 2004, 292–8.

[64] Cf. also the invisibility of the mind (*nous*) of the gods (17).

[65] This is not to deny that limiting the unlimited is after all a general feature of cultural action (an insight approached by Philolaos B2; Seaford 2004, 277 n. 52), and is found as the originating act in Greek mythical cosmogony: e. g. Orph. *frr*. 55, 56; Burkert 1972, 37–9.

[66] Aristox. fr. 16 Wehrli. In Iambl. *VP* alone see 11, 78, 133, 189, 214, 215–6, 220, 248, 266; Minar (1942) 2, 71–3.

[67] Frr. 33, 35, 38 Wehrli, from the *Pythagorean Precepts*, which have recently been

shown to be 'precisely what they purport to be, a summary of Pythagorean ethics as taught in the fourth century': Huffman 2008; Minar 1942, 99 n. 13; Burkert 1972, 101 n. 17.

[68] cf. also 645, 648–51, 156–9, 349, 926–7; Seaford 2003, 152–3.

[69] 58 DK B15, D1, D4, D8; Aristoxenos.

[70] Aristotle fr. 57.

[71] *Hubris* and excess (*koros*): Fisher 1992, 19, 21, 72–6, 187, 212–42, 272–80, 336, 350, 375–6; *hubris* and wealth: 20–1, 48, 69–72, 102–4, 273–6, 337, 350, 421, 491, 496–7.

[72] with the slight change to ἀκορέστου (or ἀκορέτου) to go with ὑγιείας.

[73] Hippocr. *Aphorismoi* 1.3 (much of this collection may derive from the fifth century BC); Dio Chrys. 1.470R; Thomson 1966, ad *Ag.* 1001–4.

[74] The transformation is beautifully expressed as a simultaneity at 1013 'filled excessively with suffering', πημονᾶς γέμων ἄγαν in which πημονᾶς may be replaced by the Doric form παμονᾶς Headlam) but not by πλησμονᾶς (Schütz, followed by e.g. Fraenkel and Page), which gives a pointless and flat pleonasm.

[75] Note the following lines (1018–24). The reciprocal violence is insatiable (ἀκόρεστος: *Ag.* 1117; 1484) and a unity of equal opposites (e.g. *Cho.* 310–14). In *Eumenides* the Furies, now upholders of the middle, pray that there never be insatiable (976 ἄπληστος) conflict in the polis.

[76] In *Ag.* alone see also 1117, 1484, 1331; Seaford 2003, 157,

[77] According to Sommerstein in his commentary (1989 ad loc.) it is so that 'we be reminded that there is another side to the case'.

[78] 927–37, 950–5, 990–1.

[79] *Eum.* 75–9, 240–1, 248–51.

[80] e.g. Janko 2001, 7 compares it with Protagoras' *Kataballontes Logoi* ('Knock-down Arguments').

[81] Baltussen 2007, 313–14.

[82] Cf. *Eum.* 589. Thomson in his commentary (1966 ad loc.) compares the wrestling contest between Kronos and Zeus at Olympia (Paus. 5.7.10; 8.2.2).

[83] 174–5, in metrical correspondence with the weight of anxiety at 165–6.

[84] Pl. *Rep.* 600b (cf. 530d).

[85] See e.g. W. K. C. Guthrie 1962, 148.

[86] B3: Huffman 1993, 118–20. For Herakleitos, by contrast, the soul has no limits (B45).

[87] For *epirrhepein* with this sense cf. *Eum.* 888; Seaford 2003, 151–4.

[88] Schol. Pi. *I.* 6.10a; Schol. Pl. *Phlb.* 66d; Pollux *Onom.* 6.15; Thomson 1966, on *Ag.* 246–7.

[89] Examples are given by Thomson 1966, on *Eum.* 759–60.

[90] *Vit. Pyth.* 28.155.

[91] Zeus *Teleios* is invoked at *Ag.* 973 and evoked at *Eum.* 214. It seems that *Sōtēr* was identified with *Teleios* in Euripides' *Andromeda* and Aristophanes' *Tēganistai*: schol. Pl. *Phlb.* 66d.

[92] 328 *FGrHist* F87.

[93] Detectable also perhaps in the recapitulation that concludes the (Pythagoreanizing) *Philebos*, where Plato re-states his view that thought is superior to pleasure, adding that neither thought nor pleasure is the good itself. Rather, 'when a third appeared more powerful than either of these, thought appeared infinitely more closely related and

naturally connected with the form of the victor' (67a7). We have encountered in *Agamemnon* the metaphor of the supervening third as athletic victor, and the power of the supervening third establishing hierarchy between the other two. Further, the recapitulation has just been introduced as 'the third for the *Sōtēr*' (66d3).

[94] The best and most comprehensive discussion of this theme is by Burian 1986, 332–42, but he mentions Pythagoreanism only in a footnote.

[95] Cf. Zeitlin 1965, 484.

[96] As observed by Clay 1969.

[97] Whereas if Klutaimestra had three specific killings in mind, they may be those of Thyestes' children, Iphigeneia, and Agamemnon.

[98] 758–60. Already at *Cho.* 244–5 the 'third Zeus' is invoked (with Power and Justice) as 'the greatest of all'.

[99] Lysias 26.6.

[100] It may or may not be relevant that Ouranos personifies the sky and Kronos was imprisoned in the underworld.

[101] Scullion 2005 argues that Aeschylus is influenced by the combination of Olympian and chthonic in the cult of the *Hausgott* Zeus *Sōtēr*.

[102] Tripartite cosmic unity is radically personified by Zeus in fragment 70 R of Aeschylus: 'Zeus is *aithēr*, Zeus is earth, Zeus is sky. Zeus is all things, and what is above them'. The idea of god as the beginning, middle, and end of all things at Pl. *Laws* 715e may have been influenced by Pythagoreanism (*pace* Burkert 1972, 467 n. 6), or alternatively may perpetuate an ancient preconception (of the kind referred to in the pre-penultimate paragraph of §4) that may have influenced Pythagoreanism. Plato's remark may derive from Orphic poetry (*Orph. Frr.* 21, 21a; Derveni papyrus 17.12): for the connections between Pythagoreanism and Orphic doctrine see Burkert 1972, 135–32.

[103] On the politico-cosmological dimension of the Orphic Zeus absorbing all things see Seaford 2004, 221–2.

3

ETEOCLES' DECISION IN AESCHYLUS' *SEVEN AGAINST THEBES*

Fritz-Gregor Herrmann

1. Eteocles' decision

The central scene of Aeschylus' *Seven against Thebes* sees the protagonist, Eteocles, the son of Oedipus, making arrangements for the defence of his city, seven-gated Thebes, by assigning defending champions to the gates of the city. At the end of this scene, Eteocles learns that, at the Seventh Gate, there is his brother Polynices. He prepares to fight him, but the Chorus of Theban maidens intervene and try to stop him. Their argument is that it need not be Eteocles himself: another can defend that gate. But, as the audience who knew the myth of the mutual fratricide of the sons of Oedipus would not have been surprised to see, the Chorus do not manage to dissuade Eteocles from fighting his brother.

Aeschylus has thus written a scene in which two parties make explicit their different opinions on and approaches to one and the same problem. The two proposed courses of action are mutually exclusive, and the situation demands that *one* must be taken. Both Eteocles and the Chorus advance arguments and reasons for their positions, but ultimately it is Eteocles on whom the outcome depends. It is in this sense that we can legitimately discuss Eteocles' decision to fight his brother Polynices.[1]

In order to see *why* Eteocles fights his brother – is it the rational thing to do? is he under a curse? is he deluded? is he just doing his duty? – it is necessary to follow his words and actions throughout the play. In the course of this discussion, we shall see what motivates and determines Eteocles in what he says and does, in how he acts and reacts in a given situation. Eteocles' facing his brother in mortal combat, just as Agamemnon's sacrifice of Iphigenia, Orestes' killing of his mother, and in the *Suppliants* Pelasgus' admitting the Danaïds and their father into his city, all these actions or events are preceded by some form of deliberation, adumbrated, reported, or witnessed immediately on stage. These deliberations,[2] together with the actions that follow, are governed by thoughts in part similar to, in part different from what could be encountered on stage, in fiction, or in life today; but they are deliberations in principle comprehensible to us.³ It is after subtracting what is humanly intelligible at all times and what is owed to specific historical circumstance that we may be able to see both aspects of Aeschylus' individuality and patterns of archaic Greek thought within and with which he was working.

2. Aeschylus' Theban plays

The *Seven against Thebes* is the third play of a thematically linked tetralogy, Aeschylus' '*Thebaïd*', comprising the tragedies *Laius*, *Oedipus*, and *Seven against Thebes*, together with the satyr play *Sphinx*.⁴ The few fragments of the earlier plays do not tell us much about their content. The *Laius* will have contained reference to the thrice-pronounced oracle of Apollo that Laius must die without offspring and save his city, Laius' disregard of this oracle, either because he desired offspring or because he desired his wife Jocasta, reference to the birth and exposal of Oedipus, and a report of the killing of Laius. The *Oedipus* may well have covered a near-identical section of the story to that covered by Sophocles in *Oedipus Rex*; the last part of the play, though, was different in important respects. Aeschylus does not know of any daughters of Oedipus and Jocasta; there are only the sons Eteocles and Polynices.⁵ And Aeschylus' *Oedipus* contained, after the self-blinding of Oedipus upon the discovery of his origins and of the nature of his marriage,⁶ a curse by Oedipus. Oedipus curses his sons because of their *trophē*, their 'conception', i.e. the fact that Oedipus begot his sons on his own mother.⁷ The content of the curse is important for the *Seven against Thebes* but must be reconstructed from references in that play alone.⁸ It may well have been something like: 'When you divide your patrimony, sword in hand, Chalybus ('a Chalybian', i.e. a stranger from the north; or: 'iron', 'steel') as arbitrator will bring reconciliation so that you get an equal share.' The play may have ended there. And as the *Seven against Thebes* begins with the city's being under siege, the audience would then have had to supply from their general knowledge of the story that Polynices had gone to Argos and that he and Tydeus and the blameless seer Amphiaraus were among the principal fighters led or at least assembled by the king of Argos, Adrastus. Alternatively, Aeschylus' *Oedipus* could have ended with the parting of the brothers, either by way of a quarrel which saw Polynices driven away and expelled, or indeed by way of a peaceful attempt to divide their inheritance and avoid the curse, for example by drawing lots for the movable wealth as one share, the kingship of the city as the other, after which Polynices would have departed from Thebes, either in an accepting or in an angry spirit.⁹ The *Seven against Thebes* opens with the city under siege and ends with the successfully accomplished defence of the land and its

3. The opening of Aeschylus' *Seven against Thebes*

The *Seven against Thebes* is a tragedy that more than any other by Aeschylus, and perhaps more than any other extant tragedy from the fifth century, focuses on one man in isolation, Eteocles.[10] In a relevant respect, Eteocles is the only *man* we see throughout this final play of Aeschylus' Labdacid trilogy: for in the prologue, when Eteocles addresses 'the citizens' as a silent mass in the opening lines, these citizens are those not yet of age and the elderly, as long as they are 'not yet decrepit', in Paley's phrase. Paley himself[11] thought that lines 10–13 addressed the young, the old, and those of fighting age in between, the adult male citizen warriors. But it is important to stress that this is not so. Eteocles' peers are at their battle stations, where they have been defending the city for some considerable time (cf. lines 21–3). Now, as the seer has pronounced, there will be the greatest onslaught yet (24–9); this requires even the very young and the very old to come to the defence (30–3); they must go to and remain on the walls and the towers and the gates; *mimnontes*, 'remaining', is a standard term for not deserting one's post; but it may here imply in addition that those who are sent now must stay where they are stationed, which enables those in their prime, the fighting force of men between, roughly, 20 and 40, to make a sortie and defeat the enemy, which is indeed what will have happened by the end of the play. The fighting and the duels take place before the city gates. The exhortations to be of good courage and not to get frightened or perturbed (34–5) accord well with the interpretation that those addressed are so young that they have never yet fought or so old that they have not fought for some time; the form of words befits an address to those age groups,[12] but not in the same way one to proud heroic warriors. It is against this background that lines 10–20 must be read:

ὑμᾶς δὲ χρὴ νῦν, καὶ τὸν ἐλλείποντ' ἔτι   10
ἥβης ἀκμαίας καὶ τὸν ἔξηβον χρόνῳ,
βλαστημὸν ἀλδαίνοντα σώματος πολύν,
ὥραν ἔχονθ' ἕκαστον ὥς τι συμπρεπές,
πόλει τ' ἀρήγειν καὶ θεῶν ἐγχωρίων
βωμοῖσι, τιμὰς μὴ 'ξαλειφθῆναί ποτε,   15
τέκνοις τε, Γῇ τε μητρί, φιλτάτῃ τροφῷ·
ἡ γὰρ νέους ἕρποντας εὐμενεῖ πέδῳ,
ἅπαντα πανδοκοῦσα παιδείας ὄτλον,
ἐθρέψατ' οἰκητῆρας ἀσπιδηφόρους,
πιστοί γ' ὅπως γένοισθε πρὸς χρέος τόδε.   20

> But you must now – both you who have not yet reached
> the prime of youth and you who have with time left youth behind,
> making the stature of your bodies strong,[13]
> each taking care as befits each –
> help both the city and the altars of the gods of our land,
> lest ever honour be wiped out,
> both for <you> the children and for Mother Land, dearest nurse:
> for she nursed you while you were young and walked with a carefree foot,
> gladly receiving all the distress that arises from bringing up the young,
> and brought you up to be spear-bearing inhabitants <of this Land>,[14]
> so that you would indeed become trustworthy for this time of need.

That it is the very young and the very old whom Eteocles addresses as being in front of him is significant in more than one regard. First, as stated at the outset, it entails that he speaks to those who are not his peers and who indeed are inferior to him at least in respect of fighting prowess, and thus in respect of the *aretē* of a citizen. Secondly, it puts Eteocles in the position in which Oedipus was when he solved the riddle of the three ages of man which the Sphinx had put to him; of course, neither the young nor the old here addressed are crawling on the floor or staggering along with their walking sticks respectively: but *herpō*, though common enough as a word for 'walking' of any sort in tragedy, may remind us of the infancy that youth has recently left behind; and the explicit qualification of the old as not yet infirm and decrepit points to that old age which will require the prop of the walking stick.

But thirdly, the scene as a whole puts Eteocles in the position of Oedipus also in another sense: the Oedipus of Sophocles' *Oedipus Tyrannus* is made to address an assembly of citizens at the beginning of the prologue of that play. A similar question of interpretation arises there. Oedipus addresses the citizens assembled as children, as befits a fatherly king, and declares that their concerns are his concerns; he then turns to one old man with the request to tell him what it is they want.[15] In response the old man replies (14–21):

> Ἀλλ', ὦ κρατύνων Οἰδίπους χώρας ἐμῆς,
> ὁρᾷς μὲν ἡμᾶς ἡλίκοι προσήμεθα   15
> βωμοῖσι τοῖς σοῖς, οἱ μὲν οὐδέπω μακρὰν
> πτέσθαι σθένοντες, οἱ δὲ σὺν γήρᾳ βαρεῖς·
> ἱερῆς, ἐγὼ μὲν Ζηνός, οἵδε τ' ἠθέων
> λεκτοί· τὸ δ' ἄλλο φῦλον ἐξεστεμμένον
> ἀγοραῖσι θακεῖ, πρός τε Παλλάδος διπλοῖς   20
> ναοῖς, ἐπ' Ἰσμηνοῦ τε μαντείᾳ σποδῷ.

> But, Oedipus, ruling over my land,
> you do see us, what age we are who have gathered here
> at your altars: some not yet having the strength to fly far,

the others heavy with old age:
priests, I of Zeus; but those the choice of the unmarried:
the other group,[16] wreathed,
sits in the squares, by the double temples of Pallas
and by the oracular ash-altar of Ismenus.

One may debate whether the priest is referring to two groups, very young and very old, namely we old priests and these chosen youths, or to three: 'Thou seest us seated at thine altar, and our years; how some are feeble still in flight, some weak with age, who are priests, as I am of Zeus; and these pure youths, a chosen few.'[17] Campbell comments: 'young children, chosen youths and aged priests; the ages most befitting supplication.' This would deprive the scene of a connection with the three ages of man. But it would not change the fact that the men of fighting age are absent: they are the other group, the other class, the other *phylon*. The adult male citizens are in the public squares to fulfil religious rites for the city, in parallel with the adult male citizens in the *Seven against Thebes*, who fulfil their citizen duties in another way.[18] Their absence in Sophocles' *Oedipus* offers indirect support for the assumption that in Aeschylus' play, too, those constituting the group to which Eteocles belonged were absent.

Fourthly, though, as has been noticed of old, Eteocles' address to the citizens and the orders he gives at the beginning of the *Seven against Thebes* are an echo of the words of Hector at *Iliad* 8. 517–28:[19]

κήρυκες δ' ἀνὰ ἄστυ Διῒ φίλοι ἀγγελλόντων
παῖδας πρωθήβας πολιοκροτάφους τε γέροντας
λέξασθαι περὶ ἄστυ θεοδμήτων ἐπὶ πύργων·
θηλύτεραι δὲ γυναῖκες ἐνὶ μεγάροισιν ἑκάστη   520
πῦρ μέγα καιόντων· φυλακὴ δέ τις ἔμπεδος ἔστω
μὴ λόχος εἰσέλθῃσι πόλιν λαῶν ἀπεόντων.
ὧδ' ἔστω Τρῶες μεγαλήτορες ὡς ἀγορεύω·
μῦθος δ' ὃς μὲν νῦν ὑγιὴς εἰρημένος ἔστω,
τὸν δ' ἠοῦς Τρώεσσι μεθ' ἱπποδάμοις ἀγορεύσω.   525
ἔλπομαι εὐχόμενος Διί τ' ἄλλοισίν τε θεοῖσιν
ἐξελάαν ἐνθένδε κύνας κηρεσσιφορήτους,
οὓς κῆρες φορέουσι μελαινάων ἐπὶ νηῶν.

And let the heralds Zeus loves give orders about the city
for the boys who are in their first youth and the grey-browed[20] elders
to take stations on the god-founded bastions that circle the city;
and as for the women, have our wives, each one in her own house,
kindle a great fire; let there be a watch kept steadily
lest a sudden attack get into the town when the fighters have left it.
Let it be thus, high-hearted men of Troy, as I tell you.
Let that word that has been spoken now be a strong one,

> with that which I speak at dawn to the Trojans, breakers of horses.
> For in good hope I pray to Zeus and the other immortals
> that we may drive from our place these dogs swept into destruction
> whom the spirits of death have carried here on their black ships.[21]

Here, Hector distinguishes clearly between, on the one hand, the men in the field, for whom he has one set of orders and exhortations, and on the other the young, the old and the women in town, for whom other orders are appropriate. We shall later, in Book 6, see Hector, too, in the city. Here, his order finishes with a prayer that displays an attitude to the attacking army not dissimilar to what Eteocles has said and will say; significantly, this prayer to Zeus and the other gods has a parallel in Eteocles' invocation of Zeus and *theos*, respectively, in lines 8–9 and line 35, which frame his address to the assembled young and old.[22] That is to say, Eteocles, from the beginning of the play, is compared, in some respect, to Hector, the model of the warrior who gives his life in defence of his city. But Hector's decision in *Iliad* 22 to defend Troy by waiting outside the Scaean Gate for Achilles is motivated not least by an overriding concern for his *timē*, his 'honour'. An expectation is thus raised by Aeschylus, and one of the questions to be addressed in an assessment of Eteocles will be whether he, too, is similarly motivated by concerns for his *timē*.

It is a distinct possibility, as Taplin has noted,[23] that these silent faces leave the stage immediately after line 35. If this is so, the last they hear is the prayer. Eteocles instils in these men the same confidence which he speaks of in addressing the women in subsequent scenes. On this reading, the arrangements he has made, his motivation for making these arrangements, and his considering the possibility of some ruse on the part of the attackers are not for the ears of the citizens: all that is difficult and dangerous, Eteocles faces alone.[24]

4. Eteocles alone

Fundamental to an assessment of Eteocles' character, his actions, and his choices is the distinction between what he says and does when in front of others and what he says and does when on his own. It has been observed, but is often not emphasized sufficiently, that lines 69 and 77 are spoken by Eteocles when he is by himself,[25] and that this is for Aeschylus a means of portraying his isolation.[26] After his last words in line 68, the Scout leaves by the *parodos* by which he had entered and Eteocles is alone in the orchestra. The precise structure and content of the words Eteocles utters here when on his own are a key to understanding what is on his mind when he dismisses the Chorus' suggestion that he could send someone else to fight against Polynices at the seventh gate. Eteocles says (69–72; 74–7):[27]

ὦ Ζεῦ τε καὶ Γῆ καὶ πολισσοῦχοι θεοί,
Ἀρά τ' Ἐρινὺς πατρὸς ἡ μεγασθενής, 70
μή μοι πόλιν γε πρυμνόθεν πανώλεθρον
ἐκθαμνίσητε δῃάλωτον Ἑλλάδος· 72
ἐλευθέραν δὲ γῆν τε καὶ Κάδμου πόλιν 74
ζεύγλῃσι δουλίῃσι μήποτε σχεθεῖν· 75
γένεσθε δ' ἀλκή· ξυνὰ δ' ἐλπίζω λέγειν·
πόλις γὰρ εὖ πράσσουσα δαίμονας τίει.

O Zeus and Land and city-protecting gods,
and Curse-Erinys of my father, mighty one,
do not for my sake root out the city, at least, from the bottom,
so that it be altogether destroyed, taken by the enemy from Greece:[28]
may <the enemy> never, with yoke-loops of slavery, hold
the land and the city of Cadmus, <now> free!
But be our defence! And I expect we have a common cause:
indeed, a city that does well honours its divinities.

Eteocles' prayer is an expression of despair. Without pre-judging the issue of why Eteocles will fight Polynices, we can observe the following: the first line unites those divinities that had been addressed or invoked already in Eteocles' first speech to the citizens, Zeus and the Land, together with the gods whose statues at the outer rim of the *orchestra* are visible to all, the gods whom the women will implore and whose images they will embrace. These gods are there for all and they can be mentioned in front of all. The second line addresses the Prayer, Imprecation, or Curse of the father as the father's mighty Erinys. Both lines are above suspicion. The second-person-plural verb form in line 72 addresses all of the divinities just invoked together. The content of Eteocles' prayer is that these gods should not utterly destroy the city. Eteocles could ask this of the Erinys: Oedipus uttered a curse against his sons, and Eteocles asks that if he and Polynices are affected by this curse, and if this is the day when that should happen, the city, at least, should be spared. It is slightly more difficult to see why the city-protecting gods should be asked not just to defend the city, but rather not to root out the city. Why should it have occurred to the city-protecting gods to root out the city?

One could argue that these gods, whose names we shall learn later on in the play, are the same gods who could be invoked by the attackers, just as in the *Iliad* the women of Troy pray to the same Athena to whom the Greeks, too, pray for help; and one could add that Eteocles' words are a veiled accusation appropriate in this prayer: 'You gods should defend the city, for a city that does well honours its gods. If you do not defend the city now, this would amount to giving it up to the enemy who will destroy it, so that the blame for the destruction of the city would fall on you, too.'

This would be a sufficient explanation for the form of words Eteocles employs. There is, however, an alternative. If Oedipus' killing his father, marrying his mother and begetting children with her constitutes pollution, *miasma*, the city could be said to be thus polluted. The women will certainly later on speak of the *miasma* of killing one's own brother (682). But if the city is polluted by the presence, then of Oedipus, now of his offspring, the prayer to Zeus and the Land and the city-protecting gods not to destroy the city would gain justification: these gods, in this poetic fiction, have reason to destroy a city that is polluted.[29]

But if this is so, then Eteocles is indeed at this point revealing both his knowledge and his intention. Whether or not the audience had heard the curse uttered by Oedipus in the preceding play, here Eteocles offers the alternatives of the city's destruction and the city's salvation. Dawson comments:[30]

> Eteokles says *mē moi polin ge*, where the particle *ge* is important; like the Latin *quidem* it usually stresses or underlines what precedes, so that Eteokles says, 'Do not, I pray you, (wipe out) my city at least'; he says nothing about himself, but he does dwell on his city's merit.

One could add that there is a loaded ambiguity in the dative of the personal pronoun: as an 'ethic' dative, *moi* can mean something like 'I pray'; but *moi* could also be a so-called 'sympathetic' dative:[31] μή μοι πόλιν γε...ἐκθαμνίσητε, 'do not destroy for me (i.e. because of me) ...the city at least' could be seen as parallel in construction to τῆισι τοκῆας μὲν φθεῖσαν θεοί, 'for them (the daughters of Pandareus) the gods destroyed their parents, ...' (*Odyssey* 20.67); the parents perish because of the daughters. On this latter understanding, the actions of the gods envisaged by Eteocles are directly affecting him, and are even seen as directed against him.[32] But however the dative of the pronoun is taken, in mentioning the curse of his father, which was a curse on him and his brother, and not asking the gods to lift the curse from him, but asking them to spare the city, Eteocles accepts that this is the point, and now is the time, to which his father's curse referred: but that, as we shall see, amounts to saying that he himself will perish on this day.

To receive confirmation for this interpretation, one need only compare Eteocles' other emotive exclamation. Parallel to his invocation of the curse in 69–77 is Eteocles' outburst at 653–7:

> ὦ θεομανές τε καὶ θεῶν μέγα στύγος,[33]
> ὦ πανδάκρυτον ἁμὸν Οἰδίπου γένος·
> ὤμοι, πατρὸς δὴ νῦν ἀραὶ τελεσφόροι.   655
> ἀλλ' οὔτε κλαίειν οὔτ' ὀδύρεσθαι πρέπει,
> μὴ καὶ τεκνωθῇ δυσφορώτερος γόος.

Ah! deranged by the gods, and great abomination to the gods,
Ah! lamentable: ours, the family of Oedipus!
Ah me! thus are the father's curses now achieving their end.
But neither crying nor lamenting befits,
lest it beget wailing even harder to bear.

This exclamation is parallel to the prayer of 69–77 most of all because Eteocles allows himself to let his guard down. When he spoke the prayer, he was alone on stage. The Scout had left. The women had not yet appeared. Here, at 653, he is not alone on stage; the women are still there. Indeed, after three lines Eteocles calls himself to order and reminds himself exactly of this, their presence. But the Scout, who to all intents and purposes is the same man who reported to Eteocles in the prologue, has left; in this respect, the scene is parallel in terms of staging and movement. The men, whether Eteocles' generals or messengers whose orders were to inform the generals, have been despatched. The men are outside the city gates with their leaders, the young and the old have taken up their posts. Eteocles himself is about to go off to defend the seventh gate, the one Polynices will attack. For three lines, overwhelmed by the situation, he gives voice to what he really thinks and feels. Once again, we see Eteocles wholly isolated. What these lines of lament share with the earlier prayer is the tone of despair. The significance of this, however, can only be assessed once we have seen what has happened in between.

5. Eteocles and the women of Thebes

In between his prayer to the gods and his lament, Eteocles encounters and has to deal with the women of Thebes, whom he perceives as wholly irrational and highly dangerous, and with the boasts of the attackers, as reported by the Scout. In contrast with the composure which Eteocles had displayed towards the young and the old, and, we presume, in contrast with the orderly manner in which these men had entered and exited the *orchestra*, the women storm on to the empty space after Eteocles as the last man has left. Their fears and anxiety are genuine, and so are their prayers. It is the manner in which they address the gods, and most of all the wailing and shrieking cries they utter, which call Eteocles back. In one respect, the exchange between the man and the women can be reduced to two simple propositions, one of them shared by the two parties, the other proposed by Eteocles but not fully comprehended on all levels by the women.

Both Eteocles and the women hold the shared belief that without the gods, there is no salvation.[34] But Eteocles adds to this that, whatever other considerations there may be, in public one must only say what strengthens the resolve of all to fight and rely on their own strength in defending the and the audience know that with each announcement of an attacker and each appointment of a defender it becomes more likely that Eteocles will face his brother Polynices. And even if that proposition as such were not present to a spectator's mind, anybody reflecting on what is going on must be aware that, as king and commanding general, Eteocles, after a long defence (23), knows who the enemy's champions are, and whom he himself has at his disposal to defend the city. Aeschylus, of course, can choose to disregard that, but we cannot assume that we are supposed to be ignorant of all that unless there is an indication in the text that the protagonists are ignorant of it and that, therefore, we too should be.

The central scene of the *Seven against Thebes* may have more functions than one within the play and the trilogy: telling the audience that Eteocles' opponent will be Polynices is not amongst them. Rather, the description of the attackers and defenders, heightening tension and leading to a dramatic climax, may be seen in parallel with the *teichoskopia* of Book 3 of the *Iliad*, where Helen identifies for Priam and the Elders of Troy who the attackers outside the city gate are: in the tenth year of war, and after the Greeks have had the upper hand and been in front of the city gates repeatedly over a long period of time. The poetic conceit allows Homer to characterize both the most prominent Greeks and Priam and the Trojan Elders, but not least also to characterize Helen, who reflects on herself as well as on her countrymen. In a similar way, in commenting on the Scout's announcements which characterize the attackers, Eteocles not only characterizes the defenders, but also and most of all himself – that is to say, this is what Aeschylus introduces him as doing. To conclude, Eteocles and all present know at the moment Lasthenes is appointed as opponent of Amphiaraus that he himself, Eteocles, will fight his brother Polynices; but Aeschylus and the audience had known that all along anyway. This circumstance as a piece of factual information is no revelation on the part of Aeschylus for his theatre audience.[47]

Against the backdrop of these considerations, then, the question of when and how the defenders of the city are chosen and assigned must be revisited. If Eteocles arrives at 374 f. with a final decision as to which one of his companions is to defend which one of the gates, his realization of an eventual confrontation with his brother must grow with every announcement by the Scout, and the Scout's as well as the Chorus' fears must grow with each announcement by Eteocles. There would, however, be nothing anyone could do to change the situation. If, on the other hand, Eteocles chooses consciously at each stage which defender to appoint for any given attacker, he must know that the earlier he names himself the better, if, that is, he wanted to avoid a direct confrontation with his brother. There would have to be strong grounds indeed which rule him out as opponent of any one of the six attackers named first if he really intended not to face his brother and nevertheless made each decision consciously and on the spot. Obviously, the implications for Eteocles' character, and for Aeschylus' view of how decisions of human beings are arrived at, will differ immensely according to which view one adopts on the matter of the appointment of the seven defenders.

In favour of the view that on entering at 374 f. Eteocles has already decided where to position whom are, among others, the following considerations. He must have done something between leaving at 287 and coming back almost one hundred lines, a tenth of the play, later, and since he left saying (282–6): ἐγὼ δέ γ' ἄνδρας ἕξ...τάξω μολών, πρὶν ἀγγέλου σπερχνούς...λόγους ἱκέσθαι, 'I shall go to appoint six men before hurried words of a messenger arrive', assuming that he has done just that may not be too far off the mark. Secondly, the way Eteocles phrases his thoughts at the announcement of the opponents suggests that, at some level at least, he regards the choices as a matter of good luck and not only as an outcome of his own adequate decisions. How else could one interpret his statement (508–511): Ἑρμῆς δ' εὐλόγως ξυνήγαγεν. | ἐχθρὸς γὰρ ἀνὴρ ἀνδρὶ τῷ ξυστήσεται, | ξυνοίσετον δὲ πολεμίους ἐπ' ἀσπίδων | θεούς. 'And Hermes has joined them with good reasoning:[48] indeed, as fiercely hostile will that man stand against the other man, the two will bring together from on their shields two gods in war with each other' – could Eteocles speak of Hermes as 'leading one to the other in an appropriate way' if he himself, Eteocles, had just chosen the defenders?

One could answer in the affirmative. The sphere of influence of Hermes, the god of the lucky find, is by no means restricted to discoveries and finds made by chance. If one strives to achieve something, in this case to find the opponent best suited, and if one then succeeds in that endeavour, that as well is Hermes, 'leading one to the other in an appropriate way'. Therefore, 'most modern scholars feel that "Eteocles is choosing, of his own volition and in the light of the opposing champions, defenders for the city, not simply witnessing in helpless and unspoken amazement the machinations whereby his previously determined choices are by some daimonic manipulation perfectly matched"'.[49] This, in itself, seems plausible enough. What, after all, would be the point of Eteocles' choosing and assigning his companions in private? From a different perspective: is it very effective in terms of drama to present two people exchanging results of appointments previously made? And on another level, is it this what Aeschylus wants to convey: on one side leaders are elected by lot, on the

7. Eteocles' lot

As the manner of appointing defenders and assigning gates and opponents does have implications for an evaluation of Aeschylus' portrayal of Eteocles' perceptions, thoughts and actions, and of the conditions that govern them, I shall, before addressing the questions of the oracle and the curse, and of Eteocles' character and his 'decision', very tentatively suggest a way of staging the central scene which would, *inter alia*, give a particular significance to the different tenses. My premises are:

1) Something must have happened on stage during the central scene.
2) The defenders were chosen and assigned at some stage.
3) It is potentially relevant how they were assigned their gates.
4) If it is relevant how the defenders were assigned their gates, the audience must clearly learn and understand how the assignments were made.

It is true that we know comparatively little about the spectacle of early fifth-century plays, and it is true that neither silent faces nor properties must be multiplied beyond necessity. But we do know something about the staging and about some of the properties Aeschylus himself used in his extant plays. The relevant points of comparison are with the *Oresteia*. Towards the end of the *Eumenides*, when Athena has instituted the court of the Areopagus to judge Orestes, we see on stage the ten or twelve[54] Athenian judges stepping forward one by one to cast their discs into the two urns, as would happen in an actual fifth-century court. This must have been a fascinating scene on stage, full of suspense. The judges are silent while the Furies and Apollo alternately speak a few words with the movement of each man.

What I propose is that a similar process was presented on stage in the *Seven against Thebes*. The action which the Scout reported from the enemy camp is repeated in front of the audience. Eteocles allots the gates with the attackers to the six men he has previously chosen, with him as the seventh. For this the men could, but need not, be on stage. How the scene could be staged may be seen from *Iliad* 6.161–99.[55] There, nine men in all had stepped forward to fight Hector in single combat. Each marks a lot and throws it into Agamemnon's helmet. All the Greeks watching pray to Zeus that he let Ajax win the draw. Nestor, as arbiter, shakes the helmet, and the lot of Ajax leaps from the helmet. Is this chance?

That selection by lot in a military context was still actual fifth-century practice, is shown by a passage in Thucydides (6.42):[56]

> οἱ δ' Ἀθηναῖοι ἤδη ἐν τῇ Κερκύρᾳ αὐτοί τε καὶ οἱ ξύμμαχοι ἅπαντες ἦσαν. καὶ πρῶτον μὲν ἐπεξέτασιν τοῦ στρατεύματος καὶ ξύνταξιν, ὥσπερ ἔμελλον ὁρμιεῖσθαί τε καὶ στρατοπεδεύεσθαι, οἱ στρατηγοὶ ἐποιήσαντο, καὶ τρία μέρη νείμαντες ἓν ἑκάστῳ ἐκλήρωσαν.

The Athenians and their allies with them were now in Corcyra. First the generals held a final review of the whole force and arranged the order in which they were to anchor and encamp. They divided the fleet into three parts and cast lots for one part to each general (trans. R. Warner).

The lot was also the instrument of democracy par excellence. Only twenty years before the *Seven against Thebes* was produced, the lot had been introduced, in 487 BC, as the virtually universal means for selecting magistrates. The lot was impartial. But at the same time, from the age of Homer onwards, selection by lot could be seen as divinely sanctioned. I do not suggest that every Athenian believed that. But I do suggest that Aeschylus gives a dignity to those newly instituted democratic measures. And from the *Eumenides*, another one of the plays with which Aeschylus won first prize, we can see how gripping for the audience this sort of scene was. An enormous tension is created although everybody knows from the start that Orestes, a model of the dutiful son in the *Odyssey* already, will walk away as a free man. Likewise here. Eteocles has his helmet with the names of the appointed defenders inside; for he has appointed who will defend the gates just as he had said he would. And one by one the names come out: 'I will appoint...' He picks up the lot and reads out the name. He picks up the next lot and announces: 'He has been appointed already...' Then, the sixth attacker, Amphiaraus, is announced by the Scout. And here, Eteocles almost breaks down; not because he did not know that Amphiaraus, the just seer and prophet, was among the attackers; he knows that just as much as he knows that his brother Polynices, too, is among them. He almost breaks down in line 597 because he knows that now he, Eteocles, must fight either the seer, the just man, or his brother Polynices. Then Lasthenes' name, his lot, comes up; he will stand against Amphiaraus. All that is left for the Scout to do is to report Polynices' boast and shield. Then he disappears, be it to convey the orders to the other generals, be it to whatever other pursuit. And Eteocles is left on his own and starts lamenting. This, too, is not because what has happened has taken him unawares, but because he is overpowered by the enormity of his fate. And he can express his terror and disgust now for the first time: because, whether or not the other generals had been on stage before, they have gone now; and so have all other male citizens. Eteocles could not have said anything beforehand, because there would have been witnesses, men, whom he must not discourage.

My contention is thus that the action on stage both reflects and echoes a famous scene in the *Iliad*, well known to the audience, and portrays what would have been a device familiar from certain military and civic contexts. Allotment on stage is both explicit and realistic on the one hand, impressive as an action with its inherent tension and suspense on the other, and it comments and reflects on Athenian practices witnessed and displayed in everyday life:[57] the poet suggests that choice by lot is not random choice, that it does reflect what is just, that it does reflect the will of the gods.

There are two places in the text which may lend specific support to this suggestion. The first has been discussed already, but deserves fresh consideration (508–11):

... Ἑρμῆς δ' εὐλόγως ξυνήγαγεν·
ἐχθρὸς γὰρ ἀνὴρ ἀνδρὶ τῷ ξυστήσεται,
ξυνοίσετον δὲ πολεμίους ἐπ' ἀσπίδων   510
θεούς.

And Hermes has joined them with good reasoning:
indeed, as fiercely hostile will that man stand against the other man,
the two will bring together from on their shields two gods in war with each other.

Hermes as the daemonic god of the lucky find has a peculiar connection with the lot.[58] This is reflected, in humorous fashion, in Aristophanes' *Peace*. There, Hermes threatens a mortal who has offended, to be rebutted with a sophism (364–6):

HERMES ἀπόλωλας, ὦ κακόδαιμον.
TRYGAEUS οὐκοῦν, ἢν λάχω·   365
     Ἑρμῆς γὰρ ὢν κλήρῳ ποιήσεις οἶδ' ὅτι.

Sommerstein translates (1978):

HERMES Miserable mortal, you shall die for this!
TRYGAEUS Oh, I don't know, Hermes.
     Being who you are you'll naturally select the victims by lot,
     and how can you be sure my number will come up?

'God playing dice'[59] and 'god drawing lots' are two old and persistent images to symbolize the vagaries and uncertainties of life; they point to unpredictability, where by contrast 'Zeus holding scales' symbolizes divine power that, while it cannot be changed, all the same seems less arbitrary and more measurable. The image of Zeus holding scales originally points to an objective order: men do not know the weight of their respective lives, but Zeus can measure and thus know it. It is a poetic twist of this image if Zeus is seen to be bound by the weighing he himself undertakes. If the weight and the weighing are objective, even Zeus cannot change this; there is a Moira, a 'fate', beyond even the Olympian gods. But this does not detract from the original force of the image, which is created to contrast the ignorance and powerlessness of mortals with the knowledge and power of the gods. Likewise with the lots of Hermes. The difference between them and the scales of Zeus is that they symbolize utter chance: mortals have no way of deciding their fate; they cannot even hope to know it. Aristophanes lets Trygaeus reinterpret this in making Hermes subject to the same uncertainty which the image was meant to illustrate for the human predicament: if Hermes is the god of the lot that decides over the life or death of a person, how can he, Hermes, know the outcome in advance?

The Aristophanic joke confirms that for a near-contemporary audience Hermes had a specific connection with the lot, and in particular with the lot in the context of life and death. Thus, if not only the attacking enemies select the assignments of their leaders by lot, but if Eteocles, too, performs this process on stage, his words that Hermes has brought together defender and attacker gain added meaning.

If the process of drawing lots is performed and acted out on stage, this would also lend additional reference and poignancy to a later passage, part of the Chorus' lament on hearing of the death of Eteocles and Polynices (727–33):

ξένος δ' ἂν κλήρους ἐπινωμᾷ,
Χάλυβος Σκυθᾶν ἄποικος,
κτεάνων χρηματοδαίτας
πικρός, ὠμόφρων Σίδαρος,   730
χθόνα ναίειν διαπήλας
ὁπόσαν καὶ φθιμένοισι † κατέχειν,
τῶν μεγάλων πεδίων ἀμοίρους.

But a stranger, it seems, distributes the lots,
a Chalybian emigrant from Scythia,
a bitter arbitrator[60] of their possessions,
Iron, of savage mind,
<for them> dividing up the earth to inhabit,
as much as can be possessed even by the departed,
lots that do not have a share in the great plains.

The passage as a whole intertwines images and metaphors from different spheres. Legal and official language is mixed with a transparent personification of the metal from which the lethal weapons of mutual fratricide were made. 'Iron' was mentioned, we must presume, in Oedipus' curse; and a *klēros* or 'lot' is a piece of land, not only in the context of Attic *apoikiai*, or 'colonies'. All of this is comprehensible in itself. But as Aeschylus also elsewhere in the *Seven against Thebes* explores semantic ambiguity and double meaning, this passage, too, would gain if the spectators had been witnesses to a double process of allotment.[61] In many ways, drawing lots on stage, while not essential to the overall interpretation of the character, actions and decisions of Eteocles here presented, would enhance, and make more immediately comprehensible, what unfolds in the last play of the trilogy.[62]

We have now reached Eteocles' final exchange on stage, his second argument with the women. These last words of the leader have been called 'the scene of decision',[63] and discussions of responsibility and free will focus to a considerable extent on 652–719. But before what is said by the Chorus and Eteocles in this scene can be assessed, the oracle and the curse must be considered. Only then can we turn to the portrayal of Eteocles by Aeschylus throughout the play as a whole.

8. Curse and oracle

We thus return to the question of what it was Eteocles knew and referred and appealed to at 69 ff. and at 653 ff. In these lines, Eteocles mentions only Oedipus and what originated from Oedipus. It is only in the expression ἁμὸν Οἰδίπου γένος, 'our family, that of Oedipus' (654), that one could see a reference not only to Oedipus and his sons, but also to previous generations. This is eventually spelt out, again by Eteocles himself, in 689–91:

ἐπεὶ τὸ πρᾶγμα κάρτ' ἐπισπέρχει θεός,
ἴτω κατ' οὖρον, κῦμα Κωκυτοῦ λαχόν, 690
Φοίβῳ στυγηθὲν πᾶν τὸ Λαΐου γένος.

Because (a/the) god strongly urges on the matter,
let go, with fair wind, gaining the wave of Cocytus,
the whole race of Laius, abhorrent to Apollo.

Here, it is the race or family or house of Laius that is said to be an object of horror to Apollo.[64] These lines form the explicit link between Apollo, Delphi, and the oracle to Laius on the one hand, and on the other Laius' forbidden offspring Oedipus, and his sons born out of the incestuous union with Oedipus' mother, Laius' wife. Here, as elsewhere in the play, Jocasta is not mentioned by name; a pregnant silence. The Chorus do not pick up this reference, but speak of the illicit desire (οὐ θεμιστοῦ) to shed kindred blood (694).[65] While Eteocles continues to speak of the curse and his fate (*moros*), what the Chorus are referring to when they speak of the *daimōn* (705) that is still boiling (708) is ambiguous. Eteocles immediately refers it to Oedipus' prayers (709), to conclude, again apparently conflating oracle and curse, that you cannot escape the bad things given by the gods (719).

It is only after this, and after Eteocles has left the stage, that the Chorus even acknowledge the existence of the curse, at least potentially, when they speak of the Erinys of the father (723). It is their song, from 720 to the final word 'Erinys' in 791, that, given the loss of the two previous plays, tells us all we are allowed to know about Apollo's oracle to Laius. And while it is certainly true that in the course of one play one and the same event of the past may be related or at least referred to, sometimes even by the same people, not only in different ways, but also differently to the point of incompatibility of aspects at least of what is reported,[66] there should not be an automatic assumption that what is reported as the oracle to Laius in 745–9 must be different from what, if anything, had been reported previously.

At 745–9, the Chorus of Theban women report that Apollo had thrice told Laius to die without offspring to save the city. The audience will have heard this oracle in the first play, *Laius*. They will not have heard it again after Laius' death. They will not have heard it in the play *Oedipus*, the topics of which were quite different events and concerns and revelations, culminating in Oedipus' cursing his sons. They did not hear it in the *Seven against Thebes*. Up until now.

The *Seven against Thebes*, by clever staging, is a play not dominated by the oracle but acted out under the cloud of the curse, which said that the sons 'would share their inheritance with iron'. The wording of the curse, or something close to it, is contained in the closing stanza sung by the Chorus, just before the Scout arrives to announce victory for the city, the death of the brothers, and thereby implicitly the fulfilment of the oracle and the curse in one double-blow (785–91):

> τέκνοις δ' ἀρχαίας 785
> ἐφῆκεν ἐπίκοτος τροφᾶς,
> αἰαῖ, πικρογλώσσους ἀράς,
> καί σφε σιδαρονόμῳ
> διὰ χερί ποτε λαχεῖν
> κτήματα· νῦν δὲ τρέω 790
> μὴ τελέσῃ καμψίπους Ἐρινύς.

But in his wrath he let loose against his children,
because of the way that they had been begotten all that time ago,
alas, bitter-tongued curses,
and <said> that one day they would get their possessions
by a hand that shares out with iron:
but now I fear lest Erinys with the bent foot complete it.

That the Erinys of Oedipus should be characterized with the physical attribute of the king is in itself a piece of Aeschylean irony. What we learn of his curse, though, is aptly described by Thalmann in his comment on 788–90:[67]

negatively to the provocative suggestion by the women that god would honour even a victory that is *kakē*, 'bad': a hoplite must not (οὐκ...χρή) acquiesce in such suggestions. Hutchinson comments on 716 (1985, 160):

> κακήν: the chorus concede what they denied in 698 f., that for Eteocles not to fight would be ignoble. In real life, such a concession would be as imprudent as it is inconsistent, but the purpose of the line is to draw forth Eteocles' response.

One could say that, when provoked in this way by a woman, any man would have reacted in this way. Eteocles' assertions at 683–5 are on a similarly generic level. A double consideration enters into our assessment of these words by Eteocles: On the one hand, if Eteocles is modelled in other respects on Hector, however profoundly or superficially, giving Eteocles some of the words of Hector may act as an efficient foil to what is distinctive in Eteocles' own reasoning. On the other hand, even if one is not convinced by the alleged parallels with the Hector of the *Iliad*, any Theban citizen, any real-life Athenian citizen would have said what Eteocles says – at least when challenged and in the presence of others.

For it is one thing to say that the concept of 'duty' is Stoic in origin, and in its modern guise informed by the neo-Stoic protestant ethics of Kant. Eteocles, conceptually, cannot be a model of duty in that sense; nor could Hector have been. But in another sense, ordinary common-or-garden duty, especially in a military context, was the order of the day, in real life as in poetry. All Athenians had performed that duty against the Persians, and all Thebans were performing it right throughout the play, by staying at their posts, where they had been posted. Equally ordinary was the ultimate sacrifice; Aeschylus' brother had made the ultimate sacrifice for Athens, and even if this is historiographic fiction, many Athenians of Aeschylus' acquaintance certainly had. Fighting for the city and giving one's life is in that sense always an *Opfertod*. But only in that sense.

What separates Eteocles from Hector is the knowledge of oracle and curse. Combined, they mean that the line of Labdacus must come to an end, because of Laius' disobedience. Eteocles realizes that the curse of Oedipus was prophetic. This is not to say that the curse predetermined events: but at the moment of realization, Oedipus, in seeing who he himself was, saw what offspring he had,[74] and his curse is a *daimōn*, an Erinys, who is *kakomantis* (722), 'a seer of ill'. Eteocles sees all that and knows that he must fight. This is not fatalistic, nor is he just deciding to fight because of the man he is. Because of the man he is, intelligent, prudent, god-fearing, caring for the citizens and the city, he knows that he will come to an end now. In fighting Polynices, he does save the city. The alternative would have been: to perish with the city. This is not least the implication of what the oracle said. The alternative was not: to save himself while the others saved the city. The women do not see this; Eteocles does.

Eteocles' talk of honour and what is fine is thus not least part of λέγειν τὰ καίρια. To that extent, it is part of his character. But what about his decision to fight his brother? There is, in Greek tragedy of the fifth century, one parallel, towards the end of a play, where different oracles and prophetic utterances come together at one point, and only the central character realizes the full implications of what has been revealed, despite the protestations and disbelief of all others; where, to the very end, the chorus and the other speaking character do not comprehend, even to the point of accusing Zeus. In Sophocles' *Trachiniae*, there are oracles and letters predicting the point of Heracles' return to Trachis, the end of his toils, the fact that he will not be killed by anyone alive. At different stages, the audience learn of the different predictions, just as no one character is aware of all of them. The exception is Heracles himself. When he learns from his son Hyllus that the poison sent by his wife Deianeira had been given to her 'as a love-charm' by the centaur Nessus in his dying moment, after he had been hit by the poisoned arrow of Heracles, Heracles suddenly realizes the convergence of all the divine predictions that foretold his end. It does not matter that, in Sophocles, some or all of these predictions are 'riddling' to a greater extent than what we find in Aeschylus. The point of comparison is the resolve, on the part of Heracles, after the sudden realization of what has been revealed.

From the moment Heracles is brought on to the orchestra after line 970, people misunderstand what is necessary. The old man wants to let Heracles sleep – as if that would change anything. Hyllus does not want to light the funeral pyre – as if Heracles were not dead already. Nor does he want to marry Iole, who is bearing Heracles' child – as if she were responsible for everything. Just as Eteocles has been said to show, in the last scene, the enraged, outrageous, impulsive bad side of Oedipus, so Heracles in the *Trachiniae* has been portrayed, in modern accounts, as harsh beyond reason, tyrannical, and everything bad that may be read out of Deianeira's words. The words of Heracles at line 1248, 'I call the gods as witnesses of this', are not seen for what they are, and the lines with which Hyllus concludes the play are left standing as an accusation (1264–78):[75]

αἴρετ', ὀπαδοί, μεγάλην μὲν ἐμοὶ
τούτων θέμενοι συγγνωμοσύνην,   1265
μεγάλην δὲ θεῶν ἀγνωμοσύνην
εἰδότες ἔργων τῶν πρασσομένων,

οἳ φύσαντες καὶ κλῃζόμενοι
πατέρες τοιαῦτ' ἐφορῶσι πάθη.
τὰ μὲν οὖν μέλλοντ' οὐδεὶς ἐφορᾷ, 1270
τὰ δὲ νῦν ἑστῶτ' οἰκτρὰ μὲν ἡμῖν,
αἰσχρὰ δ' ἐκείνοις,
χαλεπώτατα δ' οὖν ἀνδρῶν πάντων
τῷ τήνδ' ἄτην ὑπέχοντι.
λείπου μηδὲ σύ, παρθέν', ἀπ' οἴκων, 1275
μεγάλους μὲν ἰδοῦσα νέους θανάτους,
πολλὰ δὲ πήματα <καὶ> καινοπαθῆ·
κοὐδὲν τούτων ὅ τι μὴ Ζεύς.

> Lift him, men. Grant me full
> forgiveness for what has to be done,
> and fully acknowledge the [lack of concern]
> of the gods in what has been done.
> They give life, and are renowned as
> fathers, and then look on at sufferings like these.
> No one can see into the future.
> But the present for us is pitiful,
> shameful for them,
> hardest of all for the man
> who is facing his doom.
> Young woman, do not stay behind at the house.
> You have just seen a terrible death,
> great pain and suffering in the strangest shape,
> and there is nothing of this which is not Zeus (trans. Ewans).

Hyllus is full of accusation. He would like the world to be a nice place, free from suffering. Because it is not, and cruel and inexplicable things happen, he accuses the gods and Zeus. Heracles did call the gods to witness. But he does not accuse. This is not just because he knows all the oracles. It is also because he knows that some things must happen as they do. This can be said irrespective of whether we wish to attribute to him any foreknowledge of his apotheosis, which can only be achieved, it is the implication, if he is indeed burned alive. The last line of the play is true, in that there is nothing in all this that is not Zeus. But Sophocles does not write this as an accusation. Rather, the long speeches of Heracles, lines 1046–1111 and 1157–78, show that he sees his life as purposeful. The realization on his part is the realization that his life here on earth is now over; all that is left for him is to make final arrangements.

Eteocles in the *Seven against Thebes* does not realize suddenly after the naming of Polynices what his fate is and what his choices are. He knows from the beginning of the play.[76] The whole of the play consists of his final arrangements. His resolve is: not to let the city perish just because he will perish this day. The prediction by the seer that this will be the day of the greatest onslaught yet has told him everything. The allotting of gates to attack, as reported, signifies, for him as for the audience, that this is the day he will fight Polynices. The allotting, on his part, of gates and attackers to defenders builds up to the inevitable conclusion, that he will fight his brother. This is the curse of his father, but it is also the meaning of the oracle to Laius.

But when Eteocles' decision and action are interpreted in this context, there is no need to adduce the notion of 'double causation'. If it had been the case that, as a consequence and result of Oedipus' cursing his two sons Polynices and Eteocles that 'they would share their inheritance sword in hand', Apollo, say, or another god had intervened, in whatever fashion, in order and so that Polynices and Eteocles had taken up swords with the intention of killing each other and had in the event achieved his purpose and theirs, then this might count as 'double causation'. But irrespective of whether a Greek playwright of the archaic age could have presented things in this fashion, this is not what Aeschylus presents to his audience in the *Seven against Thebes*. Things are much vaguer than that. The shield scene, however interpreted, is set within the city and leaves Eteocles with the decision of whether to go to the seventh gate to fight his brother or not. The shield scene has not decided anything, it has presented and revealed realities.

And in the same way, Oedipus' curse upon his two sons, whatever its precise wording, can and should be read not as determining but as presenting and revealing what will happen. Because of their *trophē*, the way they have been brought into the world, this is what Eteocles and Polynices will do. They will come to a bitter end. What the events that lead to their actual deaths as presented in the trilogy and the play do reveal is precisely that the total working of the universe is not arbitrary but constitutes an order, a *kosmos*.[77] We do not know the background to Apollo's prophecy to Laius concerning his offspring, but we do not have any indication that the god threatened the mortal with punishment in case of transgression; in his oracle, the god simply reveals the consequences of courses of action.

What, then is Eteocles' decision? Decision is not the individual choice, in a particular situation, between a cucumber sandwich and an apple, between a walk in the countryside and an afternoon of chess, or between staying at home behind the city walls and fighting in war in defence of the city. Decision is the fundamental act that positions the individual-in-isolation for the rest of his life. As Kierkegaard, who has defined for modern thinking what it is to decide, puts it in *Either/Or*:[78]

> Men hvad er det da, jeg vælger, er det Dette eller Hiint? Nei, thi jeg vælger absolut, og absolut vælger jeg jo netop derved, at jeg har valgt ikke at vælger

> Dette eller Hiint. Jeg vælger det Absolute, og hvad er det Absolute? Det er mig selv i min evige Gyldighed. Noget Andet end mig selv kan jeg aldrig vælge som det Absolute, thi vælger jeg noget Andet, da vælger jeg det som en Endelighed, og vælger det altsaa ikke absolut (1962, 199).

> But what is it then, that I choose – is it this or that? No, for I choose absolutely, and I choose absolutely precisely by having chosen not to choose this or that. I choose the absolute, and what is the absolute? It is myself in my eternal validity. Something other than myself I can never choose as the absolute, for if I choose something else, I choose it as something finite and consequently do not choose absolutely (1987, 214).

If we expect Aeschylus to show us, in lines 653–719, the reasons why Eteocles will go out to fight Polynices, or his decision to face his brother, we will be disappointed. Eteocles' decision antedates the series of events portrayed in the play. Eteocles' resolve is firm from start to finish. He will defend his city and his land. Aeschylus allows us two glimpses beyond his façade, when Eteocles is on his own and when, towards the end, he very briefly, for three lines, loses control of himself. Eteocles is a man full of emotions at the dreadful realization of his fate and that of his family. But throughout, in word and deed, he does not let his personal feelings interfere with saving the city, at least. We do not know about Oedipus. He may have been the innocent man caught up in his father's transgression; he may have been unjust in his deranged anger. But we do know about Laius. His ill-advisedness is folly. His counsel is an expression of not following the god, but following irrational lust.[79] That was Laius' decision. Eteocles, in his character and his decision, is in every respect the opposite of Laius. And just as Sophocles, at the end of the *Trachiniae*, does not preach, nor yet even explain to the audience what has happened, so Aeschylus does not end with an explanation. The Chorus are aghast in their lament. Eteocles is not built up into a rôle model, neither within the play nor by the author for the audience. He goes to his death not understood by anyone around him. His thoughts and actions do not fall neatly into categories of duty and responsibility, decision and acceptance of necessity, freedom and fatedness. Even the genuinely Greek opposition of *hekōn* and *akōn*, *hekousios* and *akousios*, i.e. what one does unencumbered, and what one does under some constraint,[80] does not fully capture what Eteocles does and what is happening to him. The poetic mode of seeing the world of human action as structured by more than rational decision and emotive irrationality, by forces that include human motivation and decision, but also gods, daemons, oracles, curses, and pollution, is a defining part of archaic Greek thought.

Acknowledgement

Versions of this chapter have been presented, between 1997 and 2008, to audiences in Birmingham, Edinburgh, Glasgow, and Swansea. I have learnt much from ensuing discussions and am particularly grateful for criticism and suggestions to Douglas Cairns, Anton Powell, Ian Repath, and David Robinson.

Notes

[1] Decision, decision-making, and in particular the question of 'decision and responsibility' have been an integral part of the study of Greek tragedy for two centuries of Western traditions of interpretation. For the centrality of the notion of 'decision' in the interpretation of Greek tragedy, one may fruitfully adduce the recent monograph on religious and psychological aspects of Greek tragedy by Sewell-Rutter (2007), which has the subtitle *Moral inheritance and decision making in Greek tragedy*. This subtitle is dictated by an influential line of thought epitomized in Lesky's (1966) study of 'Decision and Responsibility in the Tragedy of Aeschylus', a tradition which Sewell-Rutter critically discusses (see below). This tradition within the last two or three generations of scholarship on Homer, archaic Greek literature, and in particular Greek tragedy, has by some been traced back to the overpowering influence of Bruno Snell, specifically his Habilitationsschrift of 1925 (published as Snell 1928), and his subsequent article (Snell 1930) on 'Das Bewußtsein von eigenen Entscheidungen im frühen Griechentum'. Two decades ago, Snell's views and their influence on European as well as Anglo-American Classical scholarship in this field, an influence felt in particular in the influential Anglophone studies on Greek values and Greek views of human nature by A. W. H. Adkins (Adkins 1960 and 1970), came under attack from different corners: in the context of a wide-ranging re-assessment of Greek psychology, beginning with an analysis of Homer, Schmitt 1990 traces Snell's own philosophico-psychological assumptions specifically to Kierkegaard's concept of 'decision', and beyond Kierkegaard to a post-Cartesian, post-Kantian modern understanding of what constitutes mental processes in decision and action. The same year saw the publication of a fundamental article on Homeric decision-making by R. Gaskin (Gaskin 1990). One year before that, Bernard Williams had delivered his Sather Lectures at Berkeley, published as *Shame and Necessity* in 1993. The first chapter of the book is entitled 'The liberation of antiquity', a title that could serve as the motto to much of what has preoccupied one powerful trend in the study of Classical concepts and ideas over the past few decades. Williams, too, is concerned with the question of decisions, notably in his second chapter, 'Centres of Agency'. Like Schmitt, he identifies the search for the 'will' and its connection with notions of 'duty' behind modern approaches that are fundamentally Kantian. While Williams 1993 must in many ways be regarded as a standard text in Anglophone treatments of early Greek psychology, reception of Schmitt's work is not widespread (despite positive reviews: Cairns 1992; Scodel 1992); he is quoted in Cairns's 1993 monograph on *Aidōs*, but not, for example, in Gill's 1996 volume, *Personality in Greek Epic, Tragedy, and Philosophy*. Gill, in building on two decades of his own investigations on personality and the self in Greek thought, could draw *inter alia* on Cairns 1993 and Williams 1993 for discussion of shame and guilt, shame-

culture and guilt-culture, as vital background to questions of decision-making, but his own discussion of earlier theories of decision-making, while contrasting the strand of thought embodied by Snell and Adkins with that of certain French anthropologists and their reaction to 'post-Kantian theory' (Gill 1996, 40 n. 35), does not make the fundamental connection of Snell's assumption with the protestant ethics of Kierkegaard, just as Snell himself acknowledges as his philosophical predecessors notably Schelling (Snell 1928, 28 n. 52; 32 n. 55.) and Hegel (Snell 1928, esp. 32–33, n. 56, where he adduces 'Vorlesungen über Ästhetik 1838 III 322 u. 479'), but does not mention either Kierkegaard, of whose influence on himself Snell should have been aware, or Kant, whose conscious use may be assumed; see Gill 1996, 40 n. 34 on 'Snell's explicit Hegelianism and his implicit Kantianism'; cf. 46 n. 54 on Gaskin 1990 and Williams 1993 on Kantian moral will. Cf. also Gill's summary of and critical reflection on his own position, 455–69.

It may be noted as an aside that, if Hegel is perceived as the one who introduces emphasis on decision-making and related notions into the discussion of human action among modern readers of Greek tragedy, this notion is absent from, and incompatible with, his implied interpretation of Antigone in the *Phenomenology of Spirit* of 1807 (Hegel 1807, 348–9, in a section on 'Die sittliche Handlung. Das menschliche und göttliche Wissen, die Schuld und das Schicksal'), and can only have arisen (and be derived) from his discussion, in his 1817 *Lectures on the History of Philosophy*, of Socrates, whom he seems to credit with the introduction of the possibility of individual decision in the face of Law and duty, a decision based on the contingency of the subjective (Hegel 1817, 489–92).

In a nutshell, the issue in this debate concerns the question of what constitutes decision. Decision as a free, spontaneous act presupposes a mental faculty, such as 'the will' (for the notion of free will, see now Frede 2011 and Cairns in this volume), whose capacities are in no way determined by external factors, by considerations of necessity and constraint; but, if this position is taken to its extreme, even doing one thing rather than another 'because it is better' is acting under an external constraint (as explicated with sophistication and subtle humour by Gorgias, the great teacher of oratory, in his *Defence of Helen*). Those who, like Schmitt, argue against Snell on a theoretical level are correct in stating that, in many ways, Greeks from Homer to Plato and beyond have seen the choice of what is better because it is better as the sign of the rational and prudent, in short, of the good man, not of the man who is restricted in his freedom to choose. Against this background, choosing 'freely', not constrained by such considerations, comes close to being nonsensical, and such a spontaneous decision is simply outside the realm of archaic and classical Greek thought altogether. In the fifth and the fourth centuries, the alternative to 'choosing what is rationally determined to be best' is 'to be governed by either anger or pleasure' – or its opposite, pain, which can be realized as fear or fright; while this complex of issues cannot be discussed fully in this context, impulsive anger, pleasure and fear all have their place in the conceptual framework of Aeschylus' *Seven against Thebes*.

Within more recent Anglophone debate, in some respects a precursor acknowledged by Cairns, Williams, and Gill is Dover 1974, while the other side of that debate is represented in Anglophone scholarship in particular by Dodds 1951, Lloyd-Jones 1962 and 1971, and Gould 1978a, 1978b. Sewell-Rutter's treatment of aspects of Greek tragedy (2007) is much more an applied study of the texts than primarily a reflection on modern ways of understanding the supernatural, causation, guilt, curses, Erinyes, fate, freedom and decision making (these the key terms from the six chapter headings of his study). In their thorough engagement with especially Anglophone scholarship (predominantly of the second half of the twentieth and the first lustrum of the twenty-first century), many of his chapters mark an advance over schematizing simplifications in the interpretation of particularly Aeschylean tragedy, not least because of a sensitive understanding of tragedy as literature and as acted drama. Yet, despite its historical and theoretical awareness and discussion, for example the first chapter to deal with tragedy, entitled 'Inherited Guilt', is ultimately marred by too ready an acceptance of a notion of guilt as something in principle acknowledged and accepted by all. While in many ways closely connected with questions of decision and decision-making, the question of guilt has its own history, which in some ways goes back even farther into the history of reception and interpretation of Greek tragedy. Recent surveys and interpretations include von Fritz 1962, 193–226 = 2007, aptly exploited and developed for Aeschylus by Rosenmeyer 1982, 284–307, in his own chapter 10, 'Guilt; Curse; Choice'; and see with a focus on Sophocles on a larger scale Lurje 2004. Likewise, Sewell-Rutter's notion of 'dispositions of choice', which becomes instrumental in his last chapter, 'Fate, Freedom, Decision Making: Eteocles and Others', is treated as a given, and as such can, for Sewell-Rutter, function as an *explanans* rather than as an *explanandum*. All the same, these discussions of, in particular, the *Oresteia* and the *Seven against Thebes* by Aeschylus highlight what have been and what should be major concerns to the viewer and reader of Greek tragedy. Narrowing down the scholarly controversy over decision-making in the way presented here is, of course, in many respects an illegitimate simplification. There are other voices in the continuum of classical scholarship; see, for example, the excellent assessment of choice and decision in Aeschylus in Rosenmeyer 1982, 299–307.

[2] Even just stating two dreadful alternatives can constitute 'deliberation'; use of this term does not imply a pondering and weighing up of pros and cons.

[3] Easterling's concern in her article on the 'Presentation of character in Aeschylus' (Easterling 1973) is among other things with the plausibility of the presentation of human motivation; one of her claims, which she illustrates through a convincing interpretation of the so-called carpet scene in the *Agamemnon*, is that neither ancient nor modern audiences would be captivated by watching a dramatic action on stage unless the author had succeeded in presenting this action as understandable in terms of human motivation. (On this point cf. also Cairns 1993, 178–9, with discussion of literature.) Against the modern view that recourse in our interpretations to naming supernatural elements such as a curse or an Erinys as responsible for the decision or action of a human being carries in itself any explanatory force, she is correct in concluding (Easterling 1973, 19): 'The compulsions under which men act were given an external, supernatural character by Aeschylus and his contemporaries, who interpreted human experience as part of a larger continuum, the total working of the universe... The curse is not a remote and peculiar phenomenon, untranslatable into universal experience: we are *all* under a curse in the sense that we are caught in the web of necessity. As human beings we are forced to make choices and commit ourselves, and then to take the consequences for actions over which we are not fully in control, and our sufferings are often out of all proportion to our deserts.'

[4] For concise introductions, see e.g. Winnington-Ingram 1983 and Sommerstein 2010a; for more detailed discussion e.g. Hutchison 1985.

[5] What we have now as the ending of the *Seven against Thebes* is commonly agreed to be a revised version, produced after Sophocles' *Antigone*, possibly in order to be staged in sequence with *Antigone*.

[6] We may assume, though we do not know, that, as in Sophocles' version, Jocasta kills herself before Oedipus blinds himself. She is not present and, significantly, not even mentioned in the *Seven against Thebes*.

[7] *Seven against Thebes* 786; this meaning is secured by 754; cf. also 792; see Hutchinson 1985, xxv–xxvi for discussion; cf. also Lawrence 2007, 336 with n. 3 and see n. 74 below.

[8] See Hutchinson 1985, esp. xxix, and Sommerstein 2010a, 76–80 for discussion and suggestions.

[9] See for Polynices' later perception *Seven against Thebes* 637. The issue is potentially important for an overall assessment not least of the character of Eteocles, and we shall return to it below.

[10] Cf. Regenbogen 1933, 69: Eteocles 'the first "tragic" man in world literature'. *Pace* Thalmann 1978, 146: 'It seems methodologically questionable […] to center attention on Eteocles himself. […] his character serves the plot.'; and 149: 'Eteocles' character and its quality, his freedom of choice and personal responsibility as against the requirements of the curse – these are not, it seems to me, the questions we should be asking about the *Seven*.' While I think that Thalmann overstates his case, his cautioning against a framing of the question of character in terms of 'free will' is still welcome, and was even more so at the time of publication; and Thalmann's study of the imagery of the *Seven against Thebes* remains a major contribution to our understanding of the play. For the type of verdict exemplified by Thalmann, see also n. 3 above on Easterling 1973.

[11] See Paley 1870, 252, ad loc.; cf. Hutchinson 1985, 44–5, ad loc.

[12] Or indeed, *mutatis mutandis*, an address to women; to be discussed in due course.

[13] The translation of this line by Ewans 1996, 39, is semantically less plausible: 'whose bodies are now growing rather fat'; but whether line 12 refers to the old men only or to both groups present, the text does not refer to a third group.

[14] *Gē*, 'The Land', to whom agency is ascribed here in accordance with a mythologem particularly appropriate in the case of Thebes and the Sown Men, has brought up the Thebans to become inhabitants 'of herself'.

[15] Note that *prepon* at *OT* 9 echoes *symprepes* in *Seven against Thebes* 13, thus further confirming the sense required at this place in Aeschylus' prologue.

[16] 'Group', as signifying age group, is not ideal as a translation of *phylon*, but conveys the sense sufficiently.

[17] Trans. Campbell 1871, 123.

[18] There are, as has been observed, in structure, in choice of words, and in the conceptual framework, a number of parallels between these sections of the prologues of the two plays. There is no doubt that Sophocles, in these lines of the *Oedipus Tyrannus*, owes something to Aeschylus. But perhaps one can go further. It is true that, given the scanty nature of the fragments we have of the other plays, we do not know for certain whether there were any structural parallels between the Labdacid plays that would mirror the parallels between the plays of the *Oresteia* trilogy. But it is at least

possible that Aeschylus' *Oedipus* began with a scene in which Oedipus addresses an assembly of the old and the young, be it at his first arrival at Thebes, after the Sphinx had killed many, or at another time of crisis which prevented the men of fighting age from being present. An emphasis on the separate roles of different age groups in Aeschylus' tetralogy may have carried over to the satyr-play *Sphinx*; cf. Hutchinson 1985, xxi–xxii. As regards the staging of the prologues, especially the entrances and exits, cf. Taplin 1977, 129–30, 134–6; in a production, both mask and costume would indicate, among other things, the age of the characters on stage.

[19] See e.g. Paley 1870, 252, ad loc.; it is all the more surprising that Paley, as does Hutchinson (1985, 41), all the same insists on emending the text so as to include the age group of men of military age. Wilamowitz 1914, 59–60, seems to have understood this aspect of the scene correctly. The separate question concerning the extent to which scenes in the *Iliad*, including this one, are modelled on an earlier *Thebaïd* cannot be discussed here.

[20] Literally: 'those with grey temples', which may just indicate, as LSJ suggest, those whose hair is beginning to grey, which would accord with a natural reading that Hector sends those of the older men who are 'not yet decrepit'.

[21] Trans. Lattimore.

[22] Hector's prayer to Zeus is for success in defence, to end, once and for all, a long siege; Eteocles is even more explicit when, in line 35, he closes εὖ τελεῖ θεός: one need not agree with every aspect of what Rosenmeyer says to appreciate his comment on *Zeus teleios* (1982, 278–9): 'Typically, Zeus's principal epithet is *teleios*, "completer", a term that is already found in this use in Homer, but which gains immeasurably in importance in Aeschylus. It designates Zeus in his universality and his omnipotence, and in his stewardship over the whole of the dramatic action. In other writers, especially Euripides, Zeus the Completer becomes, as it were, the divine symbol for the future-directedness of the drama. But Aeschylean dramaturgy does not exhibit the same straining for completion or resolution. The rhythm of an Aeschylean play is more like a process of exhaustion; as it unfolds, it reveals what has been there from the beginning. The Aeschylean Zeus *teleios*, then, presides over the completeness of the revelation. As the defeat of the Persians is made fully apparent, or as the necessity of Eteocles' fratricidal destruction is assured, or the house of Agamemnon is saved or restructured, we witness an unpacking of implications and of commitments which document the meaning of Zeus *teleios*.'

[23] Taplin 1977, 136–7.

[24] Opinion may be divided over an exit by the silent faces after line 35 or after line 38; see e.g. Ewans 1996, 186 n. 3; but they must leave after either 35 or 38, not later; Eteocles' own logic in his exchange with the women dictates that there are no witnesses to the Scout's grim descriptions.

[25] And if one is not persuaded that Eteocles also speaks 36–8 by himself, 69–77 are the only lines of the play where he is thus by himself; see previous note.

[26] Explicitly Hutchinson 1985, 41; cf. Dawson 1970, 36 ad loc.; Sommerstein 2010a, 68; cf. also Ewans 1996, 186–7, with n. 5; see also Wilamowitz 1914, 60, on Eteocles as the son of Oedipus.

[27] Line 73 is spurious; cf. Hutchinson 1985, 54, ad loc.

[28] Ἑλλάδος could be a separative genitive; it could, alternatively, be construed with δηάλωτον, as it is by Ewans 1996, 41; also Collard 2008, 37: 'O Zeus and Earth, and

you gods who hold the city, and you Curse, my father's powerful Fury, do not, I beg you, raze the city root and branch in total destruction, a captive of Greek foes. The land and the city of Cadmus are free: never hold them in the bonds of slavery, but be our defence! I speak of our common interest, I hope; for when a city prospers, it honours its gods.'

[29] Cf. Hutchinson 53–4, with reference to Parker 1983, 265 ff.

[30] Dawson 1970, 36–7.

[31] See Schwyzer 1950, 147–8.

[32] Cf. the context of the *Odyssey* 20.67.

[33] It is pertinent that Aeschylus will use the same phrase again when, at *Eumenides* 644, he lets Apollo address the Erinyes: ὦ παντομισῆ κνώδαλα, στύγη θεῶν, 'O beasts hated by all, abominations to the gods'. On στύγος see below.

[34] One could object that all we can say, especially in accordance with the line of argument followed here, is that Eteocles *professes* this belief; a separate argument would be needed to show that he *holds* it. While I shall not deal with this objection here, some light will be shed on the question in the course of discussion below.

[35] See also Hiltbrunner 1950, 50.

[36] Lines 674–6 are spurious.

[37] Tydeus, 381, 392–4; Capaneus, 434, shouts indirectly from his shield; Eteoclus, 643–4, shouts from his shield 468–9; Hippomedon 487, 497; Parthenopaeus 529–32, 538, 449; Polynices 633, 634–41, and indirectly from his shield 647–8.

[38] 410 against Tydeus; 442–3, 447 against Capaneus; 550–1 against Eteoclus, Hippomedon and Parthenopaeus, plus 554; no threat from Amphiaraus, rather 619, no counter-boast; against Polynices 660, 662–71.

[39] Words with the stem *komp-* are employed at 425, 436, 437, 473, 480, 500, 551, 794.

[40] In 1914, Wilamowitz declared that the incongruity of verb tenses in the defence arrangements of Eteocles, an incongruity which commentators had in various ways remarked on before, had to be taken literally. Future tenses referred to the future, past tenses to the past. Eteocles had been interrupted in making his selections of defenders and assignments for the gates. Perhaps because of the awe in which Wilamowitz was held for so long, perhaps because of what is perceived as excesses in textual criticism, it is often overlooked that a major contributor to this issue is Wecklein, who writes in the introduction to his edition of the play (1902, 9–10): 'Die Meldung eines Kundschafters, daß die feindlichen Heerführer um die Tore losen, führt dazu die Verteidiger der einzelnen Tore zu bestimmen. Zunächst aber geht Eteokles in den Palast zurück um sich zu rüsten. Bevor er ganz damit fertig ist (663), wird er durch die Hilferufe der Jungfrauen veranlaßt wieder herauszukommen. Dann (273) geht er in die Stadt um Heerführer an die Tore abzuordnen. Nachdem Eteokles bereits drei Führer, Polyphontes (435), Hyperbios (491) und Aktor (542), abgeschickt hat, kommt er mit drei anderen, Menippos (394), Megareus (459) und Lasthenes (607), zurück, um von dem mittlerweile neuerdings zurückgekehrten Kundschafter Näheres über die feindlichen Heerführer und deren Stellung zu erfahren und dem entsprechend über die drei übrigen Führer und seine eigene Person zu verfügen. In ähnlicher Weise wird Eur. Phoen. 448 Eteokles in der Aufstellung des Heeres durch die Ankunft des Polyneikes unterbrochen. – Butler und Blomfield nehmen an, daß Eteokles bei diesem Auftreten (359) von den erwählten sechs Heerführern umgeben sei um erst nach

Entgegennahme der Mitteilungen des Kundschafters und diesen entsprechend den feindlichen Führern die richtigen Männer entgegenzustellen. Blomfield verweist auf das hinweisende τόνδε 459. Ebenso hat man τόνδε 395, wofür Grotius ohne Not τῶνδε gesetzt hat. Ferner spricht dafür das Fut. ἀντιτάξω 395, ἀντιτάξομεν 608. Die entgegengesetzte Ansicht, daß die Helden bereits an die Tore abgeschickt seien, wird empfohlen durch ᾑρέθη 492, τέτακται 435, vor allem aber durch die Worte Ἑρμῆς δ' εὐλόγως ξυνήγαγεν 495. Denn wenn der glückliche Zufall die Männer zusammengebracht hat, so muß die Aufstellung des Thebanischen Führers vor der Kenntnis des feindlichen geschehen sein. Heimsöth sucht deshalb das Fut. ἀντιτάξω damit zu erklären, daß Eteokles seine Ansichten ändere und statt des bereits am Tore stehenden Mannes einen anderen, geeigneteren schicke. Aber das wäre weder poetisch noch für die Zuschauer deutlich genug. Weil meint, Eteokles könne immerhin sagen: "ich werde dem Tydeus den Melanippos entgegen stellen", wenn auch Melanippos bereits am Tore stehe, wie er 459 πέμποιμ' ἄν und darauf πέμπεται gebrauche. Aber damit ist τόνδε nicht erklärt und 460, wo eine Lücke ist, kann man annehmen, daß Megareus inzwischen an das Tor abgegangen ist. Hiernach scheint die einzige Auskunft [Ausflucht(?)] in der Annahme zu liegen, daß drei Führer bereits am Tore stehen, drei dagegen mit Eteokles auftreten und auf seine Weisung hin an ihren Posten abgehen von den Segenswünschen des Chors begleitet. Sonst würde auch der Bericht des Kundschafters zwecklos sein.' Strictly speaking, Blomfield (1817, 40, ad 404) says: 'Butlerus existimat Eteoclem in scenam ducibus stipatum prodiisse, et ex iis quosdam ad portarum custodiam selegisse. Recte: vid. 466.7.' This is important as it presents in the strictest and clearest form the alternative that Eteokles has not only not begun with the assignments, he has not even selected yet who should lead the troops; i.e., he chooses the leaders on stage from a larger group of potential leaders, presumably men of noble birth; and this should indeed be the alternative for all who argue that we witness a choice that is based exclusively on who is best suited; this position does, of course, leave out of consideration completely the notion, to be discussed in the text presently, that there were six others who, after or with Eteocles, were the best.

[41] Cf. Wilamowitz's discussion of 472–3 (1914, 76).

[42] The symmetry of the tenses from future to past and back to the future has in turn been interpreted as reflecting in geographically convincing fashion which gates have and which have not yet received their respective defender.

[43] Only those future forms which occur in Eteocles' decision-making process in his replies to the Scout are of relevance here. For a clear summary discussion of the future forms in particular, see Lenz 1981, 426–7.

[44] E.g. recently Sommerstein 2010a, 73–4, who stresses that in the report of the Scout 'there is no indication that Polyneices is among' the Seven who are about to attack the gates: some defenders have been posted, others, who have not yet been posted, are assigned their gates on stage; Sommerstein maintains that even at the point where Amphiaraus is announced as the attacker of the sixth gate, Eteocles himself still does not know 'that Polyneices is one of the Seven at all' (74). Similarly, Lesky 1961; Dawe 1963; Winnington-Ingram 1983, 16–54. A widespread opinion before Wilamowitz was the view that Eteocles appears on stage with six champions; cf. e.g. Verrall 1887, xiii–xiv. That the defenders are chosen but not yet assigned their gates is also held i.a. by von Fritz 1962, 193–226; Taplin, 1977, 153–5; and recently Ewans 1996, 190–1. Kirkwood (1969, 13) holds that it is 'essential...to a reasonable view of

the play to see that Eteocles is choosing, of his own volition and in the light of the opposing champions, defenders of the city'; i.e., Kirkwood seems to say that not even the six other defenders had been chosen when Eteocles re-enters (cf. 14: 'It is therefore not only by an irony of fate, nor at all by the fact that Eteocles has run out of capable champions, that Eteocles chooses himself.'). That everything, both the list of defenders and their positions at the seven gates, is determined in advance is argued by E. Wolff 1958; so also Patzer 1958 and Erbse 1964. Lenz 1981 suggests that Eteocles has indeed chosen the defenders and assigned them to their gates, but now, as he could previously not have been aware of the identity of the attackers of each gate, he 'assigns' each defender to his opponent.

[45] Lloyd 2007, 8–13, with discussion of secondary literature.

[46] The opposing view, that Eteocles is not aware in advance that Polynices will be one of the seven enemy leaders, has most recently been asserted again by Sommerstein 2010a, 73–5 (= first edition, 2006, 105–7); see n. 44 above.

[47] Whether and in what way it may be a revelation for Eteocles will be discussed below.

[48] Or perhaps: 'in good proportion', i.e. well matched.

[49] Ewans 1996, 190–1, quoting Kirkwood 1969, 13 (cf. n. 42 above), and adducing Taplin 1977, 154, 'and others'; similarly also Lawrence 2007, 343–5; and Demont 2000, 316–18, who interprets as a sign of Eteocles' responsibility that comes with the voluntary nature of his choices the fact that, while the attackers select by lot, he, Eteocles, chooses consciously and rationally.

[50] A subsidiary argument, in harmony with this scenario, is that he, Eteocles, has to stay behind since he is giving orders; thus he will fight whoever is announced last. Although this is in itself not a very strong point, it is fully compatible with a choice of defenders on the spot.

[51] For brief discussion of the central issues, see Allan 2005, 80–1, and Mastronarde 2005, 321–2. Cf. Cairns in this volume.

[52] E.g. Verrall 1887, xiii (Introduction); more recently Hecht and Bacon 1974.

[53] Whether or not line 472 is spurious, as has been suggested, as a matter of pragmatics, the deictic demonstrative τόνδε, 'this man', need not invariably refer to somebody actually present.

[54] *Pace* Sommerstein 1989, 221–6, Athena's vote must always decide, for the rest of time; in a voting system without the possibility to abstain, this presupposes an even number of votes, so that voting may result in a tie; visually, this is brought home to the audience by Athena's position in the *theologeion*. Correct Cairns 2005, 306.

[55] For detailed discussion of the use and significance of lots in literature from Homer to Aeschylus, and in fifth-century Greek reality as reflected in contemporary historiography, see Demont 2000, who, however, concludes that the importance of the use of the lot by the attackers in the *Seven against Thebes* lies not least in the contrast with Eteocles' choosing rationally.

[56] The word is ἐκλήρωσαν, 'cast lots for'; see Gomme et al. 1970 ad loc. for further parallels.

[57] See Parker 1996, 126–9, for qualifying statements concerning the extent to which choice by lot was seen as a secular or as a 'religious' matter; and 292–3 (with 130) on κλήρωσις ἐκ προκρίτων, 'allotment from a group of people selected beforehand'.

[58] For Hermes and the lot, see also Demont 2000, 300 n. 2, 311 n. 32.

[59] In line 414, Eteocles uses the image of the dice of Ares for what will happen when Tydeus and Melanippus meet on the battlefield.

[60] In –*daitas* there is contained, etymologically, but also visibly, the root **dai-*, 'distribute', also found in *daimōn*. Intriguingly, *chrēma* can be the word for the 'lot' used in lot oracles in Delphi. Evidence for lot oracles is fragmentary and allusory in nature (see Johnston 2008, 52–5), but among the few instances of vase paintings suggesting the early existence of a lot oracle besides the riddling conversational oracle there, one depicts Aegeus consulting Themis, presumably in the matter of offspring, which would constitute a close parallel to Laius' inquiry; another shows Oedipus (for references and illustrations, see Robbins 1916). But there is, to my knowledge, no evidence to suggest either that Aeschylus mentioned the lot in connection with Delphi in the *Laius* or the *Oedipus* or that a version of the myth linked the enquiries of Laius or Oedipus at Delphi specifically to the lot. One may note, though, that when the Chorus refer to Laius' having consulted the oracle of Apollo thrice (742–57), this could be fully compatible with practices of consulting in particular lot oracles, where one desired outcome could easily be interpreted as cancelling out all previous negative attempts. But in the case of Laius and Oedipus, in the versions of the story we have, there would have to be a discursive/conversational/'enthusiastic' answer at least in addition to whatever other form of enquiry and response.

[61] This is not to deny that the different layers of meaning have their impact regardless of how Eteocles selects the defenders; for nuanced discussion see Demont 2000, 319–24.

[62] The best discussions of the imagery and significance of the lot in the *Seven against Thebes*, far beyond what can be discussed here, are Thalmann 1978, 62–77, and Demont 2000.

[63] E.g., in a long line of tradition, Hutchinson 1985, xxxi.

[64] The Aorist passive participle στυγηθέν with the so-called 'dative of the agent' expresses here, as does the perfect otherwise, a state of affairs. Apollo has turned away in horror from the House of Laius; that is the sense of the verb. Etymologically, its root conveys the notion of 'chilling cold'. The same root is found in the name of the river Styx, on which Aeschylus is here punning, by using the verb form near to the name of the river Cocytus, the stream of 'wailing', which in turn is appropriate for Eteocles to invoke, as his name has the two etymologies of 'true fame' and 'true lament'.

[65] Are the audience here being reminded of Themis as the source of the oracle at Delphi? Cf. n. 60 above.

[66] This claim is most fervently and most frequently made for Sophocles, but often enough applied to Aeschylus, too; cf. Hutchinson 1984, xxviii–xxix.

[67] Thalmann 1978, 62–3. Cf. Demont 2000.

[68] Cf. Hutchinson 1985, xxix.

[69] Laius is mentioned at only four points in the whole play, all within the space of 152 lines: 691, 745, 802, 842.

[70] For discussion, see Sewell-Rutter 2007, 49–77.

[71] *Iliad* 22.63–4 may have a faint echo in *Seven against Thebes* 348–50; see also Hutchinson 1985, 100, ad loc. Cf. further *Iliad* 22.38, 55, 79 ff., and importantly, 6.407–39, with key terms.

[72] I do not consider here the extent to which the *Iliad* itself is modelled on a *Thebaïd*; on the basis of the extant evidence, it is fruitless to speculate whether the character of

that will avoid one-sided, partisan interpretations of the play's main characters as either exemplary heroes or unqualified villains. In order to arrive at a fuller appreciation of *Antigone*, I submit, we must realize that neither Antigone nor Creon is to be perceived as a static figure; rather, as the play evolves, the presentation of the two conflicting characters is gradually but crucially modified, and the audience are encouraged to reassess their original evaluations of those characters. At the outset of the play, as I intend to show, Antigone is cast as a threatening, anti-*polis* character insofar as she champions the cause of a traitorous blood-relative, Polynices, who turned against his own city and his own kin (cf. Creon's harsh words in *Ant*. 198–206, anticipated by the Chorus' striking imagery of the Theban host as a vulture in 110–16).[4] The world-view expounded by Antigone is distinctly archaic, in that she advocates the primacy of funeral rites both as a preserve of the family and as a domain fundamentally antithetical to the *polis*. In fifth-century (Athenian) political ideology, the primacy of the *polis* over the *genos* was a value to be ardently defended, since it constituted the foundation of democratic ideology as opposed to the aristocratic prevalence of the *genos*.[5] As has been demonstrated by a number of scholars,[6] funerary ritual provided a perfect opportunity for the public display of the power and solidarity of great families; this was not only expressed in excessive lamentation or elaborate funerary monuments, but also in acts of (symbolic or actual) aggression, especially in persistent and emotionally loaded demands for violent revenge, which could easily lead to vendetta practices and the disruption of the concord indispensable for the collectivity that is the *polis*. It was therefore imperative for the emergent city-state to deprive the individual *oikoi* of such opportunities.[7] In Athens such a tendency can be demonstrated to underlie Solonian funerary legislation, which strictly prohibited excessive expressions of mourning in private funerals.[8] It is in this context that Creon's prohibition of the burial should be placed: the interest of the community matters for the leader more than the prerogatives of the individual *oikos*. The irony of the play lies precisely in that Antigone, who sides with a traitor against the *polis*, seems at the end to prevail over the statesman Creon, who starts off as a champion of *polis* values, only to deteriorate rapidly into a tyrant and be eventually shattered in a fashion alarmingly recalling the downfall of the afflicted Labdacids, a family to which he is no blood relative.[9]

2.1. Antigone, the *polis,* and the burial of the dead

Antigone's case is forcefully presented at the very outset of the play, and with remarkable eloquence at that. The new state authority, Creon, has prohibited burial for Antigone's brother Polynices as a punishment for his expedition against his own city; however, Antigone argues that, regardless of what he did while alive, Polynices is a brother, and deserves at the very least a proper funeral from his family. The question arises whether this early and potent statement of Antigone's case is a dramatic device meant to manipulate the audience's sympathies in favour of the heroine. 'First impressions are powerful', observes a perceptive modern critic, 'and our first impression of Kreon's edict comes to us filtered through Antigone's grief and indignation'; this is achieved, according to the same critic, because Sophocles has shrewdly let Antigone 'launch a pre-emptive strike' upon the audience to win their sympathy.[10]

Moreover, it has been argued that Antigone must be by default the focus of the audience's sympathetic attention: she is the one to be threatened by Creon, and Creon is thus cast in the role of the inherently antipathetic adversary, no matter how sound his political statements may be.[11] This, however, is a reductive reading that ignores at least two crucial factors. First, Antigone's behaviour is cast from the start as transgressive, not only because it runs counter to the constraints imposed by the *polis*' leader but primarily because it promotes the ritual privileges of her (self-)destructive *oikos*, whose members have repeatedly imperilled the city (see above pp. 81–2). Secondly, if Creon is by default the play's villain, it seems puzzling that he is given the opportunity to voice such sound political principles in his opening speech. In the rest of this section, I shall explore in greater detail the transgressive character of Antigone's behaviour; in most of the following sections (2.2, 4.1, 4.2, 5) I shall concern myself with Creon, his character, his principles, and his actions.

Two *parthenoi*, or unmarried girls, meeting furtively, before dawn (*Ant.* 16, 100–5), outside the boundaries of their home (18) would have been a shocking sight for the original audience: aside from the blatant social impropriety, this clandestine encounter represents a defiant challenge to male authority, both political and familial.[12] This is a point stressed time and again by Ismene: one has to yield to the political constraints (66, βιάζομαι) imposed by the νόμος (59), which in this case is identified with the monarch's decree and power (60, ψῆφον…κράτη), and also with the body politic (79, πολιτῶν); this is, after all, what the rest of the *polis* does (44).[13] Especially the use of ψῆφος in 60 suggests, as Knox (1964, 63) has seen, 'that Creon's proclamation is no capricious gesture but the expression of a deliberate policy'; moreover, by virtue of its associations with democratic political process ψῆφος implies that 'Creon speaks for the whole body of the citizens'. It has been argued, notably by Kamerbeek, that Ismene does not care to draw subtle distinctions between the body of citizens and the monarch, or even the impersonal νόμος, as political agents: what matters is that all of them represent the will and the power of state authority (63, ἀρχόμεσθ' ἐκ κρεισσόνων; 67, τοῖς ἐν τέλει βεβῶσι) as opposed to the family.[14] We shall see later that, if Ismene regards Creon's decree as virtually a law sanctioned by the community, it is not because of a failure to make 'subtle distinctions' but rather because of an implicit belief that the representative of the body politic, once designated, literally *embodies* the will of the people, who are subsequently to be regarded as authors of each and every decision and act emanating from their representative. Creon clearly sees himself as appointed by the *polis* (666, ἀλλ' ὃν πόλις στήσειε), and thus as someone whose decisions cannot possibly be contested (666–7 τοῦδε χρὴ κλύειν | καὶ σμικρὰ καὶ δίκαια καὶ τἀναντία). True, there is a disturbing authoritarian streak here, explicitly criticized by Haemon in 635–765, and it is fair to assume that at least some audience members would have seen the force of Haemon's observations. As will be seen later, much of the dramatic impetus of *Antigone* hinges on Creon's gradual disintegration from a statesman concerned primarily about the *polis'* safety to an openly authoritarian tyrant (see further section 5 below), the more so that his rhetoric about political values is undercut by traces of monomania and a disconcerting tendency to turn issues of principle into questions of personal status. Still, it can hardly be denied that in the earlier part of the play his stance is a principled one, and his concept of the ideal *polis* ruler is one directly associated with the welfare of the body politic. This concept, which I have deliberately if anachronistically described in Hobbesian language, will be treated in greater detail in sections 4.1 and 4.2 below. Suffice it to recall here that the Greeks often considered νόμος as the work of a single man, one who was subsequently honoured as a benefactor of the community: Solon in Athens, Lycurgus in Sparta, Zaleucus in Locri Epizephyrioi, Charondas in Catane. Likewise, the sentiment that a single person's authority may also constitute a νόμος to be obeyed is memorably voiced in Heraclitus 22 B 33 Diels-Kranz: νόμος καὶ βουλῇ πείθεσθαι ἑνός.[15] After all, Ismene's implicit equation between violating Creon's νόμος (59–60, νόμου βίᾳ) and violating the will of the citizens (79, βίᾳ πολιτῶν) is a point conceded, if belatedly, by Antigone herself at 907 (βίᾳ πολιτῶν).[16] Indeed, Antigone's belated realization seems to stem from the Chorus' eventual reluctance to side with her cause (cf. 838–41): she is thus forced to reconsider her previous conviction (504–5, 509) that the Thebans would approve of her action if they were not afraid to contradict Creon.[17]

Further, those readings of *Antigone* that routinely turn the heroine into a defender of human dignity against despotic repression disregard the fundamental fact that her reaction to Creon's edict stems not from her devotion to ideals of liberty or merely of ritual propriety but mainly from concerns related to her familial privileges, that is to say to the funeral honours she bestows on Polynices.[18] Her decision is motivated by her indignation at the fact that Creon has turned against her own φίλοι in a manner appropriate to ἐχθροί: 'are you unaware', she inquires of Ismene at 9–10, 'that evils proper for our enemies are coming upon our friends?' Characteristically for Antigone, her use of ἐχθροί rather than πολέμιοι in this context subtly shifts the focus from the political to the familial. Showing oneself worthy of one's lineage is more important for Antigone than serving the commonweal or obeying those in power: 'This is how matters stand for you', she declares to Ismene, 'and you will soon have occasion to demonstrate whether you are well born or whether you are the base offspring of noble stock' (37–8). In fact, it has been suggested that much of *Antigone*'s relevance for its original audience may have consisted in its dramatizing the detriment to the community that may result from women's excessive attachment to their natal households, especially in dynastic contexts.[19]

However, the family with which Antigone associates herself all too willingly is a doomed *oikos*, where procreation is overwhelmed by self-annihilating introversion. The famous opening line, in which Antigone identifies her sister (and, by implication, herself too) by stressing that they both are the common (κοινόν) offspring of the same womb (αὐτάδελφον), has often been admired for its presumed warmth of heart, but the blood relations Antigone appeals to are surely too close for comfort. For Antigone's family is beset by an excessive, unhealthy closeness (Oedipus' and Jocasta's incestuous marriage) or by an excessive, destructive hostility (Oedipus' parricide, Eteocles' and Polynices' mutual fratricide). Far from denying the self-destructive character of her immoderate adherence to her family, Antigone confirms it repeatedly, especially in 73–6, where she envisages spending an eternity with her dead brother – in Hades:

> φίλη μετ' αὐτοῦ κείσομαι, φίλου μέτα,
> ὅσια πανουργήσασ'· ἐπεὶ πλείων χρόνος   75
> ὃν δεῖ μ' ἀρέσκειν τοῖς κάτω τῶν ἐνθάδε.
> ἐκεῖ γὰρ αἰεὶ κείσομαι

> I shall lie next to him (Polynices), a beloved woman next to a beloved man, having committed a pious crime; because it is to the dead, not to the living, that I must be agreeable for a longer time. For it is down there that I shall lie for ever.[20]

The sexual ambiguity inherent in the repeated κείσομαι, 'I shall lie' (cf. Aristophanes' *Peace* 1332–3 μετ' ἐμοῦ καλὴ | καλῶς κατακείσει, in a nuptial context) poignantly reinforces the impression of unhealthy family introversion characteristic of Antigone and of the Labdacids in general.[21] As pointed out by Zellner, if Antigone insists so much on burying Polynices, it is because she regards this as the only means of having an eternal post-mortem relationship with him.[22] The effect is further enhanced in 423–8, when Antigone's lament over her brother's body is likened to that of a bird over the loss of her fledglings: Antigone is both a sister and a mother to Polynices, just as Oedipus was both father and brother to his children.[23]

Ismene seems fully to realize that the source of her and her sister's misfortunes is their own family's excessive introversion. In her overview of the disasters that have befallen the house of Oedipus (49–57), she repeatedly brings out striking instances of this inordinate inwardness, which is expressed either as incest or as kin-killing. This is obvious especially in the case of Eteocles and Polynices: their common origin in the same incestuous birth ends in the community of their mutual death (56–7 μόρον | κοινόν). Interestingly, their mutual killing is described by αὐτοκτονοῦντε (56), which as Jebb (1900) ad 55 f. remarks, suggests that 'the deed is done with one's own hand, implying that such a use of one's own hand is unnatural'; thus, both suicide and the slaying of kinsfolk may be expressed by such words as αὐθέντης, αὐτοκτόνος, αὐτοσφαγής, αὐτοφόνος, etc.[24] This brings us to an important stylistic feature of this play, namely the occurrence of compounds with the pronoun αὐτός as their first component: for instance, Oedipus' intrafamilial crimes that he himself brought to light are αὐτοφώρων ἀμπλακημάτων (51); and his self-blinding he performed αὐτὸς αὐτουργῷ χερί (52).[25] The recurrence of αὐτο- words within the brief space of a few lines helps hammer home the Labdacids' disastrous tendency to turn in upon themselves, to annihilate themselves in incest or internecine murder. Ismene's survey of several instances of Labdacid introversion is meant to dissuade Antigone from her own excessive adherence to her kin, which only reiterates the destructive patterns that have led her family to almost complete extinction – a realization poignantly underscored by the duals of Ismene's μόνα δὴ νὼ λελειμμένα, 'the two of us left alone' (58).[26] Antigone herself may be acknowledging the significance of sexual misconduct as a source of her family woes in 857–62, assuming with Clarke 2001 that the puzzling 'thrice-ploughed woe' mentioned there refers 'to the fact that the source and focus of Antigone's misery is the sequence of sexual ploughings that has destroyed her family'.[27] These passages bring up notions of hereditary self-destruction and patterns of transgression, conflict, and suffering recurring in successive generations, which conform to a familiar and fundamentally archaic model (see further pp. 93–5).

2.2. Creon, the *polis,* and the burial of the dead

In stark contrast to Antigone's obsession with herself and her natal family, Creon shows himself, in his opening speech, as a model leader concerned exclusively with the welfare of the community. As he famously insists, what ensures individual salvation/safety (σωτηρία) is the safety of the *polis* as a whole (178–90):

> ἐμοὶ γὰρ ὅστις πᾶσαν εὐθύνων πόλιν
> μὴ τῶν ἀρίστων ἅπτεται βουλευμάτων,
> ἀλλ' ἐκ φόβου του γλῶσσαν ἐγκλήσας ἔχει,   180
> κάκιστος εἶναι νῦν τε καὶ πάλαι δοκεῖ·
> καὶ μείζον' ὅστις ἀντὶ τῆς αὑτοῦ πάτρας
> φίλον νομίζει, τοῦτον οὐδαμοῦ λέγω.
> ἐγὼ γάρ, ἴστω Ζεὺς ὁ πάνθ' ὁρῶν ἀεί,
> οὔτ' ἂν σιωπήσαιμι τὴν ἄτην ὁρῶν   185
> στείχουσαν ἀστοῖς ἀντὶ τῆς σωτηρίας,
> οὔτ' ἂν φίλον ποτ' ἄνδρα δυσμενῆ χθονὸς
> θείμην ἐμαυτῷ, τοῦτο γιγνώσκων ὅτι
> ἥδ' ἐστὶν ἡ σῴζουσα καὶ ταύτης ἔπι
> πλέοντες ὀρθῆς τοὺς φίλους ποιούμεθα.   190

The leader of a whole city who does not adhere to the best counsels but keeps his mouth shut out of fear is the worst sort; this has always been my opinion. And whoever considers his friends more important than his own homeland, he is a nobody, to my mind. As for myself, Zeus the All-Seer be my witness, I would never keep silent if I saw ruin rather than safety heading towards the citizenry, nor would I ever befriend an enemy of this land. For I know that it is she that keeps us safe, and only if her vessel sails in a prosperous course can we make our friends.

The approving quotation of these lines by Demosthenes (*On the False Embassy* [19] 247, quoting *Ant.* 175–90) shows that Creon's principles would be quite in keeping with the Athenian ideal of civic behaviour. Indeed, the lines in question are specifically proclaimed by Demosthenes (*ibid.* 246) to be 'beautifully composed and useful *to you*', meaning the Athenian citizenry (πεποιημένα ἰαμβεῖα καλῶς καὶ συμφερόντως ὑμῖν).[28] It may well be, as Yunis claims (2000, 111), that epic or tragic quotations in Greek oratory were no more than tools used to bolster a particular argument through their prestige. This, however, does not make them mere rhetorical boilerplate: to invoke the authority of classical poetry is to appeal to the community's inalienable cultural capital. In similar fashion, as Yunis (loc. cit.) points out, 'American politicians and lawyers of an earlier day used suitable passages of the Bible to support whatever case they were arguing at the moment.' Moreover, Demosthenes' approving quotation of Creon's lines implies that Creon would not have been perceived as a complete and unqualified villain: to use a modern analogy, no orator worth their salt today would quote a speech by, say, Shakespeare's Iago or Edmund as evidence for the soundness or general acceptability of this or that argument. After all, similar ideas are also expressed in the last of the Periclean speeches reported by Thucydides (2.60.2–4), where the key idea recurs that only in a *polis* that fares safely (ὀρθουμένην) can the individual be saved (διασῴζεται):

> ἐγὼ γὰρ ἡγοῦμαι πόλιν πλείω ξύμπασαν ὀρθουμένην ὠφελεῖν τοὺς ἰδιώτας ἢ καθ' ἕκαστον τῶν πολιτῶν εὐπραγοῦσαν, ἀθρόαν δὲ σφαλλομένην. καλῶς μὲν γὰρ φερόμενος ἀνὴρ τὸ καθ' ἑαυτὸν διαφθειρομένης τῆς πατρίδος οὐδὲν ἧσσον ξυναπόλλυται, κακοτυχῶν δὲ ἐν εὐτυχούσῃ πολλῷ μᾶλλον διασῴζεται.

> For I believe that a city that thrives as a whole is of more benefit to the individuals than one whose citizens prosper singly, whereas it teeters on the brink of disaster as a whole. For a man who prospers as an individual will perish along with his ruined city, whereas an unfortunate man is much more likely to be saved if he lives in a fortunate city.

Those readers who routinely repudiate Creon as a petty, power-hungry despot, ready to trample on common decency, ritual propriety, and the universal 'unwritten laws', can do so only by disregarding or explaining away the 'undeniably impressive' principles enunciated in this speech, and by applying the benefit of hindsight, in view of Creon's later deterioration.[29] As intimated above (p. 83), if Sophocles had intended to cast Creon as an unequivocally antipathetic personage, he would hardly have glorified the play's villain by enriching his first appearance with a fine piece of political rhetoric. It has been argued that, once Creon has been cast as the play's villain, or rather as the adversary of its focal character, his statements, however sound in themselves, can only serve as a foil to what we know to be his tyrannical frame of mind.[30] The argument is specious: if Creon's character were consigned to dramatic damnation from the outset, there should be little need to increase the audience's antipathy towards him; even if there were such a need, it would be ill served by the ambiguity of having an apparently unlikeable character enunciate well-grounded political principles.

On the contrary, apart from the Demosthenes quotation mentioned above, there is internal evidence from the play itself that the audience was conditioned to react favourably to Creon's speech, especially to those crucial passages in which Polynices' repulsive act of high treason is condemned in the harshest terms. For already in the parodos the Chorus had employed some strikingly disturbing imagery in their description of the Argive attack, thereby predisposing the audience into welcoming Creon's strictures against Polynices. The enemy army, led by Polynices, encircled the city of Thebes, like a shrieking vulture ready to devour its prey, gaping with its 'seven-gated mouth' (118–19, ἀμφιχανὼν...ἑπτάπυλον στόμα) around Thebes' proverbial seven gates.[31] Likewise, Creon visualizes Polynices as someone who ventured not only 'to burn down his fatherland and the gods of his race', but also literally 'to taste of kindred blood' (αἵματος | κοινοῦ πάσασθαι), as if he were a vulture or wild beast (199–202). It bears repeating that the violent imagery Creon uses would have resonated deeply with an audience already biased against Polynices by the Chorus' horrified description of his vulture-like bloodthirstiness.

Although no scholar denies the enormity of Polynices' actions against his own homeland, it is often argued that Creon is in the wrong insofar as the punishment he metes out to his dead foe is a cruel and unusual one: he has the body cast out, without funerary rites, for the vultures and dogs to prey on. However, it has long been pointed out that such a punishment, horrendous as it may be, would have been completely in line with what Athenians thought a traitor deserved.[32] To take but a few out of many examples, burial in Attic soil was prohibited, on account of treasonous acts (real or alleged), for Themistocles (Thucydides 1.138.6), for Antiphon the orator and Archeptolemus (Plutarch, *Moralia* 833a, 834a), and for Phocion (Plutarch, *Phocion* 37.2). It will not do to counter–argue that Creon should have simply thrown Polynices' body beyond the borders rather than actively to prohibit its burial.[33] For one thing, as pointed out by Holt (1999, 665), such counter–arguments are belied by the simple observation that 'no such course of action is considered in the play, where we find only the stark extremes of exposure and a full burial'; and it would be 'poor criticism to say that a character in a play ought to have done something which he is never given a chance to do and which is never proposed by anybody on stage.'[34] For another, as again Holt points out (1999, 665–6), Attic law could not prevent burial outside Athenian soil, since it was not concerned to regulate what went on outside Attic territory; however, it is unlikely that the law envisioned burial of traitors outside Attica, and it certainly did not provide for it. After all, as has been pointed out time and again,[35] active prohibition of burial for the cast-out bodies of traitors is a historically documented practice. Thus, for instance, after Phocion was executed and his body thrown out of the borders of Attica, it was specifically ordered that no Athenian cremate his body; 'as a result', remarks Plutarch, 'no φίλος of his dared to touch the body', and so a certain Conopion, who used to provide such services for money, was hired to carry the body outside Attica and cremate it. The mentality underlying such practices seems also to inform those passages of Plato's *Laws* that concern the treatment of the bodies of kin-killers (873a–c): their corpses are to be thrown naked at a crossroads out of the city's borders, pelted with stones by the city authorities, and carried outside of the country's borders to be left there uninhumed and unmourned. Similar punishments are reserved for those involved in sorcery and necromancy, and especially for those who employ such means to destroy whole cities (*Laws* 909b–c): their bodies are to be cast outside the borders, and left there without burial; if a freeborn person were to give them burial, they would be liable to punishment for impiety (δίκας ἀσεβείας). Remarkably, Plato's phrasing here, especially ὅσοι δ' ἂν... πόλεις χρημάτων χάριν ἐπιχειρῶσιν κατ' ἄκρας ἐξαιρεῖν, 'those who attempt to annihilate cities for the sake of money', is reminiscent of the language used by Creon with reference to Polynices' intentions (*Ant.* 199–201): ὃς γῆν πατρῴαν καὶ θεοὺς τοὺς ἐγγενεῖς | [...] φυγὰς κατελθὼν ἠθέλησε μὲν πυρὶ | πρῆσαι κατ' ἄκρας, 'who came back from exile wishing to burn down his native land and the gods of his country'. Likewise, the burial of Polynices, insofar as it has transcended the limits of private ritual, is treated as a grave public offence to be punished by stoning, a characteristically *public* mode of execution (36, φόνον ... δημόλευστον ἐν πόλει),[36] again reminiscent of one of the Platonic punishments mentioned above.

3. Labdacid madness against the *polis*

For all their political and moral soundness and their historical applicability, Creon's strictures against Polynices have scarcely struck readers as worthy of credit. This may be explicable by the assumption, most eloquently put forth by Malcolm Heath, that Creon's position, for all its intellectual appeal, is emotionally defective and, indeed, offensive. For the play's emotional centre of gravity is, we are told, Antigone and her devotion to the funerary honours due to her dead brother. After all, in Greek tragedy prohibition of burial is always a device meant to excite strong emotions, including the quintessentially tragic ones of pity and fear, rather than to be debated coolly and level-headedly.[37] For all its apparent attractiveness, however, this argument cannot withstand criticism, at least in the case of *Antigone*. The play's original audience, some members of which would have been exposed to several narrative and dramatic versions of the Labdacid myth, including primarily Aeschylus' *Seven*, would have been keenly aware of a persistent trait frequently associated with that family: namely, that the Labdacids are a source of pollution and danger for Thebes, and that their perverse family relations are shown time and again to be fundamentally incompatible with the welfare and even the very survival of the Theban *polis*. For one thing, in the so-called 'Pisander scholium', which may well reflect the cyclic *Oidipodeia* on this point,[38] the Sphinx was an affliction visited indiscriminately on the whole of Thebes by Hera, who had been angered by Laius' sexual misconduct. For another, in the Aeschylean treatment of the myth, Laius was advised by Apollo's oracle that he would save the city by dying without offspring (Aeschylus, *Seven against Thebes* 743–9).[39] And in Sophocles' version in *Oedipus Tyrannus*, Oedipus' homecoming, which seemingly saved the *polis* from the Sphinx, turned out to be in actuality only a means of paving the way to incest, having been preceded by parricide. Ruin can be avoided only by the dissolution of the accursed family: Jocasta dies, Oedipus is exiled, and Polynices and Eteocles slay each other, in spite of the fact that in certain versions of the myth Polynices willingly fled into exile to avoid the prophesied mutual fratricide and thus preserve the family.[40] In view of this fundamental antinomy between the welfare of the Labdacids and that of the city of Thebes, the character who comes out as profoundly anti-*polis*, at least in the first half of the play, is Antigone, not Creon, despite the latter's undeniably authoritarian strain, which is progressively exacerbated as the play unfolds (see further below).

Viewed in this light, Antigone's defiance of the laws of the *polis* is essentially a manifestation of her family's incompatibility with the public weal. When Antigone voices for the first time her opposition to Creon's edict, the Coryphaeus comments that the girl is patently the savage (ὠμός) offspring of a savage father (471–2):

(Χο.) δῆλον· τὸ γέννημ' ὠμὸν ἐξ ὠμοῦ πατρὸς
τῆς παιδός· εἴκειν δ' οὐκ ἐπίσταται κακοῖς.

    δῆλον Nauck : δηλοῖ mss.

CHORUS It is obvious: the girl is the savage offspring of a savage father; she doesn't know how to yield to misfortune.

If Antigone is 'savage' in the eyes of the Chorus, her attitude is described as ὕβρις by Creon – an indictment that receives special emphasis (*Ant.* 480–3):

(Κρ.) αὕτη δ' ὑβρίζειν μὲν τότ' ἐξηπίστατο
νόμους ὑπερβαίνουσα τοὺς προκειμένους·
ὕβρις δ', ἐπεὶ δέδρακεν, ἥδε δευτέρα,
τούτοις ἐπαυχεῖν καὶ δεδρακυῖαν γελᾶν.

CREON: She knew how to show *hubris* back then, when she transgressed the established laws; and now that she has committed the crime, this is a second instance of her *hubris*: to brag and gloat about what she has done.

Moreover, both Antigone and her sister are castigated by Creon as 'two ruinous creatures' (ἄτα), insofar as they are potential overthrowers of the legitimate ruler (*Ant.* 531–3):

(Κρ.) σὺ δ᾽, ἣ κατ᾽ οἴκους ὡς ἔχιδν᾽ ὑφειμένη
λήθουσά μ᾽ ἐξέπινες, οὐδ᾽ ἐμάνθανον
τρέφων δύ᾽ ἄτα κἀπαναστάσεις θρόνων

CREON: As for you [=Ismene], you were a viper lurking in my house and stealthily draining me dry; and I wasn't aware that I was nurturing two ruinous creatures, two overthrowers of my royal power.[41]

Especially interesting here is the comparison of Ismene to a viper. In ancient animal lore 'the most notorious belief about the echidna [...] was that the female bit the male to death in the act of mating'.[42] The image of the lurking female viper is aptly chosen by Creon as an illustration of what he perceives as Ismene's domestic treachery,[43] the more so since the coital context of the viper's aggression must have had especial resonance among an audience attuned to echoes of the Labdacids' sexual deviance and sensible to its disastrous consequences.

Both Creon's disparagements and the choral statements with respect to Antigone's behaviour touch upon central concepts of archaic Greek political thought. In particular, the association between ὕβρις, ὠμότης, and the overthrowing of political order (cf. κἀπαναστάσεις θρόνων above) occurs already in the prominently political poetry of Theognis, whose date seems to fall around the middle of the archaic era (second half of the seventh century BC):[44]

δειμαίνω μὴ τήνδε πόλιν, Πολυπαΐδη, ὕβρις   541
ἥ περ Κενταύρους ὠμοφάγους ὀλέσῃ.

I fear, son of Polypaos, lest this *polis* is destroyed by the *hubris* that ruined the Centaurs, eaters of raw flesh.

Moreover, later in the play (834–37) the Chorus, taking their cue from Antigone's self-comparison to Niobe, consider it praiseworthy that Antigone should share, both in life and in death, the lot of those who, like Niobe, Zeus' granddaughter, were equal to the gods (τοῖς ἰσοθέοις, 837). This is an extravagant claim, which Antigone herself is quick to rebut as being tantamount to an insult (839–41). But the very extravagance of this statement invites us to ponder its meaning. The Chorus' comparison of Antigone to an ἰσόθεος figure like Niobe may be meant to balance their earlier use of ὠμὸν ἐξ ὠμοῦ πατρός (471) with reference again to Antigone. Significantly, ὠμός is used in this play only once again, with reference to the 'raw-eating' (697 ὠμηστῶν) dogs that devoured Polynices.[45] If Antigone can, paradoxically, be both ἰσόθεος and ὠμός at once, it is because she combines traits that place her on a par with the gods and at the same time make her equal in savagery and brutality to the beasts. This paradox recalls Aristotle's famous aphorism, to the effect that whoever cannot form part of a political community must qualify either as a beast or as a god (*Politics* 1253a27–9, ὁ δὲ μὴ δυνάμενος κοινωνεῖν ἢ μηδὲν δεόμενος δι' αὐτάρκειαν οὐδὲν μέρος πόλεως, ὥστε ἢ θηρίον ἢ θεός). Antigone, as we have seen, refuses to keep herself within the *polis*, its structures, and its statutes. In this respect, her parallelism with Niobe may extend even further. Niobe is emphatically marginal: she is called a Phrygian ξένα (824), whose residence in Thebes was only temporary; she is now at the remotest heights of Sipylus (825–6), where she lies exposed to the rage of the natural elements (828–32). Likewise, Antigone does not fully belong to the body of Theban citizens: her life in the upper world is described as μετοικία by Creon (890), and she maintains her marginal status as μέτοικος even as she goes to her death (850–2, 868). The location of her tomb, like that of Niobe's, is also characteristically marginal: it is at a place where no mortal sets his foot (773),[46] beyond the boundaries of the *polis*.[47]

Interestingly, Antigone's rejection of collectivity and her concomitant adhesion to her implosive family is often castigated as sheer folly or even madness – first by Ismene (67–8, οὐκ ἔχει νοῦν οὐδένα; 98–9, ἄνους), then by the Chorus (381–3, ἐν ἀφροσύνῃ), then by Creon, with Ismene chiming in (561–4):

(Κρ.) τὼ παῖδε φημὶ τώδε τὴν μὲν ἀρτίως　　　　　　　　　　　561
ἄνουν πεφάνθαι, τὴν δ' ἀφ' οὗ τὰ πρῶτ' ἔφυ.
(Ἰσ.) οὐ γάρ ποτ', ὦναξ, οὐδ' ὃς ἂν βλάστῃ μένει
νοῦς τοῖς κακῶς πράσσουσιν, ἀλλ' ἐξίσταται.

CREON: I say that one of these two girls has just shown how mindless she is, whereas the other has been so since the day she was born.
ISMENE: Indeed, my king, for even what inborn sense one has goes astray in misfortunes, nor does it stay in place.[48]

By contrast, Creon the statesman had pointed out (175–7) that 'a man's soul, his counsels and his opinions' are displayed most patently in the exercise of political authority; accordingly, he had insisted on the cardinal importance of sound-mindedness (ἀρίστων ... βουλευμάτων) for the successful steering of the ship of state and the avoidance of communal ruin (178–81, quoted on p. 87 above).[49] The Chorus seem to concur with Creon when, in the second stasimon, they refer to the Labdacids as a clan that has been collectively afflicted by (self-)destructive madness (582–624):

(Χο.) εὐδαίμονες οἷσι κακῶν ἄγευστος αἰών·
οἷς γὰρ ἂν σεισθῇ θεόθεν δόμος, ἄτας
οὐδὲν ἐλλείπει γενεᾶς ἐπὶ πλῆθος ἕρπον·　　　　　　　　　　　585
...
ἀρχαῖα τὰ Λαβδακιδᾶν οἴκων ὁρῶμαι　　　　　　　　　　　594
πήματα φθιτῶν ἐπὶ πήμασι πίπτοντ',　　　　　　　　　　　595

οὐδ' ἀπαλλάσσει γενεὰν γένος, ἀλλ' ἐρείπει
θεῶν τις, οὐδ' ἔχει λύσιν.
νῦν γὰρ ἐσχάτας ὑπὲρ
ῥίζας ἐτέτατο φάος ἐν Οἰδίπου δόμοις·   600
κατ' αὖ νιν φοινία
θεῶν τῶν νερτέρων ἀμᾷ κοπίς,
λόγου τ' ἄνοια καὶ φρενῶν Ἐρινύς.
τεάν, Ζεῦ, δύνασιν τίς ἀν–
δρῶν ὑπερβασία κατάσχοι;   605
...
σοφίᾳ γὰρ ἔκ του   620
κλεινὸν ἔπος πέφανται·
τὸ κακὸν δοκεῖν ποτ' ἐσθλὸν
τῷδ' ἔμμεν, ὅτῳ φρένας
θεὸς ἄγει πρὸς ἄταν

    595 φθιτῶν Hermann : φθιμένων mss.   602 κοπίς Jortin : κόνις mss.

CHORUS: Fortunate are they whose lifetime never tastes of evil! For those whose house is shaken by the gods, no part of ruin is wanting, as it marches against the whole of the family [...] From ancient times I see the troubles of the dead of the Labdacid house falling hard upon one another, nor does one generation release another, but some one of the gods shatters them, and they have no means of deliverance. For lately the light spread out above the last root in the house of Oedipus; it too is mown down by the bloody scimitar of the gods below, folly of reasoning and an Erinys afflicting the mind. Zeus, what arrogance of men could restrict your power? [...] For in wisdom someone has revealed the famous saying, that evil seems good to him whose mind the god is driving towards disaster.

(Translation by Lloyd-Jones 1994, 59, 61, adapted.)

The 'bloody scimitar of the gods below' that strikes down the last surviving members of the Labdacid family operates through 'folly of reasoning[50] and an Erinys afflicting the mind' (603).[51] 'Folly', or infatuation, that leads to disaster is viewed in this stasimon as an inherent trait of the Labdacids; the chain reaction 'infatuation – transgression – disaster' is identified as the common denominator of the whole race's career from generation to generation. The allusion to Labdacus at the beginning of the first antistrophe (594, ἀρχαῖα τὰ Λαβδακιδᾶν etc.), as well as later in 862, is surely meant to bring out the *hereditary* nature of the evils that have beset the clan generation after generation.[52] The notion of ancestral guilt, and the concomitant belief that punishment for the sins of the ancestors may be visited upon their descendants, is of course a fundamental tenet of archaic Greek thought. Traces of it may be detectable already in Homer and archaic epic (especially the *Oedipodeia* and possibly the *Thebaid*), as was argued by H. Lloyd-Jones.[53] It surfaces most clearly, however, in Solon (fr. 13.25–32 West), who hopefully asserts that no transgression can go unpunished, since the offspring of sinners who escape punishment are certain to suffer in their stead.[54] Essentially the same idea recurs, in inverse form, in the poetry of the Theognidea (731–42), where Zeus is asked to punish sinners immediately rather than allow for the consequences of a father's wickedness (ἀτασθαλίαι) to be visited upon his children.[55] Indeed, as Dodds remarks (1951, 33), the idea that the successful sinner will be punished in his descendants is 'the characteristic archaic doctrine'; it relies on the notion of the family as an integrated structure, in which 'the son's life was a prolongation of his father's'. It is this doctrine that informs the Chorus' interpretation of the sufferings of the Labdacids, which seem to extend over a multitude of generations. This is, of course, a prominently Aeschylean idea too: in *Seven against Thebes*, for instance, each generation inherits a tendency to transgress or come to grief – a tendency memorably manifested as an Erinys of the *genos* and seen as partly the result of an ancestral curse (see esp. *Seven* 720–6, 741–91) – but still contributes to that outcome by its own deluded actions.[56]

The Chorus' emphasis on Zeus (604–5) as an agent of the destruction of the Labdacids is reflected in Antigone's own attitude towards the gods of the *polis*. While Creon, the advocate of communal σωτηρία, evokes Zeus or the Olympians on several occasions,[57] Antigone's appeals to Zeus are not to the Olympian deity but to Zeus' chthonic hypostasis – an aspect of the god already evidenced in the *Iliad* (9.457 Ζεὺς ... καταχθόνιος) and amply exampled in tragedy.[58] As MacKay points out (1962, 167), Antigone otherwise refers to Zeus only as a persecutor of her family (2–3), and generally professes no allegiance to Zeus or any other Olympian. Once again, Antigone places herself at the extreme opposite of the laws of the *polis*: her loyalties are with what constitutes the utter negation of a *polis*, namely Hades; instead of caring for salvation and welfare, she is determined to join the rest of her *philoi* in death. Admittedly, at *Ant.* 486–9 Creon does mention Zeus in an impious manner, when he declares that, even if Antigone were a closer blood-relative than Creon's closest family – τοῦ παντὸς...Ζηνὸς Ἑρκείου (487) – she would still not escape punishment; 'let her invoke Zeus of common blood' (ἐφυμνείτω Δία ξύναιμον), he adds at 658–9. However, Creon's hubristic reference to Zeus comes at a later stage, when his initial image of the high-principled leader has begun, slowly but steadily, to disintegrate (see further sections 4.1 and 4.2 below). Ironically, the self-same man who had earlier invoked Zeus (304) to witness his determination to punish the perpetrators of Polynices' burial, will descend further into impiety at 1039–44, when he declares that he will not be moved from his decision even if Zeus' eagles accepted as genuine: Polynices is a traitor whose defeat has been greeted with relief by the Chorus of Theban citizens (cf. 100–54), since it spelled the deliverance of the *polis* from mortal danger. Anyone who upholds the cause of the traitor must necessarily alienate himself or herself from the body politic, as Creon points out to Antigone in 508–10 σὺ τοῦτο μούνη τῶνδε Καδμείων ὁρᾷς ... σὺ δ' οὐκ ἐπαιδῇ τῶνδε χωρὶς εἰ φρονεῖς; ('You are the only one of the Cadmeians to see things this way... Are you not ashamed to set yourself apart from them?') The absurdity, in Creon's eyes, is further aggravated by the fact that Antigone is a woman, and so excluded by definition from the political sphere: the representative of the male-dominated, male-oriented *polis* cannot submit to a force as extraneous to it as a woman (cf. 484–5, 677–80, 740, 746, 756) – and, indeed, a woman who, by acting abnormally like a man (61–2), seeks to impose the interests of the *oikos*, the female domain *par excellence*, on those of the *polis*.[80]

More importantly, the incompatibility between Antigone's cause and the welfare of the *polis* is rendered all the more intense, to Creon's mind, because Antigone has been siding all along, by her own admission, with the 'laws' of Hades and the forces of annihilation rather than with those of the *polis* and its σωτηρία; the point is nicely brought out at the end of the pivotal third episode (780): πόνος περισσός ἐστι τὰν Ἄιδου σέβειν, 'it is useless toil to pay respect to what is in Hades'. To the communality of the *polis*, to its collective effort for σωτηρία, Antigone is simply alien: her life has been confined to the privacy of her family evils (463, κακοῖς),[81] so that death is for her the only conceivable benefit (463, 464).

5. Creon the Labdacid: re-enactments of family doom

For all his keenness on protecting the *polis* and promoting its welfare, Creon does not seem to realize that the absorption of the body politic into the person of its sovereign (cf. again p. 99 above) cannot be an end in itself. On the contrary, such an absorption is arguably legitimate only insofar as the sovereign guarantees the safety and advancement of the collective entity he embodies.[82] As we have seen, Creon's extreme position with regard to the sovereign's function leads, eventually, to the absurdity of a political leader lording it over a desolate city – an absurdity shrewdly pointed out by Haemon but never adequately answered by Creon (738–40, quoted on p. 98 above). In such an eventuality, the supposed defender of the common weal turns out in actuality to be the one who reduces it to the point of extinction. By contrast, Antigone, who has been ardently advocating the privileges of a doomed *oikos* and the 'laws' of Hades over those of the *polis*, is now seen as the one person who truly expresses the feelings of the *polis* in its entirety. The scandalous paradox is not merely ironical: it is also supremely significant for our assessment of the *polis* and its claims in *Antigone*.

Creon's deterioration into tyranny is confirmed by the very mouthpiece of the gods, Tiresias. The seer calls the king τύραννος (1056), and in the same breath adds an imputation of 'base covetousness' (αἰσχροκέρδεια). Ironically, Creon is the man who once vented his anger against his political opponents' lust for illegitimate 'gain' (κέρδος 310, 312) and for 'sordid profiteering' (αἰσχρῶν λημμάτων 313). The association of tyrants with lust for personal gain, which entails public detriment, especially since it leads to *stasis*, or factious conflict, is a well-documented *topos* of Greek political thought.[83]

A major way in which Creon's (and the *polis*') claims are surreptitiously undercut in the play is by means of Creon's gradual, almost imperceptible assimilation to the clan that brought ruin to Thebes: the Labdacids' hereditary self-destructiveness is finally catching up with him.[84] When, in the context of his altercation with Haemon, Creon states that his son stands no chance of marrying Antigone while she is alive (750), Haemon replies that 'her death will spell somebody else's destruction' (751) – an obvious allusion to his marriage-like suicide over Antigone's corpse towards the end of the play (1219–43). Creon, however, misconstrues this as threatened parricide (752): 'Do you have the nerve to come out against me with threats?'. The misunderstanding is significant insofar as it foreshadows the climactic lines 1231–4, where a 'wild-eyed' Haemon (cf. 1231, ἀγρίοις ὄσσοισι) does indeed attempt to stab his father. In its gradual assimilation to the Labdacids, Creon's house, like Laius' before him, seems to have become vulnerable to the germ of parricide.

We saw above (p. 93) that folly or madness has been seen in the course of the play as a trait typical of the Labdacids. However, Creon now finds himself accused, and by his own son at that, not merely of having unwise counsels (755, οὐκ εὖ φρονεῖν), but indeed of being nothing short of a 'madman' (765, μαίνῃ). Worse still, towards the end of the play Tiresias points in no uncertain terms to Creon's 'mind' as the source of the 'disease' that is afflicting the city (1015, καὶ ταῦτα τῆς σῆς ἐκ φρενὸς νοσεῖ πόλις), and directs further imputations of mental error against the monarch (1048–52, 1089–90; cf. also 1242, 1261–9). Creon's 'madness', Tiresias explains, consists in his having subverted cosmic order: he has sent a living person down to the Underworld, while keeping a dead man in the upper world (1068–73). The parallel with Antigone's case cannot go unnoticed: she, too, has attempted to reverse the cosmic boundaries by trying to impose the νόμοι of Hades on the upper world (cf. Creon's snide remarks in 777–80 and see p. 95 above), and her actions too have been described as 'madness'. It would appear that Creon is progressively becoming Antigone.

Creon's assimilation to the Labdacids becomes more pronounced towards the end of the play, in which the themes and patterns we have identified as typical of that doomed *oikos* are now associated with Creon and his own *oikos*. To begin with, the mental delusion (ἄτη) which has been such a conspicuous trait of the self-destructive Labdacids (see especially the second stasimon, partly quoted on pp. 93–4 above), now gets the better of Creon, despite his earnest efforts to avert it (cf. especially his opening speech, 184–91, quoted on p. 87 above).[85] At 1096–7 the man thanks to whom Thebes was led to safety (1058, 1162) finds himself dangerously close to ἄτη: ἀντιστάντα δὲ | ἄτῃ πατάξαι θυμὸν ἐν δεινῷ πάρα, 'if I resist there is danger I may crash my temper into ruin'.[86] The suspicion is eventually confirmed in a barbed choral comment shortly afterwards (1259–60): οὐκ ἀλλοτρίαν | ἄτην, ἀλλ' αὐτὸς ἁμαρτών, 'his ruin came not from others, but from his own error'.[87] What is more, Creon is now compelled to pay reverence to the infernal gods, Hecate and Pluto (1199–1200), like the self-destructive Antigone whom he himself had once mocked for revering only Hades of all gods (777–80).[88] Astonishingly, Creon goes as far as to abandon his devotion to the νόμοι of the *polis* and espouse the καθεστῶτες νόμοι, i.e. Antigone's 'unwritten laws' of Hades (1113–14):

δέδοικα γὰρ μὴ τοὺς καθεστῶτας νόμους
ἄριστον ᾖ σῴζοντα τὸν βίον τελεῖν.

CREON: For I am afraid that the best thing may be to go through life safeguarding established custom.[89]

At the end of the play, Creon even prays (like Antigone!) for death to come (1307–8, 1330–3): the safe harbour into which he once claimed to be able to lead the Ship of Thebes has now become an Ἅιδου λιμήν, a 'harbour of Hades' (1284).[90] For all his previous confident pronouncements about the gods and much else, Creon's fortunes suffer a major reversal: from champion of the welfare of the *polis* he becomes 'a living dead man' (1167, ἔμψυχον…νεκρόν). His fall exemplifies the characteristically archaic principle of mutability and alternation, according to which human fortune is precariously subject to dramatic change. As the Messenger says in 1158–60, 'it is Fortune that exalts and Fortune that brings down both the successful and the unsuccessful, as the case may be; and no one can divine the shape mortal life may take.'[91]

Most disturbingly, the self-destructive introversion that has crushed the Labdacids now becomes also a trait of Creon's own family – a development signalled again by an accumulation of αὐτο-words (cf. p. 86 above). Thus, Haemon's suicide, the first fatal blow dealt to Creon's family, is described with the phrase αὐτόχειρ…αἱμάσσεται, emphasized by the polyptoton αὐτὸς πρὸς αὑτοῦ (1175–7):[92]

(Αγ.) Αἵμων ὄλωλεν· αὐτόχειρ δ' αἱμάσσεται.　　　　　　　　　　1175
(Χο.) πότερα πατρῴας ἢ πρὸς οἰκείας χερός;
(Αγ.) αὐτὸς πρὸς αὑτοῦ, πατρὶ μηνίσας φόνου.

MESSENGER: Haemon is dead, stabbed by his own hand/by a kin's hand (αὐτόχειρ).[93]
CHORUS: By whose hand? His father's or his own?
MESSENGER: His very own; for he was enraged at his father because of (Antigone's) murder.

A similar phrase, παίσασ' ὑφ' ἧπαρ αὐτόχειρ αὑτήν (1315), is later used of Eurydice's suicide, which completes the collapse of Creon's *oikos*. The responsibility for these two deaths is put down to Creon, and so both of them are viewed as, in a way, instances of intrafamilial killing. This is made clear by Creon's first address to the Chorus, when he reappears on stage carrying the body of Haemon: both the killers, he says, and the victims are ἐμφύλιοι, members of the same family (1263–4):

ὦ κτανόντας τε καὶ
θανόντας βλέποντες ἐμφυλίους.

Being responsible for his son's death, Creon is called by Eurydice, in no uncertain terms, παιδοκτόνος, 'a murderer of his own child' (1305) – not only because he has been responsible for Haemon's death but also because, it is now implied, he may also have caused the death of his other son, Megareus:

(Εξ.) ἡ δ' ὀξυθήκτῳ βωμία περὶ ξ<ίφει>
λύει κελαινὰ βλέφαρα, κωκύσασα μὲν
τοῦ πρὶν θανόντος Μεγαρέως κενὸν λέχος,
αὖθις δὲ τοῦδε, λοίσθιον δὲ σοὶ κακὰς
πράξεις ἐφυμνήσασα τῷ παιδοκτόνῳ.　　　　　　　　　　1305

　　　1301 ὀξυθήκτῳ βωμία περὶ ξ<ίφει> Arndt : ὀξύθηκτος ἥδε βωμία πέριξ mss
　　　1303 κενόν Seyffert : κλεινόν mss.

EXANGELOS: And as she fell on the sharp-edged sword at the altar, she [sc. Eurydice] loosened her eyelids in the darkness of death, after bewailing the empty marriage-bed of Megareus, who had died before, then this boy's [sc. Haemon's] (empty marriage-bed), and finally adding curses for you, the son-killer.

Eurydice's brief appearance on stage, which is unprepared for and does not advance the plot in any way, seems to be motivated largely by emotional and symbolic considerations that bring the play's cardinal thematic concerns to an appropriate close. Eurydice must hear of Haemon's pathetic demise so that she may subsequently sacrifice herself on the house altar (1301, βωμία),[94] in a characteristically tragic perversion of sacrificial ritual that seems to seal the fate of Creon and his family. Her highly emotional lamentations, as described in the Exangelos' report, offer a harrowing if terse description of the collapse of Creon's house. As well as bewailing Haemon's 'marriage in Hades' (cf. 1240–1), which has deprived him of an actual marriage, Eurydice mentions in the same breath the earlier demise of another child of hers, Megareus, whose death seems to have been brought about by the παιδοκτόνος Creon.[95] The mention of Megareus, brief as it may be, is quite unexpected and thus stands out as a salient feature of the mother's lament: the dead boy's 'empty marriage-bed' (1303, κενὸν λέχος),[96] signifying his own cancelled marriage, only confirms that Creon's house is doomed to extinction, its male line completely and utterly obliterated, like that of Oedipus' own *oikos*. Hades has indeed stayed the weddings of Creon's sons, as the monarch himself had grimly foretold at 575.[97] Eurydice's death, for which Creon takes full responsibility (1319–20 'It was me, me, that killed you, o wretched that I am, it was me, I'm telling the truth'), merely hammers home the same point: with both his descendants and his wife dead, Creon must abandon all hope for a continuation of his bloodline.[98]

If Creon is a παιδοκτόνος, or 'killer of his own child', as Eurydice calls him, Haemon too has attempted, conversely, to be a πατροκτόνος, a 'killer of his own father': before committing suicide, he drew the sword and attempted to murder his father, who escaped at the last moment (see 1231–4). Even so, however, Creon does not escape (virtual) death: he calls himself 'a man already dead' at 1288 (ὀλωλότ' ἄνδρ' ἐπεξειργάσω) and 'nothing more than a nobody' at 1325 (τὸν οὐκ ὄντα μᾶλλον ἢ μηδένα). The last time we heard this kind of phrase was at 1029–30, when Tiresias described Creon's prohibition of the burial of Polynices as 'killing a man already dead':

(Τε.) ἀλλ' εἶκε τῷ θανόντι, μηδ' ὀλωλότα
κέντει. τίς ἀλκὴ τὸν θανόντ' ἐπικτανεῖν; 1130

TIRESIAS: Yield to the dead man, don't prod a corpse. What good is it to slay a man already dead?

Far from being mere tropes, such expressions point to an important theme that lies at the core of *Antigone*. The dead Polynices, far from being 're-killed' by Creon, becomes himself the cause of the king's 'death' by means of a fatal chain of events: first, Antigone is 'killed' by her dead brother (871, θανὼν ἔτ' οὖσαν κατήναρές με, 'you, a dead man, have destroyed me, a living person'); then, Antigone in turn 'kills' Haemon (751, ἥδ' οὖν θανεῖται, καὶ θανοῦσ' ὀλεῖ τινα, 'she will die, then, and her death will spell somebody else's destruction'); and finally Haemon, with his death, eventually 'kills' his father (1288, 1325, quoted above).[99]

Thus, the Labdacids finally get the better of Creon's *oikos*, and in a twofold manner at that. First, Creon's *oikos* collapses under the burden of multiple intrafamilial killings, as an almost exact replica of the house of Labdacus. Second, the very act by which Creon tried to 'rekill' Polynices, namely the prohibition of burial, in fact recoils upon him and leads to the destruction of his own house as well as his own death (symbolic, insofar as his bloodline becomes extinct).[100]

6. The *polis* and the gods

Put in a nutshell, the central theme of the *Antigone* is the defeat of the *polis* and its institutions by the individual, self-contained, and self-destructive *oikos*.[101] Creon starts off as an embodiment of the fundamental principle of νόμος, on which every well-governed *polis* must be grounded. His prohibition of Polynices' burial is directed both against a man who nearly destroyed his own homeland and against the excessive autonomy of the individual household, which may undermine the fundamentally collective nature of the *polis*. Nonetheless, in *Antigone* the *polis*' attempt to exert control over the autonomous house, by placing the collective σωτηρία above family or individual privileges, is tragically vitiated. Significantly, as we have seen (p. 104 above), Creon himself has to concede, eventually, that it is best to adhere to the καθεστῶτες νόμοι (1113–14), the 'unwritten laws' Antigone had professed allegiance to. This is tantamount to recognizing that he has failed to live up to his most important principle of all, that the safety of the city comes first. His absolute faith in the all-encompassing, all-absorbing Leviathan of the State concealed, inevitably, a tyrannical streak, which eventually gets the better of him. His despotic, if principled, opposition to the claims of Antigone's *polis*-endangering *oikos* results in a major transgression against cosmic order, thereby causing collective pollution and setting the whole *polis* at peril. Most disturbingly, as we have seen (section 5 above), Creon's *oikos* is finally destroyed in a fashion strikingly similar to that of the Labdacids. All in all, then, in our play it is not the anomic, unhealthy *oikos* that submits to the general interest of the *polis*, but the *polis* (as represented by the defender of its safety, Creon) that is reduced to the status of the anomic and unhealthy *oikos*.

Antigone defies easy taxonomies. On the one hand, the importance of unwritten laws in Greek civic life is historically undeniable,[102] and Antigone's vindication at the end of the play must be accepted as a consequence of this importance. On the other hand, in this particular case Antigone's championing of the unwritten laws involves defending a traitor who almost achieved the annihilation of Thebes (110–26), while she herself, the last member of a doomed *oikos*, expressly prefers Hades to the σωτηρία which is such an important part of the essence of a *polis* (see especially Plato, again a later counterpart in Hobbes, whose unwavering faith in an all-encompassing Sovereign led him to affirm that the attributes of the divine are to be determined and enjoined by the Head of State:

> And because words (and consequently the Attributes of God) have their signification by agreement, and constitution of men; those Attributes are to be held significative of Honour, that men intend shall so be; and whatsoever may be done by the wills of particular men, where there is no Law but Reason, may be done by the will of the Common-wealth, by Lawes Civill. And because a Common-wealth hath no Will, nor makes no Lawes, but those that are made by the Will of him, or them that have the Soveraign Power; it followeth, that those Attributes which the Soveraign ordaineth, in the Worship of God, for signes of Honour, ought to be taken and used for such, by private men in their publique Worship.[109]

This tension between the state and the gods can lead to acute paradoxes and even to a deadlock position, as it does in our play; and from this deadlock *Antigone* provides no way out.[110] All we can do is recognize that our intellectual resources do not allow us to proceed beyond the simple realization that human and divine laws seem to be irreconcilably different and that, worse still, abiding by either of them does not guarantee avoidance of catastrophe. The theme of late learning with which the play ends (cf. 1270, 1353) is a reminder that knowledge comes, painfully if at all, only when it is too late and when no profit can be made of it.[111]

Acknowledgement
An earlier, briefer draft of this paper was presented at the colloquium on 'Tragedy and Archaic Greek Thought' held at the University of Edinburgh from 13 to 15 June 2008. I thank the organizers, Douglas Cairns and Michael Lurje, for their hospitality, and members of the audience, especially Alex Garvie, Scott Scullion, and Richard Seaford, for their criticisms. A somewhat different version was presented at the colloquim 'De la philologie: théorie et pratique (en hommage à Jean Bollack)' held at the Université Charles de Gaulle (Lille III) from 23 to 25 October 2008. I thank Jean Bollack, Vittorio Citti, Philippe Rousseau, and Renate Schlesier for their remarks. The final draft was read and commented on by Ryan Balot, Clifford Orwin, and Anton Powell: I am deeply grateful to all of them for perceptive and often salutary remarks. A special word of thanks is owed to Douglas Cairns, who painstakingly went through multiple versions of this paper and offered shrewd advice. Naturally, none of the above can be held responsible for the use I have made of their remarks. All translations are mine, unless otherwise indicated.

Notes

[1] On the reception of *Antigone* in the literature and thought of the West, see in the first place Steiner 1984; cf. also e.g. Sommer 1998; Daskarolis 2000, esp. 48–66, 72–87, 181–4, 314–49; Rosenfield 2003; Brezzi 2004; Pöggeler 2004. For an overview of earlier scholarship on *Antigone*, especially of the 'Antigone-as-noble-martyr' approach, see Hester 1971, 11–19; cf. also Holt 1999, 659 n. 4, 660 n. 5.

[2] Quotation from Bloom 1987, 228.

[3] See especially Sourvinou-Inwood 1989a; Bollack 1999, 54; *idem* in Bollack et al. 2004, 45. For an overview of critical objections raised to Antigone's moral stance see Foley 2001, 196–200.

[4] That Antigone is cast, initially at least, as a subverter of *polis* order has been most eloquently argued by Sourvinou-Inwood 1989a, whose influence on my own reading of *Antigone* I readily admit. However, my paper is intended to be more nuanced and less polarized than hers.

[5] See further Cerri 1979.

[6] See e.g. Alexiou 2002, 18–22; Seaford 1994, 74–105. On the sociology of grave offerings and funeral display in Athens see further Morris 1992, 103–155; Humphreys 1993, 79–134.

[7] On the antagonism between the old clans and the *polis* see also Knox 1964, 76; Sorum 1981–2, 201–4; Oudemans and Lardinois 1987, 98 with further bibliography.

[8] See Alexiou 2002, 14–18; Bennett and Tyrrell 1990, 444–5, 455; Foley 1993b, 103–7; Seaford 1994, 74–5, 78–92. Admittedly, as Alexiou 2002, 19–21 and Seaford 1994, 100–1 have shown, Solonian legislation privileged the *oikos* at the expense of the larger family group or clan (*genos*). However, in *Antigone* – as in the *Oresteia* – the dichotomy is between family and state: in the *Oresteia* the antinomy seems to be resolved by the foundation of a *polis* institution, the Areopagus (cf. e.g. Knox 1964, 77–8; Seaford 1994, 74–105), whereas in our play the antinomy leads to mutual destruction and therefore remains irresolvable.

[9] Cf. the concept of the 'historical moment of tragedy' defined by Vernant in Vernant and Vidal-Naquet 1990, 23–8 as an opposition 'between legal and political thought on the one hand and the mythical and heroic traditions on the other' (quotation from p. 27). As a result of this opposition, *Antigone* – and Greek tragedy in general, according to Vernant – 'depicts...one *dikē* in conflict with another, a law that is not fixed, shifting and changing into its opposite', much as the respective evaluations of the characters of Creon and Antigone shift and change in the course of the play (cf. in the text above).

[10] The critic is Holt 1999, 673–5.

[11] The most eloquent proponent of this thesis is Heath 1987, 73–7, esp. 75.

[12] Cf. Sourvinou-Inwood 1989a, 138; *contra* Porter 2009.

[13] Cf. Podlecki 1966, 360; Knox 1983, 13. With regard to *Ant.* 44 ἦ γὰρ νοεῖς θάπτειν σφ', ἀπόρρητον πόλει; I should be inclined, with Kamerbeek 1978, ad 44, to take πόλει as dative of interest rather than *dativus auctoris*: the decree is regarded as having been issued by the monarch rather than by a body of citizens. However, the ambiguity might be significant, insofar as Ismene tends to regard Creon's decree as equivalent to one issued *by* the body politic: cf. Podlecki 1966, 363 n. 14; Blundell 1989, 111 n. 24. See also immediately below in the text.

[14] See Kamerbeek 1978, ad 58–60; cf. also Calder 1968, 392 n. 20; Knox 1964, 63, 82–3.

[15] See further Jaeger 1947, 126–7 with n. 63; Kahn 1979, 179–81; Robinson 1987, ad loc.; *contra* Kamerbeek 1948, 94. Marcovich 1967, 537 prefers to translate νόμος as 'conformable to custom and tradition' here, thus mitigating the 'totalitarian' tone of the fragment. However, aside from the fact that this is no more than one of many possibilities (see Robinson 1987, 103), it weakens the force of the fragment almost to the point of tautology. A more extreme version of this idea is attributed to Solon (fr. 30 West): ἀρχῶν ἄκουε καὶ δικαίως κἀδίκως; but the attribution is almost certainly erroneous, and occurs mainly in late paroemiographic texts (see West's *testimonia*); cf. also *P.Oxy.* xlii (1974) 3006, col. i.10 ἄρχοντι π(ε)ίθου καὶ δικαίως κἀδίκως, wrongly labelled by ed. pr. P. Parsons as 'unidentified': see Diggle 1975.

[16] Cf. Kirkwood 1958, 239 n. 21; Rohdich 1980, 171; Sourvinou-Inwood 1989a, 139–40. Cropp 1997, 150–1 shows that Creon's edict must be seen as implying communal assent; contrast, less convincingly, Blundell 1989, 147; Meier 1993, 198; Tyrrell and Bennett 1998, 77, 116. Rösler 1993, 91–2 insists that 904–20 are spurious, and so dismisses 907. However, the authenticity of 904–20 has been convincingly argued for by Neuburg 1990, esp. 66–76, who avoids culturally conditioned assumptions and focuses instead on the play's thematic concerns and structural patterns. Neuburg's excellent article not only offers a detailed account of the *status quaestionis* but also expounds some basic methodological presuppositions for its solution. Cf. also Zellner 1997; S. West 1999, 130–2; Tyrrell and Bennett 1998, 112–15; and particularly Cropp 1997, who offers an analysis of Antigone's final speech 'as a rhetorical whole', of which 904–20 form an integral part.

[17] Cf. Foley 2001, 176.

[18] Cf. Ostwald 1986, 156 against viewing Antigone as a champion of individual liberties opposing state tyranny. Holt 1999, 681 aptly remarks that Antigone 'is driven by will, pride, and family honor at least as much as by devotion to the unwritten laws.'

[19] See Maitland 1992, esp. 32–3.

[20] Cf. Benardete 1975a, 155–6; Goldhill 1986, 102–3, 105; Sourvinou-Inwood 1989a, 138, 140. Antigone's yearning for eternal physical contact with her dead brother plays on the pervading and multifarious associations between marriage and death in Greek culture: see Seaford 1987.

[21] Cf. Benardete 1975a, 159; Winnington-Ingram 1980, 130; Steiner 1984, 88, 158–60; Oudemans and Lardinois 1987, 172 with bibliography; Blundell 1989, 108 n. 12; most importantly, Seaford 1990, 78 with n. 9 for documentation. For a comparison with similar *quasi*-erotic language in E. *Pho.* see Seaford 1994, 350 n. 74; for further possible erotic undertones see Rehm 1994, 59; M. Griffith 2005, 95–6. There is no notion here of an 'afterlife' in which Antigone's piety will be 'rewarded', as Ahrensdorf 2009, 100 imagines. Antigone's obsession with the idea of spending eternity with her dead kin has nothing metaphysical about it, and nothing could be more alien to her way of thinking than the expectation of posthumous rewards.

[22] Zellner 1997, 316–17.

[23] Tyrrell and Bennett 1998, 66–8 associate the bird-imagery with augury and thus with potentially ominous developments for Creon's house, especially in relation to marriage. Ormand 1999, 91 ably discusses the passage's erotic language but refrains from pointing out its incestuous implications. At S. *El.* 1143–8 Electra is also said to have been a mother to Orestes, and in this case too the substitution of a sister for a mother evinces an anomaly (although not an incestuous one) in family relations: Clytaemestra, the physical mother, is a μήτηρ ἀμήτωρ (1154).

[24] On αὐτοκτονοῦντε see also Loraux 1986, 173–4. For αὐτοκτόνος, αὐτοφόνος, αὐτοσφαγής, and related formations see also Fraenkel 1950 on A. *Ag.* 1091 ff.; Hutchinson 1985 on A. *Th.* 734–41; Sommerstein 1989 on A. *Eum.* 211; Mastronarde 2002 on E. *Med.* 1253–4. Cf. further Parker 1983, 122 with n. 69; Belfiore 2000, 23–4, 81–100 (esp. 82–5), 127, 131, 134–5, 147. On αὐτο-compounds in *Antigone* see the exhaustive treatment of Loraux 1986; cf. also Knox 1964, 79; Else 1976, 27–8; C. P. Segal 1981, 186 with n. 103; Rehm 1994, 65–6; Bollack in Bollack et al. 2004, 82; Santagostini in Bollack et al. 2004, 83–4.

[25] Cf. again Loraux 1986, 174, 176; M. Griffith 2001, 127 and 2005, 94.

[26] On the duals as signs of the sisters' 'troubled closeness – and of the uncomfortable and intricate family history and relations that produced it' see M. Griffith 2001, 127.

[27] See Clarke 2001; quotation from his p. 371. Cf. also M. Griffith 2005, 129 n. 71.

[28] On the *Antigone* quotation in Demosthenes see further Perlman 1964, 170–1. On the uses of tragedy (including tragic quotations) in fourth-century oratory see Wilson 1996.

[29] The quotation is from Heath 1987, 75, one of Creon's detractors. See also Tyrrell and Bennett 1998, 46–7.

[30] Thus Heath 1987, 75.

[31] Though this image strictly refers to the Argive enemies as a whole, it is Polynices that is brought out as the primary instigator of the expedition: cf. Burton 1980, 93 and esp. Craik 1986, 103–4, who further shows how Polynices comes to be identified with the Argive army by means of poetic ambiguity (*contra* Davidson 1986, 108 with n. 7). For possible literary precedents for the eagle-simile see Davidson 1983, 44; the eagle-and-snake omen in *Il.* 12.200–29 (cf. Burton 1980, 93 n. 8) is particularly relevant, since it is Ares' *serpent* that is in this song a symbol of the Theban defence (124–6).

[32] For detailed discussions of relevant ancient sources see Hester 1971, 55; Rosivach 1983, 193–4; Holt 1999, 663–5; and especially Diggle 2007; for a concise statement see Liddel 2007, 147–8.

[33] Thus e.g. Heath 1987, 75; Sourvinou-Inwood 1989a, 146–7; Kirkwood 1991, 108–9; Rösler 1993, 87.

[34] Quotation from Holt 1999, 665.

[35] See notably Cerri 1979, 17–32, 43–4; Rosivach 1983, 194 with nn. 3, 4; 208 n. 49; Holt 1999, 665–6. Cf. also Hester 1971, 20–1; Oudemans and Lardinois 1987, 101, 162.

[36] On execution by stoning in Athens see further Rosivach 1987.

[37] See Heath 1987, 75.

[38] See in particular Lloyd-Jones 2002, 3–12, esp. 5–7, 10–11 = 2005, 18–33, esp. 23–6, 30–1, with detailed discussion and full doxography. For the 'Pisander-scholium' see *FGrHist* 16 F 10; Mastronarde 1988, 10–11 (no. 11): ἱστορεῖ Πείσανδρος ὅτι κατὰ χόλον τῆς Ἥρας ἐπέμφθη ἡ Σφὶγξ τοῖς Θηβαίοις..., ὅτι τὸν Λάιον ἀσεβήσαντα εἰς τὸν παράνομον ἔρωτα τοῦ Χρυσίππου, ὃν ἥρπασεν ἀπὸ τῆς Πίσης, οὐκ ἐτιμωρήσαντο {αὐτόν}.

[39] See esp. Seaford 1993, 139; 1994, 347. Hutchinson 1985, xxviii–xxix seems to underestimate the significance of the city in the oracle. For further discussion, see Herrmann, this volume.

[40] Stesichorus *PMGF* 222b (Davies), Hellanicus *FGrHist* 4 F98 Jacoby: see Gantz 1993, 503. The better-known version of the myth is that of E. *Pho.* 67–74: Polynices goes willingly into exile, having agreed with his brother to rule alternately.

[41] On Antigone as an agent of subversion see further Tyrrell and Bennett 1998, 27–8, 42, 109–10.

[42] Quotation from Borthwick 1967, 250, where the relevant evidence is to be found. The earliest instances of this idea are Hdt. 3.109 and A. *Cho.* 247–9. Thus, it is appropriate that Sophocles elsewhere (*Tr.* 770–1) 'likens Deianeira's love-gift for Heracles to an echidna's poison feeding on his flesh' (Borthwick 1967, 251).

[43] So Jebb 1900b, ad 531.

[44] On the dating of Theognis see M. L. West 1974, 65–71.

[45] Further on the semantics of ὠμός in this play see Tyrrell and Bennett 1998, 72, 110.

[46] Following Kamerbeek's suggestion 1978, ad 773, 4 I read στίβου (not στίβος) and take ἐρῆμος to refer to Antigone (cf. 919): 'taking her to such a place that there she will be destitute of the steps of men' (cf. *Phil.* 487 ἐρῆμον οὕτω χωρὶς ἀνθρώπων στίβου).

[47] Cf. Reinhardt 1979, 81: 'the rock-chamber grave in which Antigone is buried alive...becomes an image of her halfway position, her rootless hovering'; cf. also C. P. Segal 1978, 1177 and 1981, 168; Sorum 1981–2, 207; Oudemans and Lardinois 1987, 188; Hutchinson 1999, 69.

[48] On Labdacid folly see Sourvinou-Inwood 1989a, 140–1; Bollack 1999, 27–35.

[49] For Creon's emphasis on intelligence and good sense see further M. Griffith 2001, 128.

[50] Not 'of speech', as it is often translated: for λόγος as 'reckoning', 'reasoning' etc. see LSJ s.v., I and III; cf. Else 1976, 27; Blundell 1989, 144 n. 154. As Lloyd-Jones 1957, 18 has shown, λόγου ... Ἐρινύς stands in apposition to κοπίς, and denotes the agents of the nether gods' destructive action (differently Booth 1959; T. Long 1974; Easterling 1978, 147; Winnington-Ingram 1979, 7–8; Tyrrell and Bennett 1998, 82 n. 3). See also G. Müller 1967, 143; Brown 1987, ad 603. On the play's intellectual vocabulary, with its emphasis on right-mindedness and its opposites, see further Cropp 1997, 143–7.

[51] On the near-identification of ἄτη and Erinys here see Dawe 1968, 100–1; on their relation to ἄνοια cf. also Tyrrell and Bennett 1998, 81–4.

[52] Cf. Winnington-Ingram 1980, 166; Bollack 1999, 37–51; Mogyoródi 1996; on the internal corruption of the Labdacids, a family that 'is gnawing out its own heart', in the context of archaic ideas of inherited guilt see Parker 1983, 199–200. *Contra* Brown 1987, ad 593; more subtly Easterling 1978, 142, 152, 155–8. Recently, Sewell-Rutter 2007, 119 has attempted, in the wake of Parker 1999, 18–19 and M. L. West 1999, 40–1, to downplay the role of ancestral evils in Antigone's demise, arguing that references to the ancestral context of her woes are limited to 'some dozen lines of' her final *kommos*, esp. 856 where the Chorus tell Antigone that she is paying for some ancestral crime (πατρῷον δ' ἐκτίνεις τιν' ἆθλον), and Antigone does not disagree. We have just seen that intimations of ancestral doom run much deeper than that and inform a larger portion of the play than Sewell-Rutter allows.

[53] See Lloyd-Jones 2002 = 2005, 18–35.

[54] Parker 1983, 201 with n. 65 and, in his wake, Sewell-Rutter 2007, 19 suggest that essentially the same idea is detectable already in *Il.* 4. 160–5, where Agamemnon is confident that Zeus will eventually punish the truce-breaking Trojans together with their women and children. However, as Sewell-Rutter 2007, 19 n. 15 himself concedes, expanding on Parker, 'the destruction of *an offender together with his family* is distinct from the destruction of *his descendants only*, while he himself goes unpunished' (his emphasis).

[55] For the idea of inherited guilt in archaic poetry and especially in Greek tragedy see further Noussia-Fantuzzi 2010, 164–5.

[56] On the workings of Oedipus' curse and of the Labdacids' folly in *Seven* see I. Torrance 2007, 42–6.

[57] Cf. 184, ἴστω Ζεὺς ὁ πάνθ' ὁρῶν ἀεί; 304, εἴπερ ἴσχει Ζεὺς ἔτ' ἐξ ἐμοῦ σέβας; 758, ...τόνδ' Ὄλυμπον.

[58] See Knox 1964, 99 with n. 33, and cf. A. *Su.* 231, Ζεὺς ἄλλος ἐν καμοῦσιν; *Ag.* 1386–7, τοῦ κατὰ χθονὸς | Διός (Enger : Ἅιδου codd.); fr. **273a Radt, χθόνιον Δία; E. fr. 912.2–3 Kannicht, Ζεὺς εἴθ' Ἅιδης | ὀνομαζόμενος στέργεις; further sources in M. L. West 1978 on Hes. *Op.* 465; cf. also Burkert 1985, 200 with 426 n. 14.

[59] On the Chorus' 'studiously non-committal' (Winnington-Ingram 1980, 123) reply as an early warning sign of the tyrannical streak in Creon's character see Holt 1999, 676 n. 53 with further bibliography. Sourvinou-Inwood 1989a, 142 denies that there may lurk here any disturbing allusions to Creon's tyrannical mindset, because in the Thebes of tragic myth it would have been normal for a single person to sway political authority.

[60] See Holt 1999, 672–87; the quotation is from p. 672. One gradually realizes, in retrospect, that Creon was setting himself up for a fall when he proclaimed (*Ant.* 175–7) that you cannot judge a man's character until he has been tested in office: he will be tested soon enough, and found wanting.

[61] On the play's suggestions that Antigone may be enjoying supernatural help see further Tyrrell and Bennett 1998, 66–8.

[62] Cf. e.g. Adams 1957, 49–50; Kitto 1956, 153–6; Knox 1964, 68–9 with n. 14; Jordan 1979, 92–3; C. P. Segal 1981, 159–60; Minadeo 1985, 143–6. For counterarguments see Hester 1971, 25; Burton 1980, 95–6; Sourvinou-Inwood 1989a, 142 with n. 31.

[63] On the date of Theognis see again n. 44.

[64] See the commentary by Nagy 1985, 42–6.

[65] On the equivalence of divine and civic laws in Creon's political theology see G. Müller 1967, 75–6; Goldhill 1986, 95–6; Foley 2001, 183. Still, the majority of scholars disregards the political legitimacy of Creon's discourse: see e.g. Gellie 1972, 35; Winnington-Ingram 1980, 125–6; C. P. Segal 1981, 169; Scodel 1984, 52; Nussbaum 1986, 58; Blundell 1989, 129; Bennett and Tyrrell 1990, 444.

[66] S. West 1999, 127 n. 72 appositely cites, as a parallel to Creon's despotism, the Danaids' view of the monarch as identical with the body politic (A. *Su.* 370–5, cf. esp. 370, σύ τοι πόλις, σὺ δὲ τὸ δάμιον), a view rejected by Pelasgus as excessively autocratic (397–401), though not 'unhellenic' as West claims.

[67] On Hobbes' political philosophy, and on his readings of Thucydides, see Ryan 1996; Evrigenis 2006.

[68] Quotation from Hobbes 1651, 87 = Tuck 1996, 120 (italics in the original). On Hobbes' view of the sovereign as the representative of the people see further Tuck 1996, xxxiv–xxxviii. The idea found its way even into the work of the otherwise antiauthoritarian Rousseau 1762, 22 = Grimsley 1972, 117–18: 'Or le Souverain n'étant formé que des particuliers qui le composent n'a ni ne peut avoir d'intérêt contraire au leur; par conséquent la puissance Souveraine n'a nul besoin de garant envers les sujets, parce qu'il est impossible que le corps veuille nuire à tous ses membres, & nous verrons ci-après qu'il ne peut nuire à aucun en particulier. Le Souverain, par cela seul qu'il est, est toujours tout ce qu'il doit être.'

[69] Hobbes 1651, 90 = Tuck 1996, 124.

[70] I am referring to 37th US President Richard M. Nixon's infamous remark, during an interview with David Frost (aired on television on May 19, 1977), that 'when the President does it, that means that it is not illegal'.

[71] Hobbes 1651, 92 = Tuck 1996, 126.

[72] διὰ καταφρόνησιν δὲ καὶ στασιάζουσι καὶ ἐπιτίθενται, οἷον ἔν τε ταῖς ὀλιγαρχίαις, ὅταν πλείους ὦσιν οἱ μὴ μετέχοντες τῆς πολιτείας (κρείττους γὰρ οἴονται εἶναι), καὶ ἐν ταῖς δημοκρατίαις οἱ εὔποροι καταφρονήσαντες τῆς ἀταξίας καὶ ἀναρχίας, οἷον καὶ ἐν Θήβαις μετὰ τὴν ἐν Οἰνοφύτοις μάχην κακῶς πολιτευομένων ἡ δημοκρατία διεφθάρη, καὶ ἡ Μεγαρέων δι' ἀταξίαν καὶ ἀναρχίαν ἡττηθέντων, 'factional strife and aggressive action result from contempt, as happens in oligarchic regimes, when those who have no part in the government constitute the majority (for they think they are superior), and also in democratic regimes, when the wealthy grow contemptuous of disorder and anarchy; for instance, in Thebes the democratic regime was ruined due to poor government after the battle at Oenophyta [457 BC]; and in Megara [the democratic party] was defeated as a result of disorder and anarchy.' On the legend of radical democracy and disorder in archaic Megara see Forsdyke 2005.

[73] Thgn. 677, Solon 13.11W with the commentary of Levine 1985, 181–2, 184, 186. For κόσμος as the Spartan word for 'social order' see Nagy 1985, 32, 41 §25n2); for κόσμοι as an official designation of magistrates in Crete see LSJ s.v. κόσμος III; Nagy 1990, 180 n. 141.

[74] Thuc. 4.76.2; 8.48.4, 67.3, 72.2; Hdt. 1.65.4; Pl. *Prt.* 322c. See LSJ s.v. κόσμος I.4.

[75] The point is well made by C. P. Segal 1981, 188.

[76] διόπερ οὐδὲν μᾶλλον ἄρχειν ἢ ἄρχεσθαι δίκαιον, καὶ τὸ ἀνὰ μέρος τοίνυν ὡσαύτως.

[77] See Miller 1995, 234–9, with refutation of earlier views.

[78] Cf. e.g. Podlecki 1966, 362: '[Creon] must cover up his insecurity with well-sounding, if somewhat muddled, political platitudes'; Holt 1999, 681: 'Kreon's long speech in this *agon* (*Ant.* 639–80) is a remarkable piece of generality and irrelevance.'

[79] For an especially forceful statement of the orthodox view on Creon see S. West 1999, esp. 124–32. She sees Creon not only as a stereotypical stage tyrant but also as a Cambyses-like embodiment of everything the Greeks found repulsive about Oriental autocracy.

[80] For gender tensions as dramatized in *Antigone* cf. e.g. Knox 1964, 78–9; Bryson Bongie 1974, 250; C. P. Segal 1978, 1179 and 1981, 183–6, 192; Sorum 1981–2, 205–6; Steiner 1983, 87–8 and 1984, 185–6, 238–41; Goldhill 1986, 98; Sourvinou-Inwood 1989a, 140. It is true that, as Foley 1981, 148–63 warns, real life might very probably belie such too clear-cut polarities between male and female; what matters, of course, is the way the *ideology* of the *polis* represented such polarities.

[81] On the interpretation of 463 see Kamerbeek 1978, ad 463, 4 and Brown 1987, ad 463 who see here a reference to the prologue (1–6).

[82] Indeed, this point is crucial to Hobbes' argument; cf. Hobbes 1651, 114 = Tuck 1996, 153: 'The Obligation of Subjects to the Sovereign, is understood to last as long, and no longer, than the power lasteth, by which he is able to protect them. For the right men have by Nature to protect themselves, when none else can protect them, can by no Covenant be relinquished.' In this respect, Creon is perhaps best termed a Hobbesian *manqué*.

[83] See e.g. Nagy 1985, 36, 43–6, 52–3; 1990, 181–2, 263–7.

[84] On the archaic notion of ancestral guilt see again p. 94 with n. 52 above.

[85] On ἄτη in *Ant.* see Cairns's Introduction above. On the semantics of the term, see Sommerstein, this volume, arguing persuasively for 'harm' as the term's core meaning; Sommerstein also provides a useful survey of ἄτη in archaic literature. For further discussion, focusing on ἄτη in Homer, see Cairns 2012a, who argues for ἄτη having two basic senses in the Homeric poems: a focal (and 'objective') sense, 'harm', and a logically – and probably also chronologically – posterior 'subjective' sense, 'error', 'folly', 'delusion'. For an earlier treatment of ἄτη in Homer and the tragedians, focusing on its associations with mental error (ἁμαρτία), see Dawe 1968, esp. 95–123.

[86] For the textual problems here see Lloyd-Jones 1964.

[87] Translation by Lloyd-Jones 1994, 119. Cf. C. P. Segal 1981, 189–90.

[88] Cf. Oudemans and Lardinois 1987, 195.

[89] Cf. Knox 1964, 113; Dalfen 1977, 14; Bollack in Bollack et al. 2004, 75: 'L'erreur de Créon...est évidemment de sous-estimer les croyances établies'. *Pace* Calder 1968, 401–2 with n. 57, Creon's capitulation, far from redeeming him, only rounds off his tragic surrendering to his adversary.

[90] Cf. e.g. Goheen 1951, 48–9; Musurillo 1967, 59.

[91] For a recent survey of the principle of mutability in archaic literature (the *locus classicus* is *Il.* 24.525–33), see Cairns 2006, esp. 100–3, and Cairns 2011, with special emphasis on the theme's mutations in epinician poetry.

[92] Cf. Loraux 1986, 176–7.

[93] On the ambiguity of αὐτο-words, which can signify both suicide and kin-killing, see again p. 86 above.

[94] C. P. Segal 1981, 175 with n. 75 draws attention to the ancient scholion ad loc. (p. 275 Papageorgius): ὡς ἱερεῖον περὶ τὸν βωμὸν ἐσφάγη, 'she slew herself like a sacrificial victim on the altar'.

[95] Cf. Rehm 1994, 67–8; somewhat differently Steiner 1984, 245–7. It is impossible to determine which version of the myth is presupposed in the extremely concise line 1303: is it the heroic death foreshadowed at A. *Th.* 477 or the self-sacrifice described in E. *Pho.* 930–1018 (the name here is Menoeceus)? The identification of Megareus and Menoeceus has been argued most fully by Vian 1963, 208–14; doubts have been voiced by Robert 1915, I 356–9 and, more recently, Mastronarde 1994, 29. As for Haemon, in the epic tradition he was either killed by the Sphinx (*Oidipodeia*, *PEG* fr. 1 Bernabé = *EGF* 1 Davies; cf. also Pisander *FGrHist* 16 F 10 Jacoby *ap.* Σ E. *Pho.* 1760 = I, 414 Schwartz) or survived long enough to produce a son by the name of Maeon (*Il.* 4.394 Μαίων Αἱμονίδης); cf. Else 1976, 50.

[96] Seyffert's emendation of the transmitted κλεινὸν λέχος; the emendation is accepted by Lloyd-Jones and Wilson 1990b, 149 after Pearson 1928, 190. C. P. Segal's attempt (1995, 135) to make sense of the *lectio tradita* is unconvincing.

[97] Cf. C. P. Segal 1995, 128; Rehm 1994, 69. On Antigone as a 'bride of Hades' see further Tyrrell and Bennett 1998, 99–102, 111, 115–18, 141–2.

[98] The point is well made by Ahrensdorf 2009, 142–3. It would be a reductionist rationalization to imagine that Creon could remarry and have other children (thus Sourvinou-Inwood 1989b, 163).

[99] On Creon's symbolic death see Hoey 1970, 337–8; Rosivach 1979, 26 n. 31; C. P. Segal 1981, 178; Loraux 1986, 183–4; Oudemans and Lardinois 1987, 198; Blundell 1989, 142; *contra* Sourvinou-Inwood 1989b, 152 n. 57. On the peculiarly Sophoclean theme of the dead killing the living cf. e.g. *Aj.* 1026–7, *Tr.* 1163, *El.* 1420–1; Kitto 1956, 193–5; 1966, 180–8.

[100] On Creon's eventual assimilation to the Labdacids see Steiner 1983, 78; Loraux 1986, 183–4; C. P. Segal 1995, 131–2; Bollack 1999, 41–2; more fully Zeitlin 1990, 150–5.

[101] See especially MacKay 1962, 166 and *passim*. To say that Antigone, 'through her heroic devotion to her family...*evidently* redeems her family in the eyes of the gods' (Ahrensdorf 2009, 86; my italics) is an attempt wishfully to explain away the play's fundamental paradox. The gods, it eventually becomes apparent, do support Antigone; however, this in no way amounts to a 'redemption' of the Labdacid *oikos*.

[102] Cf. Thuc. 2.37.3; Pl. *Leg.* 793a–d; Isocr. 12.169; Xen. *Mem.* 4.4.19–25; Arist. *Rh.* 1373b5–18, 1375a15–1375b8. Cf. also the testimony of [Lys.] 6. 10, whose remarkable similarities with *Ant.* 453–7 have been demonstrated in detail by Cerri 1979, 36–7; see further Jebb 1900b, ad 454 f.; Ehrenberg 1954, 37–47; Podlecki 1966, 370; Bennett and Tyrrell 1990, 446–7; Foley 1995, 141. Especially on the concept of ἄγραφος νόμος see Romilly 1971, 26–38 and, in greater detail, Ostwald 1973.

[103] Thus M. Griffith 1999, ad loc.

[104] Cf. on this point especially Sourvinou-Inwood 1990.

[105] Quotations from Dover 1974, 252, 253. Cf. also Sourvinou-Inwood 1989a, 144 n. 33 and see, in greater detail, Yunis 1988, 19–28 with further bibliography.

[106] Cf. Ostwald 1986, 161–9; Sourvinou-Inwood 1989a, 137. The most notable exception to this rule, namely Plutarch's (*Alc.* 22.5) story about the priestess Theano who refused to curse Alcibiades, is arguably a fiction based on the *Antigone*: see Sourvinou-Inwood 1988. Cf. also the remarks of Kirkwood 1958, 123; Knox 1964, 101–2; Oudemans and Lardinois 1987, 160–1; Ostwald 1986, 151 with sound criticisms of Romilly 1971, 29–34.

[107] Cf. C. P. Segal 1981, 161: 'In defining the *polis* in terms of its man-made, rational structures, Creon in fact exposes their fragility.' Ostwald 1986, 170 appositely wonders whether it is 'possible that in the *Antigone* Sophocles meant to warn against the dangers inherent in too secular an interpretation of the power of the state'. And Cropp 1997, 153 states that 'Sophocles' text reflects political concerns that were real in the democratic Athens of his day: the sources and extent of the civil government's authority, the need for government to accommodate natural or traditional rights, the capacity that any government has to bring harm to a community through misconceiving its powers and acting arbitrarily and with limited vision.' Cf. also Gellie 1972, 52; Bing 1974, 98; Benardete 1975a, 175, 176, 183; Else 1976, 40; Dalfen 1977, 17; Jordan 1979, 91 n. 150; C. P. Segal 1986, 143–4.

[108] Solon fr. 17 West; Thgn. 133–42; Sem. fr. 1. 1–5 West; Sim. fr. 22 (*PMG* 527 Page).

[109] Hobbes 1651, 192 = Tuck 1996, 253. Hobbes' argument for a fundamentally civil religion, one that would take into account the interests of the body politic more than any metaphysics, earned him a reputation for atheism; see further Tuck 1996, xxxxviii–xliii.

[110] Cf. Steiner 1984, 262–3. For this deadlock, with emphasis on its ethical aspect, see Trapp 1996, 80–2.

[111] Cf. Dawe 1968, 113; Coleman 1972, 26–7; Reinhardt 1979, 91–2; Benedetto 1983, 6–9; excellent treatment in Oudemans and Lardinois 1987, 200.

5

DIVINE AND HUMAN ACTION IN THE *OEDIPUS TYRANNUS*

Douglas Cairns

The issue of the role of the gods in Sophocles' *Oedipus Tyrannus* inevitably arises in classroom discussion. Modern students come to the play with certain preconceptions about freedom of choice and the truth or otherwise of determinism, and typically find these challenged by salient aspects of the play. These modern preconceptions will certainly differ from those of ancient audiences and readers, who will similarly have approached the play with their own, no doubt varying and perhaps internally inconsistent, sets of assumptions. But various though these will have been, they will all have been in some way informed by traditional Greek views (which may themselves be both various and inconsistent). Hence, in order even to begin to approach issues which indisputably demand discussion, we need to establish the nature of the play's interaction with these traditional views. While it may be impossible to reach a new or definitive set of conclusions on these questions, I propose to tackle them nonetheless, as part of this volume's project of returning to core aspects of tragedy's content, and in particular its roots in and reaction to the thought of archaic Greece.

Though there are signs of a recent resurgence of interest,[1] debate on this issue, which goes back to the very beginnings of modern interpretations of tragedy, seems rather to have come to a standstill in the 1990s.[2] Inevitably, in such an interpretative tradition, there are very few arguments or even particular observations that have never been made before. In this study, however, I do not want just to offer modified endorsement of particular interpretative tendencies, but rather to attempt to show how even approaches that fall outside the general tendency I favour nonetheless respond to genuine and significant features of the play. I do not assume that those who favour different views from my own are merely obtuse or misguided; I credit them with a genuine attempt to come to terms with the detail of the text and to recreate its performance in the mind's eye. Despite the centuries of interpretation in which, if the truth be told, fundamental differences of approach occur only within a very limited range,[3] scholars continue to disagree on a number of core issues. Some of this disagreement we should try to resolve, using the best arguments we can muster in the proper task of rational persuasion. But a further aim in the appraisal of often polarized arguments must be to show where room for legitimate disagreement remains. What follows is not an attempt to legislate for a single right answer, but to examine the play and its interpretations especially in the light of archaic Greek thought, as outlined in the Introduction to this volume. Focusing on the traditional religious and ethical beliefs in the light of which the original audience will, one way or another, have responded to the drama in its original cultural setting does suggest a degree of limitation, but in this case it also leaves a considerable openness of texture, as warranted by the richness, complexity, and reticence of the play itself and the variety of stances which a fifth-century audience might have adopted towards the traditional material on which it is based. Though our diverging interpretations of Oedipus' downfall and the role of the gods therein no doubt do depend, to a significant extent, on our affiliations as critics and on our cultural background as citizens of the modern West, there is a real sense in which the grounds for some of the most fundamental interpretative differences of all can be located in particular features of the plot, and in particular in the frequently noted but variously interpreted tension between the events of the *fabula* that have taken place before the play begins and the action as it develops on stage.

I approach these issues by dealing first with an acknowledged classic of Sophoclean interpretation that is still, in many quarters, regarded as definitive: E. R. Dodds's 'On Misunderstanding the *Oedipus Rex*'.[4] This is not an *ad hominem* strategy. Partly it is a means of addressing problematic aspects of what remains the dominant strand of contemporary interpretation. But more broadly it is to such classic formulations that we must return in order to rediscover and renew our focus upon the central issues of tragic interpretation; we may not find answers that satisfy us, but we shall find a stimulus to reformulate central questions that have been neglected in much recent scholarship.

Dodds defines his own approach in contradistinction to others. Though all the views he discusses could be represented by the published work of one scholar or another, Dodds prefers to assail them in the form in which they were presented by his students '[o]n the last occasion when [he] had the misfortune to examine in Honour Moderations at Oxford'.[5] To Dodds's question, 'In what sense, if in any, does the *Oedipus Rex* attempt to justify the ways of God to man?' the students gave three main kinds of answer: most argued that Oedipus' sufferings were warranted by his defects of character: either he was a thoroughly bad lot ('look how he treated

Creon') or he was vitiated by his Aristotelian *hamartia*; others that the *OT* was 'a tragedy of destiny', demonstrating human helplessness in the hands of the gods; while a third group held that Sophocles was 'not interested in justifying the gods', who 'are simply part of the machinery of the plot'. Dodds is shocked 'that all these young persons...could read this great and moving play and so completely miss the point. For all the views...just summarized are in fact demonstrably false.'[6] It is not my aim to vindicate the views of any of the three groups of students in their entirety, but I shall try to demonstrate that Dodds's own view, too, is 'demonstrably false'.

Dodds's interpretation has two main aspects: the first concerns the issue of divine involvement both in the actions of the *fabula* presupposed by the onstage action and in those of the onstage action itself; the second is a matter of the play's perlocutionary force – the view of the world that it (*qua* text or performance) presupposes and that its audience must presuppose in order properly to understand it. One way in which Dodds's view distinguishes itself from those of the students he castigates is that where some of the latter (allegedly) believe that dramatists are 'for ever running about delivering banal "messages"', Dodds instead finds in the play 'a vision of man's estate' – 'I do not wish to describe it as a "message". But I find in it an enlargement of sensibility.'[7] This 'vision' (which is indeed a 'message', though perhaps not, at least in Dodds's own view, banal) he expresses in the following two propositions about 'Sophocles' opinions':

> First, he did not believe (or did not always believe) that the gods are in any human sense 'just'; Secondly, he did always believe that the gods exist and that man should revere them.

He finds the evidence for the second proposition above all in the second stasimon:

> If men are to lose all respect for the gods, in that case, the Chorus asks, τί δεῖ με χορεύειν (895). If by this they mean merely 'Why should I, a Theban elder, dance?', the question is irrelevant and even slightly ludicrous; the meaning is surely 'Why should I, an Athenian citizen, continue to serve in a chorus?' In speaking of themselves as a chorus they step out of the play into the contemporary world, as Aristophanes' choruses do in the parabasis.[8]

We shall discuss the second stasimon later in this chapter. We shall also postpone substantive discussion of the first of Dodds's two propositions (on the issue of the gods' justice 'in any human sense'). For the moment, let us attend to some implications of these propositions. First, if the issue of the gods' justice is to be relevant at all, even in a negative sense, then they must be regarded as agents – an entity which is never the cause, whether by commission or omission, of states of affairs in the world is not the kind of subject of which the adjectives 'just' or 'unjust' can be predicated. The second proposition seems to me likewise to presuppose divine influence over our lives – if the gods exist but have no influence at all over our lives, we might contemplate and admire them, but we should not fear or revere them. Reverence implies power. The crucial state of affairs which raises questions of divine power and justice in the *OT* is Oedipus' downfall; we must therefore ask ourselves whether, or how, the gods manifest agency and power in respect of that.

Dodds claims: 'Certain of Oedipus' past actions were fate-bound; but everything that he does on the stage from first to last he does as a free agent' (p. 42). Dodds prefers 'fate-bound' to 'determined' because, according to him, determinism is a creation of later (Hellenistic) philosophical debate;[9] by contrast

> fifth-century Greeks did not think in these terms any more than Homer did... Homeric heroes have their predetermined 'portion of life' (μοῖρα); they must die on their 'appointed day' (αἴσιμον ἦμαρ); but it never occurs to the poet or his audience that this prevents them from being free agents. Nor did Sophocles intend that it should occur to readers of the *Oedipus Rex*. Neither in Homer nor in Sophocles does divine foreknowledge of certain events imply that all human actions are predetermined. If explicit confirmation of this is required, we have only to turn to lines 1230 f., where the Messenger emphatically distinguishes Oedipus' self-blinding as 'voluntary' and 'self-chosen' from the 'involuntary' parricide and incest.

Dodds's view on the relation between the question of divine agency and its justice to that of fate and determinism becomes clear in his next point:

> Even in calling the parricide and the incest 'fate-bound' I have perhaps implied more than the average Athenian of Sophocles' day would have recognized. As A. W. Gomme put it, 'the gods know the future, but they do not order it: they know who will win the next Scotland and England football match, but that does not alter the fact that the victory will depend on the skill, the determination, the fitness of the players, and a little on luck'. That may not satisfy the analytical philosopher, but it seems to have satisfied the ordinary man at all periods.

There are several problems in these formulations. First, while we can agree that it is anachronistic to apply later philosophical formulations of an antithesis between 'free agency' and determinism to Homer or to tragedy, this should apply to both terms, to the notion of 'free agency' as well as to that of determinism.[10] Free agency is a concept that requires examination in its own right; its baggage needs to be unpacked, and the range of senses that it is capable of bearing needs to be explored. One cannot simply assume that an unproblematic notion of 'free agency' obtains as the default position whenever a developed concept of determinism is absent. Second, Dodds assumes that any form of determinism must be incompatible with what he calls 'free agency'; archaic and classical Greeks (allegedly) believed in the latter, therefore they could not have believed in the former. But among contemporary philosophical determinists, incompatibilism is a distinctly minority view;[11] the Stoic theory to which Dodds principally alludes was itself a compatibilist one.[12] Proving (or assuming) something like a belief in 'free agency' does not prove the absence of something like determinism.

Beyond these general considerations, the inadequacy of Dodds's position is highlighted first by a tension between his own view and his endorsement of Gomme, and second by tensions within Gomme's position. The view that Dodds advances in his own person implies a future of which only some (indeed very few) aspects are determined and thus knowable in advance, while the one that is buttressed by the quotation from Gomme seems on the surface to imply that all outcomes are in principle predictable, provided that sufficient information is available. The latter is the stronger thesis; but if this were the view implied by the play, it would be difficult to say in what way it differed from the variety of determinism supposedly first advanced by Hellenistic philosophers. If something like this thesis were inherent in Sophocles' play, then one can see how it could give rise to a view of divine knowledge that is at least in principle tenable: if everything is determined in a complex chain of cause and effect, so that at any one time there is precisely one possible future that can succeed the present state of affairs, then a being, if there were one, that understood all the properties of all potential causal factors would be able to predict the future. This knowledge – that of Laplace's demon[13] – would not be in any way a cause of that future and would not detract in any way from the sufficiency of all the causes that combine, in a unique collocation of circumstances, to create that future; it is simply that each of these causes would itself be caused, and so on in an unbreakable chain of cause and effect. Such a view would be, in the eyes of many, perfectly compatible with a notion of human responsibility.

This, however, is not precisely what Gomme says, nor is it what Dodds appears to want him to say. For Gomme admits one causal factor that is apparently both knowable in advance and yet not part of a predictable chain of cause and effect – namely 'luck'. There are two ways of resolving the conundrum thrown up by the use of this term: 'luck' may just be a way of referring to some concatenation of causal factors that is undetected by the casual observer, yet still predictable by a Laplacean divinity; in that way, these factors would be in principle knowable, but they would not have the last he does as a free agent'. But before we examine that proposition, we should consider the way that Dodds contrasts this notion of free agency with an alternative type of action, action that is 'fate-bound'. This distinction entails a contrast between the things that Oedipus does within the play and some of those, i.e. the crimes of parricide and incest, that he did before the play begins; it is the former that are free, while the latter are 'fate-bound'. What it is to be 'fate-bound', as we have seen, is then explained with the aid of the quotation from Gomme, so that a 'fate-bound' future appears to be one of which the gods have advance knowledge, but which they do not intervene to arrange. This, however, immediately sets up an inconsistency, to which we have already alluded, with Dodds's two central theses, (a) that the gods are not 'in any human sense' just, but (b) that they exist and human beings should revere them (an injunction which Dodds finds enunciated in the second stasimon). But if it is a premiss of the play that the gods demand worship, we must ask ourselves whether it is likely that the poet will have sought to support that premiss by presenting the gods as knowing what will happen, but not influencing events. Why should the infallibility of divine foreknowledge compel an audience's reverence? If everything the gods know is going to happen, but the gods have no role either in determining or effecting those outcomes, it would not seem to matter what one chooses to believe about the gods or how one chooses to interact with them. And if the gods merely knew that Oedipus would kill his father and marry his mother, and had no role either in bringing these things about or in the sufferings of Oedipus that result from them, to what extent does the question of measuring the gods (positively, negatively, or neither) by the yardstick of human justice even arise? In raising the issue of divine justice, and in referring to the power of the gods that should compel mortals' reverence, Dodds suggests that the ways in which the gods order the world and treat human beings, as evidenced by the depiction of the world and the gods' treatment of Oedipus in *OT*, raises fundamental questions about how the gods exercise their power. A substantial failing of his account, therefore, is that his explanation of the gods' role in the play is inconsistent with his view that the gods are potential subjects of moral evaluation and that they can manifest the sort of power that should command our reverence.[22]

But this is not the main failing of that account. Dodds argues that Oedipus' parricide and incest are necessary, but not forced upon him: the gods know that he will do these things, but they do not cause him to do them. Oedipus himself causes and is solely responsible for everything he does in the play. There is a difference between events outside the play (some of which are determined) and those within it (which are free). Influential though it has been, however, this is a view that could be held only by someone who adopted the radical hermeneutic stance of refusing to believe anything that is said by any character in the play.[23]

There is, of course, an issue here. As a purely mimetic genre, tragedy offers no direct guidance in the *persona* of author or narrator on the reliability of its characters' opinions.[24] In the *OT* in particular, characters' pronouncements on the role of the gods in the events of the play are subject not only to the partiality and imperfection of any human perspective on such issues but also to a degree of inscrutability and reticence about the ultimate purposes of the divine that is greater in Sophocles (even) than it is in Aeschylus and Euripides.[25] This does not, however, mean that we approach characters' utterances with the scepticism with which we should evaluate the claims of real individuals in everyday social interaction. People say all kinds of things; often they have no particular proof of or evidence for their assertions. We are right to be cautious. But in drama, everything that a character is made to say is said for a reason as part of an overall dramatic design. Characters' utterances call not for uncritical acceptance, for clearly characters can be misinformed, deluded, partial, and unreliable in all sorts of other ways, but for evaluation, and such evaluation must bring the specific judgement in context into a relation with the overall impact of the action and events of the play. In the *OT*, this raises particular questions about the authority with which characters are to be credited,[26] about the perspective of the Chorus,[27] and about the play's pervasive irony, by which characters words' often have one meaning for the audience and another for the characters themselves.[28]

Zeus and Apollo are wise and know the affairs of mortals, sing the Chorus in the final stanza of the first stasimon (498–9),[29] and the certainty of Apollo's knowledge of Oedipus' future is confirmed beyond all doubt by the action of the play. In the first stasimon, however, the Chorus' certainty regarding what seems to be a statement of divine omniscience contrasts with uncertainty about the pronouncements of human prophets (499–506). Superior audience knowledge, however, confirms that they are wrong and that the prophet in this case, Tiresias, who has just named Oedipus the murderer of Laius, is correct. This exchange alone proves that Dodds is unequivocally wrong about the difference in status between events within and beyond the action of the play, for in this scene one of the former, namely the self-blinding of Oedipus, is accurately foretold, as were his parricide and incest. Tiresias alludes to the self-blinding at 372–3 (σὺ δ' ἄθλιός γε ταῦτ' ὀνειδίζων, ἃ σοὶ | οὐδεὶς ὃς οὐχὶ τῶνδ' ὀνειδιεῖ τάχα, 'you are the wretched one, making reproaches that everyone here will soon level at

you') and foretells it outright at 419 (βλέποντα νῦν μὲν ὄρθ', ἔπειτα δὲ σκότον...,
'now you see aright, but in future blind...') and 454–6:

> τυφλὸς γὰρ ἐκ δεδορκότος
> καὶ πτωχὸς ἀντὶ πλουσίου ξένην ἔπι   455
> σκήπτρῳ προδεικνὺς γαῖαν ἐμπορεύσεται.

> For blind who once was sighted and a beggar instead of a rich man he will make his way onto foreign soil, using his sceptre to point the way.

He has already correctly named Oedipus as the murderer of Laius (350–3, 362), and the whole of their exchange is predicated on his possession of accurate knowledge of Oedipus' parricide, incest, and their imminent revelation – see his allusions at 366–7 (and cf. 337–8, 341, 435–8), and his more open denunciations and predictions at 412–25, 449–60.[30]

The audience already knows that Tiresias is in the right in this exchange, and the prophecy of self-blinding will be fulfilled by the end of the play.[31] These are μέλλοντα that have the status, *qua* objects of knowledge, of ὄντα. Whatever the status of Oedipus' self-blinding ('fate-bound', 'free', neither, or both), it is identical to that of the parricide and incest.[32]

Tiresias also has information for us on the role of the gods in bringing about the events that he says will happen (374–7):

> Οι. μιᾶς τρέφῃ πρὸς νυκτός, ὥστε μήτ' ἐμὲ
> μήτ' ἄλλον, ὅστις φῶς ὁρᾷ, βλάψαι ποτ' ἄν.   375
> Τε. οὐ γάρ σε μοῖρα πρός γ' ἐμοῦ πεσεῖν,[33]
> ἱκανὸς Ἀπόλλων, ᾧ τάδ' ἐκπρᾶξαι μέλει.

> OEDIPUS: You are nourished by one long night, and so you could never harm me or anyone else who sees the light.
> TIRESIAS: It is not your fate (*moira*) to fall at my hands: Apollo is sufficient; it is his task to effect this outcome.

Tiresias is the prophet of Apollo, and he is right about so much else that an audience cannot be expected to regard him as mistaken in this assertion about his patron's motivation.[34] This passage suggests that Apollo is actively involved in the events that are unfolding in the play and that he will be involved – in an adversarial way – in Oedipus' downfall: it is Oedipus' *moira* to fall at the hands of Apollo, and Apollo is seeing to it that this will in fact happen.[35] This is, to be sure, Tiresias' perspective; but it is not merely one of fallible human conjecture. Both in Tiresias' status and in the congruence between his explanations, the development of the plot, and the wider background of events against which that plot develops there are the strongest possible reasons for accepting what he says.

Tiresias' is not an isolated perspective. Other characters make pronouncements about the intentions and actions of the gods that are as confident as his are. In a play of a different sort, we might not make very much of these remarks, but in the *OT* the existence of gods and their influence on human affairs is a given. Thus, while only one other character (see below) achieves an authority as a commentator on divine actions that bears comparison with that enjoyed by Tiresias, nonetheless what the other characters (including the Chorus) say about the gods, their ways, and their motives must be evaluated. Such evaluation will take place both in the light of the audience's fundamental knowledge that Oedipus has already fulfilled an oracle by killing his father and marrying his mother and against a background supposition that the divine order revealed in these actions is reflected in the unfolding events of the play.

As is often noted, no divine action takes place on stage. Divine efficacy, however, is presupposed, if not by the plague which is the focus of the opening scene,[36] then certainly by the response of the Delphic oracle, which Creon has undertaken to consult, at Oedipus' bidding, in the hope of finding a remedy. The presentation of this consultation is in many respects characteristic. Oedipus' statement that Creon has already been sent (70–2) is followed immediately by his arrival, a coincidence on which the Priest comments (78–9). Oedipus' own comment is a prayer to Apollo (80–1):

ὦναξ Ἄπολλον, εἰ γὰρ ἐν τύχῃ γέ τῳ   80
σωτῆρι βαίη λαμπρὸς ὥσπερ ὄμματι.

Lord Apollo, may he come as bright in salutary good fortune (*tychē*) as he does in his countenance.

The development of the plot depends explicitly on an apparently fortunate coincidence, and Oedipus' hope that the outcome should prove equally fortunate is addressed to Apollo on the evident assumption that a positive resolution is in his hands. If the audience's knowledge of the Oedipus myth has already led them, as well it might, to expect that a play that begins by presenting an Oedipus who is at the height of his powers, the once and potentially future saviour of his people (14, 35–57), will end with his ruin, then that audience may suspect that Oedipus' hope is misplaced, that the coincidence which seems so opportune for the movement of the plot is in fact more than that, and that the design which such coincidence may betray is that of Apollo.

The oracle itself is reported in the form of a divine command (96–8):

ἄνωγεν ἡμᾶς Φοῖβος ἐμφανῶς ἄναξ
μίασμα χώρας ὡς τεθραμμένον χθονὶ
ἐν τῇδ' ἐλαύνειν μηδ' ἀνήκεστον τρέφειν.

> Lord Phoebus clearly orders us to expel from the country the contagion, a contagion that has been nurtured in this land, and not to feed it and make it incurable.

If the audience had not already surmised that Oedipus is the source of the plague, the detail that its remedy depends on finding the murderer of Laius (103–11) makes it clear that he is. Thus the god has initiated a search of which Oedipus is the object, with the result that Oedipus' own conviction that he is acting in concert with the god in pursuit of a common end (136, 244–5) impresses the audience with an ominous sense that this is indeed a common enterprise in which Oedipus is acting to further a divine purpose that entails his own downfall. This sense, that the project upon which Oedipus has embarked furthers aims of Apollo that may not yet be perfectly understood and may be at variance with the purposes of Oedipus himself, is powerfully and ominously confirmed by lines 278–81, where, in response to the Chorus-leader's observation that Apollo's oracle could perfectly well have divulged the killer's identity, Oedipus replies (280–1):

δίκαι' ἔλεξας· ἀλλ' ἀναγκάσαι θεοὺς   280
ἄν μὴ θέλωσιν οὐδ' ἂν εἷς δύναιτ' ἀνήρ.

You're right; but no man can compel the gods against their will.

A conventional truth, but a significant and resonant claim in a context in which a god has just acted to set in motion a train of events whose outcomes will reveal a yawning gulf between the god's plans and those of humans.

Other characters are no less convinced that release from the plague and finding the killer of Laius depend on the gods. The Priest whose words close the play's opening scene prays that Apollo be active in saving the city and ending the plague (149–50), i.e. in the process of revealing Oedipus as the murderer of Laius, as an incestuous parricide. The parodos that immediately follows invokes a number of deities, including Apollo (154–7, 162, 203–6) in a prayer for release, and the hope that divine power will be manifest in the fulfilment of oracles is maintained in each of the two subsequent choral songs. In the first stasimon the Chorus conjure up an image of the killer in headlong flight from an Apollo armed with fire and thunderbolt and attended by the unerring Keres (467–72). Tiresias, of course, has just named that killer as Oedipus himself, but the Chorus suspend judgement: though Zeus and Apollo, as they know the affairs of mortals in general, will know for sure who the killer is, mortal seers may be fallible (498–506). The irony confirms what the audience already knows, that Tiresias is right, and thus the Chorus confirm the explicit statements of Tiresias in the previous scene, that Apollo is in pursuit of the killer, i.e. Oedipus.[37] Though it would be wrong to assume as a general rule that pronouncements of this kind on the part of a Sophoclean Chorus are necessarily true, in this case they are confirmed by statements (on the part of Tiresias) that the audience already knows to be true and which are confirmed by the action of the play.

By the second stasimon, the Chorus' faith in the certainty of divine action has been shaken, but again their anxiety is expressed in the form of prayer (863–71, 879–81, 883–8), a speech-act predicated upon its potential for efficacy. Belief in divine support for human morality is in any case strongly affirmed in concluding each stanza of the first strophic pair (872, 882). Two hypotheses would shake the Chorus' conviction: wrongdoers' evasion of punishment (strophe 2, 883–96) and the failure of oracles, specifically the oracle given to Laius that he should die at the hands of his son, to be proved true (antistrophe 2, 897–910). The Chorus' religious faith, therefore, will be confirmed by the identification and suffering of the killer of Laius and by the proof that that killer was his son. The Chorus, ironically, ask the gods to demonstrate that Oedipus is guilty of parricide – precisely what Apollo proposes to do, according to the authoritative statements of Tiresias.

The role of dramatic irony in allowing the partial and fallible perspectives of characters such as Oedipus, the Priest, and the Chorus to point towards a greater divine purpose is considerable. This is especially clear in the scene between Oedipus and Jocasta (679–862) that prompts the choral reflections on the maintenance of divine law and the fulfilment of oracles to which we have just referred. In that scene, Jocasta uses the failure, as she sees it, of the oracle that Laius should die at the hands of his son to assuage Oedipus' anxiety that Tiresias spoke the truth when he named him as the murderer of Laius. An oracle had come, not from Apollo, but from his human interpreters, that Laius should be killed by his and Jocasta's son. Yet Laius was killed by brigands, and the son exposed on a deserted hillside (711–19). Jocasta goes on (720–2):

> κἀνταῦθ' Ἀπόλλων οὔτ' ἐκεῖνον ἤνυσεν   720
> φονέα γενέσθαι πατρός, οὔτε Λάϊον,
> τὸ δεινὸν οὑφοβεῖτο, πρὸς παιδὸς θανεῖν.

And so Apollo brought it to pass neither that he should become the murderer of his father nor that Laius should die at the hands of his son, the terrible fate he feared.

Jocasta has been careful to distinguish between the god and his mortal servants (712), but here she elides the distinction. Formally, there is no disparagement of Apollo in her statement that he did not bring to pass something that he did not actually prophesy,[38] though it is possible to read the line as undermining her previous disjunction rather than maintaining the distance between Apollo and his interpreters. But of course Jocasta is wrong: both the fulfilment of the prophecy and its source as an authentic pronouncement of the god are facts. And so her words ironically imply their opposite – that Apollo not only foresaw that Laius would be killed by his son, but that he actually brought that event to pass (ἤνυσεν).[39]

Jocasta concludes her remarks on the fallibility of seercraft with the thought ὧν γὰρ ἂν θεὸς | χρείαν ἐρευνᾷ ῥᾳδίως αὐτὸς φανεῖ ('everything whose need the god seeks he will easily reveal by himself', 724–5). In the ironic application that these words are surely intended to bear, Apollo thus 'needs' Oedipus' downfall, Oedipus himself is the victim of a 'hunt', and Apollo is 'easily revealing' the truth about Oedipus.[40] The final revelation of the truth then begins with immediate effect: Oedipus seizes on Jocasta's reference to the crossroads at which Laius was killed, and on learning the location and chronology of this event, begins to suspect that he may indeed be the murderer of Laius (726–38). Fearing what he thinks is the worst, he also senses a divine plan (738):

ὦ Ζεῦ, τί μου δρᾶσαι βεβούλευσαι πέρι;

O Zeus, what have you resolved to do about me?

Again, Oedipus is wrong, but the audience is likely to conclude that there is an element of truth in his words, that the gods do indeed have a plan for him.[41] Similarly, at 828–9, Oedipus suggests that it would be a reasonable conjecture from his apparent predicament – soon to be exiled from Thebes, under the terms of his own proclamation, as the murderer of Laius, yet unable to return to Corinth for fear of fulfilling prophecies of parricide and incest – that his troubles were sent by a cruel *daimōn*:

ἆρ' οὐκ ἀπ' ὠμοῦ ταῦτα δαίμονός τις ἂν
κρίνων ἐπ' ἀνδρὶ τῷδ' ἂν ὀρθοίη λόγον;

Would one not be correct in concluding that a cruel *daimōn* is the source of my troubles?

Again, the detail is wrong (and the thought may itself be conventional), but the assumption of divine influence appears to be correct, and so the thought in context is much more than a cliché.[42]

A similar reflection of popular belief in divine intervention surfaces in the Messenger's speech at 1258–61: as the furious Oedipus bellows to be given a sword and to be directed towards his wife/mother, some *daimōn* shows him the way –

λυσσῶντι δ' αὐτῷ δαιμόνων δείκνυσί τις·
οὐδεὶς γὰρ ἀνδρῶν, οἳ παρῆμεν ἐγγύθεν.

δεινὸν δ' ἀΰσας, ὡς ὑφηγητοῦ τινος   1260
πύλαις διπλαῖς ἐνήλατ' (κτλ.)

> In his fury some *daimōn* showed him – it was none of us men who were present nearby. With a terrible cry, he leapt, as if someone were guiding him, upon the double doors, and...

Ordinary mortals, then, ordinarily expect the divine to be at work, especially in significant and terrifying events; in other contexts we might not make too much of this, but in a play in which a divine prophet has delivered an accurate prophecy of an outcome that he says his divine patron actively seeks to bring about and in which events onstage tend inexorably towards that end, we should be very unwise to play it down.[43]

The irony by which the words of the characters confirm a pattern of divinely inspired events that the characters themselves cannot yet comprehend reaches its peak, as we saw, in the scene between Oedipus and Jocasta in which are presented all the indications needed to conclude that Oedipus, in fulfilment both of Laius' oracle and his own, is the exposed child who killed his father, but the only conclusion drawn is that Oedipus may have killed Laius. This is the pivotal scene. It is followed by an ode in which the Chorus pray for Laius' oracle to be proved true, and then Jocasta reappears, intent on praying to the gods for a resolution of the anxieties that beset Oedipus and his household (911–23). She turns first of all to Lycian Apollo, for he is nearest (ἄγχιστος γὰρ εἶ, 919): not only is some object associated with Apollo conveniently close at hand,[44] but Apollo's presence is, as we have seen, intensely felt as the drama develops. Jocasta's is a prayer for action, for *lysis* (solution, resolution, 921). Action then follows, with far greater rapidity than in the play so far, and the solution to the quest for the murderer of Laius becomes the solution to the puzzle of Oedipus' identity. The sequence of events onstage encourages us to think that Sophocles' disposition is also Apollo's design, that Apollo has indeed been ἄγχιστος throughout and that now, with the entry of the Corinthian Messenger, he delivers his *lysis*. The coincidence of the Corinthian Messenger's arrival is determined by the coincidence of Polybus' recent death. Coincidentally, the Corinthian Messenger is also the shepherd who first received the infant Oedipus from his Theban counterpart and gave him to his adoptive parents. Coincidentally, the Theban shepherd who gave the child away is the survivor of Laius' party who has already been summoned (859–61) for reasons that now no longer matter. One cannot equal many, says Oedipus at 845, but here four roles are played by two men. Coincidence? These are daring dramatic expedients that test the limits of plausible plot construction. There are more convenient coincidences of the same kind: Oedipus' consultation of the Delphic oracle leads to his departure from Corinth just in time to encounter Laius, proceeding from Thebes to Delphi on some form of religious business (114–15), at the ominous and fateful crossroads (794–813);[45] the plague caused by Oedipus' pollution occurs not immediately after the parricide and incest, but years later, just in time for the search for a remedy to coincide with the death of Polybus; and so on. Any audience-member or reader who reflects on these coincidences will realize that they are artefacts of the plot's design; but dramaturgical artifice performs a simultaneous thematic function in a play in which the attribution of events to mere chance is repeatedly shown to be mistaken. Oedipus is not the son of Tyche (1080–1); there can be foreknowledge of events, and chance does not rule human life, *pace* Jocasta (977–8).[46] Throughout the play, references to chance hint ironically at divine design.[47] In the same way, at the dramaturgical level, what might otherwise appear as implausible coincidences emerge, because of the presuppositions that drive the plot, as manifestations of divine purpose.[48]

We remember that the self-blinding, like the parricide and incest, is foretold; in Dodds's terminology, since they are accurately predicted by an oracle or a prophecy, these actions are all 'fate-bound'; but Dodds would have us believe that such actions, though they are the object of divine foreknowledge, are neither divinely willed nor divinely caused. Tiresias and others, however, have seen divine will and divine agency in actions that appear to be conceived and executed entirely by human beings. The self-blinding is not only a prophesied action which must happen but also a consequence of a revelation which Apollo (according to Tiresias) has an interest in bringing about. Its status as 'free', 'fate-bound', or divinely inspired is not so easily encompassed.

At 1227–31 the Messenger describes Jocasta's suicide and Oedipus' self-blinding as κακά that are ἑκόντα κοὐκ ἄκοντα and as πήμονες αὐθαίρετοι. We remember, however, that the same Messenger sees the hand of god at work in Oedipus' ability to locate Jocasta's corpse despite the intensity of his rage and the lack of human assistance (1258–61). When Oedipus finally enters, blind, to reveal these κακὰ ἑκόντα at 1297, the Chorus immediately ask, in horror at his self-mutilation (1299–1302):

> τίς σ', ὦ τλῆμον,
> προσέβη μανία; τίς ὁ πηδήσας   1300
> μείζονα δαίμων τῶν μηκίστων
> πρὸς σῇ δυσδαίμονι μοίρᾳ;

Poor man, what madness has come upon you? Who is the *daimōn* who leapt further than the longest leap onto your ill-*daimōn*ed fate (*moira*)?

Oedipus' existing troubles, i.e. his revelation as an incestuous parricide, stem from *moira*, and such *moira* depends in some way on a *daimōn*. Only an abnormal state of mind (*mania*) could have led him to add to these by blinding himself, and such *mania* must also depend in some way on a *daimōn*. This question elicits only lamentation, and so the Chorus repeat it (1327–8):

> ὦ δεινὰ δράσας, πῶς ἔτλης τοιαῦτα σὰς
> ὄψεις μαρᾶναι; τίς σ' ἐπῆρε δαιμόνων;

> Doer of terrible deeds, how could you bring yourself to put out your eyes like that? Which *daimōn* urged you on?

And Oedipus immediately answers (1329–35):

> Ἀπόλλων τάδ' ἦν, Ἀπόλλων, φίλοι,
> ὁ κακὰ κακὰ τελῶν ἐμὰ τάδ' ἐμὰ πάθεα.   1330
> ἔπαισε δ' αὐτόχειρ νιν οὔ-
> τις, ἀλλ' ἐγὼ τλάμων.
> τί γὰρ ἔδει μ' ὁρᾶν,
> ὅτῳ γ' ὁρῶντι μηδὲν ἦν ἰδεῖν γλυκύ;   1335

> These things were Apollo; it was Apollo, my friends, who brought to pass these sufferings of mine. But no one but I, poor wretch, struck them the actual blow. For what need had I of sight, for whom, sighted, there was nothing sweet to see?

There are many interpretations of these lines that acquit Apollo of any role in the self-blinding,[49] but all these have to be forced on the Greek, which says only, 'these things were Apollo, but my hand did the deed'. In answer to the question, 'Which *daimōn* urged you to blind yourself', Oedipus says 'Apollo'; but he also goes on to say that he did the deed himself, and then gives a reason for his action, a reason he amplifies in the sequel (1337–9, 1369–90).[50] Like others in the play, Oedipus sees divine influence in human actions that are adequately motivated by human reasons; in doing so he sees Apollonian influence in an outcome which Apollo's priest predicted. This outcome is part of the downfall which that same priest said Apollo had an interest in bringing about. Oedipus once thought that his misfortunes, such as he thought they were at the time, were part of a plan of Zeus; now that he sees fully what his misfortunes are, he thinks that they are part of a plan of Apollo. The Chorus accept this explanation (ἦν ταῦθ' ὅπωσπερ καὶ σὺ φής, 'It was just as you say,' 1336),[51] and we must accept it too.[52] Its truth is confirmed by the prophecy of Tiresias at 376–7, and the way that Oedipus' pronouncement signals the fulfilment of Tiresias' prophecy gives it a special status not shared by the opinions of other characters. Yet the perspective that Oedipus and Tiresias now share corroborates the speculative, partial, and sometimes ironic indications given by other characters that the divine is at work; and this sense of divine power both confirms and is confirmed by the audience's sense that the play's dramatic design presents not a series of strange coincidences but an overarching divine plan.[53]

Oedipus' self-blinding is thus something that Apollo causes; but it is also something that Oedipus himself causes. He himself struck the blow, with his own hand, αὐτόχειρ (1331). As Bernard Williams has pointed out,[54] a link is thus made to the horrendous deeds that Oedipus performed long before, for αὐτόχειρ is 'the same word that he applied at 266 to the murderer of Laius'. Both actions are those of Oedipus' own hand. These deeds, as we have seen, are of the same order, carried out by a human being acting for intelligible human reasons but simultaneously fulfilling prophecies whose logic entails that these aspects of the future, at least, are necessary and unavoidable. These prophecies, moreover, are presented not merely as objects of divine knowledge but projects of divine intention. The difference is that when Oedipus blinded himself, this, as such, was what he himself wanted to do. When he killed Laius he may have wanted to kill his assailant, but he surely did not want to kill his own father. When he married Jocasta, he equally did not do so with the deliberate intention of marrying his mother. This is why the Messenger can describe the parricide and incest as *akonta* and Oedipus' self-blinding (along with Jocasta's suicide) as *hekonta* and as πήμονες αὐθαίρετοι ('self-chosen ills', 1230–1). The terms *hekonta* and *akonta* do not equate to 'free' *versus* 'determined'. As we have seen, both the self-blinding and the parricide and incest are determined, in that they are known in advance and a god acts to help bring them about. It is simply that in the case of the self-blinding Oedipus' wishes coincide with those of Apollo, whereas in that of the parricide and incest they did not. The Corinthian Messenger's words at 1008 are emblematic of Oedipus' life thus far: he did not know what he was doing; after the revelation, he does, and so acts, this time, as the god's willing rather than unwitting accomplice.

The phenomenon here is the familiar one of over-determination. This notion is familiar in two senses. First, it is something all of us encounter in our daily lives: the boss orders the secretary to carry out some task, but he had already begun to do it anyway. If the boss had not asked, it would still have been done. Five members of a firing squad simultaneously fire at a target pinned on the condemned man's chest. The shots of each are sufficient to kill the victim, but none is necessary; if one should fail, any one of the four others will do. But over-determination is also familiar as a term of art in the study of archaic Greek thought. In that context, explanations in terms of over-determination have perhaps become too familiar, and the concept is arguably due for a root and branch re-examination (of a sort that cannot be attempted here). So far, however, classic formulations, though perhaps unsatisfactory in some respects, have proved resistant to rejection or to extensive reformulation.[55] Suffice it to say, for the moment, that the kind of over-determination operative in the deeds of Oedipus is not the same as that described in our everyday modern examples. The secretary may execute both his own decision and the boss's in (say) calling the photocopier repair man, but his doing so is not normally seen as the boss somehow performing the action of calling the engineer *via* the action of the secretary. Oedipus does execute Apollo's will, both in the self-blinding and in the parricide and incest, but even in the self-blinding he is not simply carrying out an order that happens to coincide with his own decision. The god's will is not merely prior to but immanent in the human action. This is especially apparent in the parricide and incest, where what Apollo wants is not what Oedipus wants, yet it is the actions that Oedipus and others choose to take that bring those events to pass.

When a human action, such as the self-blinding, is simultaneously an action of the unseen god we are dealing with a distinctly supernatural form of causation, albeit one that is based on everyday forms of inference about causation and agency.[56] But though the concept of gods is presumably always a concept of the supernatural (for even if gods are believed to be immanent in nature it is not in fact true that they are), not all the ways in which these supernatural beings interact with humans are in themselves supernatural. An action of a god, for example, need not be simultaneously an action of a human being through whom the god acts, but may simply be a factor that causes a reaction in a human being in the same way as another human's action might. This type of divine intervention in human affairs is also very much in evidence in the *OT*. Apollo's initial oracle to Laius, for example, led him to have his infant son exposed; this meant that, having been saved from extinction (by another human being acting for the best of human motives), Oedipus grew up not at Thebes, with knowledge of who his natural parents were, but at Corinth. Similarly, it is in reaction to another pronouncement of the god at Delphi that Oedipus resolves to put as much distance between himself and Corinth as he can, thus delivering himself to the crossroads in time for his encounter with Laius.[57] A third oracle, reported by Creon at the beginning of the play, causes Oedipus, as any good leader would, to initiate the actions that lead to his own identification as killer and incestuous parricide. There is thus some purchase for Kovacs's explanation of the role of Apollo in the events of Oedipus' life, that Apollo is like a chess grand master pitted against a novice opponent: 'All of [the novice's] moves in the game are freely chosen, and [the novice is] in every sense the author of them, yet the grand master can beat [the novice] easily – indeed, can confidently predict the result of the match beforehand... All of Oedipus' actions are free, but because Apollo knows more than Oedipus and because he can withhold information from him when he wants and supply it where it will be most misleading, he easily engineers the result.'[58] This account of Apollo's role is an advance upon the quasi-Laplacean demon, the god who knows but does not cause, of Dodds's version. But it is insufficient: Apollo does not merely 'confidently predict' parricide, incest, and self-blinding; those things are bound to happen. Apollo, we are encouraged to think, ensured that they did, but also knew for certain that they would; for him, these are objects not of confident belief but of knowledge. Nor is Apollo's intervention limited to eliciting human reactions that will further his own plans: the self-blinding is not a reaction by Oedipus to something that Apollo did; it *is* something that Apollo did, *as well as* Oedipus. Divine power in the *OT* is manifested not only in the few direct interventions that influence human behaviour, but also in a grand design that encompasses those interventions; and it includes occurrences that appear initially to be the result of chance as well as apparently spontaneous human actions. The analogy is less that of a grand master against a novice but of a grand master against a rather basic chess-playing computer programme in whose design the grand master has himself participated and in whose moves he is able directly to intervene.

In standard, everyday cases of over-determination, each cause is sufficient, but none is in itself necessary: if the boss had not asked the secretary to call the repair man, the secretary would have anyway; no single member of the firing squad needs to hit the target as long as at least one other member does. Just so, if Apollo had not wanted Oedipus to blind himself, Oedipus himself had sufficient reasons to do so anyway. In such cases, however, one cause is often more effective than the others: the boss's decision to call the repair main trumps that of the secretary; had the secretary been against the idea, the boss could have issued a command that overrode his opinion; had the secretary wanted to call the repair man, but the boss forbade him to do so, the repair man would not have been called. Similarly (but purely hypothetically), had Oedipus not wanted to blind himself – had the self-blinding been, like the parricide and incest, something that he did not ἑκών but ἄκων, we assume that it would have been as much in Apollo's power to ensure, as he did in the case of the prophecies of parricide and incest, that it should still happen despite human opposition (e.g. in a fit of madness such as that which overcomes Heracles in Euripides' play or Ajax in Sophocles'). In this case, though both causes are sufficient and neither is, given the other, necessary, nonetheless one of the two causes, the divine one, is more truly effective than the other.[59] We see this in the case of the parricide and incest, where the aims of the god and those of the human characters are at variance: the human agents – Oedipus' parents when they expose the child they had rather than abstain from sex or kill the child at birth, the Theban shepherd who takes pity on the infant he is despatched to expose, Oedipus himself when he receives Apollo's oracle – take action which contributes to the prophesied outcome, but do so with the specific intention of frustrating that outcome. The outcome that is prophesied and desired by the god comes about in spite of what they do. If they have a degree of freedom, they are nonetheless not free to frustrate that outcome. This is a commonplace of archaic Greek thought. Bernd Manuwald has pointed out the close resemblance between the Oedipus myth as dramatized by Sophocles and other examples, chiefly the tale of Croesus, Atys, and Adrastus in Herodotus Book 1, in which human beings try but fail to evade a fated outcome.[60] This is not by any means the logic of all myths or of all tragic dramatizations of myth, but in the *OT* this particular mythical pattern is confirmed by events both onstage and off.[61] A similar sense of the true effectiveness of divine causation emerges in a case such as that of Patroclus in *Iliad* 16. This is a case of over-determination: Patroclus' disregard, in the heat of battle, of Achilles' warning not to attack Troy (16. 88–96) is adequately motivated by his desire for glory and by the elation of his success so far, but it is also a requirement of Zeus' plan, first enunciated in Book 8, that the Trojans' success should continue for a further day and Achilles not return to battle until Patroclus has been slain (8. 472–6). What Patroclus wants does not conflict with what Zeus wants; but if it did, Zeus would prevail (16. 684–91):

Πάτροκλος δ' ἵπποισι καὶ Αὐτομέδοντι κελεύσας
Τρῶας καὶ Λυκίους μετεκίαθε, καὶ μέγ' ἀάσθη   685
νήπιος· εἰ δὲ ἔπος Πηληϊάδαο φύλαξεν
ἦ τ' ἂν ὑπέκφυγε κῆρα κακὴν μέλανος θανάτοιο.
ἀλλ' αἰεί τε Διὸς κρείσσων νόος ἠέ περ ἀνδρῶν·
ὅς τε καὶ ἄλκιμον ἄνδρα φοβεῖ καὶ ἀφείλετο νίκην
ῥηϊδίως, ὅτε δ' αὐτὸς ἐποτρύνῃσι μάχεσθαι·   690
ὅς οἱ καὶ τότε θυμὸν ἐνὶ στήθεσσιν ἐνῆκεν.

With a shout to the horses and Automedon, Patroclus went after the Lycians; so, poor fool, he was greatly afflicted by *atē*.[62] Had he remembered the words of Peleus' son he might have escaped the evil doom of black death. But the mind of Zeus is always stronger than that of men. It puts even a brave man to flight and easily deprives him of victory, when he himself drives him on to fight. Then too he put spirit in Patroclus' chest.

The counterfactual, as in the examples discussed above, reveals that the effective cause of Patroclus' forgetting, and thus of his death, is Zeus: Patroclus might have escaped with his life, had he remembered Achilles' warning; but the mind of Zeus is stronger than that of men, so he did not. Though Patroclus is 'foolish' (νήπιος, 686) in forgetting, he could not really have remembered; Zeus intervenes to ensure that he does not (691).[63] Here, over-determination is presented hypothetically as a struggle between god and man, and in such circumstances the god will always prevail.

In this case, however, as in that of Oedipus' self-blinding, the divine cause is sufficient but, given its coincidence with human motivation, not necessary. But the case of the parricide and incest is different. Here, the divine cause remains effective: Oedipus did not want to kill his father and marry his mother, indeed he did all in his power not to do so; but still he did. Yet if Apollo had not wanted Oedipus to commit these acts, if he had not intervened in ways that led him to commit them, it is hard to imagine that Oedipus would have committed them anyway. Though similarly over-determined by supernatural factors and human choice, the parricide and incest differ from the self-blinding in that in these cases the divine cause appears essential; take away that cause, and it is difficult to imagine a possible world in which there exists a cause or set of causes sufficient to bring about those results. In these cases it is the divine input that makes the human action, adequately motivated in normal human terms though it may be, contribute to ends that the god foresees and wants and that the human beings do not. In such cases, one cannot say, as scholars sometimes do, that divine causation leaves human freedom (or 'free will') unaffected, because in these cases divine causation imposes considerable limitations upon what human beings are free to do or not to do. The human agents may will the means, but not the ends; the ends are set by the gods and are in conflict with the desires and projects of the human agents. In so far as the actions of humans promote the gods' ends rather than their own, even the means are more truly the gods' than the humans'. In such situations human beings may still be answerable for their actions, but that is another matter.

In the case of the self-blinding, what Apollo wants is also what Oedipus wants. Though in a sense this action 'was Apollo', Oedipus takes full ownership; in full realization of how forces beyond his control have brought him to this point, Oedipus endorses and appropriates the self-blinding. The revelation of who he is and what he has done makes all the difference; he is now able to choose to act consciously and deliberately in accordance with the ends chosen by Apollo. Thus the responsibility he takes for the self-blinding entails a kind of responsibility for the parricide and incest to which the self-blinding reacts. The self-blinding is itself a way of recognizing that the parricide and incest are *his* acts, even if he committed them in ignorance and despite his efforts to avoid them. Within limits severely circumscribed by fate, Oedipus takes responsibility for his past. The abhorrence that the Chorus express for his actions and his person is something that he himself shares;[64] the knowledge that he is the man who did these things is something that he knows he has to bear; indeed, he says, only he *can* bear it (1414–15).[65] There is thus a strong sense that Oedipus the man must be answerable for his actions, despite their conformity to a pattern that was set before his birth and even though they were performed in ignorance. This is not blame, and indeed moral and legal culpability can be denied, as in *OC* (258–74, 525–6, 545–8, 960–99);[66] but it is a strong and impressive assertion of Oedipus' sense of agency.

For a variety of reasons, moreover, the kinds of over-determination presented in the *OT* are compatible with the retention of a degree of human freedom. First, though human freedom to act is circumscribed, it is not wholly circumscribed. Though there are cases, such as Oedipus' self-blinding, when a self-chosen human action is at the same time an action caused by a god, it does not appear that all human choice is micro-managed in this way. There remains room for considerable disagreement (among ancient Athenians and modern interpreters) about how far, how many, and which individual human actions are determined as part of an overall divine plan. But in any case, even where they are so determined (as in the case of the self-blinding), human motives can remain causally sufficient. Second, as we have already noted, it is a basic fact that the belief in humans' responsibility for their actions is deeply engrained in language and thought. Such beliefs survive even when held in conjunction with other, incompatible beliefs. In no literary genre at any period does a belief in effective divine causation entirely remove the sense that human beings are, at least to some extent, answerable for what they do. One reason for this is that the sort of insight into divine causation that is possible in drama and in other forms of imaginative literature is not available in daily life. Though it is possible for an audience to do as Peradotto (1992) urges and reject the premises on which the plot of Sophocles' play is constructed (that the gods exist, that they are capable of knowing the future, and that they act, both in their own persons and through human action, to cause events in the world), an audience that accepts those premises enters a fictional world in which divine causation has a much more concrete and less contested explanatory power than it ever does in the real world, even if the belief in divine causation is a feature of the real world too. Yet the real world remains the one in which all of us live: we modify, but do not wholly override, our intuitions as to how the world works when we enter the imaginative worlds of fiction. But even in the real world, divine causation is fiction, a network of metaphor based on ordinary human experience of causation and agency. In a belief-system in which gods, like persons, are agents, effective human action, in which humans are able to act, of their own volition, to bring about changes in the world, is the source domain which provides the material for the concept of the agency of personal divinities. Even a culture that holds that such divine agency severely limits the room for genuine and responsible human agency cannot be said to lack the latter concept; for that concept is in fact prior to the notion of divine causation which is felt to undermine it.[67] If, therefore, the view of human agency implicit in the *OT* is one in which human freedom is drastically limited, this is an artefact of two levels of fictionality, that of ancient Greek belief and that of Sophocles' play, and not an indication that the Athenians of Sophocles' day do not (or 'not yet', as the progressivists would say) have a concept of effective human agency. Yet whatever residue of the belief that human beings are effective causes of their own actions remains in the structure of the play and the minds of its audience, that residue must co-exist, for anyone who accepts the play's fictional world, with an acceptance that human beings' ability to forge their own futures can be radically limited. At no stage of his life was Oedipus free not to commit parricide and incest. Both because his self-blinding is, before it occurs, an object of certain knowledge and because it is the product of Apollo's designs as well as Oedipus' own, Oedipus is not free not to blind himself either. Anyone who accepts that the parricide and incest are less than free must accept that Oedipus is also less than free in what he does on stage. 'Free agency' is not a notion that adequately encapsulates Oedipus' career, onstage or off.

Oedipus' freedom is circumscribed not because all events are causally determined, but because there are forces (or rather agents) at work in the world that are set on his destruction. We have seen already that the design of the play supports the pronouncements and intuitions of its characters that Apollo or the gods are as active in the revelation that brings Oedipus down as they were in the horrors that are revealed. This impression of an order that is ranged against Oedipus is confirmed as much by the language of fate as it is by the language used of the gods. For in fact there is no hard and fast distinction between the two. This is true in two ways. First, powers with a degree of agency and personality can be used as metonyms for the notion of individual destiny. Second, the mechanism of personification that is fundamental to the conceptualization of both major and minor divinities is also regularly employed for entities such as fate and fortune, even when these are not being represented as fully anthropomorphic agents. Hence, although in *OT* the term *daimōn* can be used of personally motivated divine agents (as when the *daimōn* who leapt upon Oedipus' fate or portion, i.e. his *moira*, at 1300–2, who 'leapt out' at him at 1311, and who 'urged [him] on' to blind himself at 1328, is named as Apollo in 1329),[68] that term itself can, because one's lot in life can be said to depend on the good will of one or more *daimones*,[69] be used as a way of referring to one's lot in life as such. This is how the Chorus use the word at 1193–5:

> τὸν σόν τοι παράδειγμ' ἔχων,
> τὸν σὸν δαίμονα, τὸν σόν, ὦ
> τλᾶμον Οἰδιπόδα, βροτῶν
> οὐδὲν μακαρίζω.   1195

With your *daimōn* as my example, yours, O wretched Oedipus, I consider nothing that mortals have to be fortunate.

This is a regular archaic and classical use of the word: the divine power which is envisaged as the dispenser of good and bad fortune becomes a metonomy for that good or bad fortune itself.[70] In such a conception, the notion of fate and that of divine agency are very closely intertwined. The same is true in a complementary way of *moira*, 'fate'. *Moira* is basically 'share' or 'portion', and the reference to one's lot in life is simply a particular application of this general sense.[71] Within this subset of uses, one's *moira* in life can be spoken of as if it were an impersonal and objective state of affairs, as when it is said to be one's *moira* to act or to be affected in a certain way.[72] At the other end of the spectrum, *moira* can be a fully personified supernatural agent, endowed with substantial mythological personality, as in the case of the Moira who joined with Zeus and 'the Erinys who walks in mist' to inspire Agamemnon's *atē* (*Il.* 19. 87–8),[73] the Moirai who endow human beings with a spirit of endurance (*Il.* 14. 49), or the powerful Moira who spun the thread of Hector's life at the moment of his birth, according to Hecuba at *Iliad* 24. 209–12.[74] Personification, indeed, is regular in the case of *moira*, even where *moira* is less a minor divinity than a name for one's fate in general or that aspect of fate that unites all mortals, namely death; for *moira* in these senses regularly meets or comes to a person, leads a person to a certain end, takes hold of, binds, or subdues a person.[75] How closely such metaphors of agency coalesce with the notion of *moira* not as an agent but as a state of affairs is shown by *Iliad* 18. 117–21:

> οὐδὲ γὰρ οὐδὲ βίη Ἡρακλῆος φύγε κῆρα,
> ὅς περ φίλτατος ἔσκε Διὶ Κρονίωνι ἄνακτι·
> ἀλλά ἑ μοῖρα δάμασσε καὶ ἀργαλέος χόλος Ἥρης.
> ὣς καὶ ἐγών, εἰ δή μοι ὁμοίη μοῖρα τέτυκται,   120
> κείσομ' ἐπεί κε θάνω.

> For not even mighty Heracles escaped death, who was dearest of all to lord Zeus, son of Cronus, but *moira* overcame him, and the troublesome anger of Hera. So I, too, if indeed a like *moira* is fashioned for me, shall lie when I die.

In this passage the event of death is figured in three ways: as a supernatural force that one cannot avoid (οὐδὲ βίη Ἡρακλῆος φύγε κῆρα, 117), as an opponent that subdues a person (μοῖρα δάμασσε, 119), and as an artefact that is fashioned for a person (μοῖρα τέτυκται, 120). One's fate is not merely an event, a series of events, or a state of affairs, but an active force. These are, of course, metaphors (in which the experiential world of human agents furnishes models for the unseen world of supernatural causation), but they are theory-constitutive or conceptual metaphors that are fundamental to the archaic Greek world view.[76]

The *OT* is permeated by such modes of thought. *Moira* can be spoken of as if it were an impersonal state of affairs, but can also be presented as an active force. Tiresias' words at 376–7 show how these conceptions, the apparently static and the dynamic, interact:

> οὐ γάρ σε μοῖρα πρός γ' ἐμοῦ πεσεῖν, ἐπεὶ
> ἱκανὸς Ἀπόλλων ᾧ τάδ' ἐκπρᾶξαι μέλει.

> No, it is not your *moira* to fall at my hands: Apollo suffices for that, whose concern it is to bring these things to pass.

The main clause presents *moira* simply as a future state of affairs of which Tiresias has knowledge, but the subordinate clauses entail that that state of affairs is a product of deliberate divine activity. The same is true of 1300–2, where the Chorus ask

> τίς ὁ πηδήσας   1300
> μείζονα δαίμων τῶν μακίστων
> πρὸς σῇ δυσδαίμονι μοίρᾳ;

> Who is the *daimōn* who leapt further than the longest leap onto your ill-*daimōn*ed fate (*moira*)?

Oedipus' *moira* consists of everything that has happened to him so far, and in particular the parricide and incest; but that *moira* is itself *dysdaimōn*, and the explicit statement that the self-blinding, which has made that *moira* even worse, is the work of a *daimōn* that has 'leapt upon' Oedipus' life positively requires us to give *dysdaimōn* its most literal sense, 'produced by a hostile *daimōn*'.

Elsewhere *moira* refers to whatever it may be that awaits one in the future, but that state of affairs is at the same time endowed with the capacity of self-motion: there was an oracle, says Jocasta, not that it would *be* Laius' *moira* to be slain by his son, but that such a *moira* would *come*, ἥξοι μοῖρα (713); 'let my *moira* go wherever it will go', says Oedipus at 1458 (ἡ μὲν ἡμῶν μοῖρ' ὅποιπερ εἶσ' ἴτω). Such personification is unremarkable in itself (as unremarkable as my use of 'awaits' immediately above), but the tendency to personify takes on more specific and pronounced connotations of agency in two passages of the second stasimon, where the Chorus pray first that a certain *moira* should remain with, i.e. not abandon them (εἴ μοι ξυνείη...μοῖρα, 863) and then that a contrary, bad *moira* seize the impious (κακά νιν ἕλοιτο μοῖρα, 887). One's lot, for good and for ill, is thus spoken of in terms which might also be used of the god or *daimōn* felt to dispense or to symbolize that lot.[77] In a similar way, the Keres, personifications of death and so divinities in some respects analogous to the Moirai, join with Apollo in pursuing the murderer of Laius, according to the Chorus at 469–72, while in the fourth stasimon the Chorus memorably sing that Time, who sees all things, has discovered Oedipus 'against his will' and now judges his incestuous marriage (ἐφηῦρέ σ' ἄκονθ' ὁ πάνθ' ὁρῶν χρόνος· | δικάζει τὸν ἄγαμον γάμον πάλαι | τεκνοῦντα καὶ τεκνούμενον, 1213–15).[78] As we have seen,[79] much of the play's language about chance (*tychē*) sustains this impression of a world permeated by non-human agents: not only does much of the language of *tychē* point ironically at design rather than chance, and not only is Tyche described, erroneously and ironically, as Oedipus' mother at 1080, but *tychē* itself is regularly presented as an agent: *tychē* leapt on Laius' head (263), much as the *daimōn* leaps on Oedipus (1299–1302, 1311),[80] and Laius died 'at the hands of *tychē*' (948–9); just so Oedipus' *tychē* has destroyed him (442), while in the past a certain *tychē* stood over him (776–7).[81] Such metaphors can point to the operation of a divine intention of which the speaker is unaware: hence Jocasta, as she prepares to offer the prayers and sacrifices that are followed immediately by the entry of the Corinthian Messenger (and thus confirm that Apollo is even closer than she thinks, 919), unwittingly refers to her decision to propitiate the gods as if it were itself some kind of supernatural agent (δόξα μοι παρεστάθη | ναοὺς ἱκέσθαι δαιμόνων, 911–12); and Oedipus, determined to pursue the truth of his origins despite the Chorus-leader's fears that Jocasta's sudden exit bodes ill, speaks of the evils that may burst forth as if they themselves had wishes or needs (ὁποῖα χρῄζει ῥηγνύτω, 1076). His sense that he has been the unwitting object of the attentions of external agents is vividly expressed in his extended apostrophe of the decisive events and locations in his life (Cithaeron, Corinth, Polybus' palace, the crossroads, his marriage) as if they had been active participants in his downfall at 1391–1408:

ἰὼ Κιθαιρών, τί μ' ἐδέχου; τί μ' οὐ λαβὼν
ἔκτεινας εὐθύς, ὡς ἔδειξα μήποτε

ἐμαυτὸν ἀνθρώποισιν ἔνθεν ἦ γεγώς;
ὦ Πόλυβε καὶ Κόρινθε καὶ τὰ πάτρια
λόγῳ παλαιὰ δώμαθ', οἷον ἄρά με   1395
κάλλος κακῶν ὕπουλον ἐξεθρέψατε.
νῦν γὰρ κακός τ' ὢν κἀκ κακῶν εὑρίσκομαι.
ὦ τρεῖς κέλευθοι καὶ κεκρυμμένη νάπη,
δρυμός τε καὶ στενωπὸς ἐν τριπλαῖς ὁδοῖς,
αἳ τοὐμὸν αἷμα τῶν ἐμῶν χειρῶν ἄπο   1400
ἐπίετε πατρός, ἆρά μου μέμνησθ' ἔτι
οἷ' ἔργα δράσας ὑμὶν εἶτα δεῦρ' ἰὼν
ὁποῖ' ἔπρασσον αὖθις; ὦ γάμοι, γάμοι,
ἐφύσαθ' ἡμᾶς, καὶ φυτεύσαντες πάλιν
ἀνεῖτε ταὐτὸν σπέρμα, κἀπεδείξατε   1405
πατέρας ἀδελφούς, παῖδας αἷμ' ἐμφύλιον,
νύμφας γυναῖκας μητέρας τε, χὠπόσα
αἴσχιστ' ἐν ἀνθρώποισιν ἔργα γίγνεται.

O Cithaeron, why did you receive me? Why did you not take me and kill me at once, that I might never have revealed to mortals whence I was born? O Polybus and Corinth and my alleged ancient ancestral home, what a beauty was I, this festering wound of hidden evils that you reared! For now I am found to be the evil offspring of evil progenitors. O three roads and hidden glen, copse and defile at the crossroads, you roads who drank my own blood, father's blood, from my own hands, do you still remember what deeds I did before you, and then again what I did when I came here? O marriage, marriage, you gave me birth, and having done so you sent forth the same seed again, and displayed father-brothers, children of incestuous blood, brides both wives and mothers, and all the things that are most shameful among humans.

Again, these are metaphors, an aspect of tragedy's elevated poetic idiom; but they are not mere *façons de parler*. Ontological metaphor, especially personification, pervades the language of the play and coalesces with the sense of active divine presence created both by the play's dramaturgy and by the explicit pronouncements of its characters. The cumulative impression created by these elements is not simply of the occasional intervention of a single divinity but of a universe that is actively ranged against and indeed hostile to the plans and actions of the play's central character.[82] This is a vision of a universe that is not merely ordered and in principle knowable, not merely beyond the control of the human will, but actually formed by the expression of the will of opposing forms of agency. It is a vision in which there is no sharp disjunction between the gods on the one hand and fate in the other; the notion of agency unites both.

Though there is a sense in which Oedipus' actions can be characterized as manifesting one kind of what ordinary English calls 'free will' and at the same time a sense in which the major events of his life are determined, the precise kinds of human action presupposed by the *OT* are not well captured in terms of either pole of the later philosophical antithesis of free will and determinism. Even though Oedipus takes ownership of his actions, the circumstances in which those actions were performed are such that it would be perverse to call them 'free'. And though the gods' foreknowledge of parricide, incest, and self-blinding means that those events are necessary rather than contingent, this necessity is not simply the working out of an unbroken causal chain but rather the product of the agency of hostile forces in a hostile universe.

This raises possibly the biggest question of all in the scholarship on this play: if the gods, especially as represented by Apollo, have an interest in bringing about Oedipus' downfall, *why* should this be so? Does Dodds's question about divine justice arise, and if so, how? Is there any sense in which what happens to Oedipus can be regarded as condign punishment? Perhaps there is no final answer, but the question is inevitable, and there are important considerations that should guide any attempt at an answer.[83]

In this case, there *is* an important distinction to be drawn between the plot's *Vorgeschichte* and its onstage action. There are many interpretations that adduce aspects of Oedipus' behaviour as presented onstage as factors that warrant his suffering: he is rash, he is over-confident in his intellectual prowess, he jumps to premature conclusions, he is quick to anger, and he is unfair in his treatment of Tiresias and Creon.[84] But in expressing their horror at what has happened, Oedipus himself, the Chorus, and the Exangelos mention none of these things; the reactions of the characters themselves all focus on the facts of what Oedipus has done in killing his father and marrying his mother. These abominations were perpetrated before the action portrayed on stage began and neither could be in any way exacerbated or ameliorated by anything that Oedipus does or does not do during the play itself.[85] Hence some interpreters locate Oedipus' responsibility for his own downfall, the fault that would warrant Apollo's determination to hunt him down, in those acts themselves.[86] And these are indeed crimes of the most heinous kind; but (as we have seen) Oedipus had no choice but to commit them, and when he did, he did so in ignorance. For some, this ignorance is itself culpable – Oedipus should have questioned the oracle that led him to leave Corinth;[87] he should have avoided violent conflict with a man old enough to be his father and marriage with a woman old enough to be his mother.[88] Or perhaps the rage he displays in killing the man who turned out to be his father is excessive, a sign of an intemperate and violent character.[89] But even if Oedipus is guilty of a homicide in which his hot-headedness and acute concern for his status play a substantial contributory role,[90] and even though his objective guilt as the murderer of Laius makes him a polluted individual, subject to the decree that he himself issued, still the crime of homicide *qua* homicide pales into insignificance beside those of parricide and incest. These are the essentials; and the logic both of the mythical pattern to which his story belongs and the play in which it is dramatized is that these were things he had to do, that this necessity obtained even before his birth. If Oedipus is born at all, he *will* kill his father and marry his mother.[91] These things had to happen, and in the play they have already happened; since they have happened, all that remains is for them to be discovered to have happened; and once they have been discovered, suffering is inevitable. If, in a godless universe, Oedipus had killed a man who turned out to be his father and fathered children upon that man's wife, later revealed to be his own mother, he would (one can only believe) have reacted no differently and suffered no less. In that sense, the suffering that follows the discovery belongs within the same sequence of objective misfortune that includes the acts themselves. Oedipus does take ownership of these acts in the act of his self-blinding, but also makes it clear that his horror at what he has done is simultaneously horror at what has happened to him, what has been done to him by the *daimōn*, by Apollo. The issue of the justification, if any, for Oedipus' suffering is therefore to be located not in the legitimacy of the 'punishment' of his crimes, but in the nature of a universe in which a man can be destined, from birth, to suffer both these crimes and their consequences.

This perspective dominates the play once the truth of Oedipus' deeds and identity become known. The first evaluation, once all the facts are known, is that of the Theban servant: if Oedipus is indeed the child whom he once saved from death, then Oedipus was 'born ill-fated' (δύσποτμος γεγώς, 1181). Oedipus himself agrees: the horror of his existence lies not only in his parricide and incest, but in his birth (1184–5):

πέφασμαι φύς τ' ἀφ' ὧν οὐ χρῆν, ξὺν οἷς τ'
οὐ χρῆν ὁμιλῶν, οὕς τέ μ' οὐκ ἔδει κτανών.[92]   1185

> I am revealed as born of parents I should not have been born of, the consort of those I should not have consorted with, the killer of those I should not have killed.

This idea, that Oedipus' suffering manifests a pattern that has governed his life from the moment of his birth is then taken up by the Chorus in the fourth stasimon, where the nature of Oedipus' *daimōn* – both the pattern that defines his life and the supernatural agency that lies behind that pattern – is taken as a paradigm for the vulnerability of all human *eudaimonia*: if

Oedipus can rise so high and sink so low, then mortal existence, all the cycles of birth, generation, and death, amount to nothing (1186–1222). Oedipus is a paradigm not of human wickedness, not of culpable negligence, obtuseness, or intemperance, but simply of the instability of human happiness, of the principle of alternation that governs all human lives.[93] This principle, enunciated in such memorable formulations as Achilles' image of the jars of Zeus in *Iliad* 24. 525–34, the lapidary coda to Pindar's last datable poem (*P*. 8. 95–7), and Bacchylides' use of the meeting of Heracles and Meleager in Hades to illustrate the *gnōmē* that no man is *eudaimōn* in all respects (Ode 5. 50–175), is the cornerstone of the popular ethics of archaic and classical Greece. It is this that explains why one should count no man happy until he is dead, a notion prominent enough in Greek popular ethics to receive extended discussion in the first book of Aristotle's *Nicomachean Ethics*.[94] It is a pessimistic view, but also one that promotes empathy, understanding, and resilience: it reminds us that suffering is the shared lot of all humankind, even the most fortunate, and underpins that sense, central to the Greek conceptualization of pity, that we ourselves are vulnerable to the misfortunes that plague others;[95] and since all inevitably suffer, the correct response to one's own suffering is not despair but endurance.[96] In the *OT*, the Chorus' affirmation that Oedipus' sufferings are illustrative of a vulnerability that all share (1186–95) is taken up by the Exangelos, who similarly presents him as a paradigm of alternation (1282–5), and though there is also genuine horror and revulsion at what Oedipus has done,[97] still the dominant note in the responses of others to his misfortunes is one of sympathy (1194, 1211, 1216–21, 1286, 1296, 1299, 1303, 1347).[98] Oedipus himself, meanwhile, though he understandably gives expression to a great deal of lamentation and self-loathing, also forcefully affirms the rightness of his self-mutilation as a response to his deeds (1331–5, 1337–9, 1369–90), declares his ability to bear not only his present sufferings (1414–15) but also any more that may be to come (1455–7), and assumes (from 1432) a desire to master events that requires a pointed reminder from Creon that the authority he once enjoyed is no longer his to dispose (1522–3). In this paradigmatic presentation of the lessons of alternation – that suffering is the common lot of humanity, that shared vulnerability is a reason for empathy, and that human beings must endure – there is no purchase whatever for the view that Oedipus is a malefactor (or the son of a malefactor) whose punishment illustrates the justice of the gods. And this matters: these are the notes on which the play ends.[99]

But the onstage actions that have led up to the discovery of Oedipus' parentage and his deeds matter too, and we must assume that they are presented as they are for a reason. Oedipus' actions demonstrate a progressive unravelling of his initially positive presentation as a concerned, competent, and public-spirited leader at the height of his powers. The insistent irony of his determination to root out the murderer of Laius attests to his ignorance of his own true position. He is quick to anger towards Tiresias and Creon and accuses them both of involvement in a wholly imaginary plot to remove him from power. His eventual suspicion that Tiresias may have been correct in naming him as the murderer promotes a scepticism about oracles that is misplaced and ominous. Throughout the earlier part of the play, prior to the entrance of the Corinthian messenger, he overlooks what appear to the audience as blatantly obvious indications of the true situation. The anger, sensitivity to insult, and brutality that he displays on stage towards Tiresias, Creon, and the Theban shepherd are mirrored in his own description of the way in which he killed the man at the crossroads. This is the material for what Michael Lurje has referred to as 'die Suche nach der Schuld'; and, in a sense, none of it matters – none of these things is a cause of Oedipus' downfall, and none would be sufficient to warrant the intensity of suffering in which the play reaches its conclusion. Yet this presentation does have an effect – the sense that some scholars have, and no doubt some ordinary readers and spectators too, that Oedipus' shortcomings bear directly on his downfall, although mistaken, is evidence enough of that. As many have noticed, from Heraclitus onwards, what we see with our own eyes makes a greater impression than what we merely hear about.[100] Had Sophocles wished to sustain the wholly positive impression of Oedipus with which the play begins, he could presumably have done so. So why does he make him rash, irascible, insecure, and unable to see the truth when it is staring him in the face?

If the 'faults' that Oedipus manifests in the course of his search are causally irrelevant, they cannot be dramatically or thematically irrelevant. Fundamentally, these characteristics are aspects of Oedipus' ignorance.[101] Because of their impact as visible aspects of the onstage action, they act as a kind of 'optical illusion' that complicates an audience's response. The effect is to underline the irony – we know that Oedipus has already done what he was fated to do and that he is now fated to discover that he has done so, yet the sympathy elicited by his initially positive characterization is mixed with dismay that he can be so misguided and nervousness that his erroneous grasp of events should be expressed in ways that undercut the positive impression that he initially created. Some audience members may even begin to believe that his shortcomings are material to the suffering that awaits him when truth is revealed. It is important not to see the action of the play as if it were merely a series of propositions, as scholars such as Lefèvre and Schmitt tend to do; the mood, pace, and sequence of the action as it develops on stage all matter very much.[102] But this is also why it is important not to ignore the action of the play entirely and concentrate only on the logic of the *Vorgeschichte*, according to which the only relevant facts are that Oedipus was doomed, from the moment of his birth, to kill his father and marry his mother. To be sure, it is essential to keep that proposition in mind, but doing so creates a tension between the audience's knowledge of what is causally significant and its tendency to assume that the failings that Oedipus demonstrates in the course of his search are not merely red herrings.

Audience members seduced by the temptation to moralize Oedipus' downfall receive a degree of encouragement from the second stasimon, for however one interprets this ode in detail,[103] it is undeniable that it links the maintenance of morality to that of religion, and the maintenance of religion to the infallibility of oracles that has been questioned by Jocasta, and to a lesser extent Oedipus, in the previous scene.[104] Whether the hybristic and tyrannical wrongdoer of 873–96 (or the transgressor of the divine laws that are extolled in 863–72), is Oedipus, merely the unknown murderer of Laius, or neither, the ode is relevant to Oedipus in three main ways. First, there is the central irony that if the Chorus' prayer of 903–10 is fulfilled, and Zeus sees to it that the oracle received by Laius is vindicated, then Oedipus will be revealed as an incestuous parricide. Second, the crimes of parricide and incest are ironically present in the Chorus' words: they sing of purity (864), and Oedipus not only fears that he may be impure (823) but is much more impure than he knows; the occurrence of this theme takes an audience back to the plague which is the manifestation of Oedipus' pollution and the catalyst for the search. The facts of Oedipus' career are likewise recalled in the song's references to childbirth, generation, fatherhood, and growth (867–70), to lying down to sleep (871), and to the untouchable (891). Characteristic also are the punning references to feet (866, 878–9), an ironically indirect method of naming the man who is in fact the object of the search.[105] Third, and most important, the strophe and antistrophos of the ode each consist of prayers, and each prayer is for a certain kind of *moira* – that it may be the singers' own *moira* always to observe the august laws of the gods (863–72), and that an evil *moira* take anyone who despises morality and religion (883–96). These two prayers are fundamental to that blend of error and accuracy that make the ode so difficult.[106] In broad terms, the Chorus' hope that the truth of Laius' oracle will vindicate the power of the gods and the value of religious practice is fulfilled – the immediate sequel shows that the divine whose lives consist either of total misery or of an admixture of misery and happiness, and gods, who live without care. Even the *Odyssey*, a much more moralistic and morally comforting poem than the *Iliad* or the *OT*, makes it programmatically clear that while mortals may bring misfortune (including divine punishment) beyond what is fated upon themselves by virtue of their own recklessness, there is a large element of human suffering that lies within their portion and which does not proceed from their transgressions (*Od*. 1. 32–43). As Zeus' speech in the first book of the *Odyssey* juxtaposes two models of human suffering, that which is caused by their *atasthaliē* and that which is inherent in the human condition, so too does the *OT*, the second stasimon concentrating on human *hybris* and the fourth solely on vicissitude. But in the *Iliad*, the *Odyssey*, and the *OT* human suffering is part of a world order that exists by divine dispensation and which the gods police because that order in itself defines the difference between god and human.

This gulf in status between man and god is manifested not only in the perpetual felicity of the divine and the vulnerability and instability of the human, but in terms of power, authority, and knowledge. If, on the one hand, Oedipus' self-blinding is his own personal reaction to the intrinsic horror of his condition, a reaction to which the status of his acts as voluntary or involuntary is of no significance, it is still, on the other, part of a pattern laid down by Apollo that Tiresias is able to foresee in advance. We have seen, moreover, that the pattern that obtains in Oedipus' life is not merely one of a chain of events that unfold by virtue of their own internal logic of causal necessity, but a divine plan in whose elaboration the gods themselves, especially Apollo, are intimately involved. We are explicitly and authoritatively informed that Apollo wants Oedipus' fall (376–7; cf. above); it is no step at all to assume that he also wants Oedipus' blindness. And if he does, the reason is clear: the literal blindness that follows Oedipus' discovery of the truth emphasizes the metaphorical, intellectual blindness that has been Oedipus' lot from the day of his birth to the moment of discovery. The self-blinding symbolizes the human limitations that are also the subject of the fourth stasimon.[112] Using mathematical imagery that has hitherto been characteristic of Oedipus' faith in his own powers of reasoning,[113] the Chorus pronounce that the generations of mortals add up to nothing (1186–8); what our lives seem to be is not really what they are (1189–92); Oedipus, the searcher and revealer, has been revealed – Time sees all, human beings do not, and what Time has revealed is precisely what Oedipus strove to avoid (1213). He did what he did *akōn*; he did not know what he was doing (as the Corinthian messenger earlier observed, 1008); he was not in control.

There is thus a link between Oedipus as a symbol of human fallibility, especially of the fallibility of human knowledge and the limitations of human powers, and his behaviour in the first and second episodes, where it is his failures of reasoning, his ignorance of the truth, and his blindness to everything that does not conform to his own limited perspective that lie behind the genuine shortcomings that have troubled many commentators and which must make at least some impression on any audience. The fourth stasimon underlines the point that man's knowledge is limited and contrasts it with a source of knowledge and vision of which man is not the subject, but an object. Oedipus' mistakes, misjudgements, and mistreatment of others ignore these human limitations and thus involve a degree of presumption, an arrogation to oneself of prerogatives that truly belong only to the gods. Confidence in one's own powers of perception, insight, and reasoning threatens the division between man and god in the same way as does the appearance of total or perpetual felicity.[114] As a paradigm of the instability of human happiness Oedipus is also a paradigm of the limitations of human knowledge; the idea of human limitation is defined by contrast with the divine.

The notion that, in his apparent success and felicity as well as in his confidence in his abilities and sense of himself as master of his destiny, Oedipus is implicated in status-rivalry with the gods receives a degree of explicit support in the text. Oedipus' initial appearance in response to his subjects' supplication already presents him, in his own mind and in that of the suppliants, as a potential source of salvation, and the implication that there is something quasi-divine about the position in which this places him receives some encouragement from the Priest's reference to *his* (Oedipus') altars (βωμοῖσι τοῖς σοῖς) at 16. Oedipus appears in response to his subjects' prayers again at 216, and this time explicitly presents himself as a source of the release for which the Chorus have prayed (216–18):

αἰτεῖς· ἃ δ' αἰτεῖς, τἄμ' ἐὰν θέλῃς ἔπη
κλύων δέχεσθαι τῇ νόσῳ θ' ὑπηρετεῖν,
ἀλκὴν λάβοις ἂν κἀνακούφισιν κακῶν.

> You make a request. With respect to your request, if you are willing to hear and accept my words and to minister to the disease, you may receive protection and alleviation of your ills.

It would be going too far to say that Oedipus thinks he is a god; but such are his apparent authority and confidence in his own abilities, born of his position as king and his status as saviour of Thebes, that the initial position from which he later falls could be seen as arrogating a kind of claim to efficacy and control that properly belongs only to a god.[115] This impression, indeed, is one that the Priest is careful to counteract in the play's opening scene: the suppliants have come to Oedipus not because they think he is the equal of the gods (θεοῖσι μέν νυν οὐκ ἰσούμενός σ', 31), but because he is the best man to assist them in time of trouble and in dealings with the divine (33–4), since he is the one who freed the city from the Sphinx, even though he 'knew no more' nor received any instruction from the Thebans, but was assisted by a god (35–9). This is not Oedipus' own evaluation of that achievement. To solve the riddle of the Sphinx, he observes, was a task for no ordinary man (393–4), but Tiresias' mantic skill proved useless: he could bring no bird sign nor divine knowledge to bear (394–6). It took Oedipus, the ignorant,[116] to solve the riddle by his own intelligence alone, with no help from divination (396–8).[117] For Tiresias this was *tychē*, albeit a *tychē* that plays a role in the disastrous pattern of Oedipus' life (442), but for Oedipus it is a sign of his greatness (441). It is a maxim of archaic thought, visible especially in epinician poetry, that all human success is with god;[118] the suggestion that a human being can succeed without god is what arouses Athena's anger against Ajax in that play (*Aj.* 764–77).[119] These hints – much less salient than (e.g.) Ajax's outright boast – of a confidence in his own intellectual ability, command of his own destiny, and independence from divine influence that put Oedipus in a position of rivalry with the gods are supported by Oedipus' form of words at 788–9. He went to Delphi to ascertain his true parentage, but Apollo sent him away 'dishonoured in what he had come for' (καί μ' ὁ Φοῖβος ὧν μὲν ἱκόμην ἄτιμον ἐξέπεμψεν). Oedipus the mortal feels that the god has dishonoured him by refusing to answer his question; there is enough here to suggest that his conceit of himself and his expectations of the god could be seen as somewhat too high.[120] If so, then it is worth noticing that one of the links between the second stasimon and the fourth is the issue of the relative status of the gods and mortals. In the second, *hybris*, i.e. deliberate overvaluation of one's own honour and under-valuation of that of others, is a characteristic of rulers who climb too high (873–9). Punishment of such *hybris* will vindicate religion (883–96); and if religion is vindicated, especially by the fulfilment of oracles, Apollo will be manifest in his honours (909). Though the second stasimon does not provide an authoritative assessment of Oedipus' position, it does, as we saw, have a considerable ironic application to his case; and when that authoritative assessment comes in the fourth stasimon,[121] it is notable that the humiliation of Oedipus, from the highest of honours (1202–3, especially τὰ μέγιστ' ἐτιμάθης) to the utmost in wretchedness (1204, τανῦν ἀκούειν τίς ἀθλιώτερος;) figures prominently. It is the humbling of Oedipus that vindicates Apollo's honour.[122]

One could perhaps see this in terms of a form of divine *phthonos*, not that which focuses on prosperity alone (if there is such a form), but one that is aroused by the failure to give appropriate credit to the role of divine favour in one's success.[123] Such a reaction presupposes at least a minimal notion of offence, at least in the eyes of the gods themselves.[124] But Oedipus' unavoidable fate is declared even before his birth. In order, therefore, for Oedipus' presumption to be a material factor in his downfall, one would have to suppose that Apollo's foreknowledge of Oedipus' future presumption led him to set his punishment in motion before the offences were committed.[125] Punishment which preceded the crime would not be wholly 'unGreek' or 'unarchaic': we see something of that sort in Aeschylus' *Agamemnon*, where the portent of the eagles and the hare is so clear a symbol of the brutality of the Atreidae in the destruction of Troy that Agamemnon must pay for it in advance by committing an act which is both punishment for a future crime and a crime that calls forth future punishment.[126] But in the *Agamemnon* the sequence of cause and effect is preserved; the eagles' slaughter of the hare precedes the anger of Artemis, and the latter remains reactive rather than prospective. The symbolic prolepsis of the future offence, moreover, puts Agamemnon in a position in which he has to choose – if he does not want to be the sort of man who will commit the offences which the omen portends, then he can spare his daughter and return home. Not only that, but the links between the portent, the sacrifice, the destruction of Troy, and Agamemnon's own sufferings are salient in the text. In the *OT*, by contrast, effect would have to precede cause, the 'punishment' would be in place before any aspect, symbolic or otherwise, of the 'crime' had been perpetrated, and the explanation in terms of proleptic punishment would have to be drawn by an audience with no guidance whatever from the text. There is no hint in the play that Oedipus is doomed to commit parricide and incest because he will grow up to be over-confident in his intellectual abilities and insufficiently cognizant of the role of the divine in all human achievement. Oedipus' presumption is much more like Agamemnon's act of walking on the crimson tapestries, causally irrelevant to the fate that is about to befall him, but still thematically significant.

Oedipus' presumption, his concern for his status, his failure to avoid the appearance of rivalry with the gods are illustrative rather than causally material: Oedipus is not the only one to leap to the wrong conclusions, to assume that he knows when he does not; so too do the Chorus (especially in the second and third stasima), and so does Jocasta when she expresses the conviction that the manner in which both Laius and Polybus died confirms the fallibility of prophecy (710–25, 851–8, 946–9, 952–3, 973, 977–83, 987). If Oedipus is proud of his abilities and quick to anger, then so is Tiresias (350–462 *passim*). Oedipus is not the only one to believe that he can avoid what appears to be an unequivocal divine prophecy; so too do Laius, Jocasta, and the Theban shepherd. And so on. The point of this is not to suggest, as Schmitt has argued, that the guilt that precipitates Oedipus' downfall is shared,[127] but that he is what the Chorus in the fourth stasimon say he is, a paradigm of human fallibility.[128] The pity that is the dominant tone of the play's closing scenes requires no less; for the requirement that the recipient of pity should be relevantly like ourselves is not just an Aristotelian one; in particular, the sense of shared vulnerability is central to the pity that is inherent in the principle of alternation in texts from Homer to Sophocles and beyond.[129] Oedipus' story illustrates the fragility of human existence, man's dependence on god, the unbridgeable gulf between the power of god and the insignificance of man. If Oedipus is to be a paradigm of these fundamental human limitations, it is understandable that he should exhibit others as well. Oedipus rose higher than most, and thus had further to fall; in the detail of his fate and in the extent of his fall he differs from others, but in the most fundamental regard he is not atypical. If thinking we know what we are doing in running our lives, pursuing our ambitions, and trying to secure our own happiness is *hybris* then it is a *hybris* that tempts us all. Oedipus challenges the gods in the way that any successful human is a potential rival to the gods. The humanity that is part of the explanation for Apollo's hostility is the basis for many of Oedipus' negative qualities, but it is also, despite those qualities, central to our sympathy.

Oedipus' presumptuous sense that he is in control of his life is merely an aspect of the ignorance in which he commits the heinous but involuntary offences of parricide and incest. It is an aspect of his status as paradigm.[130] Whether one sees Oedipus as a *pharmakos* either in a ritual sense or in terms of various mythical patterns that may be related to that ritual depends on how strictly one interprets the various kinds of mythical and ritual evidence.[131] But he may be, in the end and in our ordinary modern sense of the word, a sort of scapegoat, an everyman whose fate is imposed upon him not because of what he has done, but in order to set an example. The gods have made Oedipus a paradigmatic human being, destined to suffer, destined to be limited in knowledge, destined to demonstrate that the gulf in status that separates god and man cannot really be tested. By the end of the play, he knows this, and so do we.

This is a typically archaic vision of the nothingness of mankind, of the evanescence of human hopes and achievements. But the play does not simply illustrate human vulnerability to vicissitude; it presupposes a belief-system that seeks to explain that vulnerability in terms of a divine order, a hierarchy of human and divine status, that the gods police and of which they resent and punish infringements.[132] Such a dispensation might be seen as a basis for divine justice. Yet in this play, the gods choose to illustrate that dispensation by making an example of a man who is doomed before any of his human weaknesses, delusions, or presumptions have a chance to assert themselves. They may regard themselves as just in this; but their demonstration of that justice by means of the vindication of an objective divine order in which the dice are loaded against humans raises fundamental questions that are not easy to answer. The alternation of success and failure and the dependence of each of these upon the gods take on sinister overtones in this play, as the sequence appears to be less one of favour and disfavour, support and abandonment, than of building up in order to knock down.

This is not a benign or providential vision, but nor is it a random one: human vulnerability and suffering are part of a dispensation that gods intervene to uphold, because vulnerability and suffering are themselves fundamental to the distinction in status between gods and men. This model may derive from attempts to explain what appears to be, from a human perspective, a random and absurd universe, but it is not itself descriptive of such a universe. This is an order based on hierarchy and power; such power may be justly distributed, if we believe that the gods exist and are vastly superior to men, and it may be justly exercised, if we believe that gods have the right to demonstrate how wide the gulf is between them and us; but it is not an order which pays much heed to the rights, claims, or interests of human beings. In answering Dodds's essay question, we need to separate (at least) modern ideas of justice, varying ancient notions of the justice of the gods, and the gods' own (hypothetical) sense of the justice of their own actions.[133] Whatever justice there is in the play is far from edifying;[134] it is a much rougher justice than envisaged by moralizing critics such as Lefèvre and Schmitt, rougher even than that envisaged by Lloyd-Jones, Griffith, and Kovacs.[135] It is a depressing and terrifying form of justice.[136]

In the argument presented above I have discussed the what, the how, and the why of divine involvement in the story of Oedipus, as dramatized in the *OT*. I am as confident as I can be that my interpretation of the what and the how is correct: if we want to understand the play as a meaningful utterance, we need to accept the reality of a divine purpose that is immanent in human action as well as manifested in direct intervention. The explanation of the why is necessarily more tentative, though a proper interpretation of the what and the how does decisively eliminate some of the possibilities and markedly favour others. I argue that Oedipus' shortcomings underscore his human fallibility; they are not causal factors in his suffering, but aspects of that condition of being human to which suffering is intrinsic; in his actions, in his sufferings, and in his character he encapsulates both the strengths and the weaknesses of humanity, and serves as a reminder that even the highest achievements fall far short of the divine. The play presupposes an order in which this is so, and rightly so; we must suppose that its demonstration is Apollo's purpose, and that the demonstration of Apollo's purpose is Sophocles' purpose. The world of the play is a world of gods both awesome and awful, gods who have their reasons for enforcing the terms of the order over which they preside. This oppressive vision is no doubt not one that we should like to see projected as a model for the world that we inhabit; no doubt, too, there were some, perhaps even many, in the play's original audience who felt the same. Peradotto's anti-theocratic reading is as valid a reading of the *OT* as is a feminist reading of Euripides' *Medea*; but it is as valid an exercise in cultural history to study Sophocles' theocratic vision as it is to study Euripides' misogyny. The *OT*'s theocratic worldview is a powerful image of a world that is neither subject to human control nor ordered, on morally edifying lines, for humans' benefit. But my primary concern has been to reconstruct a plausible account of the picture of human beings' place in the world that is presupposed by the text. This is not to legislate for one single authentic interpretation; nor does the location of the ideas that underpin the play's plot in a wider nexus of archaic Greek thought mean that archaic thought provides the only matrix on which to interpret the play. I attempt only to pin down the phenomena from which the range of possible interpretations must proceed.

Notes

[1] See Lawrence 2008; Kovacs 2009b; cf. also Lurje 2004, who, however, regards the central issues as having been settled by Wilamowitz in 1899, until the twentieth-century consensus was disturbed by Lefèvre 1987 and Schmitt 1988; see Lurje, 2004, 1–4, 241–80, and *passim*.

[2] See, e.g., Manuwald 1992 against Lefèvre 1987 and Schmitt 1988; Williams 1993 in reaction to the progressivist approaches of 19th- and 20th-century scholarship and philosophy; R. D. Griffith 1996 in opposition to the Wilamowitzian interpretation cited in n. 1 above. Beyond these, the last works of mainstream interpretative scholarship to deal comprehensively and incisively with the evidence of the play and the issues of divine and human action it raises are those of Winnington-Ingram 1980 and Scodel 1984. For the history of the play's interpretation up to the beginning of the present century, see above all Lurje 2004.

[3] Again, see Lurje 2004.

[4] Dodds 1966. Lloyd-Jones in 1971 called this essay 'the clearest statement known to me of one of the central problems of Sophoclean interpretation' (Lloyd-Jones 1971, 104). On its classic status, cf. Stinton 1975, 240; Saïd 1978, 30; Lefèvre 1987, 38–9;

Divine and human action in the Oedipus Tyrannus

Burkert 1991, 15–16, 18; R. D. Griffith 1996, 29, 45; C. P. Segal 2001, 169; Lurje 2004, 2, 245–6, 252, 254; E. M. Harris 2010, 122–3. Dodds himself (1966, 38) acknowledged the influence of Wilamowitz 1899 on his own interpretation; for this as the 20th-century orthodoxy (as represented by the similarly classic studies of e.g. Pohlenz 1954, i. 213–20, von Fritz 1962, 1–21, Schadewaldt 1970, and Reinhardt 1979, 94–134) see Lurje 2004, 241–54. More recently, Dodds's essay forms the starting point of Kovacs 2009b, a discussion which is in some respects complementary to mine, at least in its diagnosis of the contradictions of Dodds's account, if not entirely in the alternatives that it offers. See also Lawrence 2008, a fine article with which I am happy to find myself in close agreement (see his pp. 1, 13, on Dodds 1966).

[5] Dodds 1966, 37.

[6] Dodds 1966, 37–8. Dodds's strictures had a special relevance for Professor D. M. MacDowell, with whom I studied the *OT* in the Higher Ordinary class of Greek at Glasgow in 1980–1, for he had been one of the hapless cohort whose failings provided the starting point for Dodds's analysis. MacDowell could not remember what he had written, but had clearly been persuaded of the error of his ways, for he advised us that if we were to read only one critical essay on the play, it should be Dodds's. MacDowell never patronized his students, and if he regarded it as a misfortune to have to read our work, he never let it show. It is a pleasure to dedicate this chapter to the memory of a great scholar and dedicated teacher.

[7] Dodds 1966, 45, 49.

[8] Both quotations from Dodds 1966, 46.

[9] Dodds 1966, 42; for the same point, cf. Wilamowitz 1899, 57; Schadewaldt 1970, 466–7; Lloyd-Jones 1971, 106; Reinhardt 1979, 98; Schmitt 1988, 10–11; Lurje 2004, 244–5; Sewell-Rutter 2007, 139, 151; Lawrence 2008, 2; cf. in general Latte 1968, 18; Dodds 1951, 7; Sewell-Rutter 2007, 137–50. But note the caution of Winnington-Ingram 1965, 47–8 = 1980, 154.

[10] Cf. Schmitt 1988, 10–11. On the difference between ancient and modern notions of the kind of freedom that makes for responsible human action, see Bobzien 1998b; Brennan 2005, 288–304; Frede 2011, 9–10, 66–9; cf. also Gill 1995, 5–19.

[11] For a recent defence of compatibilism, see Dennett 2003; for compatibilism as the dominant contemporary position, see Sarkissian et al. 2010, 347; cf. Eidinow 2011, 16–19.

[12] See Bobzien 1998a; Brennan 2005, 235–87; Frede 2011, 14–15, 77–86, 175–6.

[13] Laplace 1902; cf. Dennett 2003, 28–9; Peradotto 1992, 4.

[14] See e.g. *Il.* 1. 70 (Calchas ᾔδη τά τ' ἐόντα τά τ' ἐσσόμενα πρό τ' ἐόντα); cf. E. *Ion* 7 (Apollo at Delphi pronounces to mortals τά τ' ὄντα καὶ μέλλοντα), *Hel.* 13–14 (Theonoe τὰ θεῖα...τά τ' ὄντα καὶ μέλλοντα πάντ' ἠπίστατο, cf. 922–3); Pl. *Chrm.* 174a (τὸν εἰδότα τὰ μέλλοντα ἔσεσθαι πάντα, τὸν μάντιν).

[15] For the issues here, cf. and contrast Sewell-Rutter 2007, 137–71, esp. 139, 154–6. See also Frede 2011, 14 on the differences between Stoic and modern versions of determinism, particularly with regard to the role of divine agency in the former.

[16] Searle 1999, 9–20, 30–1, 107–9.

[17] Pinker 2007, 86–7 (quotation p. 86), 162–3, 206–8, 219–25, 228–33, 431; cf. Williams 1993, 57 on ancient Greek. On the mental modules involved (especially in agency detection), see also Boyer 2001, 96–106 (144–8 on the extension to supernatural agents); Atran 2002, 59–71, 78–9 (93–5, 266–7 on supernatural agents).

[18] Sarkissian et al. 2010. For the ideas of 'cause, intention, state, and response' as 'universal materials' of 'any conception of responsibility', cf. Williams 1993, 55–6; contrast (e.g.) Latte 1968, 9: 'Kausalität wird in dieser Periode [i.e. 5th–4th cent. BC] nur ganz primitiv erfaßt.'

[19] The subject is so vast that only the most basic bibliographic orientation can be offered here: see e.g. Kane 2005a and 2005b; for a very short introduction, including a brief history, see Pink 2004.

[20] For the specificity of modern notions of the will and the lack of an exact ancient Greek equivalent, see Dihle 1982, 20–67 *passim*; Vernant 1990a; Frede 2011, 2–9, 19–30, and *passim* (e.g. p. 98 on Dihle's notion of the will as something 'which decides or chooses in some mysterious way that is independent not only of the external objects of desire but also of the desires and beliefs of the person'). See also Bobzien 1998b and Brennan 2005, 288–305, cited in n. 10 above, and cf. Herrmann, this volume.

[21] See Frede 2011, esp. 11–48, 66–88; cf. Williams 1993, 5–7, 29, 36–7, 46, 67–8 (on *OT*), 133, 151–2. For Williams (cf. Dover 1974, 150–1), the will is a concept that the Greeks were fortunate to lack; contrast Vernant 1990a, who, despite his recognition of the peculiarity and historical particularity of modern notions of the will, retains a teleological approach in which these are the goal towards which their ancient Greek 'intimations' tend; cf. Hall 2010, 304: 'the Greeks had only an emergent sense of an autonomous individual will'. For a (more or less) positive assessment of the value of the Stoic notion of free will, at least, see Frede 2011, 177–9.

[22] Cf. Kovacs 2009b, 358–9.

[23] On the falsity of the claim that, in *OT*, the gods know the future but do not order it, see Cameron 1968, 71, 78–9; Lloyd-Jones 1971, 197–8 n. 112; Winnington-Ingram 1980, 178; Manuwald 1992, 8, 13–14; Peradotto 1992, 8; Lawrence 2008, 1–3; Kovacs 2009b, 359, 363, and *passim*; cf. the implicit criticism in Halliwell 1990, 173. Dodds's view is shared by (among others) Kitto 1956, 75–6; Knox 1957, 5–14, 33, 51 (cf. Knox 1979, 106); Kirkwood 1958, 276; Gellie 1972, 103–5. A version of this thesis (together with the view that what is known is not necessarily fixed), is advanced by R. D. Griffith 1996, 53–4, 62–6. I am not sure how well this fits with his insistence (pp. 26, 42–3, 82) on the involvement of Apollo, both in his own right and through the actions of human beings. But it is noteworthy that his claim that 'foreknowledge by a timeless God [*sic*] of an indeterminate universe...entails no compulsion for his creatures' requires him to observe that 'Sophocles' language is insufficiently rigorous in this regard, for he reports the prophecies in terms suggestive more of compulsion than of mere futurity (μοῖρα 713, χρείη 791)' (R. D. Griffith 1996, 64).

[24] Cf. Halliwell 1990, 170–1.

[25] See esp. Halliwell 1990; Parker 1999; Budelmann 2000, 133–94; cf. Buxton 1987; Schein 1997.

[26] See Parker 1999, 15–17 (rather too insistent, in my view, on the unreliability of characters' judgements).

[27] On the role of the Chorus (which will be discussed in detail below with regard to the interpretation of the 2nd and 4th stasima) see above all Rosenmeyer 1993, Calame 1999, and Budelmann 2000, 197–272; for a summary of recent approaches, cf. Kitzinger 2008, 1–10. Specifically on the Chorus' theological pronouncements, see Parker 1999, 17–18.

[28] There is a taxonomy and discussion of forms of irony in Sophocles in Jouanna 2007, 469–85. For the importance of irony in the interpretation of *OT*, cf. Winnington-Ingram 1965, 39.

[29] Cf. *El.* 657–9 (also with irony).

[30] I see no reason to suppose that Oedipus does not hear the open denunciations at 449–60 (as claimed by Knox 1980; cf. R. D. Griffith 1996, 22); if the Chorus can hear the charge of murder and yet, in the ensuing stasimon, suspend judgement out of good will towards Oedipus, then Oedipus can, out of anger, ignore denunciations which might be thought to chime with the prophecies he has received in the past and with his uncertainty about his parentage (437). The gradual nature of the revelation and the retardation of the movement between the plot's two phases (1. Who killed Laius? 2. Who is Oedipus?) are fundamental to the play's design. This being so, an audience that succumbs to the poet's spell will be content with any reasons for the delay which seem to them to be plausible, even if only minimally so. Considerations of this sort go a long way towards refuting those, such as Lefèvre 1987 and Schmitt 1988, for whom the slowness of Oedipus (and, for Schmitt, the Chorus) to put two and two together shows culpable failings of intellect. See rather Scodel 1984, 63–5; Manuwald 1992, 22–36, esp. 27–8; Lawrence 2008, 8–9.

[31] Cf. R. D. Griffith 1996, 26. Tragic seers in general are always right: see Mikalson 1991, 92–101 (with 110–13 on prophecy in the *OT* in general); cf. R. D. Griffith 1996, 34 ('in all literature antecedent to Sophocles, whenever a dispute arises between a seer and a layman, the seer is proved by the sequel to be correct'). For Tiresias' authority, cf. 284–6, 297–9, 300–4; also 563. Parker observes (1997, 146): 'the spectator's anticipation that any prophecy by Tiresias will prove correct is based not on a general faith in seers (regular objects of scepticism and mockery) but on Tiresias' particular reputation, canonized in earlier myth and literature, as one seer who "has never spoken falsehood in the city" [*Ant.* 1094].' Tiresias, of course, also prophesies exile at 418 and 455–6, closely tied to the prophecy of blindness on each occasion, but despite the strong expectation created by these passages, by Apollo's oracle (96–101, 305–9), by Oedipus' own pronouncement against the murderer of Laius (228–9, 236–7; cf. 816–20), and by repeated references in the exodos (1409–15, 1436–7, 1449–54, 1518; cf. the expectation of immediate departure created by 1446–75, 1478–1514 in general), Oedipus does not actually go into exile at the end of the play. Dawe's argument (2001b, 3–11, 2006, 192–203) that the exodos has suffered extensive interpolation has recently been challenged by Finglass 2009 and Kovacs 2009a (cf. Sommerstein 2011b, who follows Finglass and goes beyond Kovacs in defence of the paradosis), but, as far as the defeated expectation of exile is concerned, the hypothesis that the end of *OT* has been modified at least partly with the aim of bringing it into line with *OC* (perhaps for a revival in association with the latter's posthumous production by the poet's grandson, perhaps later) remains a possible, if unverifiable, one: see Hester 1984, March 1987, 148–54 and C. W. Müller 1996, offering stronger, though not unassailable, support for a suggestion first made by Graffunder 1885, dismissed without argument by Davies 1982, 278 n. 26, and endorsed more recently by Dawe 2001b, 12, 21 (cf. 2006, 200, on *OT* 1507). For my purposes, however, it is enough that Oedipus' exile is still expected at some time in the future (Kovacs 2009a, 51, 64; cf. Sommerstein 2011b, 90); and note Tiresias' use of ποτε at 418: Oedipus' ruin must

a discussion of Lesky's explanations in the light of the alternatives offered by Schmitt 1990, see Cairns 2001b, 14–20. For the widespread tendency of beliefs in divine causation to co-exist with robust and perfectly ordinary notions of non-supernatural causation (and cultures' tendency not to employ divine causation as a consistently over-arching explanatory principle), cf. Boyer 2001, 137–67 and *passim*; Atran 2002, 93–100, 107–13, 141–6.

[56] All language about gods is in some sense an extrapolation from ordinary human experience, involving a form of metaphor that does not simply map from a source to a target domain, but creates that target domain. See e.g. S. Guthrie 1993; Boyer 2001; Atran 2002; cf. Williams 2006. For more on metaphorical god-talk, see Boeve and Feyaerts 1999; Pender 2000, 27–34. For the ordinary concept of hidden causation as a model for the actions of supernatural powers, see Williams 1993, 32; Pinker 2007, 217; on supernatural agency as a product of the mind's agency-detection capacities, cf. again Boyer 2001, 144–8; Atran 2002, 93–5, 266–7.

[57] Cf. Kovacs 2009b, 361.

[58] Kovacs 2009b, 359–60.

[59] For this idea, see Dennett 2003, 72–3.

[60] Manuwald 1992; cf. Williams 1993, 141–3; Ugolini 2000, 178; contrast C. P. Segal 2001, 55.

[61] If *OT* presupposes a fate that cannot be avoided, this cannot be generalized as *the* Sophoclean view of all human action. E.g. where the tragedy of the *OT* depends on a sense that Oedipus could not have done otherwise, in *Antigone* by contrast it depends on a sense that Creon could (i.e. that he might have reached Antigone before her suicide). But the subject in general is too large to explore here.

[62] On *atē*, cf. Sommerstein, this volume, my comments in the Introduction above, and (on *atē* in Homer in general) Cairns 2012a (esp. 7, 29–30 on this passage).

[63] On such counterfactuals in epic, see Reinhardt 1961, 107–10; De Jong 1987, 68–81; Nesselrath 1992.

[64] See 1207–12, 1217–18, 1297–9, 1303–4, 1306, 1312, 1348 (Chorus); 1340–6, 1362–6, 1384, 1395–7, 1407–12, 1436–7, 1484–5, 1496–9, 1519 (Oedipus).

[65] Cf. Williams 1993, 69–70.

[66] See the discussion of Allan, this volume.

[67] Williams (1993, 31) makes a similar point. On the metaphorical nature of all language about gods, see above, n. 56.

[68] Cf. 34 (*daimones* = gods and other powers with whom humans have 'dealings'), 244 (a reference to Apollo which ironically confirms his hostility to Oedipus), 816 and 828 (human misery seen as the result of *daimones*' hostility), 912 (Apollo among the *daimones* to whom Jocasta addresses her appeals; cf. 1378–9, the sacred *agalmata* of *daimones* from which Oedipus is cut off), 1258 (some *daimōn* leads Oedipus to the chamber in which Jocasta has hanged herself).

[69] As at 1478–9, where Oedipus wishes Creon well in conventional terms that take on considerable additional resonance in the circumstances:

ἀλλ' εὐτυχοίης, καί σε τῆσδε τῆς ὁδοῦ
δαίμων ἄμεινον ἢ 'μὲ φρουρήσας τύχοι.

May you have good luck, and may a *daimōn* chance to guard you on this journey better than I was guarded.

⁷⁰ Cf. esp. *Il.* 8. 166; A. *Pers.* 158, 601–2, 824–6; Pi. *P.* 3. 108–9, 5. 122–3; see further Richardson 1974 on *h.Cer.* 300 and cf. Cairns 2010 on B. 3. 37. On *daimōn* in the play in general, cf. Mikalson 1991, 28–9; Eidinow 2011, 59–60.

⁷¹ The standard works in English on fate and related notions in Greek literature (Greene 1944; Dietrich 1965) have recently been supplemented by the valuable contemporary perspective of Eidinow 2011, but a detailed and comprehensive re-examination remains desirable. For discussions of fate in tragedy, esp. Sophocles, see Winnington-Ingram 1980, 150–78; Lurje 2004, 244–51; Sewell-Rutter 2007, 136–71. For a discussion of some of the relevant issues as they apply to A. *Th.*, cf. Herrmann, this volume.

⁷² See e.g. *Il.* 7. 52, 15. 117–18, 17. 421–2, *Od.* 4. 475–6, 5. 41–2, 5. 114–15, 5. 345, 9. 532–3. Cf. *Il.* 21. 110: *moira* and *thanatos* 'are over' all men.

⁷³ Cf. the 'great god and powerful Moira' who are responsible, *via* the death of Patroclus, for Achilles' own imminent death, according to the horse Xanthus at *Il.* 19. 410.

⁷⁴ Cf. the *Kēr* who got Patroclus as her lot at the moment of his birth, *Il.* 23. 79–80. See in general Eidinow 2011, 30–44.

⁷⁵ *Moira* binds: *Il.* 4. 517, 22. 5, *Od.* 3. 269 (specifically μιν μοῖρα θεῶν ἐπέδησε δαμῆναι, 'fate from the gods bound her to be overcome'), 11. 292; takes (hold of): *Il.* 5. 82–3, 16. 334, 20. 476–7, *Od.* 2. 100, 3. 237–8, 17. 326, 24. 134–5; leads: *Il.* 13. 602–3; comes upon/meets: *Il.* 17. 478, 22. 303, 22. 436; subdues: *Il.* 18. 119, *Od.* 22. 413 (cf. *kēr* at *Od.* 11. 171, 398). For other personifications, see *Il.* 5. 628–9 (*moira* arouses Tlepolemus to face Sarpedon); *Il.* 16. 852–4, 24. 131–2, *Od.* 24. 28–9 (the *moira* [that he will be slain by Achilles] that stands beside Hector even as he kills Patroclus; that which stands beside Achilles as he mourns Patroclus; and that which stood beside Agamemnon); *Il.* 16. 849 (the *moira* that kills Patroclus); *Il.* 21. 82–3 (the *moira* that puts Lycaon in the hands of Achilles, i.q. 'Zeus gave me to you', ibid. 83–4). At *Il.* 12. 116–17, the *moira* that 'envelops' Asius is probably not a personified agent (*pace* Dyer 1964, 36), but the enveloping garment itself, as in the common locution with θάνατος, τέλος θανάτοιο, or θανάτου νέφος (so Leaf 1900–2, on 12. 116, Onians 1954, 425, Cairns 2012b, n. 30).

⁷⁶ On conceptual metaphor, Lakoff and Johnson 1980 remains fundamental.

⁷⁷ With 863 cf. e.g. 273–5, where Oedipus prays that Dike and all the gods remain forever (εὖ ξυνεῖεν εἰσαεί) with those who abide by his edict. For a brief survey of the uses of *moira* in the play, cf. Eidinow 2011, 55–7.

⁷⁸ This notion of Time as an agent thus bears comparison with, but also emphasizes the irony in, Oedipus' conviction at 1080–3 that he is the son of Tyche and the months who are his kinsmen have defined the magnitude of his life so far.

⁷⁹ See n. 47 above.

⁸⁰ And Oedipus himself, as if at a *daimōn*'s prompting, leaps on the doors of Jocasta's chamber at 1260–1; cf. Apollo's leaping on the unknown killer at 469–70.

⁸¹ Personification and irony coalesce also at 337–8, where, in Tiresias' reference to Oedipus' temper (*orgē*) as 'cohabiting' with him, the feminine participle facilitates the allusion to Jocasta.

⁸² Cf. Dodds 1951, 48 and 62 n. 108; also Williams 1993, 150–1, 165.

⁸³ On the inevitability of the question, see Bowra 1944, 176; Lloyd-Jones 1971, 108–9; Scodel 1984, 65; contrast Reinhardt 1979, 133–4; Lurje 2004, 389.

[84] For recent interpretations along these lines, see especially Lefèvre 1987, Schmitt 1988, and R. D. Griffith 1996; there are traces also in Cameron 1968. The phenomena are noted, but in the right perspective, by Allan (this volume, 178 and n. 19).

[85] Cf. von Fritz 1962, 7; Lloyd-Jones 1971, 105–6; Manuwald 1992, 33; Lurje 2004, 5, 93, 257, 266.

[86] For the parricide and incest as at least culpable, though not necessarily criminal, see Lefèvre 1987, 49, 51–2; R. D. Griffith 1996, 52, 54–5; cf. Cameron 1968, 132–3, 139–40.

[87] Erbse 1993, 60; R. D. Griffith 1996, 52.

[88] Vellacott 1964, 140, 143–4; Erbse 1993, 60.

[89] Cameron 1968, 125, 128–9; Schmitt 1988, 22; R. D. Griffith 49–51.

[90] It is often stated that Oedipus would be acquitted in an Attic court on the grounds that the homicide of Laius was justifiable (e.g. Wilamowitz 1899, 55; Bowra 1944, 164–6; Pohlenz 1954, i. 213; Fisher 1992, 340; C. P. Segal 2001, 90). This is not, in fact, clear: the speaker for the defence at Ant. 4.δ.2–3 argues that one should be acquitted of homicide if the victim struck the first blow, but his opponent disagrees (4.γ.2, 4); Demosthenes, in emphasizing his own forbearance against Meidias (21. 71–5), has an interest in exaggerating the extent to which juries approve of lethal retaliation for even a single blow, and in fact when Euaeon killed Boeotus in such circumstances, he was convicted (by one vote); cf. R. D. Griffith 1996, 47–8; Lawrence 2008, 10; Burian 2009, 104; and see now E. M. Harris 2010, esp. 135–6. On the general distinction between 'self-defence' (as in Ant. 4 and D. 21. 71–5) and *phonos dikaios*, see Gagarin 1978. But whether the killing of Laius is *phonos hekousios* or *phonos dikaios*, it is *qua* parricide and not *qua* homicide that it really matters. Oedipus suffers as he does not because he killed a man, but because the man he killed was his father; his anger and haste may have caused the killing *qua* killing, but not *qua* parricide. A tendency to anger and an acute concern for his status are, of course, salient traits of Oedipus' character: on the latter, cf. below, pp. 150, 154–6, and n. 120.

[91] Kovacs (2009b, 366) is right to emphasize that the original oracle to Laius, as represented by Jocasta at 711–14, is indefinite: Laius will be killed by any child who might be born to him (cf. Lawrence 2008, 3). Though (as Jebb 1893 on 714 suggests) this may indicate only that the oracle was delivered before Oedipus' birth (and perhaps also before Jocasta's pregnancy), it does leave room to believe that parricide, incest, and Oedipus' subsequent suffering could have been avoided had Laius and Jocasta seen to it that they remained childless (contrast Dodds 1966, 41; Eidinow 2011, 186–7 n. 20). But still the oracle is not presented as a command that Laius disobeys, much less as an element in a sequence of crime and punishment originating in the rape of Chrysippus. The point is not in any way salient, and it would require much more prominence and emphasis to support the hypothesis that Oedipus is punished for Laius' guilt (as claimed by Lloyd-Jones 1971, 119–23; Kovacs 2009b, 367; see rather M. L. West 1999, 41–3; Sewell-Rutter 2007, 63–6, 126; cf. Allan, this volume, 174).

[92] It is possible, even likely, that we are to connect these lines (and the similar sentiments at 1360–1) with 711–14 (see above n. 91), in that it at least seems to be the case that Laius might have avoided his fate and Oedipus' had he remained childless; hence Laius 'should not' have had a child. We should see this, however, not in terms of a curse arising from the rape of Chrysippus, nor as Laius' disobedience of a divine command (see n. 91), but rather as a symptom of human beings' misplaced belief that

they have the power to circumvent prophecy, a belief of which Oedipus' career furnishes multiple examples. The parents of a man destined to kill his father and marry his mother are as ill-fated as he is, and so the divine hostility which has attended Oedipus since birth also encompasses his parents (as he is *atheos* so they were *anosioi*, 1360), but the play provides no explanation of this in a single transgression on Laius' part.

[93] Thus the riddle of Oedipus' identity converges with the riddle of the Sphinx: both tell us something about Man (Cameron 1968, 22; Vernant 1990c, 124; C. P. Segal 1995, 141, 171).

[94] Arist. *EN* 1. 9–10, 1100a4–1101b9; cf. A. *Ag.* 928–9; E. *Andr.* 100–2, *Hcld.* 865–6, *Tro.* 509–10; Hdt. 1. 32. 7. See further my Introduction to this volume.

[95] See *Il.* 24. 485–512; B. 5. 155–62 (esp. 160–2 and cf. 89–92); S. *Aj.* 121–6, *Phil.* 501–6, *OC* 566–8; E. *Hec.* 282–7; Hdt. 1. 86. 6, 7. 46. 2; Arist. *Rhet.* 1385b13–1386a3, 1386b25–9; Dover 1974, 272; Pelling 2005, 289, 291–2.

[96] See esp. *Il.* 24. 524, 549–50; B. 5. 162–4.

[97] Especially the Chorus at 1217–18, 1297–9, 1303–6, 1348, all, significantly, associated in context with their pity; cf. Creon at 1424–31, prefaced by the (relative) magnanimity of 1422–3.

[98] Cf. 1321–6, where Oedipus rightly interprets the Chorus' attitude as one of concern, and 1473–7, where Creon confirms Oedipus' conjecture that it was pity that led him to accede to his request to be reunited with his daughters.

[99] The final lines, 1524–30, seem too poor to be genuine, but the sentiments expressed are entirely in keeping with those of the fourth stasimon and the speech of the Exangelos (Dawe 2006, 202–3).

[100] See Hclt. B 101a DK; Hdt. 1. 8. 1; Xen. *Mem.* 3. 11. 1.

[101] Cf. Wilamowitz 1899, 61.

[102] Cf. n. 30 above. It is a paradox – but a thoroughly Aristotelian one – that some mitigation of sympathy towards Oedipus is required if his suffering is to attract sympathy, as opposed to revulsion or outrage, at all (see Aristotle, *Poetics* 1452b34–6, and cf. below, p. 158).

[103] Important discussions include Winnington-Ingram 1980, 179–204; Scodel 1982; Carey 1986; Fisher 1992, 329–42; Sidwell 1992.

[104] This point is accepted even by those (such as Carey 1986, 179 and Burkert 1991, 22) who deny that the ode responds specifically to the events of the preceding episode.

[105] On the ode's latent reference and ironic application to Oedipus, see Bowra 1944, 206; Winnington-Ingram 1965, 40, 1980, 197–8, 200–4; Scodel 1982, 220–3, 1984, 67; Fisher 1992, 337; Budelmann 2000, 222–3; C. P. Segal 2001, 92; Sewell-Rutter 2007, 127–9.

[106] Thus, while I see what he means, I am not sure that it is enough, with Allan (this volume, p. 175) just to label the Chorus' view '*simplistic*' (original emphasis). Though the chorus' analysis is, at the surface level, an over-simplification, there are deeper levels of significance that also require investigation. As Easterling (1978, 158) pertinently asks (expecting the answer 'no'): 'Does Sophocles ever, in fact, make his lyrics unequivocally false, even in *Philoctetes*?' On the multiple functions of the choral persona, cf. esp. Calame 1999.

[107] See C. P. Segal 1995, 190, 194–5; 2001, 104.

[108] 1196–7: ὅστις καθ' ὑπερβολὰν | τοξεύσας ἐκράτησας τοῦ πάντ' εὐδαίμονος ὄλβου ('you who shot your arrow to excess and took control of that prosperity that was

eudaimōn in all respects'). With the transmitted text (printed and translated here, but suspect both in its use of the article and on metrical grounds), with Dawe's ἐκράτησας ἐς πᾶν (2006, 175–6), and even with Reisig's ἐκράτησας οὐ ('you took control of a prosperity that was not in all respects *eudaimōn*', adopted by Lloyd-Jones and Wilson 1990a, cf. 1990b, 107), this is non-culpable, but nonetheless dangerous excess.

[109] Cf. also τεκνωθέντες (867) and ἔτικτεν (870) with τεκνοῦντα καὶ τεκνούμενον (1215); πατήρ (868) with παιδὶ καὶ πατρί (1210); κατακοιμάσῃ (871) with κατεκοίμησα (1221); Ζεῦ (904) with ὦ Ζεῦ (1198); ἀνάσσων (of Zeus, 904) with ἀνάσσων (of Oedipus, 1203).

[110] See Henrichs 1996, 44–50, 55–6; Calame 1999, 135–7. The exemplary force of the line is emphasized (before Dodds) in e.g. Wilamowitz 1899, 58, Pohlenz 1954, i. 219–20, ii. 92–3.

[111] Allan (this volume, p. 177) writes: 'this pattern of alternation is only one aspect of Oedipus' life, and the audience can see that Oedipus' downfall is also due to his own actions', and goes on to explain this in terms of 'double motivation'. But, as the ode itself makes clear and in general, this is a false antithesis: the vicissitudes entailed by the principle of alternation may have a wide range of causes, from divine to human and from offence, through culpable and non-culpable ignorance, to misadventure. Alternation is not solely a matter of divine causation.

[112] For Oedipus as a paradigm of the gulf between divine and human knowledge and an instantiation of the Delphic maxim, know thyself (especially in the context of fifth-century claims to intellectual and scientific progress), cf. Ehrenberg 1954, 66–74; Knox 1957, 53–158 *passim*; Winnington-Ingram 1980, 319–20; Ugolini 1987, esp. 25–30 (cf. id. 2000, 157–84); Burkert 1991, 26–7; C. P. Segal 1995, 141, 176–7, 195–6; R. D. Griffith 1996, 69, 78.

[113] See Knox 1957, 147–58; Ugolini 1987, 2000, 170; Jouanna 2007, 493.

[114] For a simple statement of the traditional norm here, see e.g. Thgn. 659–60: οὐδ' ὁμόσαι χρὴ τοῦθ', ὅτι "μήποτε πρῆγμα τόδ' ἔσται". | θεοὶ γάρ τοι νεμεσῶσ', οἷσιν ἔπεστι τέλος ('and you should never swear, "this thing will never be". For the gods feel *nemesis*: the fulfilment, the *telos*, is theirs'). The wider context (657–66) is one of the mutability of fortune and the need for endurance.

[115] Cf. Whitman 1951, 125; Ehrenberg 1954, 67; Knox 1957, 159–60; Bushnell 1988, 73–4; Vernant 1990c, 125; R. D. Griffith 1996, 6, 18, 77.

[116] Ironically meant, but also ironically true: note the correspondence between Oedipus' ὁ μηδὲν εἰδὼς Οἰδίπους (397) and the Priest's οὐδὲν ἐξειδὼς πλέον (37).

[117] Cf. 964–7; Bowra 1944, 189; C. P. Segal 1995, 149. True, 'without the help of prophecy' is not the same as 'without the aid of the divine', but still Oedipus disparages a form of communication with the divine that is being vividly vindicated in the very scene in which his remarks occur.

[118] For a large number of references, see Schmid-Stählin 1929–34, i. 1, 564 n. 4, 588 n. 2. Cf. e.g. A. *Pers.* 158, 164, 825, with the corollary, that the gods abandon those who fail to appreciate their need for divine assistance, at 101–5, 345–7, 353–4, 362, 373, 454–5, 472–7, 515–16, 724–5, 739–42, 845, 909–12, 921, 942–3.

[119] Cf. Cairns 2006, 109, 112–13.

[120] He is, of course, a competitive and status-conscious character: he thinks that the plot that Creon has conceived against him arises from ambition and envy (380–6); he is incensed by the Corinthian drunk's slight on his parentage, and the insult still rankles after the event (779–86); his angry retaliation against Laius and his men is

prodigious in its extent (800–13); and he assumes that Jocasta shares his concern for honour and status when he attributes her sudden departure to shame at his low birth (1077–9). Cf. Schmitt 1988, 22, 27; Gregory 1995.

[121] On this point, see C. P. Segal 1995, 197–8.

[122] Cf. in general Winnington-Ingram 1980, 203–4.

[123] Cf. Bowra 1944, 189. On more and less 'moralized' forms of divine *phthonos* see Cairns 1996, 20.

[124] See Cairns 1996, 17–22; 2003, 249–50.

[125] For an argument along these lines, see Letters 1953, 225; against, Scodel 1984, 67.

[126] A. *Ag.* 108–247; for the comparison, see Lawrence 2008, 1–2 n. 3.

[127] Schmitt 1988, 17–18, 22, 26–7, 29.

[128] Cf. Manuwald 1992, 36.

[129] See n. 95 above.

[130] By this statement, I mean of course to reject the suggestion that the downfall of Oedipus is merely a tale of presumption punished – this is the point of the preceding paragraphs. My point appears to be misunderstood by Lloyd, this volume, p. 213. Equally, I do not think it is at all helpful to label my interpretation 'an extreme "pietist"' one (Lloyd p. 208): see the immediately following paragraphs of my discussion, where my interpretation should be distinguished from the others that I mention in the text to n. 135. I would fully endorse Bernard Knox's view (quoted by Lloyd p. 222) that the *OT* 'is concerned not only with the greatness of the gods but also with the greatness of man', and so wonder whether Lloyd is in fact attributing to me something like the view of Oedipus that I attribute to Apollo.

[131] For various views of the ways in which Oedipus is or is not like a *pharmakos*, see Bowra 1944, 183; Girard 1977, 68–88 and *passim*; 1986, 24–44, 121–3; Vernant and Vidal-Naquet 1990, 17–18; Vernant 1990b, 106; 1990c; Burkert 1991, 19–21; Foley 1993a; R. D. Griffith 1993 (cf. 1996, 29–44); C. P. Segal 1995, 154; 2001, 114, 140, 164–6; Burian 2009, 103–5, 108, 114–15. For *pharmakos* rituals see Bremmer 1983 (now incorporated in a larger study at Bremmer 2008, 169–214); and for possible reflections of the scapegoat mechanism in ritual, myth, and literature see Parker 1983, 257–80.

[132] Cf. Winnington-Ingram 1980, 322; C. P. Segal 2001, 58–9, 61.

[133] Cf. Mikalson 1991, *passim*.

[134] Cf. Winnington-Ingram 1980, 322–4.

[135] See Lloyd-Jones 1971, 107–28; R. D. Griffith 1996, 52, 54–7, 82–5; Kovacs 2009b, 367–8.

[136] Cf. C. P. Segal 1995, 196.

6

'ARCHAIC' GUILT IN SOPHOCLES' *OEDIPUS TYRANNUS* AND *OEDIPUS AT COLONUS*

William Allan

In Sophocles' treatment of the Oedipus myth, Oedipus' knowledge and lack of knowledge are crucial, not only to his ruin, but also to how the audience react to his suffering. Yet it is also striking that Oedipus himself reacts to his ignorance and suffering in very different ways in Sophocles' two plays about him. For in *OT* Oedipus accepts responsibility for what he did unwittingly, whereas in *OC* he vehemently denies that he can be blamed at all. The aim of this chapter, then, is to look at the nexus of issues surrounding Oedipus' knowledge, intentions, and responsibility in the two plays. And more specifically, with a view to the volume's theme of tragedy and archaic Greek thought, we will also consider the claim that the differences between the two Oedipus plays can be explained in terms of a movement *away* from an archaic worldview to a more modern one. This idea was neatly expressed by Cedric Whitman: 'Oedipus [at Colonus] is a landmark in Greek morality, for he presents the first really clear exposition of the independence of the inner life, that doctrine which in Socrates and his followers became the cornerstone of a whole new phase of civilization.'[1] This 'developmental model' (as I shall call it) remains influential, so that, for example, in the Introduction to the recent reprint of Jebb's *Oedipus Coloneus*, Rush Rehm can take for granted 'the change in Oedipus' attitude towards his unintentional crimes, from an archaic acceptance of guilt [in *OT*] to a progressive notion of extenuating circumstance [in *OC*]'.[2]

We will look in more detail later at the problems surrounding this developmental model of *OC*, but let us begin by focusing on its implications for *OT*. For it implies that only later (that is, in *OC*) could Sophocles make something of the fact that Oedipus' guilt, and the audience's response to it, are affected by his acting in ignorance. Yet the central point of *OT*, and the reason it is so powerful, is that the audience know he has acted unwittingly. If there was *no* interest in the concepts of intention and responsibility in *OT*, the play would simply be a matter of Oedipus getting his comeuppance for his terrible crimes. Yet, as we shall

173

see, this is not the case, and the play's power comes from the conflict between Oedipus' horrific deeds and his state of mind when he did them. In short, *OT* is so terrifying because we see someone being punished for acts he did not intend.

Moreover, Sophocles' version of the myth has two features which make Oedipus' downfall particularly disturbing and thus encourage us to dwell on questions of responsibility and intention: the first is the opacity of divine motivation, which is achieved by excluding any mention of a curse on Laius' descendants and by downplaying the oracle given to Laius at Delphi; the second is the conflict between the audience's knowledge of Apollo's role and the Chorus' simple trust in righteous divine punishment (seen most clearly in the second stasimon, which I discuss below).[3]

Let us first consider the absent curse and the oracle. As many scholars have noted, Sophocles' gods are far more remote and enigmatic than those of Aeschylus and Euripides.[4] But in the case of Oedipus, what is the point of this silence about the gods', and especially Apollo's, motives? The curse on Laius and his descendants for the rape of Chrysippus is also absent from Aeschylus' *Seven Against Thebes* trilogy and Euripides' *Phoenician Women*, but there is no doubt that, in the words of a recent book on the blighted families of tragedy, 'Aeschylus and Euripides never allow us to forget that their protagonists are accursed members of a certain line.'[5] Rather than invoke the curse, Aeschylus and Euripides stress Laius' flagrant disregard for the oracle, and present Oedipus as paying for his father's disobedience. By contrast, Sophocles does not at all stress that Oedipus is paying for the crimes of his ancestor. For not only is the curse on Laius not mentioned at all, but the oracle too is mentioned only briefly by Jocasta (*OT* 711–14):

> χρησμὸς γὰρ ἦλθε Λαΐῳ ποτ', οὐκ ἐρῶ
> Φοίβου γ' ἀπ' αὐτοῦ, τῶν δ' ὑπηρετῶν ἄπο,
> ὡς αὐτὸν ἥξοι μοῖρα πρὸς παιδὸς θανεῖν,
> ὅστις γένοιτ' ἐμοῦ τε κἀκείνου πάρα.

> JOCASTA: An oracle once came to Laius – I won't say from Phoebus himself, but from his servants – saying that the fate would overtake him to die at the hands of any child who would be born to him and me.

Unlike Aeschylus' and Euripides' versions of the myth, where Laius is warned three times by the oracle[6] or sires Oedipus in drunken lust,[7] Sophocles does not spell out what Laius had done to deserve his punishment. Sophocles leaves implicit the idea that Oedipus is the bearer of his father's guilt and will suffer for it, and the whole structure of *OT* leads us *not* to be satisfied with the idea that Oedipus is merely an instrument of divine punishment.

The actual purpose of the curse's absence and the oracle's brief appearance, I would argue, is precisely so that we do *not* focus on Laius' wickedness but on Oedipus' downfall. We know that Oedipus did terrible wrongs and needs to be punished, but we are also terrified by the picture of him doing these things *unwittingly* and yet still paying the price. This form of harsh justice is central to *OT* (indeed it is implicit in the whole action) and it is then spelled out even further in *OC*, where (as we shall see) Oedipus explicitly complains about it. The opacity of divine motivation in *OT* focuses the audience's attention on the chilling fact that terrible things can happen to basically sympathetic people. This is not to deny that Oedipus' life is shaped by something that resembles a curse (namely the prophecy made to Laius that he would be killed by his son), but by making the gods' reasons for punishing Oedipus far less explicit, Oedipus' ruin becomes all the more shocking.

The search for Oedipus' 'guilt', or *Die Suche nach der Schuld*, as Michael Lurje has called it, may be in certain respects misguided,[8] but it does have some purchase in the play, namely in the view of human wickedness and divine punishment expressed by the Chorus in the second stasimon (863–910), especially in its second strophe, where they condemn the sinful and arrogant man who despises justice and the gods (883–96):

> εἰ δέ τις ὑπέροπτα χερσὶν
> ἢ λόγῳ πορεύεται,
> Δίκας ἀφόβητος, οὐδὲ   885
> δαιμόνων ἕδη σέβων,
> κακά νιν ἕλοιτο μοῖρα,
> δυσπότμου χάριν χλιδᾶς,
> εἰ μὴ τὸ κέρδος κερδανεῖ δικαίως
> καὶ τῶν ἀσέπτων ἕρξεται,   890
> ἢ τῶν ἀθίκτων θίξεται ματᾴζων.
> τίς ἔτι ποτ' ἐν τοῖσδ' ἀνὴρ θυμοῦ βέλη
> τεύξεται ψυχᾶς ἀμύνων;
> εἰ γὰρ αἱ τοιαίδε πράξεις τίμιαι,   895
> τί δεῖ με χορεύειν;

CHORUS: But if someone proceeds arrogantly in deed or word, with no fear of Justice, and no reverence for the seats of the gods, may an evil fate seize him for his ill-destined decadence, if he will not gain what he gains with justice and restrain himself from unholy acts, or if he foolishly lays hands on things which are untouchable. What man in such a case will succeed in warding off shafts of anger from his life? For if such deeds are held in honour, why should I dance in the chorus?

Here the Chorus present a *simplistic* view of divine justice (evil people are punished by the gods) which the audience know to be not quite the whole story, since Oedipus too (they know) will suffer, but he is not exactly the arrogant and impious figure the Chorus have described. Moreover, the Chorus' analysis leaves no space for the *moral ambiguity* of someone who transgresses unintentionally, as in the case of Oedipus. So when Oedipus' identity is revealed, our feelings towards his punishment are not the righteous trust in the system of divine punishment which the second stasimon assumes. In short, the Chorus' moral scheme is too simple and clear-cut, and there is a disturbing gap between their pious vision and what we actually see on stage, where even basically well-meaning people can face horrific suffering, and where the punishment of the guilty (Oedipus did commit parricide and incest after all) can be terrifying and not simply reassuring.[9]

Nonetheless, it must be stressed that there are further layers of irony in the Chorus' song which are far less flattering to Oedipus, since although he acted in ignorance, his retaliation against Laius has by this point already been marked as *excessive*. For as Oedipus tells Jocasta just before the second stasimon (810–13):

οὐ μὴν ἴσην γ' ἔτεισεν, ἀλλὰ συντόμως
σκήπτρῳ τυπεὶς ἐκ τῆσδε χειρὸς ὕπτιος
μέσης ἀπήνης εὐθὺς ἐκκυλίνδεται·
κτείνω δὲ τοὺς ξύμπαντας.

OEDIPUS: *Not at all equal was the penalty he paid*, but swiftly struck by the staff in this hand he rolled right out of the carriage onto his back. I killed every one of them.[10]

So when the Chorus sing in the second stanza of the second stasimon that '*hybris* begets a tyrant' (ὕβρις φυτεύει τύραννον, 873),[11] the audience (if not the Chorus) can see the appropriateness of this to Oedipus, whose propensity to anger and disproportionate violence marks him out as a potentially dangerous ruler.[12] Such an association is aided by the fact that fifth-century Athenians themselves considered acts of excessive retaliation (such as Oedipus' killing of Laius) to be instances of *hybris*.[13] Oedipus is far from being a monstrous tyrant figure like Phalaris – indeed, he is one of the more sympathetic heroes of tragedy – but the emphasis on his anger (first underlined in the Teiresias and Creon scenes, where his suspicions of a plot to overthrow him recall the paranoia that is typical of historical tyrants)[14] shows that for Sophocles' Oedipus, as for Heraclitus, a man's character determines his destiny: ἦθος ἀνθρώπῳ δαίμων (Heraclitus DK 22 B 119). In other words, the fifth-century audience, attuned to stories of excessively violent autocrats who come to a sticky end, can see the truth in the Chorus' remarks (Oedipus' anger and violence *have* determined his fate), even if the audience can also see that the Chorus' simple picture of crime and punishment leaves no room for Oedipus' ignorance.

We find a similarly incomplete view of Oedipus' destruction in the fourth and final stasimon, as the Chorus react to the revelation of Oedipus' identity (1196–1200):

ὅστις καθ' ὑπερβολὰν
τοξεύσας ἐκράτησας οὐ
πάντ' εὐδαίμονος ὄλβου,
ὦ Ζεῦ, κατὰ μὲν φθίσας
τὰν γαμψώνυχα παρθένον
χρησμῳδόν.   1200

CHORUS: You shot your arrow beyond the limit and took control of a prosperity not destined for happiness in every way – O Zeus! – when you destroyed the hook-taloned maiden, singer of oracles.

Here the Chorus search for an explanation of Oedipus' downfall and come up with the standard model of excessive human success incurring divine anger, and they go on to stress Oedipus' once elevated status and his great honours as king of Thebes (1202–4). However, as in the second stasimon, the audience can see how limited the Chorus' view is, and can contrast it with the more disturbing reality of Oedipus' experience of divine punishment, whereby he is brought low not so much because of his success, but because of acts he committed in ignorance. It is made clear from the very start of the play that Oedipus has risen to the height of mortal fortune (ὁ πᾶσι κλεινὸς Οἰδίπους καλούμενος, 8; cf. 33–4, 40, 46). However, while the Chorus come to view him as an exemplar of human frailty and the dangers of mortal success (τὸν σόν τοι παράδειγμ' ἔχων, | τὸν σὸν δαίμονα, τὸν σόν, ὦ | τλάμον Οἰδιπόδα, βροτῶν | οὐδὲν μακαρίζω, 1193–6) – an idea they repeat in the final words of the play, again with reference to his success in solving the riddle of the Sphinx (1524–30) – this pattern of alternation[15] is only one aspect of Oedipus' life, and the audience can see that Oedipus' downfall is also due to his own actions. The double motivation (human and divine: cf. n. 3 above) underpinning Oedipus' ruin is best summed up by Oedipus' own response to the Chorus, when they ask (at 1327–8; cf. 1300–2) which of the gods incited him to blind himself (1329–32):

Ἀπόλλων τάδ' ἦν, Ἀπόλλων, φίλοι,
ὁ κακὰ κακὰ τελῶν ἐμὰ τάδ' ἐμὰ πάθεα.   1330
ἔπαισε δ' αὐτόχειρ νιν οὔ-
τις, ἀλλ' ἐγὼ τλάμων.

OEDIPUS: It was Apollo, Apollo, my friends, who brought these cruel, cruel sufferings of mine to pass. But the hand that struck me was no one's but my own, wretch that I am!

As these words make clear, divine punishment can be carried out by human agents – that is to say, by Oedipus' own choices and actions.[16]

As I argued above, Sophocles presents us with a less than comprehensive picture of the divine in order to make us think about the fairness of Oedipus' suffering. In his influential article, 'On Misunderstanding the *Oedipus Rex*', E. R. Dodds argued that Sophocles portrays mortals seeking mistakenly for divine justice: 'he did not believe (or did not always believe) that the gods are in any human sense "just".'[17] However, I think the point is less that gods and humans have different conceptions of justice, but that, as we see from *OT*, the gods do not care about intention the way humans do. In other words, there *is* a basic form of justice at work in *OT* (namely, the doer must pay) and this is a system of punishment which the audience would have accepted; the problem is that it is also pretty harsh and terrifying, because it means that we can pay enormously even for things we do not intend to do. So if we ask 'Is there any justice, as humans understand justice, in Oedipus' downfall?', the answer is *yes*, but the emphasis in *OT* is on the *negative* and harsh side of this justice, that is, not on good people being rewarded, but on wrongdoers being punished, even if they have committed their crimes in ignorance.[18]

Moralizing critics, too influenced perhaps by the Chorus – not to mention misinterpretation of Aristotle's comments on *hamartia* (*Po.* 1453a7–17) – seek to find some fault in Oedipus that justifies his demise. I do not mean to deny that Oedipus' bad qualities, principally his anger, do indeed contribute to his ruin – note especially his recollection of the encounter at the crossroads (*OT* 810–13, discussed above).[19] However, these bad qualities hardly justify his downfall in the righteous terms envisioned by the Chorus. For in contrast to their vision of human crime and divine punishment, Oedipus is not a terrible villain whose comeuppance we get to see and approve, but a man who does terrible things unwittingly and yet must be (and is) brought to account for them by the gods. We may be shown Oedipus' anger, but we are also shown his positive qualities: his intelligence, and his sense of responsibility to the city, and it is these positive qualities just as much as the negative ones which bring his downfall to pass.[20]

Moreover, Oedipus actually tries to avoid his prophesied crimes, yet by leaving Corinth to avoid parricide and incest he ends up bringing them about. In other words, there is a bracing parallelism between Oedipus' angry punishment of Laius being 'not equal' to Laius' offence (810) and the disproportionate (that is, complete) ruin of Oedipus himself because of crimes he did not intend to commit. Yet while it may be 'just' that the killer is punished, the audience's emotional response is crucially affected by Oedipus' ignorance, and his suffering is terrifying precisely because anyone could do wrong unintentionally.[21] Thus the developmental model is wrong to treat Oedipus' so-called 'archaic acceptance of guilt' in *OT* (n. 2 above) as if the audience's response to it were straightforward and uncomplicated, or as if the tragic gap between Oedipus' ignorance and his responsibilty were any less central to *OT* than to *OC*.

Turning now to *Oedipus at Colonus*, we can see even more serious errors in the developmental model. Whereas Oedipus never denies responsibility for his actions in *OT*, he presents a very different attitude in the later play. But to explain this change by saying that the later play embodies a more advanced view of moral guilt is incorrect, for two main reasons: firstly, such a 'progressive' approach neglects the extent to which Oedipus uses highly traditional strategies of self-exculpation in *OC*, as he (like Agamemnon or Priam in the *Iliad*; cf. n. 28 below) exploits the indeterminacy of double motivation for his own ends; secondly, it takes Oedipus' rhetoric of extenuating circumstances at face value, as if the audience simply believe his defence. This is not the case, however, and the audience is brought to see both the rhetorical purpose and *limitations* of Oedipus' arguments.

Rather than showing a development in Athenian moral thought, Oedipus' rejection of responsibility in *OC* is best accounted for in the terms which are spelled out by Oedipus himself. Speaking to Ismene, he complains of his sons' failure to save him from exile, and contrasts his initial reaction to the discovery of his identity with his later desire to live on in Thebes (*OC* 431–44):

εἴποις ἂν ὡς θέλοντι τοῦτ' ἐμοὶ τότε
πόλις τὸ δῶρον εἰκότως κατήνεσεν;
οὐ δῆτ', ἐπεί τοι τὴν μὲν αὐτίχ' ἡμέραν,
ὁπηνίκ' ἔζει θυμός, ἥδιστον δέ μοι
τὸ κατθανεῖν ἦν καὶ τὸ λευσθῆναι πέτροις,   435
οὐδεὶς ἔρωτ' ἐς τόνδ' ἐφαίνετ' ὠφελῶν·
χρόνῳ δ', ὅτ' ἤδη πᾶς ὁ μόχθος ἦν πέπων,
κἀμάνθανον τὸν θυμὸν ἐκδραμόντα μοι
μείζω κολαστὴν τῶν πρὶν ἡμαρτημένων,
τὸ τηνίκ' ἤδη τοῦτο μὲν πόλις βίᾳ   440
ἤλαυνέ μ' ἐκ γῆς χρόνιον, οἱ δ' ἐπωφελεῖν,
οἱ τοῦ πατρός, τῷ πατρὶ δυνάμενοι, τὸ δρᾶν
οὐκ ἠθέλησαν, ἀλλ' ἔπους σμικροῦ χάριν
φυγάς σφιν ἔξω πτωχὸς ἠλώμην ἀεί·

Trachiniae, the only way to contain such an excessive figure is through posthumous cult.[42]

So, Oedipus fails in his attempts to shift the blame for what has happened to him onto the gods, and yet their role in his downfall remains clear. At the same time, however, the gods' support for the harsh system of justice that engulfs Oedipus *is* combined with some concern on their part, a point made clear when Ismene first tells Oedipus of recent prophecies that predict his posthumous powers (*OC* 394):

> νῦν γὰρ θεοί σ' ὀρθοῦσι, πρόσθε δ' ὤλλυσαν.
>
> ISMENE: For now the gods are raising you up, though earlier they destroyed you.

Oedipus' ultimate heroization does offer some divinely-granted compensation for his suffering, and the Chorus stress the consolation of his cult (*OC* 1565–7):

> πολλῶν γὰρ ἂν καὶ μάταν   1565
> πημάτων ἱκνουμένων
> πάλιν σφε δαίμων δίκαιος αὔξοι.
>
> CHORUS: For despite the many sorrows that have come upon him in vain, a just divinity may raise him up again.[43]

Moreover, Oedipus himself presents Apollo's attitude to him in a more positive light, and praises the god's oracle for directing him to Athens (84–105; cf. 664–5).

In conclusion, Sophocles' Oedipus plays both understand Oedipus' experience in terms of his culpability for what he has done, but they offer very different perspectives on the hero's attitude to his past, with Oedipus in the later play defending his innocence and denying responsibility for his actions. For some this is a sign of moral development beyond a 'primitive' or 'archaic' worldview.[44] Thus, for example, one scholar notes how, in comparison to the *Oedipus Tyrannus*, both Sophocles' *Oedipus at Colonus* and Euripides' *Phoenician Women* downplay Oedipus' guilt and shame, and concludes: 'The move by both Sophokles [*OC*] and Euripides [*Pho.*] to an acceptance of the essential guiltlessness of Iokaste and Oidipous is easy to understand, given the questioning spirit of the later fifth century.'[45] However, it is not the case that *OC* illustrates Oedipus' 'essential guiltlessness'. On the contrary, as we have seen, Oedipus uses *traditional* techniques of exculpation to evade the responsibility and blame for his actions, but the audience do *not* necessarily believe him (any more than an audience of epic would believe Agamemnon or Priam).[46] So Sophocles' *Oedipus at Colonus* does indeed describe a possible challenge to so-called archaic ideas of responsibility and pollution, but in the end the drama rejects that challenge and adheres to a traditional (or 'archaic') idea of both.[47] Oedipus' attempt at self-exculpation is seen to be invalid, and this invalidity is an essential part of the play's meaning. For it marks the gulf between Oedipus' rationalization of his mistakes and the reality of his condition, since he *is* both responsible and polluted, not only by the standards of the divine and heroic world of the play, but also by those of fifth-century Athens.

Moreover, Oedipus' markedly fifth-century legal language (of ignorance, intention, self-defence, and law) underlines this gulf, since arguments from intention may count in Athenian courts in cases where people have done wrong unwittingly, but they do not work in tragedy's world of extreme crimes. Oedipus' use of fifth-century legal language is inappropriate for his world because, for all his rhetoric, he still feels himself polluted by what he has done. It might be possible for a court to acquit Oedipus of intentionally killing his father on the grounds that he did not know who Laius was (though he would remain guilty of *phonos akousios*, unintentional homicide), but no court could remove the shame and pollution incurred by his parricide and incest. Thus Sophocles is not debunking out-of-date views of responsibility or pollution – rather he is using contemporary language and ideas to underline the *harshness* of Oedipus' fate, but also its basic *justice* (he did what he did and must face the consequences). In *Oedipus Tyrannus* our sympathy for Oedipus is enhanced by his acceptance of responsibility; in *Oedipus at Colonus*, by contrast, the hero's denial of it is understandable but ultimately futile. For in the latter work Sophocles exploits the 'developmental model' – whereby extenuating circumstances exclude archaic guilt – for a variety of dramatic ends, but Oedipus' actions and character as a whole express Sophocles', and his audience's, *rejection* of such a narrow (legalistic) model of ethical experience. Far from endorsing a vision of moral 'progress', Sophocles' Oedipus plays depict a world in which the 'archaic' ideas of responsibility, guilt, blame, and shame endure.

Notes

[1] Whitman 1951, 204.

[2] Rehm 2004, 50. For Oedipus' moral or legal 'innocence' in the *OC*, see (influentially) Jebb 2004, xxi; cf. e.g. Seidensticker 1972, 262–3; Finkelberg 1997, 576; and most recently E. M. Harris 2010, 138–9; also nn. 44–5 below. For the no less mistaken view of Oedipus' 'innocence' in *OT*, cf. e.g. Dodds 1966, 42; Winnington-Ingram 1980, 201–3; Rehm 2003, 69. A great deal of scholarship along these lines is catalogued and effectively analysed by Hester 1977; Altmeyer 2001, 127–69, 263–99; and Bernard 2001, 104–21.

[3] The audience are made aware of Apollo's guiding role in a variety of ways well before it is finally acknowledged by Oedipus himself at 1329–31 (see below); the most explicit is Teiresias' statement οὐ γάρ σε μοῖρα πρός γ' ἐμοῦ πεσεῖν, ἐπεὶ | ἱκανὸς Ἀπόλλων, ᾧ τάδ' ἐκπρᾶξαι μέλει ('It is not your fate to fall at my hand, since Apollo is sufficient, whose care it is to bring this about', 376–7); cf. Oedipus' unconsciously ironic remark that Apollo's help will determine whether he (and the Thebans) live or die (ἢ γὰρ εὐτυχεῖς | σὺν τῷ θεῷ φανούμεθ', ἢ πεπτωκότες, 145–6). Indeed, by bringing the plague upon Thebes at this point and so choosing to intervene many years after Laius' murder, Apollo is shown to be crucially involved in Oedipus' downfall, just as he was in the timing of Laius' murder itself (cf. 112–15: Οι. πότερα δ' ἐν οἴκοις, ἢ 'ν ἀγροῖς ὁ Λάιος, | ἢ γῆς ἐπ' ἄλλης τῷδε συμπίπτει φόνῳ; | Κρ. θεωρός, ὡς ἔφασκεν, ἐκδημῶν πάλιν | πρὸς οἶκον οὐκέθ' ἵκεθ', ὡς ἀπεστάλη). Similarly, when Jocasta's prayer to Apollo that he should help reassure Oedipus is immediately answered by the entry of the Messenger from Corinth (919–26), the audience can see the close connection between god and victim, and so too when the second Messenger reports that 'some god' revealed the hanged Jocasta to Oedipus (λυσσῶντι δ' αὐτῷ δαιμόνων δείκνυσί τις· | οὐδεὶς γὰρ ἀνδρῶν, οἳ παρῆμεν ἐγγύθεν, 1258–9). Thus Oedipus' suspicion that 'a cruel deity' may be working against him is truer than he realizes (828–9): ἆρ' οὐκ ἀπ' ὠμοῦ ταῦτα δαίμονός τις ἂν | κρίνων ἐπ' ἀνδρὶ τῷδ' ἂν ὀρθοίη λόγον; The play ends, as it began, with Oedipus waiting for a response from Apollo, though now it is Creon who sends for the god's advice (68–77, 1438–45); on mirroring effects (i.e. motifs repeated and reversed) in the play's opening and closing scenes, cf. Sommerstein 2011b, 91–2 and Burian 2009. For the god's role in shaping the action of the play, see Kovacs 2009b; Cairns (this volume).

[4] Cf. Parker 1999, with further bibliography.

[5] Sewell-Rutter 2007, 128.

[6] τρὶς εἰπόντος ἐν | μεσομφάλοις Πυθικοῖς χρηστηρίοις | θνᾴσκοντα γέννας ἄτερ σῴζειν πόλιν (A. *Th.* 746–9).

[7] ὁ δ' ἡδονῇ 'νδοὺς ἔς τε βακχείαν πεσὼν | ἔσπειρεν ἡμῖν παῖδα, καὶ σπείρας †βρέφος† | γνοὺς τἀμπλάκημα τοῦ θεοῦ τε τὴν φάτιν (E. *Pho.* 21–3).

[8] Lurje 2004.

[9] As Swift 2010, 74–90 has shown, the Chorus' songs throughout the play serve to emphasize the cruelty of Apollo (often by ironic inversion of the god's paeanic role as healer and saviour).

[10] Cf. E. M. Harris 2010, 139 'His retaliation is greater than the harm he suffers, and he is therefore guilty of deliberate homicide.'

[11] For a defence of the manuscript text as superior to Blaydes' conjecture ὕβριν φυτεύει τυραννίς ('royal power begets *hybris*'), see Scodel 1982, 215–16; Carey 1986, 175–6; Lloyd-Jones and Wilson 1990b, 100; contrast Winnington-Ingram 1980, 191–2.

[12] It is clear that the Chorus themselves do not mean Oedipus since in the same stanza they praise his achievement in protecting Thebes (τὸ καλῶς δ' ἔχον | πόλει πάλαισμα μήποτε λῦ|σαι θεὸν αἰτοῦμαι, 879–81). The audience, however, are encouraged to see the connection; cf. W. V. Harris 2001, 172 on the link between anger and *hybris* in the *OT*. The phrase '*hybris* begets a tyrant' has a further irony in the sense that Oedipus' (hybristic) killing of Laius (his own begetter) does indeed lead to his becoming *tyrannos* of Thebes. Fisher (1992) 339–40 denies that Oedipus' killing of Laius can be described as 'hybristic', but he incorrectly describes it as self-defence

(cf. nn. 34–5 below) and misses Oedipus' crucial admission that his reaction was disproportionate to the offence. As Gregory 1995, 144–5 shows, Laius' treatment of Oedipus (striking him with a goad) reduces him to the status of an animal or slave, so Oedipus' violent reaction is a defence of his status. Nonetheless, his own recollection here suggests an *overreaction*. So when, for example, Nussbaum 1986, 385 states that 'We pity Oedipus, because the *appropriate* action to which his character led him was not the terrible crime that he, out of ignorance, committed' (emphasis added), it is important to qualify such a view of Oedipus' response – 'appropriate' yes, but excessive all the same.

[13] For violence and *hybris* in Athenian courts, see Fisher 1992, 38–40, 86–8; for *hybris* used to describe excessive revenge elsewhere in tragedy, cf. *Ajax* 301–4, E. *Hec.* 1257, Fisher 1992, 116, 424–7, 430–2.

[14] Cf. 330–1, 346–9, 380–403, 532–42, 618–30; note especially Creon's reminder that the city does not belong to Oedipus alone (κἀμοὶ πόλεως μέτεστιν, οὐχὶ σοὶ μόνῳ, 630).

[15] For the pervasive idea of human 'alternation' or 'mutability' in archaic and classical Greek literature, see the discussions of Cairns and Lloyd in this volume; cf. also Nussbaum 1986, 1–84 on tragedy's portrayal of human life as dependent on things that humans cannot control. Long 1968, 39–40 notes the echo of contemporary philosophical language in the Chorus' meditations upon Oedipus at 1186–96.

[16] In contrast to his unintentional crimes, Oedipus' self-blinding is emphatically described as ἑκόντα κοὐκ ἄκοντα ('willed and not unwilled', 1230). On the meaning of these terms *hekōn* and *akōn*, see Rickert 1989 and Herrmann (this volume). The self-blinding expresses Oedipus' inability to meet the gaze of others now that his shameful identity is revealed (1371–83); cf. Cairns 1993, 217–19. As Budelmann 2000, 175 observes, 1329–31 are the last time Oedipus mentions a god in the play: 'Apollo, to put it metaphorically, is there to give his oracles but withdraws when he is blamed, placing responsibility all the more firmly with Oedipus.'

[17] Dodds 1966, 46.

[18] Cf. also Cairns (this volume, p. 160) on the *OT*'s 'theocratic worldview'.

[19] Cf. also 673–5 (Creon to Oedipus) στυγνὸς μὲν εἴκων δῆλος εἶ, βαρὺς δ' ὅταν | θυμοῦ περάσῃς. αἱ δὲ τοιαῦται φύσεις | αὑταῖς δικαίως εἰσὶν ἄλγισται φέρειν ('You clearly hate to yield, and you are oppressive when far gone in rage. Such natures are most painful for themselves to bear, and justly so').

[20] This combination of good and bad qualities is perhaps most clearly seen in Oedipus' encounter with Teiresias, where Oedipus' concern for the city (312, 322–3, 330–1, 339–40, 443) is counterbalanced by his extreme (and misplaced) anger at the venerable prophet (334–8, 343–6, 364, 404–5), and where Teiresias points out that Oedipus' intelligence (in solving the riddle of the Sphinx) is also an essential part of his ruin (αὕτη γε μέντοι σ' ἡ τύχη διώλεσεν, 442). The latter remark generates considerable irony in the Chorus' following stasimon, as they praise the cleverness of Oedipus in saving the city from the Sphinx (502–12) with no awareness of its ambivalent role in Oedipus' life.

[21] One can see why *OT* appealed so much to Aristotle (e.g. *Po.* 1453b5–7: simply hearing the plot of *OT* is enough to arouse horror and pity), since we will feel particular pity and fear for someone who commits such great wrongs (parricide and incest) unknowingly. The audience's sympathy and pity for the blinded Oedipus are succinctly cued by the Messenger's introduction: θέαμα δ' εἰσόψῃ τάχα | τοιοῦτον οἷον καὶ στυγοῦντ'

ἐποικτίσαι (1295–6).

[22] For the intertextual relationship between *OT* and *OC*, see Seidensticker 1972, 255–6, Bernard 2001, 58–83.

[23] Though parricide was treated like any other form of homicide from a legal perspective, it was naturally considered a peculiarly horrendous crime; Solon is said to have fixed no penalty for parricide, believing that no one would ever commit it (Diog. Laert. 1.59): cf. MacDowell 1963, 9–10, 116.

[24] If a man beat (let alone killed) his parents, he was barred from addressing the assembly, council, and law courts (e.g. Aeschin. 1.28).

[25] Bernard 2001, 107 encapsulates the weaknesses in Oedipus' logic here (266 ff.), at the central point of his opening speech of self-justification: 'Entweder er hat nicht gewußt, daß der Mann an der Weggabelung sein Vater war (und so war es ja tatsächlich), dann hat er im Affekt einfach einen Fremden erschlagen und die Tat ist zumindest als Totschlag zu bewerten, oder er war zur Rache an seinen Eltern berechtigt, dann hätte er aber wissen müssen, wer diese sind.'

[26] Cf. οὐδὲν εἰδώς above (273); also τούτων δ' αὐθαίρετον οὐδέν (523), ἄκων (964), τό γ' ἆκον πρᾶγμ' (977), ἄκων (987), all spoken by Oedipus, though it is Antigone who first makes the plea that Oedipus' actions were 'unwilled': ἔργων | ἀκόντων ἀίοντες αὐδάν (239–40).

[27] Building on Hermann's change of the MSS ἄλλους to ἁλούς; cf. Lloyd-Jones and Wilson 1990b, 235. For a detailed review of the textual problems in 547, and the various solutions proposed, see Finkelberg 1997, 567–73.

[28] Agamemnon, notoriously, uses the influence of *atē* in Book 19 of the *Iliad* to excuse his conduct towards Achilles (19.85–90, 134–8). Agamemnon does not deny responsibility (after all he pays compensation), but uses the language of *atē* for his own rhetorical end, which is to save face before his fellow Achaeans. However, his audience (both internal and external) can see the tendentiousness of his claim that he is οὐκ αἴτιος, not to blame (19.86). Similarly, in Book 3 of the *Iliad*, the audience can see Priam's bias when he says to Helen, 'It's not you I blame, I blame the gods, who brought upon me sorrowful war with the Achaeans' (*Iliad* 3.164–5). Priam seeks to comfort Helen, but by blaming the gods he is abnegating both Helen's responsibility and his own for the fall of Troy. Thus Oedipus is exploiting a highly traditional way of evading blame or downplaying the extent to which an agent is *aitios* for what he has done, but a Greek audience are attuned to considering such arguments in their rhetorical context. Thus when Helen in the *Trojan Women* seeks to excuse her elopement with Paris by appealing to the power of Aphrodite, 'Zeus has power over the other divinities, but is a slave to her; so it is pardonable in me' (E. *Tro.* 949–50), the audience can see through her attempts to evade responsibility and will sympathize with Hecuba's counter-argument: 'My son was outstandingly handsome, and when you saw him your mind was turned into Kypris' (*Tro.* 987–8). Unlike Helen, who did wrong knowingly, we feel sympathy in the case of Oedipus, who did wrong in ignorance. On *atē*, see Cairns 2012a, Sommerstein's discussion in this volume, and Cairns's Introduction above.

[29] E. M. Harris 2010, 128.

[30] Cf. MacDowell 1963, 141–50, Parker 1983, 104–43. Only by proving that his killing of Laius was just could Oedipus escape pollution; however, as we shall see, he fails to do this (*pace* E. M. Harris 2010, 137–9).

[31] As Parker 1983, 320 observes, Oedipus' personal pollution remains, but 'by a contrast of beautiful plausibility, to Creon, who taunts him with it, he makes no admission of pollution, but before Theseus, his saviour, he feels himself impure.'

[32] In classical Athens those found guilty (on the Areopagus) of deliberate homicide (φόνος ἐκ προνοίας) faced death or permanent exile, while those found guilty (at the Palladion) of unwilled (*akousios*) killing had to go into exile until pardoned by the relatives of the dead; Oedipus' claim of self-defence (*OC* 992–6) was the preserve of yet another court, the Delphinion, which heard cases of justifiable homicide: cf. MacDowell 1963, 45–7, 58–81, 110–25; Harrison 1971, 36–43; Lanni 2006, 87–96, 105–14; E. M. Harris 2010, 131–3.

[33] For the unsettling intertext with *OT* 800–13, see Bernard 2001, 116–17 (including a bibliography of scholars who accept at face value Oedipus' claim of self-defence); Kelly 2009, 54.

[34] Kelly 2009, 57.

[35] As does, most recently, E. M. Harris 2010, 138–9.

[36] Not all spectators were Athenian and the heroic world is not the world of the audience. E. M. Harris 2010 is right to stress that the claim of self-defence marks an important difference between the *OT*'s and *OC*'s accounts of Oedipus' encounter with Laius, but he exaggerates the extent to which the Athenian legal system guides the audience's reaction to the plays.

[37] For authenticity and date (composed in 430s, if not earlier), see Gagarin 1997, 8–9. The *Second Tetralogy* deals with accidental homicide, while the *Third* presents an argument from provocation and self-defence, akin to the plea used by Oedipus at *OC* 992–6.

[38] Williams 1993, 69.

[39] Oedipus' propensity to anger, crucial for the development of *OT*, continues here. Theseus rebukes Oedipus for his temper (ὦ μῶρε, θυμὸς δ' ἐν κακοῖς οὐ ξύμφορον, *OC* 592) and Antigone warns him of the threat to their family posed by Oedipus' angry rejection of Polynices (οἶδ' ἐγώ, γνώσῃ κακοῦ | θυμοῦ τελευτὴν ὡς κακὴ προσγίγνεται, 1197–8).

[40] The death of Antigone as a result of her father's curse is foreshadowed as well: ἀλλ' εἰ τάδ' ἔχει κατὰ νοῦν κείνῳ, | ταῦτ' ἂν ἀπαρκοῖ· Θήβας δ' ἡμᾶς | τὰς ὠγυγίους πέμψον, ἐάν πως | διακωλύσωμεν ἰόντα φόνον | τοῖσιν ὁμαίμοις (1768–72, Antigone speaking).

[41] As Rosenmeyer 1952, 110 says of Oedipus' angry curse upon his sons, 'The wrath of Oedipus gives a foretaste of what may be expected of him when he has become an avenging hero.' Cf. also Blundell 1989, 256 on the similarities between Oedipus' anger and that of the gods: 'His wrath, like theirs, is harsh, unforgiving and effective.'

[42] And importantly, as Bernard 2001, 57 says of such figures, 'Ihr Verhalten im Leben erhält durch die Heroisierung keine höhere Weihe oder Rechtfertigung.'

[43] For the Chorus' sense of shared suffering with Oedipus at the end of the *OC*, see Carey 2009.

[44] Reinhardt 1979, 221 describes Oedipus' heroization at the end of *OC* in similar terms: 'The Greek belief in heroes is here raised from its primitive, magical significance to a higher, spiritual and ethical significance.'

[45] March 1987, 130.

[46] Cf. n. 28.

[47] For the continuity in Greek attitudes to the recognition of responsibility throughout the archaic and classical periods, see Williams 1993, 50–74; Allan 2005, 80–1.

7

SOPHOCLES AND THE WISDOM OF SILENUS: A READING OF *OEDIPUS AT COLONUS* 1211–48

P. E. Easterling

The starting point for this chapter[1] is a short passage in *Oedipus at Colonus* (1224–7):

μὴ φῦναι τὸν ἅπαντα νι-
κᾷ λόγον· τὸ δ', ἐπεὶ φανῇ,
βῆναι κεῖθεν ὅθεν περ ἥ-
κει πολὺ δεύτερον ὡς τάχιστα.

The old men of Colonus who form the Chorus of Sophocles' last surviving play devote their fourth song to a reflection on old age, which includes the memorable saying: 'Not to be born is best (literally 'exceeds every possible estimate'), and once a man is born the next best thing by far is to go back as quickly as possible to wherever he came from'. These famous lines echo a view of life which the Greeks attributed to one of their favourite wisdom figures, Silenus, father or leader of the satyrs.[2] In a way, Silenus – ugly, playful, undignified – can be seen as a sort of prototype for other sources of authority such as Aesop and Socrates.[3]

Perhaps it is not a matter of chance that 'Not to be born is best' is associated with the advice that Silenus gave to the Phrygian king Midas, just as 'Call no man happy' was associated with Solon's advice to the Lydian king Croesus, both examples of individuals who had reached the heights of power and material prosperity. Each seems to have asked a similar sort of question: 'What is best for human beings and most to be wished for?' in Midas' case, while Croesus asked 'Who is most fortunate (*olbios*)?' (Hdt.1.30).[4] And although there is a good deal of difference between a Dionysiac *daimōn* and an Athenian statesman, their answers reflect a comparable attitude to material values and a similarly unblinking but witty recognition of human vulnerability.

The idea 'best not to be born at all, or to die as soon as possible' is part, of course, of a larger complex of attitudes traditional in Greek literature from Homer onwards. Compare, for example, the following:

193

(i) Of all creatures that breathe and walk on the earth there is nothing more miserable than man, *Il.* 17.446; cf. *Od.* 18.130.
(ii) Man is *ephēmeros*, 'for a day', meaning both subject to sudden rapid changes of fortune from one day to the next (don't talk about tomorrow till today has been got through), and 'creature of a day', insubstantial and short-lived.[5] One of the most frequently repeated ideas from Homer onwards is that human beings are like leaves that flourish and fall; and the lyric and elegiac poets as well as the tragedians extend the imagery to dreams, shadows, and phantoms.[6]
(iii) Within the life-span that any mortal has, the time for joy and freedom from care is short: 'Youth is short as a dream' (Mimnermus 5.4–5 W) and old age is likely to be troubled by weakness, pain, disease, dishonour, not to mention white hair and bad teeth (Anacreon *PMG* 395).

How should human beings react, what message is to be drawn from these reflections? First, it's no good complaining. The lyric poets often talk of endurance; sometimes they suggest temporary compensations of the *carpe diem* kind, or use the dark imagery of mortality as foil for the rare bright moments of success and fame (as in Pindar *P.* 8.95–7). But mainly it is a matter of putting up with the way things are. Sometimes, like Aesop, you can use a kind of wit to help you deal with the bleak facts of existence. So here, the formulation 'Best not to be born', like 'Call no man happy till he's dead', depends on paradox, a provocative way of seeing the contradictions in the human condition. You take what is normally seen as an evil to be shunned and feared – death or non-being – and call it 'best' or 'happy'. Similarly with the second best – to die young. Untimely death, normally the kind that provokes the bitterest laments, is seen as a paradoxical good, as in Menander ('He whom the gods love dies young', *Dis Exapaton* fr. 4 Sandbach).

The fullest surviving account of the story of Silenus and Midas is given in a passage of Aristotle (= fr. 65 Gigon, 44 Rose) from *Eudemus* or *On the Soul*, quoted by ps-Plutarch in *Consolatio ad Apollonium* (27, 115b–e). This was certainly current before Aristotle's time: he refers to it himself as a familiar old anecdote, and the language he uses in paraphrasing the words of Silenus[7] recalls that of the early, more elliptical, sources, Theognis 425–8 and Bacchylides 5.155–62, which quote them without attributing them to an author and give the impression that they refer to an already well-known saying. Theognis' version is our oldest surviving text on this theme:

πάντων μὲν μὴ φῦναι ἐπιχθονίοισιν ἄριστον 425
  μηδ' ἐσιδεῖν αὐγὰς ὀξέος ἠελίου,
φύντα δ' ὅπως ὤκιστα πύλας Ἀίδαο περῆσαι
καὶ κεῖσθαι πολλὴν γῆν ἐπαμησάμενον.

> Of all things the best for earth-dwellers is not to be born and not to look on the rays of the dazzling sun; but once he is born (it is best for a man) to pass through the gates of Hades and lie covered by a great heap of earth.

There was presumably also an early hexameter tradition,[8] traces of which have survived in Alcidamas;[9] this was evidently the source for the *Certamen Homeri et Hesiodi*, which (74–9) has 'Hesiod' ask the question τί φέρτατον ἐστι βροτοῖσιν; 'What is best for mortals?' and gives 'Homer' a version of Theognis 427–8 in reply. Bacchylides' lyric recasting is put in the mouth of Heracles, weeping for pity at the sight of Meleager in the Underworld, and draws on the same version as Theognis: θνατοῖσι μὴ φῦναι φέριστον | μηδ' ἀελίου προσιδεῖν | φέγγος, 'For mortals not to be born is best and not to look on the light of the sun'. The essential point for my purposes is that variations on the story and the saying were extremely well known from an early date.

Scholars attempting to reconstruct the story of Midas and Silenus also invoke a passage of Theopompus' *Philippica*[10] for the detail (not given by Aristotle) that Silenus was captured by a couple of Midas' shepherds who had been sent by the king to find him; they spiked the water of a spring with wine and made him drunk, then tied him up and forced him to answer the crucial question.[11] The site of Silenus' capture was identified by Herodotus (8.138.2, in the context of Macedonian foundation stories) as Midas' wonderful rose gardens below Mt Bermion in Macedonia; but for other authors the important feature was the spring where Silenus was caught.[12] There is artistic evidence, too, for the popularity of the story. A magnificent black-figured cup by Ergotimos (*ABV* 79, c.560 BC) shows a drunken 'Silenos' led by two named figures: on the left 'Therytai' holding a coiled rope for binding him, and on the right 'Oreios', carrying a wineskin.[13] Another, by the Acheloos painter (*ABV* 384, 19 = *LIMC* s.v. Midas, 9), shows the spring, with Silenus drinking and two figures with hunting spears ready to catch him.[14]

There are many strands of association here: popular stories of a wise creature – divine or human – being trapped and forced to give advice, accounts of riddle-competitions[15] as in the *Certamen*, anecdotes of the sayings and advice of the Seven Sages. Silenus is particularly interesting as a figure who embodies the polar opposites of nature and culture. For example, as a practitioner of cultivated arts he is the teacher of Dionysus (in bee-keeping and the fermenting of grapes, Diodorus 4.4.3) and the adviser to the *aulos*-player Olympus (Pindar fr. 157 M).[16] He has parallels with figures like the centaur Chiron as teacher (of Achilles, Jason, Asclepius), or Proteus, the prophet who has to be bound before he will utter his wisdom (cf. Numa catching Picus and Faunus in Ovid, *Fasti* 3. 285–311). Plato's famous comparison between Socrates and Silenus in the *Symposium* (216 c–e) shows how easily this wisdom figure could metamorphose into a philosopher. But he was always a *daimōn*, too, and liable to give rude answers to human beings, as in his dismissive words to Olympus: ὦ τάλας ἐφάμερε νήπια βάζεις | χρήματα μοι διακομπέων (Pindar fr. 157 M), 'You wretched mortal, you're talking foolish nonsense, boasting to me about wealth'. (The tone recalls that of the Muses to Hesiod at *Theogony* 26: ποιμένες ἄγραυλοι, κάκ' ἐλέγχεα, γαστέρες οἶον, 'shepherds of the fields, shameful wretches, mere bellies'). And of course he never lost either his wildness, symbolized by his animal tail and ears and his snub nose, or his creativity and rumbustiousness as a Dionysiac performer. By Sophocles' time his central role in satyr-play was perhaps the most familiar thing about him.[17]

Silenus' answer is quoted with many variations, but there is a standard pattern that makes the saying recognisably one and the same, while using a variety of words for 'being born' (φῦναι, γενέσθαι, γεννᾶσθαι); 'best' or 'better' (ἄριστον, φέριστον, κράτιστον, κρεῖσσον, ἄμεινον); 'for mortals' (ἐπιχθονίοισιν, θνατοῖσι, βρότοις, βρότῳ, ἀνθρώποις, ἡμᾶς); and 'as quickly as possible' (ὅπως ὤκιστα, ὡς τάχιστα).

What, we might ask, does Sophocles gain by allusively invoking Silenus' wisdom in this play? He certainly echoes the famous dictum, but re-casts it in a distinctive way, making his allusion a little more oblique than (for example) at the opening of *Trachiniae*, where he introduces his version of 'Call no man happy' with λόγος μὲν ἐστ' ἀρχαῖος : 'It is an old saying...', or at *OC* 139, where the striking phrase φωνῇ γὰρ ὁρῶ ('I see by the voice') is qualified by τὸ φατιζόμενον ('as the saying goes'). Here the wording, especially μὴ φῦναι and ὡς τάχιστα, are enough to give the relevant signals in an ode which makes many intertextual references, seeming to evoke a long tradition of thought about life and death, youth and age, and condensing it into this short sequence of intense reflection. It is worth exploring the structure and logic of the whole lyric before trying to tease out the meaning of this passage for the play more generally, and to make the discussion clearer I supply the text, and a rather literal translation, of strophe, antistrophe, and epode.

Strophe (1211–1223)
ὅστις τοῦ πλέονος μέρους
χρῄζει τοῦ μετρίου παρεὶς
ζώειν, σκαιοσύναν φυλάσ-
σων ἐν ἐμοὶ κατάδηλος ἔσται.

ἐπεὶ πολλὰ μὲν αἱ μακραὶ 1215
ἁμέραι κατέθεντο δὴ
λύπας ἐγγυτέρω, τὰ τέρ-
ποντα δ'οὐκ ἂν ἴδοις ὅπου,
ὅταν τις ἐς πλέον πέσῃ
τοῦ δέοντος· ὁ δ' ἐπίκουρος ἰσοτέλεστος, 1220
Ἄϊδος ὅτε μοῖρ' ἀνυμέναιος
ἄλυρος ἄχορος ἀναπέφηνε,
θάνατος ἐς τελευτάν.

> Whoever longs for the greater share of life, having neglected (to desire) a moderate portion, he in my judgement will be clearly shown to cherish a foolish attitude. For the long days, of course (δή), store up many things that are nearer to pain, and as for the things that give pleasure, you can't find them (lit. 'see where') when someone happens to fall into more (of life) than is needed. The helper constitutes an end for all alike,[18] when the doom of Hades, without marriage, without lyre music, without dancing, is revealed: death at the last.

The Chorus look at Oedipus as he waits for the arrival of his latest and most threatening visitor, his son Polyneices. Their reflection on his situation, as one who has lived long and suffered much, is informed by their own old age (they have been introduced in the prologue as 'advanced in age', χρόνῳ παλαιοί, at 112, and the image of a group of old men has been before the spectators ever since). The syntax of the whole ode brings out very clearly the fact that what is true for Oedipus is true not only for him and for them, but for all humanity. Here in the strophe we are introduced to a range of subjects: 'anyone', 'me', time ('long days'), 'you', 'death', with the implication that the observer is also the participant, since there is no way of keeping them separate in the face of 'the deliverer' (ὁ ἐπίκουρος, 1220), who turns out, of course, to be death.

The style is rather plain until the final section (1220 ff.) brings a change of rhythm[19] and a climactic tricolon, ἀνυμέναιος ἄλυρος ἄχορος, 'without marriage, without lyre music, without dancing', rounded off with the alliterative ἀναπέφηνε 'is revealed'. The strongest presence[20] is that of the mysterious ἐπίκουρος, 'ally', 'helper' (at *OT* 496 almost 'avenger'), but here used of the agency which takes charge of every human being in the end, and which turns out to be hard to separate from the 'doom of Hades', that is, death. The insistent nominative endings, all effectively relating to the same ineluctable force, create a more resonant effect than the first nine lines, building up to the finality of ἐς τελευτάν, and also preparing the mood for the reflection to come in the antistrophe (1223–38).

Antistrophe
μὴ φῦναι τὸν ἅπαντα νι-
κᾷ λόγον· τὸ δ', ἐπεὶ φανῇ, 1225
βῆναι κεῖθεν ὅθεν περ ἥ-
κει πολὺ δεύτερον ὡς τάχιστα.
ὡς εὖτ' ἂν τὸ νέον παρῇ
κούφας ἀφροσύνας φέρον, 1230
τίς πλαγὰ πολύμοχθος ἔ-
ξω; τίς οὐ καμάτων ἔνι;
φόνοι, στάσεις, ἔρις, μάχαι
καὶ φθόνος· τό τε κατάμεμπτον ἐπιλέλογχε 1235
πύματον ἀκρατὲς ἀπροσόμιλον
γῆρας ἄφιλον, ἵνα πρόπαντα
κακὰ κακῶν ξυνοικεῖ.

Not to be born comes first by every reckoning,[21] and once (someone) is born the next best thing by far is to go back as quickly as possible to wherever he came from.[22] For when he lets go by/sees go by youth that brings cheerful unconcern, what painful blow (stays) outside?[23] What suffering is not there (with him)? Murders, factions, conflict, battles, and envy. And the final allotment[24] is disparaged old age: lacking strength, lacking sociability, lacking friends, where all evils of evils have their home.

I have already sketched the literary context of the opening reflection; it is marked as an intertextual allusion by μὴ φῦναι, 'not to be born', and by most of βῆναι κεῖθεν ὅθεν περ ἥκει πολὺ δεύτερον ὡς τάχιστα, 'the next best thing by far is to go back as quickly as possible to wherever he came from', although τὸν ἅπαντα νικᾷ λόγον, 'comes first by every reckoning', is a striking innovation in place of some phrase like 'is best' – φέρτατον, ἄριστον, κτλ. – and prevents the passage from sounding like the cliché it had probably already become.[25] The treatment of both youth and old age is also evocative of other texts in interesting ways. Like most interpreters, I take παρῇ at 1229 as aorist subjunctive of παρίημι 'let slip by', with 'someone', τις, understood as the subject (the same person who is the subject of φανῇ in 1225). The alternative is to take παρῇ as the present subjunctive of πάρειμι, with τὸ νέον as its subject, 'while youth is with one'.[26] The main objection to this is that 'youth bringing light heedlessness' is not a bad thing, to be associated with the kind of troubles listed in 1232–5: it is the one brief time of freedom from care that human beings can enjoy, and the language used to describe it – κούφας ἀφροσύνας φέρον – is reminiscent of other passages which use similar language to evoke the insouciant joys of youth. Compare, for example, Mimnermus 2.3–5 or Simonides 20.5–8 West (which uses κοῦφος, 'light', 'cheerful', of the mind of a young person, who has no notion of growing old or dying, and in health has no worry about κάματος, 'suffering'), and two passages in Sophocles: particularly *Aj.* 552–9, where Ajax speaks in some of the same terms to his son, and (less directly comparable) *Tr.* 144–7. Old age, too, is characterized in ways that evoke the earlier tradition: the phrasing of 1236–7 in particular (ἀκρατὲς ἀπροσόμιλον | γῆρας ἄφιλον, 'old age lacking strength, lacking sociability, lacking friends', brings to mind Mimnermus 5.5–6: τὸ δ' ἀργαλέον καὶ ἄμορφον | γῆρας, 'painful and ugly old age'.

But there are new perspectives here, too: in the gloss that the Chorus put on the idea of the distress and indignity of old age the emphasis is not on the traditional evils of poverty, infirmity, pain or sexual humiliation (as in, say, Mimnermus 1, 2, and 5, or Anacreon *PMG* 395), but on social isolation and powerlessness, and at the centre, between youth and old age, stands the stark list of troubles besetting life in the community. 'Murders, factions, conflict, battles, and envy' (1233–4)[27] sounds more like Solon or Theognis reflecting on the problems of the *polis*[28] than like traditional meditations on mortality, and the phrasing perhaps owes something to the atmosphere of tense scenes in the *Iliad*: αἰεὶ γάρ τοι ἔρις τε φίλη, πολεμοί τε, μάχαι τε, 'For strife is always dear to you, and wars and battles' (1.177: used by Agamemnon to Achilles; 5.891: Zeus to Ares). The implication is surely that human society for all its civilization is liable to make things worse, not better, for those who live long in it, and the Homeric resonance stresses the continuing validity of the idea. All this is closely relevant to Oedipus, of course, but it is certainly not specific to him, as the first verse of the epode will confirm.

The syntax of the first part of the antistrophe contrasts with that of the strophe: there is no personal noun or pronoun here, though one has to understand 'any human being' as the main subject, and the dominant presences are expressed by abstract nouns that are relevant to everyone: (fleeting) light-hearted youth, the painful blows of experience, the afflictions of human rivalry, conflict, and envy, and worst of all, old age. The stylistic echo of the strophe in 1235–8, with the list of alpha-privatives closely patterned on those describing the 'doom of Hades' in 1221–2, marks the inexorable similarity between old age and death and the paradox of absence ('no strength, no interaction, no friends') being a way of stressing presence ('all evils of evils').

Epode (1239–48)
ἐν ᾧ τλάμων ὅδ᾽, οὐκ ἐγὼ μόνος,
πάντοθεν βόρειος ὥς τις ἀκτὰ   1240
κυματοπλὴξ χειμερία κλονεῖται,
ὡς καὶ τόνδε κατ᾽ ἄκρας
δειναὶ κυματοαγεῖς
ἆται κλονέουσιν ἀεὶ ξυνοῦσαι,

Sophocles' words at 1224–7 would carry, though I hope the first part of this paper has shown that the story of Silenus' encounter with Midas continued to be widely known. What I want to suggest is that Sophocles' evocation of the saying has so much authority because it captures the Dionysiac truth on which tragedy is founded. Silenus was himself the embodiment of contradictory extremes – wisdom teacher, Dionysiac *daimōn* and reveller – and as such a source of creative inspiration, one might guess, to dramatists who regularly made plays for him to take part in, at the same festivals and with the same performers as the tragedies.[34] His wisdom could serve as a model for tragedy's power to work creatively with contradiction, condensing the stories and sayings of the past into urgent contemporary form.

Notes

[1] Originally published in Ἀντιφίλησις: *Studies on Classical, Byzantine, and Modern Greek Literature and Culture in Honour of John-Theophanes A. Papademetriou*, eds Eleni Karamalengou and Eugenia Makrygianni, Stuttgart 2009, 161–70. I am grateful to the editors and to the publishers, Franz Steiner Verlag, for permission to reproduce it here, and to Douglas Cairns for the invitation.

[2] Silenus is a distinctive individual from the time of satyr-play onwards, but it is not impossible that in the earliest versions of the story Σιληνός (or Σειληνός) was used generically; cf. *Hom. Hymn Aphr.* (= 5 in Allen 1912) 262, where the dancing companions of the nymphs are Σειληνοί, not satyrs. See Gantz 1993, 137–8; Conrad 1997; Seidensticker 2003, 100–21, esp. 104–5.

[3] See Papademetriou 1997, 34–5 for the satyr-like features shared by Aesop and Socrates.

[4] Giannini 1982 has suggested that the famous questions τί δέ τις; τί δ'οὔ τις; are abbreviated variations on a similar question as formulated in the scholia: 'Who is considered great and rich? Who is thought to be a nothing, valueless?' (Drachmann 1910, 218).

[5] Cf. Fränkel 1946; Cairns 2006, 100–2; and Lloyd's chapter in this volume.

[6] See e.g. Mimnermus 5.4–5 W = Theognis 1020–1; Pindar, *P.* 8.95–6 (with D. Iakob's note ad loc. (1994, 307); Aeschylus, *Ag.* 1328; Sophocles, *Aj.* 126, *Phil.* 946–7.

[7] δαίμονος ἐπιπόνου καὶ τύχης χαλεπῆς ἐφήμερον σπέρμα, τί με βιάζεσθε λέγειν ἃ ὑμῖν ἄρειον μὴ γνῶναι; μετ' ἀγνοίας γὰρ τῶν οἰκείων κακῶν ἀλυπότατος ὁ βίος. ἀνθρώποις δὲ πάμπαν οὐκ ἔστι γενέσθαι τὸ πάντων ἄριστον οὐδὲ μετασχεῖν τῆς τοῦ βελτίονος φύσεως (ἄριστον γὰρ πᾶσι καὶ πάσαις τὸ μὴ γενέσθαι)· τὸ μέντοι μετὰ τοῦτο καὶ τὸ πρῶτον τῶν ἀνθρώποις ἀνυστῶν, δεύτερον δέ, τὸ γενομένους ἀποθανεῖν ὡς τάχιστα. 'Ephemeral offspring of a toilsome destiny and harsh fortune, why do you force me to say things it would be better for you not to know? For a life spent in ignorance of one's own troubles is the most free from sorrow. But for human beings it is completely impossible to get the best thing of all or even have a share in its nature (lit.: of the better) – for the best thing for all men and women is not to be born – but the next after this, and the first that human beings can achieve, though it is only the second best, is to die as soon as possible once they have been born' (115d–e).

[8] Cf. Maehler 1982, on 160–2 for further references; also M. L. West 1998, app. crit. to Theognis 425–8.

[9] The hexameter lines we know as Theognis 425 and 427 are quoted by Stobaeus (4.52.22) as from the *Mouseion* of Alcidamas: cf. P.Lit.Lond. 191.

[10] Quoted in part by Aelian (*VH* 3.18), alluded to by Athenaeus (II 45c), and summarized by Servius auctus on Virgil, *Ecl.* 6.13 (=*FGrHist* 115 F75).

[11] In Theopompus as summarized by Aelian the answer was all about the existence of a world full of marvels beyond Europe, Asia, and Libya; but cf. Cicero, *Tusc.* 1.48.114: 'Adfertur etiam de Sileno fabella quaedam; qui cum a Mida captus esset, hoc ei muneris pro sua missione dedisse scribitur: docuisse regem non nasci homini longe optimum esse, proximum autem quam primum mori' ('A tale is told also about Silenus: it is recorded that after he had been taken captive by Midas he gave him this reward for his deliverance: he taught the king that not to be born is by far the best thing for a mortal, and the next best to die as soon as possible').

[12] Xenophon (*Anab.* 1.2.13) locates this at Thymbrium in Phrygia; Bion of Proconnesus gave it a name (Inna) and put it further East ('between the Maiadoi and the Paeonians' *FGrHist* 14 F3); by Pausanias' time it was shown at the city of Ancyra (1.4.5) and perhaps had become a tourist attraction.

[13] Alan Griffiths suggests to me that the implausible ΘΕΡΥΤΑΙ is a corruption of a more general caption ΘΗΡΕΥΤΑΙ, 'Hunters', which the painter mistook for the personal name of the figure on the left. These figures become Chromis and Mnasyllus in Virgil's famous re-imagination of the scene in *Ecl.* 6.

[14] For more examples see Brommer 1941, 36–52, Gantz 1993, 138, and *LIMC* s.v. Midas.

[15] See M. Griffith 1990, esp. 192.

[16] It is interesting that Midas himself had musical associations: according to Pliny the Elder he invented the *obliqua tibia* (*Nat.* 7.204).

[17] See Seidensticker 2003.

[18] ἰσοτέλεστος at 1220 might be active 'makes a *telos* for all alike', or passive 'is accomplished for all alike', and it is better not to have to choose a translation which comes down too firmly on either side.

[19] The aeolic (mainly glyconic) rhythms of 1211–18 give way to an iambic dimeter at 1219, but then heavily resolved trochaics dominate the rest of the strophe.

[20] For the language in which divine forces are evoked in Sophocles cf. Budelmann 2000, ch. 4.

[21] This is Hugh Lloyd-Jones's (1994) neat rendering of τὸν ἅπαντα νικᾷ λόγον. Cf. Jebb 1900a, ad loc.: 'lit., "Not to be born exceeds every possible estimate," – of the gain, as compared with the loss, of being born.'

[22] The sense is not in doubt here, but many critics are suspicious of the illogical (though still intelligible) κεῖθεν ὅθεν περ; for a full discussion see Lloyd-Jones and Wilson 1990b, 251.

[23] πλαγά is the most commonly accepted emendation here for the problematic πλάγχθη of the MSS; see further Lloyd-Jones and Wilson 1990b, 251–2.

[24] I have borrowed this phrase from Blundell 1990, 68. This gets round the difficulty of deciding which is the subject of ἐπιλέλογχε: old age, which could 'fall to the lot' of the mortal, or the man himself, who gets old age as his portion.

[25] The sentiment was already so familiar when Euripides wrote *Bellerophon* that it could be identified as a cliché: ἐγὼ τὸ μὲν δὴ πανταχοῦ θρυλούμενον | κράτιστον εἶναι

φημὶ μὴ φῦναι βροτῷ , 'Myself, I echo the common refrain (heard) everywhere, that best for a mortal is not to be born' (fr. 285. 1–2 Kannicht). On the dating of *Bellerophon* see Collard, Cropp, and Lee 1995, 101.

[26] As does Lloyd-Jones 1994; also, but more hesitantly, Blundell 1990. Lloyd-Jones makes the passage logical by translating ἔξω in 1233 as 'far away' and τίς οὐ καμάτων ἔνι in 1234 as 'What hardship is not near', with the implication that the troubles are impending, and will be there as soon as youth's short time of heedless bliss is over; but this seems to strain the meaning of ἔνι.

[27] This is the transmitted reading; many editors have followed Faehse in transposing φόνοι and φθόνος, but see Lloyd-Jones 1994, 252; Carey 2009, 126. On φθόνος see Konstan and Rutter 2003.

[28] E.g. Solon 4 West; Theognis 39–52, 780–2 (adesp.).

[29] For clear references to *Antigone* elsewhere in *OC* see 1405–13; 1768–72. On ἄτη in *Ant.* see Cairns's Introduction to this volume.

[30] Alcman *PMG* 90: Ῥίπας, ὄρος ἀνθέον ὕλαι | νυκτὸς μελαίνας στέρνον, 'Rhipai, mountain blossoming with forest, | bosom of black night'.

[31] Cf. *Ant.* 332–75 (πολλὰ τὰ δεινά), which mentions only Earth (338) and Hades (361), with a comparably universalizing effect.

[32] 607–28, cf. 575–80, 593–4; 1518–39.

[33] Cf. above, n. 25.

[34] Cf. my comments in a more general context in Easterling 1997, 38–44, 52–3.

8

THE MUTABILITY OF FORTUNE IN EURIPIDES

Michael Lloyd

E. R. Dodds observed that for the purposes of political history the archaic age is usually thought to end with the Persian Wars, but with the rise of the sophistic movement about thirty years later for the purposes of the history of thought.[1] Sophocles, Pindar, and Herodotus thus belong in significant respects to the archaic age. Sophocles was for Dodds 'the last great exponent of the archaic world-view, who expressed the full tragic significance of the old religious themes in their unsoftened, unmoralised forms – the overwhelming sense of human helplessness in the face of the divine mystery, and of the *ate* [disaster] that waits on all human achievement'.[2] The characteristic features of this outlook were insecurity and helplessness (ἀμηχανία) on the part of humans, with the corresponding view of the deity, 'the gods resent any success, any happiness, which might for a moment lift our mortality above its mortal status, and so encroach on their prerogative'.[3]

An example of the kind of outlook that Dodds had in mind is the following passage from Solon (13.63–70 W):

Μοῖρα δέ τοι θνητοῖσι κακὸν φέρει ἠδὲ καὶ ἐσθλόν,
    δῶρα δ' ἄφυκτα θεῶν γίγνεται ἀθανάτων.
πᾶσι δέ τοι κίνδυνος ἐπ' ἔργμασιν, οὐδέ τις οἶδεν   65
    ᾗ μέλλει σχήσειν χρήματος ἀρχομένου·
ἀλλ' ὁ μὲν εὖ ἔρδειν πειρώμενος οὐ προνοήσας
    ἐς μεγάλην ἄτην καὶ χαλεπὴν ἔπεσεν,
τῷ δὲ κακῶς ἔρδοντι θεὸς περὶ πάντα δίδωσιν
    συντυχίην ἀγαθήν, ἔκλυσιν ἀφροσύνης.   70

Fate brings good and ill to mortals, and the gifts of the immortal gods are ineluctable. There is risk in all actions, and no one knows when a matter is beginning how things will turn out. The man who tries to act well falls unexpectedly into great and harsh disaster [*atē*], while to the man who acts badly the god gives good fortune in everything, an escape from his folly.

Two crucial points here are the lack of connexion between human effort and success, and our fundamental dependence on the gods. This kind of view, which recurs in 'archaic' contexts in Euripides, can co-exist with confidence in the ultimate justice of the gods.[4] Similarly, Archilochus (130 W) writes that the gods frequently raise those lying on the ground and overthrow (ἀνατρέπουσι) even those who stand firmly. The lesson is to be moderate both when things are going well and when they are going badly (Archilochus 128.4–7 W). Mark Griffith observes that 'much Greek lyric exhibits a similar sense of uncertainty and insecurity about the biological, economic and political realities governing society'. He points out that 'this was a period of remarkable change and social instability', while recognizing that 'expressions of insecurity and anxiety about the human condition' are also to be found in earlier poetry, and that their apparently greater prominence in lyric may be more a matter of genre than of any fundamental difference of world-view.[5]

A similar sequence of thought can be found in Semonides (1.1–7 W):

ὦ παῖ, τέλος μὲν Ζεὺς ἔχει βαρύκτυπος
πάντων ὅσ' ἐστὶ καὶ τίθησ' ὅκῃ θέλει,
νοῦς δ' οὐκ ἐπ' ἀνθρώποισιν, ἀλλ' ἐπήμεροι
ἃ δὴ βοτὰ ζόουσιν, οὐδὲν εἰδότες
ὅκως ἕκαστον ἐκτελευτήσει θεός.   5
ἐλπὶς δὲ πάντας κἀπιπειθείη τρέφει
ἄπρηκτον ὁρμαίνοντας.

> Boy, loud-thundering Zeus controls the outcome of everything that is and disposes it as he wishes. Humans have no reason, but live for the day like beasts, knowing nothing of how the god will bring each thing to fulfilment. Hope and confidence nourish everyone in their eagerness for the impossible.

The word ἐφήμερος (line 3) was central to Hermann Fränkel's influential account of the archaic outlook: 'it is not merely our external condition that is liable to abrupt vicissitudes: we are ἐφήμεροι ourselves; our thoughts and feelings, our attitude and behavior, our ways and actions – in short, our entire personality is shifting and at the mercy of the day'.[6] Fränkel argued that the word always means 'unstable', 'changing with the day', and he has been criticized for denying that it can also mean 'lasting one day, short-lived'.[7] Fränkel traces this archaic view of man's 'ephemeral' nature back to Odysseus' advice to Amphinomus (Hom., *Od.* 18.130–7, in Fränkel's translation):

> Of all creatures that breathe and creep on earth, man is the most miserable. While we are young and strong, and while the gods grant us *aretê* [prowess, success], we refuse to believe that misfortune may ever hit us. And yet, when the gods make reality dark and painful for us, we bear our lot in a temper of submissive endurance. For such is the mind (νόος) of men on earth, as is the day that the father of men and gods sends upon them.[8]

It is important to contrast the archaic outlook sketched above with later views that the world is governed by chance (τύχη). Bernard Williams expresses the distinction as follows: 'For Solon and other archaic writers, human beings were largely powerless against fate and chance, but this was not simply because there were conditions of life that were unmanageably complex or, as it happened, inaccessible. Fate and chance were forces, and they were deeply, necessarily, significantly, mysterious...they belong to an order of things that has the shape and the discouraging effect of a hostile plan, a plan that remains incurably hidden from us'.[9] Williams contrasts events as described by Thucydides, which may be hard to control or predict but which are random or complex rather than governed by a malevolent divine power.[10]

There is an element of paradox in the presence of a chapter on Euripides in a book on tragedy and archaic Greek thought. A long tradition of interpretation treats him as an innovator both in thought and in dramatic style, whose commitment to the ideas of the sophists implies a corresponding rejection of earlier modes of thought.[11] This modernist Euripides gives voice to characters regarded as below the social status appropriate to serious literature, undermines received morality, and questions the behaviour or even the very existence of the gods. The agonistic style of Euripidean drama, with all kinds of opinions expressed with rhetorical sophistication, tends to undermine belief in inherited wisdom. This view of Euripides is prominent in ancient scholarship, with its frequent references to him as 'the philosopher of the stage' (σκηνικὸς φιλόσοφος).[12] It does indeed go back to his own lifetime, and in particular to the caricature of him in the plays of Aristophanes. This comic Euripides appears in *Acharnians*, *Thesmophoriazusae*, and above all in the contest with Aeschylus in *Frogs*. Aristophanes' criticisms, along with his association of Euripides with Socrates, were influentially taken up by the Schlegel brothers and then by Nietzsche in *The Birth of Tragedy* (1872).[13] Euripides' reputation as a playwright of the enlightenment was reinforced in the later nineteenth century by his perceived similarities to progressive playwrights of the time, especially Ibsen and Shaw.[14]

A reaction against this innovative and subversive Euripides can be dated, so far as English-language scholarship is concerned, to two books published in 1971: Hugh Lloyd-Jones's *The Justice of Zeus* and Anne Pippin Burnett's *Catastrophe Survived*. Both were influenced by mid-twentieth-century German scholarship, which tended to take a less ironic view of Euripides.[15] These 'traditionalist' scholars frequently argue that apparently innovative features in Euripides' plays are in fact also present in earlier poetry. Lloyd-Jones thus observes: 'the inscrutability of the divine purpose is an ancient commonplace of Greek religion, whose content is not altered by describing it in modern terms; and the expurgation of the myths has a long history, in which Pindar and Aeschylus play an important part'.[16] Lloyd-Jones did not deny that there are modernist utterances in Euripides, such as Hecuba's famous prayer to Zeus (*Tro.* 884–8), but argued that they are to be understood in the context of a fundamentally traditional world-view: 'General reflections that echo contemporary speculation are abundant in his works; but they coexist with others of a more traditional kind, and in virtually every instance can be shown to express a mood or an attitude closely related to a character, to a chorus, to a particular and perhaps momentary situation, which it is unsafe to assume to be the poet's own.'[17] This is a useful corrective to the tendency of ancient scholarship to attribute to Euripides himself views which are expressed by characters in his plays.

Later scholars have developed the implications of Lloyd-Jones's emphasis on the dramatic context of modernist views in Euripides. Malcolm Heath thus argues that expressions of progressive theology (e.g. *Hipp.* 120; *Ba.* 1348) are shown to be tragically at variance with the all-too-traditional gods represented in those plays.[18] Mary Lefkowitz takes a similar view: 'But although Euripides' "philosophizing" made him seem impious, at least to the comic poets and the biographers who used their works as "evidence", I believe that it can be shown that any character in Euripides who expresses "philosophical" notions about the gods does so out of desperation, and that ultimately, the gods in that play will prove – not always to the characters' satisfaction – that the gods still retain their traditional powers'.[19] Compare the following statement by Donald Mastronarde: 'Despite all the modernity of Euripides' language and rhetoric and of the issues of his plays, he remains, in most of his work, a poet of the traditional tragic genre, a genre which carries on the pessimistic emphasis on man's limits and frailties which characterizes much of archaic literature and myth'.[20] A similar approach to Sophocles is taken by Douglas Cairns in his interpretation of *Oedipus Tyrannus* in this volume: 'This is a typically archaic vision of the nothingness of mankind, of the evanescence of human hopes and achievements...human vulnerability and suffering are part of a dispensation that gods intervene to uphold, because vulnerability and suffering are themselves fundamental to the distinction in status between gods and men'.[21] This is an extreme 'pietist' interpretation of Sophocles, and one which takes a particularly harsh view of divine justice in his plays.[22]

Supplices is the play by Euripides in which the theme of the mutability of fortune is most explicitly a central issue. It is introduced at the very beginning of the play, when Aethra's prayer to Demeter is prompted by the sight of the mothers of the Seven with their cropped hair and mourning clothes (1–11; cf. 95–7). There is a strong contrast between the prosperity for which she prays and the sufferings of the mothers, with the implication that her pity (34) is due to awareness that she could be in a similar plight herself. Aethra offers various reasons for helping them in her speech to Theseus, but it is striking that her concluding words are that the Thebans may now be prospering but that they will have different luck if they throw the dice again, ὁ γὰρ θεὸς πάντ' ἀναστρέφει πάλιν ('for the god turns everything upside down', 331).

Adrastus, in his appeal to Theseus, describes himself as 'a grey-haired man who was once a prosperous king' (166). He goes on to argue that it is wise for the rich man to look upon poverty, and for those who are not unfortunate to look upon what is pitiable (176–9). After the Thebans have been defeated, he develops the idea that people lose the prosperity which they have by seeking for more, and draws a comparison between the Thebans and the Argives (734–49). The Argives thought they were irresistible, and rejected a conciliatory proposal by Eteocles. Adrastus also expresses other archaic ideas. His speech begins by stressing the dependence of 'miserable mortals' (949; cf. 744) on Zeus, and he adds the further idea of fools only learning after the event (747).

Theseus' rejection of Adrastus' plea (195–249) begins with the confident, and decidedly unarchaic, statement that mortals have more good than bad in their lives, for otherwise they would not remain alive. He then gives a 'modern' account of progress, including the gift of augury. Adrastus culpably ignored the prophecies, and made the further error of associating with bad men (223–8; cf. 589–94; *El.* 1355; A. *Th.* 597–614).

Theseus' reply to the Theban herald, however, takes a more 'archaic' view (549–57):

ἀλλ' ὦ μάταιοι, γνῶτε τἀνθρώπων κακά·
παλαίσμαθ' ἡμῶν ὁ βίος· εὐτυχοῦσι δὲ   550
οἱ μὲν τάχ', οἱ δ' ἐσαῦθις, οἱ δ' ἤδη βροτῶν·
τρυφᾷ δ' ὁ δαίμων· πρός τε γὰρ τοῦ δυστυχοῦς,
ὡς εὐτυχήσῃ, τίμιος γεραίρεται,
ὅ τ' ὄλβιός νιν πνεῦμα δειμαίνων λιπεῖν
ὑψηλὸν αἴρει. γνόντας οὖν χρεὼν τάδε   555
ἀδικουμένους τε μέτρια μὴ θυμῷ φέρειν
ἀδικεῖν τε τοιαῦθ' οἷα μὴ βλάψει πάλιν.[23]

Foolish men, recognize human suffering! Our life is a struggle. Some have good fortune now, others will in the future, and yet others have already had it. The deity is capricious. He is honoured by the unfortunate man who hopes for good fortune, while the prosperous man exalts him from fear that the favouring wind will leave him. We should recognize this, and not get angry when we suffer moderate wrong and do such wrongs as will not harm us in return.

Kovacs deletes these lines, partly on the grounds that their content is inconsistent with the views which Theseus expressed earlier. 'In his speech to Adrastus (195–215) he describes the gods as benevolently supplying all the necessities of human life... We are spoiled (τρυφῶμεν), he says, if we are not satisfied with this. Here, by contrast, man's lot is described as uncertain, and the god is spoiled (τρυφᾷ) by mortals who try to win or retain his favor'.[24] Mastronarde gives a more satisfactory interpretation of the change in Theseus' attitude. He characterizes the views expressed in Theseus' speech to Adrastus (195–249) as those of an 'optimistic rationalist', who believes that 'the world is orderly and comprehensible and that there are elements in that order which have been fashioned for the good of man'.[25] The inadequacy of these views is, however, demonstrated by the fact that they prompt Theseus to such a blunt rejection of a suppliant. He learns both from Aethra and from Adrastus, but the correct attitude at which he eventually arrives is more complex than either. In this speech, he combines justice with pity, and an understanding of mutability with decisiveness in insisting on the burial of the corpses.[26]

The reversal of Theseus' position is underlined by the use of τρυφάω in the two passages.[27] At line 214, it clearly means 'to be choosy, not satisfied with what is perfectly acceptable', applied to people like Adrastus who are not satisfied with divine providence. The meaning at line 552 is less immediately obvious. Collard offers two possible meanings: (1) translating 'luxuriates, is spoiled', with the explanation 'the god...has an easy, careless time at man's expense, for he is fawned upon by the prosperous and unlucky alike'; (2) translating 'is random, fickle', with the explanation 'the god treats men's fortunes like a game in which he moves the pieces on impulse'.[28] It is perhaps not necessary to choose between these two senses, as fickle and arbitrary behaviour tends to follow from being spoiled. Compare Demosthenes 8.34, rebuking the assembly that it has been indulged by politicians to the extent that ἐν μὲν ταῖς ἐκκλησίαις τρυφᾶν καὶ κολακεύεσθαι πάντα πρὸς ἡδονὴν ἀκούοντας, ἐν δὲ τοῖς πράγμασι καὶ τοῖς γιγνομένοις περὶ τῶν ἐσχάτων ἤδη κινδυνεύειν ('in your assemblies you are spoiled and flattered, always being told what you want to hear, while running the gravest risks in your policy'). Similarly, at Plato *Meno* 76b, the handsome Meno gives orders ὅπερ ποιοῦσιν οἱ τρυφῶντες, ἅτε τυραννεύοντες, ἕως ἂν ἐν ὥρᾳ ὦσι ('like those who are spoiled, playing the tyrant so long as the bloom is on them').

Supplices explains the sufferings of both Thebans and Argives in terms of the mutability of fortune, which is expressed in language which highlights the archaic provenance of the ideas involved. This theme is especially marked because of the emphasis given to Theseus' change of mind, and it also contrasts significantly with other elements in the play. The final part of the play (from line 778) introduces the distinctively Euripidean portrayal of extreme psychological states, especially in female characters, which contrasts in interesting ways with the nexus of archaic ideas discussed so far in this chapter. Some indication of what is involved may be given by means of a contrast with the following statement by Hermann Fränkel: 'throughout the archaic period, down to Pindar, the idea of the passive and pliable self was a major element in the general feeling of human helplessness (ἀμηχανία) of which we hear so much in the literature of the time'.[29] Euripides often portrays characters who are anything but helpless and passive, even when the world of mutability is treating them most harshly. His tragic vision seems to have been particularly attracted by the ways in which human beings maintain the integrity and autonomy of their character in extreme circumstances. What all these individuals have in common is a strong sense of identity persisting through time, passionate commitment to subjective feelings and beliefs, and the refusal to diverge from the behaviour which they regard as demanded by these.

Supplices culminates in one of Euripides' most remarkable scenes, in which Evadne, dressed as a bride, 'sings a song which explicitly recalls her marriage and is itself suggestive of the wedding-song, and envisages her proposed suicide on the pyre of her husband Kapaneus as an erotic union'.[30] She describes herself as καλλίνικος ('glorious in victory'), an epithet especially associated with Heracles (e.g. E. *HF* 49, 180, 570, etc.), because she triumphs over all other women in *aretē*, i.e. devotion to her husband (1060–3). Her self-sacrifice may be compared to that of the Maiden in *Heraclidae* (discussed further below).[31] Her action has been interpreted in many different ways, but there is no doubt that she contrasts strikingly with the passivity of the mothers of the Seven and of her father Iphis, all of whom seem broken by their bereavements (e.g. 960–2, 1104–6).[32] Voluntary self-sacrifice is one of Euripides' favourite themes, and it is sometimes presented as a response to the mutability of fortune which preserves the agent's autonomy and dignity. This is especially clear in Polyxena's explanation of her willingness to die in *Hecuba* (342–78). She describes her previously pre-eminent position among the women of Troy and her expectation that royal bridegrooms would compete for her hand. She then dwells, in equal detail, on the life of slavery which would await her were she to live. The contrast in her fortune could not be more extreme. Talthybius' later description of her death stresses the freedom with which she died (547–52), and the Greek soldiers pay tribute to her surpassing courage and nobility.[33]

The mutability of fortune is also a prominent theme in *Heraclidae*, and the second stasimon gives a very full and explicit exposition of archaic ideas

(608–28). Demophon reports to Iolaus that a noble virgin must be sacrificed to ensure success in the forthcoming battle against Eurystheus. An anonymous daughter of Heracles ('the Maiden', identified in some sources as Macaria) volunteers, and departs with Demophon. Iolaus collapses in despair, and the Chorus consoles him in a brief ode. The strophe presents a remarkably full exposition of the archaic outlook as outlined above (608–18):

> οὔτινά φημι θεῶν ἄτερ ὄλβιον, οὐ βαρύποτμον,
> ἄνδρα γενέσθαι·
> οὐδὲ τὸν αὐτὸν ἀεὶ 'μβεβάναι δόμον   610
> εὐτυχίᾳ· παρὰ δ' ἄλλαν ἄλλα
> μοῖρα διώκει.
> τὸν μὲν ἀφ' ὑψηλῶν βραχὺν ᾤκισε,
> τὸν δ' † ἀλήταν † εὐδαίμονα τεύχει.
> μόρσιμα δ' οὔτι φυγεῖν θέμις, οὐ σοφί-   615
> ᾳ τις ἀπώσεται, ἀλλὰ μάταν ὁ πρό-
> θυμος ἀεὶ πόνον ἕξει.

No man, I say, is prosperous (*olbios*) or ill-fated without the gods. Nor is the same house always established in good fortune, but one fate after another pursues it. It removes one man from high to low estate, and makes another, †a wanderer†, happy. It is not permitted (*themis*) to evade what is fated. No one can repel it by cleverness (*sophia*), and the man who is eager (*prothumos*) to do so will always labour in vain.

The stanza begins with the traditional idea, common in prayer, that nothing is accomplished without the gods. The standard rhetorical form is: negative (or rhetorical question equivalent to negative) + 'without' (here ἄτερ) + 'the gods', or name of a particular god, often Zeus. See, for example, A. *Ag.* 1487 τί γὰρ βροτοῖς ἄνευ Διὸς τελεῖται; ('What is accomplished for mortals without Zeus?') The power of the gods is traditionally contrasted with the futility of human effort, as at E. *Peleus* fr. 617a Kannicht: τὰς θνητῶν δ' ἐγώ / χαίρειν κελεύω θεῶν ἄτερ προθυμίας ('I dismiss human eagerness without the gods'). πρόθυμος ('eager') or προθυμία ('eagerness') are formulaic in such contexts (cf. *HF* 310),[34] as are πόνος ('toil') and σπουδή ('zeal'). The idea that no one can escape misfortune is also common in archaic thought, especially in consolatory contexts. M. L. West offers many parallels for the gods making the great small and the small great: 'Usually it is not represented as a question of what one deserves but simply as one of God's whim or private purposes'.[35]

The mutability theme is also made explicit at the end of the messenger's account of the battle, when he describes Iolaus' capture of Eurystheus (862–6):

ἥκει τὸν στρατηλάτην ἄγων
τὸν ὄλβιον πάροιθε. τῇ δὲ νῦν τύχῃ
βροτοῖς ἅπασι λαμπρὰ κηρύσσει μαθεῖν,
τὸν εὐτυχεῖν δοκοῦντα μὴ ζηλοῦν πρὶν ἂν   865
θανόντ' ἴδῃ τις· ὡς ἐφήμεροι τύχαι.

He has come bringing the general who was formerly prosperous (*olbios*). By his present fortune he proclaims a clear lesson for all mortals to learn, not to envy the man who seems fortunate until one sees him die. For our fortunes are changeable with the day (*ephēmeroi*).

There is further stress on the reversal of fortune in the Servant's speech when he brings on Eurystheus (928–40). The emphasis on mutability in these passages is supplemented by expressions of confidence in divine justice by the Chorus (especially lines 766–9, 901–9, 919–27), which seem to be vindicated by the defeat of the villainous Eurystheus. Zuntz concludes his interpretation of the play by stating that Euripides 'presents the concept of a rationally ordered universe created for the best of man by a benevolent deity'.[36] He is of course well aware that mutability cannot be aligned so neatly with divine justice in all Euripides' plays. Burian accepts that much of the play is remarkably orthodox in its view of the gods, but disputes Zuntz's confidence in divine justice in the play on the grounds of the troubling ending, when Alcmena orders the killing of Eurystheus: 'Moral certitude, and the assumption of divine justice that underlies it, are brought sharply into question in the final scene'.[37] The mutability of fortune is indubitable, but the justice of the gods is less clear.

Douglas Cairns stresses the moral aspect of mutability when he writes of Sophocles' *Oedipus Tyrannus*: 'Oedipus' presumptuous sense that he is in control of his life is merely an aspect of the ignorance in which he commits the heinous but involuntary offences of parricide and incest'.[38] We are invited to interpret Eurystheus' fate in similar terms, with the qualification that his offences are not involuntary. Iolaus relates in his prologue speech how Eurystheus was confident of his prosperity and of the strength of his city Argos, and proceeded on that basis to commit *hybris* against the apparently weak children of Heracles (17–25). Eurystheus himself explains that he persecuted Heracles' children in order to make himself secure from possible retaliation from them (1000–8). It may have been proverbially foolish to spare the children of defeated enemies, but this policy is only adopted by Euripides' least attractive characters: Menelaus (*Andr.* 519–22), Polymestor (*Hec.* 1138–44), Lycus (*HF* 168–9), and Odysseus (*Tro.* 723).[39] Furthermore, Eurystheus' policy is counterproductive even in terms of *Realpolitik* since he comes to grief considerably sooner than he would have done even on the most pessimistic view of what the children of Heracles would have done to him when they grew up.

There are a number of striking examples in Euripides of the downfall of a character because of his 'presumptuous sense that he is in control of his life'.[40] The Argives and Thebans in *Supplices* were discussed above. In *Andromache*, Menelaus' plot to murder Andromache's son, far from removing fear from the house as he hopes, is responsible for his daughter Hermione's terror later in the play (*Andr.* 804–13, 866–8). She herself recognizes that she already had everything she needed (*Andr.* 938–42), but she loses it all in the futile attempt to make her position even more secure. Polymestor (*Hecuba*) treacherously murders the innocent and defenceless Polydorus in order to acquire further wealth. This crime seems to involve no danger to himself, but the unforeseen result is that he is blinded and his sons are killed. He sees Hecuba's fate in terms of the mutability of fortune (*Hec.* 953–60; cf. 282–5, 488–98), but it will prove to be equally applicable to him. Hecuba (*Troades*) remarks: 'I see the behaviour of the gods, how they build up the man who is nothing but destroy the man who appears powerful' (612–13). Hecuba is thinking of the fate of Troy, but the audience knows from the prologue that this also applies to the Greeks who had apparently reached their goal by sacking Troy but will suffer shipwreck for their failure to punish the *hybris* of the Lesser Ajax (*Tro.* 69–73).[41] Jason (*Medea*) aspires to improve his fortunes by deserting Medea and marrying the daughter of the king of Corinth. As a result, he loses both his new bride and the sons he had with Medea, and ends up considerably worse off than he was before. These are all characters who believe their position to be secure, but commit *hybris* against weaker individuals who apparently lack the ability to retaliate, and finally 'fall unexpectedly into great and harsh disaster' (Solon 13.67–8 W). This pattern is distinctive of Euripides, and is not so prominent either in Aeschylus or in Sophocles.

The train of thought in the stanza from *Heraclidae* quoted above is especially close to Theognis 165–8:

οὐδεὶς ἀνθρώπων οὔτ' ὄλβιος οὔτε πενιχρὸς   165
   οὔτε κακὸς νόσφιν δαίμονος οὔτ' ἀγαθός.
ἀλλ' ἄλλῳ ἄλλον κακόν ἐστι, τὸ δ' ἀτρεκὲς ὄλβιος οὐδεὶς
   ἀνθρώπων ὁπόσους ἠέλιος καθορᾷ.

No man is prosperous (*olbios*) or poor, or bad or good, without a god. A man has one misfortune or another, and no one is truly prosperous (*olbios*) of all upon whom the sun looks down.

Theognis goes on to dismiss human σπουδή ('zeal', 'effort'), and to stress that there is no good or bad for mortals without the gods (ἄτερ θεῶν, 171).

The eloquent comparison of the two passages by Zuntz argues that Euripides' Chorus finds less consolation in piety than does Theognis, and looks rather to the beauty of the Maiden's self-sacrifice. He draws attention to an important function of archaic-sounding passages in Euripides like this ode when he refers to 'its calm music and the comfort of traditional wisdom'.[42] He suggests that more traditional members of the audience would have been content with this aspect of the ode, while 'the enlightened hearer' would have been more alert to its deficiencies in conventional piety. Zuntz distinguishes traditionalist and enlightened members of the audience, but Euripides' handling of archaic ideas suggests rather that they can coexist without contradiction with a more modern emphasis on the efficacy of human action. This certainly includes the Maiden's heroism: 'the dignity and beauty of such sacrifice shines only the brighter in a world no longer illuminated by the presence of the divine'.[43] The divine does, as it turns out, play a significant part in the outcome, but there is also considerable stress on the zeal, effort, and honour of Iolaus, Hyllus, and the Athenians. The play ends with Alcmene's troubling decision to execute the captive Eurystheus (972–80):

Θε. οὐκ ἔστι τοῦτον ὅστις ἂν κατακτάνοι.
Αλ. ἔγωγε· καίτοι φημὶ κἄμ' εἶναι τινα.
Θε. πολλὴν ἄρ' ἕξεις μέμψιν, εἰ δράσεις τόδε.
Αλ. φιλῶ πόλιν τήνδ'· οὐδὲν ἀντιλεκτέον.   975
     τοῦτον δ', ἐπείπερ χεῖρας ἦλθεν εἰς ἐμάς,
     οὐκ ἔστι θνητῶν ὅστις ἐξαιρήσεται.
     πρὸς ταῦτα τὴν θρασεῖαν ὅστις ἂν θέλῃ
     καὶ τὴν φρονοῦσαν μεῖζον ἢ γυναῖκα χρὴ
     λέξει· τὸ δ' ἔργον τοῦτ' ἐμοὶ πεπράξεται.   980

SERVANT: There is no one who would kill him.
ALCMENE: I shall – and I say that I am someone.
SERVANT: You will incur great reproach if you do this.
ALCMENE: I love this city, there is no denying it. But as for this man, now that he has come into my hands, there is no mortal who will rescue him. In response to this, whoever wishes will call me 'bold' and 'prouder than a woman should be', but by then this deed will nonetheless have been done by me.[44]

Alcmene's determination to kill Eurystheus is open to criticism, as the Servant points out, but the force of her self-assertion is nevertheless remarkable. Daniel Mendelsohn, from a somewhat different point of view, compares her unexpected intervention to that of Evadne in *Supplices*: 'Each, we might say, represents a tragic residue remaining in the individual, subjective, and emotional realms, which the smooth operations of the newly defined state cannot accommodate'.[45] This is a distinctively political reading of the behaviour of these two characters, which can also be seen in more universal terms as a demonstration of human intransigence in the face of changing circumstances.

David Kovacs's 'traditionalist' reading of *Medea* does well to point to the importance in the play of the mutability of fortune: 'The plot, the characters, the *dianoia*, all draw our attention to the radical insecurity of human life, the opaqueness of the future, and the impotence of human reason and human contrivance to control circumstance even when the grounds for confidence are the strongest.'[46] This undoubtedly applies to Jason, and there is no need to attach too much interpretative weight to the formulaic concluding lines of the play (1415–19):

πολλῶν ταμίας Ζεὺς ἐν Ὀλύμπῳ,　　　　　　　　　　　　　　1415
πολλὰ δ᾽ ἀέλπτως κραίνουσι θεοί·
καὶ τὰ δοκηθέντ᾽ οὐκ ἐτελέσθη,
τῶν δ᾽ ἀδοκήτων πόρον ηὗρε θεός.
τοιόνδ᾽ ἀπέβη τόδε πρᾶγμα.

Zeus on Olympus is the dispenser of many things, and many are the surprising things which the gods accomplish. What was expected does not come to fulfilment, while a god finds a way for the unexpected. That is how this matter turned out.

Helen, *Alcestis*, *Andromache*, and *Bacchae* end in the same way, except for a different opening line, πολλαὶ μορφαὶ τῶν δαιμονίων ('Many are the forms of the miraculous').[47] The lines are indeed very much in keeping with an 'archaic' interpretation, but their generic nature, applied as they are to five very different plays, makes it unlikely that they contain any particular insight and counts in favour of Deborah Roberts's argument that they are conventional indicators of the end of the play.[48] It is nevertheless interesting that Euripides chose such sentiments as an appropriate conclusion, resembling as they do the passage of Solon quoted above.[49]

Kovacs also argues that the play shows the working out of a plan by Zeus to punish Jason for breaking his oaths and Medea for the murder of Apsyrtus. This is inevitably more speculative, depending as it does on seeing the hand of Zeus in (e.g.) the apparently coincidental arrival of Aegeus. It is a feature of archaic thought, as sketched above, that the mutability of fortune is an indisputable fact of human life while the operation of divine justice leaves more room for speculation. Kovacs gives an admirably detailed account of those aspects of *Medea* which can plausibly be interpreted in 'archaic' terms. His article is also interesting for the moves it needs to make in trying to establish the case that this can give a comprehensive account of the play. In particular, he questions the integrity of the character of Medea herself. He recognizes her heroic stature, but sees it as being both manipulated and distorted by Zeus' plan: 'this heroic nature is pushed a step beyond even heroism to the point where Medea, without being able to explain why she is doing so, acts in ways that not only *risk* destroying her happiness but are certain to do so'.[50] The main objection to this argument is that there is very little evidence in the play that Medea is being manipulated by Zeus in the manner suggested by Kovacs.[51] It is also worth noting that it is she rather than one of the Olympian gods who plays the part of *deus ex machina*.[52] Kovacs downplays the human as much as he emphasizes the divine, arguing that Euripides' psychological portrayal is rudimentary and that Medea's behaviour is too extreme to be of general interest.[53] In the context of the present discussion, her self-assertive 'let no one think me contemptible or weak' (*Med.* 807) resembles Alcmene's 'I say that I am someone' (*Hcld.* 973), although her character is elaborated with vastly more complexity and force.

Heracles is the play by Euripides which offers the starkest contrast between human resources and unpredictable and malignant divine power. Heracles is brought down at the moment of apparent triumph because of Hera's resentment that he was a child of Zeus with a mortal woman (1307–10). This particular motive is not very prominent in the play, and the emphasis is more on the malignity of Hera itself (1189, 1253, 1263–8, 1311–12, 1393). Iris says that Heracles must be punished so that 'he may know the nature of Hera's wrath against him and may know mine. Else – if he be not punished – the gods will be of no account and it is mortals who will be great' (840–2). Martin Cropp argues that this passage expresses Hera's grudge in a rhetorically generalized form, and should not be taken as evidence that divine *phthonos* is really an important issue in the play.[54] This is doubtless true if *phthonos* is interpreted in a relatively primitive sense, as (e.g.) in the story of Polycrates' ring (Herodotus 3.40–3), but the effect, if not the purpose, of Hera's persecution of Heracles is to emphasize the gulf between human and god. Michael Silk argues that Heracles' original status was anomalous: 'The combination of god and man is unstable and must be blown apart to permit a new, simpler and comprehensible stability, whereby Heracles becomes a suffering man in whom we can believe and to whom we can relate'.[55] The last part of the play is devoted to this entirely human Heracles, with his strong sense of his own life story, character, and obligations (1255–1310, 1347–52). This results in his decision to reject suicide, and to go to Athens with Theseus. Interpretations of the last part of the play usually, and rightly, argue in one way or another that it shows the value of friendship in coping with the uncertainty of life and the hostility of the gods who rule the world.[56]

Pessimism is prominent in archaic poetry, but the passage from Solon quoted above also allows for the gods bestowing unpredictable success (13.69–70 W). The old servant in *Helen* expounds this more positive aspect of them to Helen, having just realized that the Greeks and Trojans had been fighting over a cloud while she was in Egypt all along (711–21):

ὦ θύγατερ, ὁ θεὸς ὡς ἔφυ τι ποικίλον
καὶ δυστέκμαρτον, εὖ δέ πως πάντα στρέφει
ἐκεῖσε κἀκεῖσ' ἀναφέρων· ὁ μὲν πονεῖ,
ὁ δ' οὐ πονήσας αὖθις ὄλλυται κακῶς,
βέβαιον οὐδὲν τῆς ἀεὶ τύχης ἔχων.   715
σὺ γὰρ πόσις τε σὸς πόνων μετέσχετε,
σὺ μὲν λόγοισιν, ὁ δὲ δορὸς προθυμίᾳ.
σπεύδων δ' ὅτ' ἔσπευδ' οὐδὲν εἶχε· νῦν δ' ἔχει
αὐτόματα πράξας τἀγάθ' εὐτυχέστατα.
οὐκ ἄρα γέροντα πατέρα καὶ Διοσκόρω   720
ᾔσχυνας οὐδ' ἔδρασας οἷα κλήζεται.[57]

My daughter, how complex and inscrutable god is! He well and truly twists and (?) everything this way and that. One man toils, while another, who has not toiled, dies a miserable death, since nothing in his fortune is ever secure. You and your husband had your share of toils, you in your reputation, he in the effort of war. He got nothing from his exertions (σπεύδων) at the time, but now success comes to him of itself. You did not bring shame on your old father and the Dioscuri after all, nor did you do the things which were rumoured of you.

The concept of the gods 'twisting' (στρέφω or ἀναστρέφω, especially with πάντα, 'everything') human affairs is common in contexts of mutability (cf. *Supp.* 331; *Rh.* 332). εὖ πως ('well and truly', 712) 'in late Eur. appears to suggest something evidently well planned but not fully understood'.[58] The emphasis is on uncertainty rather than providence. The passage also contains several of the terms standardly used in such contexts for pointless human activity: 'effort' (προθυμία, 717), 'exertions' (σπεύδων, 718), 'toil' (πονεῖ, 713; πονήσας, 714; πόνων, 716). This context suggests that the emphasis of the passage is on mutability rather than providence, although in this case the mismatch between effort and result does not prevent a happy outcome. The providential interpretation needs ἀναφέρων (713) to be translated as something like 'bringing back' (Burian 2007, 236, translating 'Yet somehow it all comes out right when he [sc. god] twists our affairs this way and that, and back again'). Plausible parallels are elusive, and Kannicht may be right to obelize (suggesting ἀνατρέπων, 'overturning').[59]

Attitudes to this speech are a revealing indication of scholars' views of traditional elements in Euripides. Dale suggests that there may be 'a degree of artlessness deliberately intended to characterize the speaker', which she goes on to describe more robustly as 'awkwardness and doddering irrelevance'.[60] Burnett, on the other hand, is impressed by an interpretation of events in terms of ineffective human bungling being redeemed by the unexpected grace of the gods.[61] Her interpretation of *Helen*, and the other plays which she discusses, does indeed show the implications of taking seriously a Solonian view of the kind expressed here by the Servant. 'Each play shows human exertion to be blind and ineffective at best, sordid sometimes, and occasionally contemptible and cruel. And each play meanwhile depicts a divine pity and purpose that can, when it is ready, turn disaster into bliss'.[62] Critics of Burnett have tended to focus on her unduly favourable view of Euripides' gods, and she also tends to underestimate the effectiveness of human action.[63] More recently, William Allan is also inclined to take the Servant seriously: 'Eur. has paused the action because he wants the audience, like the Servant, to reflect in all seriousness upon the wider ramifications of the phantom's existence, and to do so from the "ordinary" perspective of a non-heroic figure'.[64] The Servant's speech does indeed have something in common with views of the gods in archaic poetry in that he has no privileged access to what the gods are actually doing. The rest of the play gives us more insight. Euripides resembles Aeschylus and Homer, while differing from Sophocles, in his explicitness about the gods' motives and behaviour. *Helen* gives three quite detailed accounts of the gods' activities (23–55, 876–91, 1642–61), none of which we are given any reason to doubt. These passages show that human action takes place in the context of a normally incomprehensible divine framework, which makes its significance very different from how it appears to the agents.

Helen thus lends itself to a 'pietist' interpretation, stressing such decidedly archaic concepts as 'the gulf between divine and human knowledge' and '[h]uman ignorance and powerlessness'.[65] Nothing could illustrate this better than Zeus' plan for the Trojan War to relieve the goddess Earth of the weight of mortals upon her (38–40). On the other hand, the war may have been fought for a phantom, but this is apparently not incompatible with the glorification of Achilles (41). Menelaus continues to be motivated by the glory which he gained as conqueror of Troy (806–8, 845, 1560, 1603). He survived his travels (765–71), is courageously prepared to die (842–54), and is resourceful in making his escape from Egypt with Helen.[66] Helen has virtuously resisted Theoclymenus (60–7), will take her own life if it is confirmed that Menelaus is dead (348–59), and is ingenious in initiating and developing the escape plan (813, 1034). Different views can certainly be taken of Menelaus' heroic credentials, but it is difficult to deny that he and Helen have a robust sense of identity persisting through the vicissitudes of their lives, and retain the willingness and the ability to act decisively on the basis of it. Euripides emphasizes both the futility and delusion of human life and its intense significance to those involved in it.[67]

Euripides' late plays *Orestes* and *Phoenissae* show his modernism at its most extreme, but also contain more explicitly archaic elements than any of his other plays. *Phoenissae* combines a strikingly contemporary treatment of the conflict between Eteocles and Polynices with archaic features such as the inherited guilt deriving from the original transgression of Laius (*Pho.* 17–20) and Oedipus' curse on his sons (66–8, 473–80, 624, 1611).[68] The modernist aspects of *Orestes* have been much discussed, including its realistic portrayal of human behaviour, its innovative treatment of myth, and the influence on it of contemporary politics.[69] The play also highlights archaic ideas of ancestral guilt and the mutability of fortune. Electra's prologue speech traces the problems of the family back to Tantalus, the great-grandfather of Agamemnon and Menelaus (4–10). He was proverbially rich and blessed (μακάριος), but now endures eternal punishment, and his descendants have suffered one disaster after another.[70] Electra later goes over this family background in detail, and explains her own and Orestes' present sufferings in terms of it (982–1012). The house has been persecuted by an *alastōr* since Pelops' treacherous murder of Myrtilus (1547–8; cf. 337, 1669).[71] The Erinyes are as real as ever they were in Aeschylus (37–8, 238, 255–74, 316–31, 408–13, 423, 579–84, 791, 836, 845, 1648–50).[72] The Chorus reflects on the impermanence of great prosperity (μέγας ὄλβος), and on how some god (*daimōn*) shakes and submerges it like a ship in a storm (340–4; cf. A. *Eum.* 550–65). The next ode reverts to the house of Atreus' loss of its great prosperity (μέγας ὄλβος again), tracing the source of the woes this time to Atreus' murder of the children of Thyestes (807–18).

The Chorus's explanation of events in terms of the mutability of fortune affecting the family over generations reaches its culmination in the lament after Orestes' defeat in the Argive assembly (971–81):[73]

βέβακε γὰρ βέβακεν, οἴχεται τέκνων
πρόπασα γέννα Πέλοπος ὅ τ' ἐπὶ μακαρίοις
ζῆλος ὤν ποτ' οἴκοις·
φθόνος νιν εἷλε θεόθεν ἅ τε δυσμενὴς
φοινία ψῆφος ἐν πολίταις.   975
ἰώ, ὦ πανδάκρυτ'
ἐφαμέρων ἔθνη πολύπονα, λεύσσεθ' ὡς παρ' ἐλπίδας
μοῖρα βαίνει.
ἕτερα δ' ἕτερον ἀμείβεται
πήματ' ἐν χρόνῳ μακρῷ·   980
βροτῶν δ' ὁ πᾶς ἀστάθμητος αἰών.

> Gone, gone is the whole line of Pelops' children, and the honour which once attended his blessed house. It was destroyed by the envy (*phthonos*) of the gods and the hateful murderous vote of the citizens. Ah, ah, you creatures of a day (*ephēmeroi*), laden with tears and toils, see how fate comes against expectations. Different woes come to different people in turn in the length of time, and the whole life of mortals is unpredictable.

West remarks of 976–8: 'the tone is lofty, as if from a superhuman level of perception', with its derisive address to 'ephemerals' (cf. Ar. *Nub.* 223, *Av.* 687, and ὦ μάταιοι, 'Foolish men!', at E. *Supp.* 549).[74] The fallibility of hope is another archaic commonplace,[75] but the point here is less the dangers of hope than the failure of human understanding to grasp the workings of the gods. ἐν χρόνῳ μακρῷ ('in the length of time') recalls Herodotus 1.32.2, soon after Solon's reference to divine *phthonos*.[76] The explanatory power attributed in this ode to the *phthonos* (envy, jealousy) of the gods is unusual in Euripides. Robert Parker writes: 'The harshness of the tragic gods is normally associated, if in complex ways, with considerations of justice; they are punishers and avengers, not forces of arbitrary cruelty.'[77] He then considers divine *phthonos* in tragedy: 'It is explicitly rejected in Aesch. *Ag.* 750–62 (cf. *Eum.* 532–8) and by implication through the contrast of *Pers.* 362 and 808–15.' Parker finds only a couple of hints in Sophocles (*Ant.* 613–14, *El.* 1466), but remarks, 'The old doctrine seems to creep back in Euripides, though mostly without great emphasis.'[78] The only play in the Euripidean corpus in which divine *phthonos* may be significant as a large-scale explanatory factor is perhaps significantly the probably spurious *Rhesus*. Hector is confident that he has defeated the Greeks, and is warned by the Chorus: 'Look to the future: the god overturns many things' (ὅρα τὸ μέλλον· πόλλ' ἀναστρέφει θεός, 332; cf. *Supp.* 331). He decides to accept Rhesus as an ally, and the Chorus sings an enthusiastic ode (342–79) beginning: 'May Adrasteia, the daughter of Zeus, keep envy (*phthonos*) from my words! For I shall say all that my soul wishes to express.' The ode is followed by a flattering address (380–7), the fulsomeness of which seems all too likely to invite divine *phthonos*.[79] Rhesus' own vaunting confidence (443–53) is followed by the Chorus singing μόνον / φθόνον ἄμαχον ὕπατος / Ζεὺς θέλοι ἀμφὶ σοῖς λόγοισιν εἴργειν ('Only may Zeus on high grant that the gods not feel *phthonos* at your words!', 455–7). The Trojan over-confidence leads to a disastrous failure to post sentries (762–9). Contrast the caution of Odysseus, and his awareness that success comes from gods (582–4).[80]

Phthonos in this rather unsophisticated sense is not prominent in *Orestes*, although the Chorus dwells on the mutability of fortune and the danger of divine hostility. Some scholars have seen a dissonance in the play between the mythical background and the action itself. Seth Schein thus writes, 'there is no real connection or continuity between anything said in these odes [332–47, 807–43, 960–1012] and the behavior of the principal characters'.[81] This is only plausible if we focus narrowly on Orestes and Electra, who have indeed never been prosperous and suffer unremitting ill fortune for most of the play. On the other hand, Euripides portrays their troubles in the context of the history of their family, and the play's combination of archaic and modern explanations is encapsulated in the reason given by the Chorus for the fall of the house of Atreus: 'the envy of the gods and the hateful murderous vote of the citizens'.[82] Furthermore, the mutability theme applies, as so often in Euripides, to characters who do wrong in the confident belief that nothing bad will ever happen to them. In *Orestes*, the Chorus's announcement and greeting of Menelaus stresses his extraordinary prosperity (348–55). He is entreated by the desperate Orestes: 'Fortunate as you are, give your relatives (*philoi*) in their wretchedness a share of your success, and do not take all the benefit and keep it to yourself. Share in effort too in your turn, repaying to those you ought the favour you owe to my father' (*Or.* 449–53). He selfishly refuses to help, and as an unforeseen result is on the point of losing his wife, daughter, and palace, when he is saved by the arrival of Apollo as *deus ex machina*.

Euripides puts more stress on the uncertainty of human life than do either Aeschylus or Sophocles. He expresses this theme in specifically archaic terms in such passages as *Heraclidae* 608–28, with their frequent use of traditional vocabulary for the futility of human effort and the 'ephemerality' of human life. This network of archaic ideas is an essential part of the fabric of Euripides' tragedies, and it defines other elements by contrast. The present chapter has inevitably focused on these archaic features of Euripides' plays, and thus on those aspects of them which respond best to a 'traditionalist' interpretation. These aspects are often underestimated in Euripides, and indeed also in Sophocles as is argued in several other chapters in the present volume. Awareness of the mutability of fortune leads inevitably to consideration of the appropriate human response to this uncertainty. Interpretations of Sophocles in terms of archaic thought have a tendency to the 'pietist', and sometimes overlook those aspects of his plays which appeal to the 'hero worshipper'. A better balance is struck by Bernard Knox in his book on *Oedipus Tyrannus*: 'The play is concerned not only with the greatness of the gods but also with the greatness of man.'[83] It is undoubtedly possible to relate this, as Knox does, to fifth-century history: 'It was in Athens that the new anthropological and anthropocentric attitude reached its high point of confidence and assumed its most authoritative tone.'[84] Euripides does not on the whole give much encouragement to the hero-worshipper, but many of his characters

The mutability of fortune in Euripides

nevertheless display remarkable resilience. The mutability of fortune is a prominent element in his plays, and along with it goes an archaic view of the gulf between mortals and gods, but it would not be a fully tragic vision that ended with 'the passive and pliable self' of Fränkel's archaic human being.[85] One of Euripides' most distinctive features is his portrayal of human beings *in extremis*, and his examination of what they can find, over and above mere endurance, to set against their circumstances.

Notes

[1] Dodds 1951, 50 n. 1.

[2] Dodds 1951, 49. On *atē* in Aeschylus, see Sommerstein (this volume), ch. 1; cf. Cairns's Introduction on *atē* in S. *Ant.*

[3] Dodds 1951, 29.

[4] Cf. Mastronarde 2010, 156.

[5] M. Griffith 2009, 80–1. Cf. Fowler 1987, 4–13.

[6] Fränkel 1946, 133; cf. Fränkel 1975, 134–5. Cf. Easterling (this volume, p. 194).

[7] See Dickie 1976; Fowler 1987, 114 n. 80.

[8] Fränkel 1946, 135.

[9] Williams 1993, 150. Cf. Cairns (this volume), pp. 146, 158–9.

[10] For τύχη ('chance') in Euripides, see *Alc.* 785–6 (with the common contrast with τέχνη, 'skill'); *Hec.* 488–91 (with Collard 1991, 157); *IT* 89 (with Kyriakou 2006, 75–6); *Ion* 1513 (with Giannopoulou 1999–2000, 261); *Phrixus B* fr. 820b Kannicht (discussed by Bond 1963, 136–7, when the fragment was wrongly thought to be from *Hypsipyle*); Wright 2005, 362–84.

[11] On Euripides and the sophists, see Conacher 1998; Allan 1999–2000; Dillon 2004; Wright 2005, 235–60. For an argument that *Orestes* was influenced by Empedocles' concept of *eris* (strife), as well as by the more recent cosmological theories of Anaxagoras, see Hall 1993, 271–82.

[12] On ancient references to Euripides as 'philosopher of the stage', see Kannicht 2004, 122–3 (T 166–9); as 'student and friend of philosophers', see Kannicht 2004, 69–73 (T 35–48); as 'atheist', see Kannicht 2004, 123–4 (T 170–1).

[13] See Snell 1953, 113–35; Michelini 1987, 3–10; Kovacs 1994, 22–32.

[14] See Lloyd-Jones 1971, 144–6.

[15] E.g. Spira 1960, Rohdich 1968, Steidle 1968.

[16] Lloyd-Jones 1971, 146; cf. Allan 2005, 76–7.

[17] Lloyd-Jones 1971, 146–7.

[18] Heath 1987, 51–2.

[19] Lefkowitz 1989, 72 = Mossman 2003, 105.

[20] Mastronarde 1986, 207.

[21] Cairns (this volume), pp. 158–9; cf. Allan 2000, 239–42.

[22] For the terms 'pietist' and 'hero-worshipper' in Sophoclean scholarship, see Friis Johansen 1962, 152–62; Winnington-Ingram 1980, 322; Lloyd 2005a, 78–9. The following summarizes perhaps the most extreme pietist interpretation of Sophocles: 'the central idea of a Sophoclean tragedy is that through suffering a man learns to be modest before the gods' (Bowra 1944, 365). An example of a hero-worshipper is

A. F. Garvie in his edition of *Ajax*: 'Ajax falls not because he is wicked but because he is a great man, or rather because of the qualities which make him a great man' (Garvie 1998, 11).

[23] Quotations from Euripides are taken, except where stated, from James Diggle's Oxford Classical Text.

[24] Kovacs 1996, 86.

[25] Mastronarde 1986, 202.

[26] Cf. Lloyd 1992, 82–3.

[27] Cf. Mastronarde 1986, 210 n. 16.

[28] Collard 1975, ii. 254–5, note on lines 552–5a.

[29] Fränkel 1946, 136.

[30] Seaford 1987, 121. Cf. Rehm 1994, 110–21.

[31] Cf. Mendelsohn 2002, 204.

[32] Cf. Mendelsohn 2002, 197–211; Storey 2008, 73–7. On the subjective character of Euripidean monody, see Barlow 1986, 43–60.

[33] On voluntary self-sacrifice in Euripides, see O'Connor-Visser 1987; Wilkins 1990.

[34] See also fr. 391 Kannicht (*Thyestes*). For προθυμία meaning 'eager (but futile) good intention', see Mastronarde 1994, 320, note on *Pho.* 588–9.

[35] M. L. West 1978, 140, note on Hes. *Op.* 5 ff.

[36] Zuntz 1955, 54.

[37] Burian 1977, 15. Cf. Allan 2001, 28–9; Mendelsohn 2002, 126–32.

[38] Cairns (this volume), p. 158.

[39] See Lloyd 2005b, 139, note on *Andr.* 519–22; Allan 2001, 212–13, note on *Hcld.* 1000–8.

[40] On Oedipus' 'presumptuous sense that he is in control of his life' in Sophocles' *Oedipus Tyrannus*, see Cairns (this volume), p. 158.

[41] See Lee 1976, 182, note on *Tro.* 612–13.

[42] Zuntz 1955, 44.

[43] Zuntz 1955, 46.

[44] The future perfect πεπράξεται (980) seems to be of the type which 'denotes that an action will be *already finished* at some future time' (Goodwin 1897, §77), i.e. it is the future of the perfect πέπρακται ('it has been done'). Less likely is the view of Allan (2001, 211) that it is of the type which 'denotes certainty or likelihood that an action will *immediately* take place' (Goodwin 1897, §79, emphases original).

[45] Mendelsohn 2002, 209.

[46] Kovacs 1993, 68.

[47] Kovacs 1993, 65–6. Cf. Lefkowitz 1989, 81 = Mossman 2003, 119: 'There is perhaps no more concise statement of the unpredictability of human life, and of the weakness of the human condition'.

[48] Roberts 1987. Many scholars accept Hartung's deletion of the lines: see (e.g.) Mastronarde 2002, 386, note on lines 1415–19.

[49] On the resemblance between Euripides' tailpieces and Solon 13.63–70 W, see Lattimore 1947, 169 n. 24.

[50] Kovacs 1993, 67 (emphasis original); cf. 54, 59–60.

[51] Cf. Mastronarde 2002, 33–4.

[52] On Medea as *deus ex machina*, see (e.g.) Knox 1977.

[53] Kovacs 1993, 46; cf. 59. For criticism of Kovacs's earlier treatment of *Hippolytus*, in the context of 'the articulation of the self' in the play, see Gill 1990, 105 n. 75.

[54] Cf. Cropp *apud* Bond 1981, xxvi.

[55] Silk 1985, 18 = McAuslan & Walcot 1993, 133.

[56] On Heracles' rejection of suicide, see (e.g.) Chalk 1962, Yoshitake 1994, Papadopoulou 2005, 173–87.

[57] The structure is well explained by Kannicht 1969, ii. 204, note on 711–21. There is no need for a lacuna after 713 (e.g. Kovacs 2003, 39–40) where the missing transition to prosperity was made explicit (Kovacs suggests 'but afterwards finds happiness and heaven's blessing'). Kannicht points out that the missing completion is supplied by 716–21 (cf. *Hcld*. 2–5). Kovacs is, however, right to query Diggle's deletion of 713–19.

[58] Burian 2007, 235, note on lines 712–13, comparing *Pho*. 1126; *IA* 66. Allan (2008, 228, note on lines 711–13) rightly says 'no approval is implied'.

[59] Kannicht 1969, ii. 205, note on lines 711–13.

[60] Dale 1967, 116, note on lines 711 ff. Arnott (1973, 62 = McAuslan & Walcot 1993, 149) envisages 'an audience growing more and more impatient for this windbag to depart and for the plot to get moving again'.

[61] Burnett 1971, 85–8, 95, 100.

[62] Burnett 1971, 14. Burnett was much influenced by Spira 1960, on which see the perceptive review by Conacher (1962). Spira's book was enthusiastically endorsed by Lloyd-Jones 1971, 155.

[63] E.g. Knox 1972. See Lloyd 1986 for an interpretation of *Ion* that gives more value to the human contribution than Burnett does.

[64] Allan 2008, 227, note on lines 700–60. Allan 2008, 61–6 offers a strongly traditionalist reading of the role of the gods in the play; contrast his reservations about a traditionalist reading of *Andromache* in Allan 2000, 234–5.

[65] Allan 2008, 63 n. 283.

[66] 'The Trojan war is fought again, in miniature' (E. Segal 1971, 606; cf. Burian 2007, 34) in Menelaus' victory over the Egyptians.

[67] For a well-balanced view of the more positive aspects of Menelaus and Helen, see Burian 2007, 32–5. On the antithesis between reality and illusion in the play, see E. Segal 1971.

[68] On archaic elements in *Phoenissae*, see Sewell-Rutter 2007, 35–48, 128; Allan (this volume), p. 174. On Euripides and Aeschylus more generally, see Aélion 1983, i. 197–228; Michelini 1987, 95–116.

[69] See above all Reinhardt 1957; the English translation in Mossman 2003, 16–46, is unreliable and, in places, barely intelligible. There is a useful critical discussion of interpretations of *Orestes* in Porter 1994, 1–44.

[70] On Tantalus in *Orestes*, see further Willink 1986, 79–80, note on *Or*. 4–10; O'Brien 1988, esp. 38–41.

[71] On the *alastōr* (avenging spirit) in Euripides, see Mastronarde 1994, 583, note on *Pho*. 1556.

[72] Heath 1987, 57, stresses the 'objective reality' of the Erinyes in the play, while Porter 1994, 301–2, no less convincingly, draws attention to the realistic medical details of Orestes' madness.

[73] M. L. West 1987, 249 argues convincingly that these lines were sung by the

Chorus, remarking 'the moralizing in 976–81 is typically choral'. Swift 2010, 408, includes this ode in her catalogue of examples of 'tragic evocation of *thrēnos*, funerary song, and ritual lament', observing that the lament here is unusual in that it is sung before rather than after death.

[74] M. L. West 1987, 250–1, note on lines 976–8. Willi 2010, 300 suggests that the register is 'oracular', citing Empedocles DK 31 B 124.1 and 31 B 141. See also Easterling (this volume), p. 196.

[75] See Collard 1975, ii. 237–8, on E. *Supp.* 479–80, M. L. West 1978, 169–70, on Hes. *Op.* 96.

[76] Cf. Fränkel 1946, 134: 'The greater the number of our years, the more are we likely to see the day of a complete reversal', citing this passage.

[77] Parker 1997, 151. Cairns 1996, 20–2 argues, however, that divine *phthonos* is never entirely unmoralized, as it can always also be interpreted in terms of human *hybris* or transgression of limits.

[78] Parker 1997, 151 n. 30. Cf. M. L. West 1987, 250, note on E. *Or.* 974.

[79] Cf. Denniston 1939, 172, note on *El.* 988–97; O'Brien 1988, 38 n. 18; Lloyd 1992, 60–1.

[80] Ritchie 1964, 96–8, rather implausibly denies that either Rhesus or Hector shows unwarranted confidence or presumption. The significance of divine *phthonos* in *Rhesus* is played down by Liapis 2012, 196, note on lines 455–7: '[t]he chorus' reference to the gods' φθόνος is merely an expression of their anxiety lest Rhesus fail to give them back their pre-war peace'.

[81] Schein 1975, 51. Cf. C. Wolff 1968.

[82] See (e.g.) Willink 1986, 244, note on *Or.* 974–5.

[83] Knox 1957, 50; cf. 195–6. Cf. Easterling (this volume) p. 201 on the contrast in Sophocles' *Oedipus Coloneus* between the Colonus ode (668–719) and the pessimistic 'not to be born is best' ode (1211–48): 'Neither ode cancels out the other; it is the function of tragedy to accommodate such contradictions'.

[84] Knox 1957, 107.

[85] Fränkel 1946, 136.

BIBLIOGRAPHY

Adams, S. M.
    1957   *Sophocles the Playwright, Phoenix* Suppl. 3, Toronto.
Adkins, A. W. H.
    1960   *Merit and Responsibility. A study in Greek values*, Oxford.
    1970   'Morals and values in Homer', *JHS* 90, 121–39.
Aélion, R.
    1983   *Euripide héritier d'Eschyle*, 2 vols, Paris.
Ahrensdorf, P. J.
    2009   *Greek Tragedy and Political Philosophy: Rationalism and religion in Sophocles' Theban plays*, Cambridge.
Alexiou, M.
    2002   *The Ritual Lament in Greek Tradition*, 2nd edn revised by D. Yatromanolakis and P. Roilos, Lanham MD.
Allan, W.
    1999–2000 'Euripides and the sophists: society and the theatre of war', in Cropp, M. J., Lee, K. H., Sansone, D. (eds) 1999–2000, 145–56.
    2000   *The* Andromache *and Euripidean Tragedy*, Oxford.
    2001   (ed.) *Euripides:* The Children of Heracles, Warminster.
    2005   'Tragedy and the early Greek philosophical tradition', in Gregory (ed.) 2005, 71–82.
    2008   (ed.) *Euripides:* Helen, Cambridge.
Allen, T. W.
    1912   *Homeri Opera*, vol. v, Oxford.
Altmeyer, M.
    2001   *Unzeitgemäßes Denken bei Sophokles*, Stuttgart.
Apfel, L.
    2011   *The Advent of Pluralism: Diversity and conflict in the age of Sophocles*, Oxford.
Arnott, W. G.
    1973   'Euripides and the unexpected', *G&R* 20, 49–64. Reprinted in McAuslan & Walcot (eds) 1993, 138–52.
Atran, S.
    2002   *In Gods We Trust: The evolutionary landscape of religion*, Oxford.
Baltussen, H.
    2007   'Playing the Pythagorean: Ion's *Triagmos*', in Jennings and Katsaros (eds) 2007, 295–318.
Barlow, S. A.
    1986   *The Imagery of Euripides*, 2nd edn, Bristol; 1st edn, London, 1971.
Bees, R.
    1993   *Zur Datierung des* Prometheus Desmotes, Stuttgart.
Belfiore, E. S.
    2000   *Murder Among Friends: Violation of* philia *in Greek tragedy*, Oxford.

Benardete, S.
- 1975a 'A reading of Sophocles' *Antigone*: I', *Interpretation* 4.3, 148–96.
- 1975b 'A reading of Sophocles' *Antigone*: II', *Interpretation* 5.1, 1–55.
- 1975c 'A reading of Sophocles' *Antigone*: III', *Interpretation* 5.2, 148–84.

Benedetto, V. di
- 1983 *Sofocle*, Florence.

Bennett, L. J. and Tyrrell, W. B.
- 1990 'Sophocles' *Antigone* and funeral oratory', *AJP* 111, 441–56.

Bernard, W.
- 2001 *Das Ende des Ödipus bei Sophokles: Untersuchung zur Interpretation des* Ödipus auf Kolonos, Munich.

Bing, J. D.
- 1974 'A note on *Antigone* 1043–44', *CW* 68, 97–9.

Blomfield, C. J.
- 1817 (ed.) *Aeschylus:* Septem Contra Thebas, Cambridge.

Bloom, A.
- 1987 *The Closing of the American Mind*, New York.

Blundell, M. W.
- 1989 *Helping Friends and Harming Enemies: A study in Sophocles and Greek ethics*, Cambridge.
- 1990 *Sophocles'* Oedipus at Colonus, *translated with introduction, notes and interpretive essay*, Newburyport CT.

Bobzien, S.
- 1998a *Determinism and Freedom in Stoic Philosophy*, Oxford.
- 1998b 'The inadvertent conception and late birth of the free-will problem', *Phronesis* 43, 133–75.

Boeve, L. and Feyaerts, K.
- 1999 *Metaphor and God-Talk*, Berne.

Bollack, J.
- 1990 *L'*Oedipe Roi *de Sophocle: le texte et ses interpretations*, 4 vols, Lille.
- 1999 *La Mort d'Antigone: la tragédie de Créon*, Paris.

Bollack, J. et al.
- 2004 Antigone: *enjeux d'une traduction*, Paris.

Bond, G. W.
- 1963 (ed.) *Euripides:* Hypsipyle, Oxford.
- 1981 (ed.) *Euripides:* Heracles, Oxford.

Booth, N. B.
- 1959 'Sophocles, *Antigone* 599–603: a positive argument for κόνις', *CQ* 9, 76–7.

Borthwick, E. K.
- 1967 'A "femme fatale" in Asclepiades', *CR* 17, 250–4.

Bowra, C. M.
- 1944 *Sophoclean Tragedy*, Oxford.

Boyer, P.
- 2001 *Religion Explained: The evolutionary origins of religious thought*, New York.

Bremer, J. M.
- 1969 *Hamartia: Tragic error in the* Poetics *of Aristotle and in Greek tragedy*, Amsterdam.

Bremmer, J. N.
- 1983 'Scapegoat rituals in ancient Greece', *HSCP* 87, 299–320.
- 2008 *Greek Religion and Culture, the Bible and the Ancient Near East*, Jerusalem Studies in Religion and Culture 8, Leiden.

Brennan, T.
- 2005 *The Stoic Life: Emotions, duties, and fate*, Oxford.

Brezzi, F.
- 2004 *Antigone e la* philia: *le passioni tra etica e politica*, Milan.

Brock, R. W.
- Forthcoming *Greek Political Imagery from Homer to Aristotle*, London.

Brommer, F.
- 1941 'Bilder der Midassage', *Archäologischer Anzeiger* 56, 36–52.

Brown, A. L.
- 1987 (ed.) *Sophocles*: Antigone, Warminster.

Bryson Bongie, E.
- 1974 'The daughter of Oedipus' in J. L. Heller & J. K. Newman (eds), *Serta Turyniana: Studies in Greek literature and palaeography in honor of Alexander Turyn*, Urbana IL, 239–67.

Budelmann, F.
- 2000 *The Language of Sophocles: Community, communication and involvement*, Cambridge.
- 2006 'The mediated ending of Sophocles' *Oedipus Tyrannus*', *MD* 57, 43–61.
- 2009 (ed.) *The Cambridge Companion to Greek Lyric*, Cambridge.

Burian, P.
- 1977 'Euripides' *Heraclidae*: an interpretation', *CP* 72, 1–21.
- 1986 'ΣΩΤΗΡ ΤΡΙΤΟΣ and some triadisms in Aeschylus' *Oresteia*', *AJP* 107, 332–42.
- 2007 (ed.) *Euripides:* Helen, Warminster.
- 2009 'Inconclusive conclusion: the ending(s) of *Oedipus Tyrannus*', in Goldhill and Hall (eds) 2009, 99–118.

Burkert, W.
- 1972 *Lore and Science in Ancient Pythagoreanism*, Cambridge MA.
- 1985 *Greek Religion*, trans. J. Raffan, Cambridge MA.
- 1991 *Oedipus, Oracles, and Meaning: From Sophocles to Umberto Eco*, Toronto.

Burnett, A. P.
- 1971 *Catastrophe Survived: Euripides' plays of mixed reversal*, Oxford.

Burton, R. W. B.
- 1980 *The Chorus in Sophocles' Tragedies*, Oxford.

Bushnell, R. W.
- 1988 *Prophesying Tragedy: Sign and voice in Sophocles' Theban Plays*, Ithaca NY.

Buxton, R. G. A.
- 1987 'The gods in Sophocles', in P. Nearchou (ed.), *International Meeting of Ancient Greek Drama, Delphi 8–12 April 1984, Delphi 4–25 June 1985*, Athens, 9–14.

Cairns, D. L.
- 1992 'Homeric Psychology' (review of Schmitt 1990), *CR* 42, 1–3.
- 1993 *Aidōs: The psychology and ethics of honour and shame in ancient Greek literature*, Oxford.
- 1996 '*Hybris*, dishonour, and thinking big', *JHS* 116, 1–32.

2001a   (ed.) *Oxford Readings in Homer's* Iliad, Oxford.
2001b   'Introduction', in Cairns (ed.) 2001a, 1–56.
2003   'The politics of envy: envy and equality in classical Greece', in Konstan and Rutter (eds) 2003, 235–52.
2005   'Values', in Gregory (ed.) 2005, 321–32.
2006   'Virtue and vicissitude: the paradoxes of the *Ajax*', in Cairns and Liapis (eds), 99–132.
2010   (ed.) *Bacchylides: Five Epinician odes (3, 5, 9, 11, 13)*, Cambridge.
2011   'The principle of alternation and the tyrant's happiness in Bacchylidean Epinician', *SO* 85, 17–32.
2012a   '*Atē* in the Homeric poems', *Papers of the Langford Latin Seminar* 15, 1–52.
2012b   'Vêtu d'impudeur et enveloppé de chagrin. Le rôle des métaphores de "l'habillement" dans les concepts d'émotion en Grèce ancienne', in F. Gherchanoc and V. Huet (eds), *Les vêtements antiques: s'habiller, se déshabiller dans les mondes anciens*, Paris, 149–62.

Cairns, D. L. and Liapis, V.
2006   (eds), *Dionysalexandros: Essays on Aeschylus and his fellow tragedians in honour of A. F. Garvie*, Swansea.

Calame, C.
1999   'Performative aspects of the choral voice in Greek tragedy: civic identity in performance', in S. Goldhill and R. Osborne (eds), *Performance Culture and Athenian Democracy*, Cambridge, 125–53.

Calder, W. M. III
1968   'Sophokles' political tragedy, *Antigone*', *GRBS* 9, 389–407.

Cameron, A.
1968   *The Identity of Oedipus the King: Five essays on the* Oedipus Tyrannus, New York.

Campbell, L.
1871   (ed.) *Sophocles. The plays and fragments*, 2 vols, Oxford.

Canevaro, M.
2013   *The Documents in the Public Speeches of Demosthenes*, Oxford.

Carey, C.
1986   'The second stasimon of Sophocles' *Oedipus Tyrannus*', *JHS* 106, 175–9.
2009   'The third stasimon of *Oedipus at Colonus*', in Goldhill and Hall (eds) 2009, 119–33.

Cerri, G.
1979   *Legislazione orale e tragedia greca. Studi sull'* Antigone *di Sofocle e sulle* Supplici *di Euripide*, Naples.

Chalk, H. H. O.
1962   '*Arete* and *bia* in Euripides' *Herakles*', *JHS* 82, 7–18.

Clarke, M.
1999   *Flesh and Spirit in the Songs of Homer: A study of words and myths*, Oxford.
2001   'Thrice-ploughed woe (Sophocles, *Antigone* 859)', *CQ* 51, 368–73.

Clay, D.
1969   'Aeschylus' *trigeron mythos*', *Hermes* 97, 1–9.

Coleman, R.
1972   'The role of the chorus in Sophocles' *Antigone*', *PCPS* 18, 4–27.

Collard, C.
 1975 (ed.) *Euripides:* Supplices, 2 vols, Groningen.
 1991 (ed.) *Euripides:* Hecuba, Warminster.
Collard, C., Cropp, M. J., Lee, K. H.
 1995 (eds) *Euripides: Selected fragmentary plays,* vol. i, Warminster.
Conacher, D. J.
 1962 Review of Spira 1960, *Phoenix* 16, 127–9.
 1967 *Euripidean Drama: Myth, theme and structure,* Toronto.
 1998 *Euripides and the Sophists,* London.
Conrad, G.
 1997 *Der Silen: Wandlungen einer Gestalt,* Trier.
Cousland, J. R. C. and Hume, J. R.
 2009 (eds) *The Play of Texts and Fragments: Essays in honour of Martin Cropp,* Leiden.
Craik, E. M.
 1986 'Sophokles' *Antigone* 100–109', *Eranos* 84, 101–5.
Cropp, M.
 1997 'Antigone's final speech (Sophocles, *Antigone* 891–928)', *G&R* 44, 137–60.
Cropp, M. J., Lee, K. H., Sansone, D.
 1999–2000 (eds) *Euripides and Tragic Theatre in the Late Fifth Century, ICS* 24–5, Urbana IL.
Dale, A. M.
 1954 (ed.) *Euripides:* Alcestis, Oxford.
 1967 (ed.) *Euripides:* Helen, Oxford.
Dalfen, J.
 1977 'Gesetz ist nicht Gesetz und fromm ist nicht fromm. Die Sprache der Personen in der sophokleischen *Antigone*', *WS* 11, 5–26.
Daskarolis, A.
 2000 *Die Wiedergeburt des Sophokles aus dem Geist des Humanismus: Studien zur Sophokles-Rezeption in Deutschland vom Beginn des 16. bis zur Mitte des 17. Jahrhunderts,* Tübingen.
Davidson, J. F.
 1983 'The *parodos* of the *Antigone*: A poetic study', *BICS* 30, 41–51.
 1986 'The Sophoclean battleground', *Eranos* 84, 107–17.
Davies, M.
 1982 'The end of Sophocles' *OT*', *Hermes* 110, 268–78.
 1991 'The end of Sophocles' *OT* revisited', *Prometheus* 17, 1–18.
Dawe, R. D.
 1963 'Inconsistency of plot and character in Aeschylus', *PCPS* 189, 21–62.
 1968 'Some reflections on *ate* and *hamartia*', *HSCP* 72, 89–123. [The bound volume containing this article is dated 1967 on its spine, but the prelims. give its date of publication as 1968, which is the date adopted in JSTOR.]
 1978 *Studies on the Text of Sophocles* vol. iii, Leiden.
 1982 (ed.) *Sophocles:* Oedipus Rex, Cambridge.
 1985 (ed.) *Sophoclis tragoediae,* vol. 2, Trachiniae, Antigone, Philoctetes, Oedipus Coloneus, 2nd edn, Leipzig.

Bibliography

    1988   'Miscellanea critica', *CP* 83, 97–111.
    2001a   'Casaubon and Camb. Univ. Adv. B.3.3', *Lexis* 19, 183–4.
    2001b   'On interpolation in the two Oedipus plays of Sophocles', *RM* 144, 1–21.
    2006   (ed.) *Sophocles:* Oedipus Rex, 2nd edn, Cambridge.

Dawson, C. M.
    1970   *The* Seven against Thebes *by Aeschylus*, Englewood Cliffs NJ.

De Jong, I. J. F.
    1987   *Narrators and Focalizers: The presentation of the story in the* Iliad, Amsterdam.

Demont, P.
    2000   'Lots héroïques: remarques sur le tirage au sort de l'*Iliade* aux *Sept contre Thèbes* d'Eschyle', *REG* 113, 299–325.

Dennett, D. C.
    2003   *Freedom Evolves*, London.

Denniston, J. D.
    1939   (ed.) *Euripides:* Electra, Oxford.

DeVito, A.
    1999   'Eteocles, Amphiaraus, and necessity in Aeschylus' *Seven against Thebes*', *Hermes* 127, 165–71.

Dickie, M. W.
    1976   'On the meaning of ἐφήμερος', *ICS* 1, 7–14.

Dietrich, B. C.
    1965   *Death, Fate, and the Gods: The development of a religious idea in Greek popular belief and in Homer*, London.

Diggle, J.
    1975   '*Pap. Oxy.* XLII (1974), 3006 (Gnomology)', *ZPE* 16, 76.
    2007   'Creon and the burial of traitors: some thoughts on the *Antigone*', in *European Cultural Centre of Delphi XII International Meeting on Ancient Greek Drama 2004: Symposium proceedings,* Athens, 79–86.

Dihle, A.
    1982   *The Theory of Will in Classical Antiquity*, Berkeley and Los Angeles.

Dillon, J.
    2004   'Euripides and the philosophy of his time', *Classics Ireland* 11, 47–73.

Dodds, E. R.
    1951   *The Greeks and the Irrational*, Berkeley and Los Angeles.
    1966   'On misunderstanding the *Oedipus Rex*', *G&R* 13, 37–49.

Dover, K. J.
    1974   *Greek Popular Morality in the Time of Plato and Aristotle*, Oxford.
    1986   'Ion of Chios: his place in the history of Greek literature', in Boardman, J. and Vaphopoulou-Richardson, C. E. (eds), *Chios: A conference at the Homereion in Chios 1984*, Oxford, 27–37.
    1988   *The Greeks and their Legacy*, collected papers, vol. 2, Oxford.

Doyle, R. E.
    1983   *Ate: Its use and meaning*, New York.

Drachmann, A. B.
    1910   *Scholia Vetera in Pindari Carmina*, vol. II, Leipzig.

Dyer, R. R.
    1964   'The use of καλύπτω in Homer', *Glotta* 42, 29–38.

Easterling, P. E.
- 1973 'Presentation of character in Aeschylus', *G&R* 20, 3–19.
- 1978 'The second stasimon of *Antigone*' in R. D. Dawe, J. Diggle, and P. E. Easterling (eds), *Dionysiaca: Nine studies in Greek poetry by former pupils presented to Sir Denys Page on his seventieth birthday*, Cambridge, 141–58.
- 1997 (ed.) *The Cambridge Companion to Greek Tragedy*, Cambridge.

Ehrenberg, V.
- 1954 *Sophocles and Pericles*, Oxford.

Eidinow, E.
- 2011 *Luck, Fate, and Fortune: Antiquity and its legacy*, London.

Else, G. F.
- 1976 *The Madness of Antigone*, Abhandlungen der Heidelberger Akademie der Wissenschaften, 1976.1, Heidelberg.

Erbse, H.
- 1964 'Interpretationsprobleme in den *Septem* des Aischylos', *Hermes* 92, 1–22.
- 1993 'Sophokles über die geistige Blindheit der Menschen,' *ICS* 28, 57–71.

Ewans, M.
- 1995 *Aeschylus:* The Oresteia, London.
- 1996 *Aeschylus:* Suppliants *and Other Dramas*, London.

Eyrigenis, I. D.
- 2006 'Hobbes's Thucydides', *Journal of Military Ethics* 5.4, 303–16.

Figueira, T. and Nagy, G.
- 1985 (eds) *Theognis of Megara: Poetry and the polis*, Baltimore.

Finglass, P. J.
- 2007 (ed.) *Sophocles:* Electra, Cambridge.
- 2009 'The ending of Sophocles' *Oedipus Rex*', *Philologus* 153, 42–62.

Finkelberg, M.
- 1997 'Oedipus' apology and Sophoclean criticism: *OC* 521 and 547', *Mnemosyne* 50, 561–76.

Fisher, N. R. E.
- 1992 *Hybris: A study in the values of honour and shame in ancient Greece*, Warminster.
- 2001 *Aeschines:* Against Timarchos, Oxford.

Foley, H. P.
- 1981 (ed.) *Reflections of Women in Antiquity*, New York.
- 1993a 'Oedipus as *pharmakos*', in Rosen and Farrell (eds) 1993, 525–38.
- 1993b 'The politics of tragic lamentation', in Sommerstein et al. (eds) 1993, 101–43. Reprinted in Foley 2001, 19–55.
- 1995 'Tragedy and democratic ideology. The case of Sophocles' *Antigone*' in B. Goff (ed.), *History, Tragedy, Theory: Dialogues on Athenian drama*, Austin, TX, 131–50.
- 2001 *Female Acts in Greek Tragedy*, Princeton.

Forsdyke, S.
- 2005 'Revelry and riot in archaic Megara: democratic disorder or ritual reversal?', *JHS* 125, 73–92.

Fortenbaugh, W. W.
- 2008 'Aristotle and Theophrastus on the emotions', in J. T. Fitzgerald (ed.), *Passions and Moral Progress in Greco-Roman Thought*, London.

Bibliography

Foucart, P.
    1899   'La Course aux flambeaux', *Rev. Phil.* 23, 112–26.
Fowler, R. L.
    1987   *The Nature of Early Greek Lyric: Three preliminary studies*, Toronto.
Fraenkel, E.
    1950   (ed.) *Aeschylus: Agamemnon*, 3 vols, Oxford.
    1957   'Die Sieben Redepaare im Thebanerdrama des Aeschylus', *SBBAW*, Phil.-hist. Kl., Heft 3, Munich.
Francis, E. D.
    1983   'Virtue, folly, and Greek etymology', in C. A. Rubino and C. W. Shelmerdine (eds), *Approaches to Homer*, Austin, TX, 74–121.
Fränkel, H.
    1946   'Man's "ephemeros" nature according to Pindar and others', *TAPA* 77, 131–45.
    1975   *Early Greek Poetry and Philosophy*, tr. M. Hadas and J. Willis, Oxford.
Frede, M.
    2011   *A Free Will: Origins of the notion in ancient thought*, Berkeley and Los Angeles.
Friis Johansen, H.
    1962   'Sophocles 1939–1959', *Lustrum* 7, 94–288, 335–42.
Fritz, K. von
    1962   *Antike und moderne Tragödie*, Berlin.
    2007   'The character of Eteocles in Aeschylus' *Seven against Thebes*', in Lloyd (ed.) 2007, 141–73 (orig. 'Die Gestalt des Eteokles in Aeschylus' *Sieben gegen Theben*', in von Fritz 1962, 193–226).
Fuqua, C.
    1978   'The world of myth in Euripides' *Orestes*', *Traditio* 34, 1–28.
Gagarin, M.
    1978   'Self-defense in Athenian homicide law', *GRBS* 1, 111–20.
    1997   (ed.) *Antiphon: The speeches*. Cambridge.
Galeotti Papi, D.
    1987   'Victors and sufferers in Euripides' *Helen*', *AJP* 108, 27–40.
Gantz, T. N.
    1993   *Early Greek Myth: A guide to literary and artistic sources*, Baltimore.
Garvie, A. F.
    1986   (ed.) *Aeschylus:* Choephori, Oxford.
    1998   (ed.) *Sophocles:* Ajax, Warminster.
    2005   *The Plays of Sophocles*, London.
    2009   (ed.) *Aeschylus:* Persae, Oxford.
Gaskin, R.
    1990   'Do Homeric heroes make real decisions?', *CQ* 40, 1–15.
Gellie, G. H.
    1972   *Sophocles: A reading*, Melbourne.
Giannini, P.
    1982   '"Qualcuno" e "nessuno" in Pind. *P.* 8.95', *QUUC* 11, 69–76.
Giannopoulou, V.
    1999–2000 'Divine agency and *tyche* in Euripides' *Ion*: ambiguity and shifting perspectives', in Cropp, Lee, and Sansone (eds) 1999–2000, 257–71.

Gill, C.
　1990　'The articulation of the self in Euripides' *Hippolytus*', in Powell (ed.) 1990, 76–107.
　1995　*Greek Thought, Greece & Rome* New Surveys in the Classics, 25, Oxford.
　1996　*Personality in Greek Epic, Tragedy, and Philosophy: The self in dialogue*, Oxford.
Girard, R.
　1977　*Violence and the Sacred*, Eng. trans. Baltimore (Fr. orig. 1972).
　1986　*The Scapegoat*, Eng. trans. Baltimore (Fr. orig. 1982).
Goebel, A.
　1877　'Homerische Etymologien', *Philologus* 36, 32–63.
Goheen, R. F.
　1951　*The Imagery of Sophocles' Antigone: A study of poetic language and structure*, Princeton.
Goldhill, S.
　1986　*Reading Greek Tragedy*, Cambridge.
　2012　*Sophocles and the Language of Tragedy*, Cambridge.
Goldhill, S. and Hall, E.
　2009　(eds) *Sophocles and the Greek Tragic Tradition*, Cambridge.
Gomme, A. W., Andrewes, A., Dover, K. J.
　1970　(eds) *A Historical Commentary on Thucydides* vol. iv, Books v. 25 – vii, Oxford.
Goodwin, W. W.
　1897　*Syntax of the Moods and Tenses of the Greek Verb*, 8th revised and enlarged edn, revised and corrected, London.
Gould, J.
　1978a　'Dramatic character and "human intelligibility" in Greek tragedy', *PCPS* 204, 43–67.
　1978b　Review of Dover 1974, *CR* 28, 285–7.
Graffunder, P. L. W.
　1885　'Über den Ausgang des *König Oedipus* von Sophokles', *NJbb* 132, 389–408.
Greene, W. C.
　1944　*Moira: Fate, good, and evil in Greek thought*, Cambridge MA.
Gregory, J.
　1991　*Euripides and the Instruction of the Athenians*, Ann Arbor MI.
　1995　'The encounter at the crossroads in Sophocles' *Oedipus Tyrannus*', *JHS* 115, 141–6.
　2005　(ed.) *A Companion to Greek Tragedy*, Oxford.
Griffin, J.
　1999　(ed.) *Sophocles Revisited: Essays presented to Sir Hugh Lloyd-Jones*, Oxford.
Griffith, M.
　1977　*The Authenticity of* Prometheus Bound, Cambridge.
　1983　*Aeschylus:* Prometheus Bound, Cambridge.
　1990　'Contest and contradiction in early Greek poetry', in M. Griffith and D. Mastronarde (eds), *The Cabinet of the Muses*, Atlanta GA, 185–207.
　1999　(ed.) *Sophocles:* Antigone, Cambridge.
　2001　'Antigone and her sister(s): embodying women in Greek tragedy', in A. Lardinois and L. McClure (eds), *Making Silence Speak: Women's voices in Greek literature and society*, Princeton, 117–36.

Bibliography

    2005   'The subject of desire in Sophocles' *Antigone*', in V. Pedrick and S. M. Oberhelman (eds), *The Soul of Tragedy: Essays on Athenian drama*, Chicago, 91–135.

    2009   'Greek lyric and the place of humans in the world', in Budelmann (ed.) 2009, 72–94.

Griffith, R. D.
    1993   'Oedipus *pharmakos*? Alleged scapegoating in Sophocles' *Oedipus the King*', *Phoenix* 47, 95–114.
    1996   *The Theatre of Apollo: Divine justice and Sophocles'* Oedipus the King, Montreal and Kingston.

Grimsley, R.
    1972   (ed.) *J. J. Rousseau:* Du contrat social, Oxford.

Gruber, J.
    1988   Review of Doyle 1983, *Gnomon* 60, 385–9.

Guthrie, S.
    1993   *Faces in the Clouds: A new theory of religion*, Oxford.

Guthrie, W. K. C.
    1962   *A History of Greek Philosophy*, vol. i, Cambridge.

Hall, E.
    1993   'Political and cosmic turbulence in Euripides' *Orestes*', in Sommerstein et al. (eds) 1993, 263–85.
    2010   *Greek Tragedy: Suffering under the sun*, Oxford.

Halliwell, S.
    1986   'Where three roads meet: a neglected detail in the *Oedipus Tyrannus*', *JHS* 106, 187–90.
    1990   'Human limits and the religion of Greek tragedy', *Journal of Literature and Theology* 4, 169–80.

Harris, E. M.
    1992   Review of MacDowell 1990, *CP* 87, 71–80.
    2010   'Is Oedipus guilty? Sophocles and Athenian homicide law', in E. M. Harris, D. F. Leão, and P. J. Rhodes (eds), *Law and Drama in Ancient Greece*, London, 122–46.

Harris, W. V.
    2001   *Restraining Rage: The ideology of anger control in classical antiquity*, Cambridge, MA.

Harrison, A. R. W.
    1971   *The Law of Athens*, Vol. ii: *Procedure*, Cambridge.

Havers, W.
    1910   'Zur Semasiologie von griechischer ἄτη', *Zeitschrift für vergleichende Sprachforschung* 43, 225–44.

Heath, M. F.
    1987   *The Poetics of Greek Tragedy*, London.
    Forthcoming
          'Aristotle on the best kind of tragic plot: *Poetics* 13–14'.

Hecht, A. and Bacon, H. H.
    1974   *Aeschylus:* Seven against Thebes, Oxford.

Hegel, G. W. F.
    1807/1986 *Phänomenologie des Geistes*, edited by E. Moldenhauer and K. M. Michel, Frankfurt/Main.
    1817/1986 *Vorlesungen über die Geschichte der Philosophie*, edited by E. Moldenhauer and K. M. Michel, Frankfurt/Main.

Henrichs, A.
    1995 'Why should I dance? Choral self-referentiality in Greek tragedy', *Arion* 3rd series, 3, 56–111.
    1996 *'Warum soll ich denn tanzen?' Dionysisches im Chor der griechischen Tragödie*, Stuttgart and Leipzig.

Hester, D. A.
    1971 'Sophocles the unphilosophical. A study in the *Antigone*', *Mnemosyne* 24, 11–59.
    1977 'Oedipus and Jonah', *PCPS* 23, 32–61.
    1984 'The banishment of Oedipus', *Antichthon* 18, 13–23.

Heubeck, A.
    1989 'Books ix–xii', in A. Heubeck and A. Hoekstra, *A Commentary on Homer's Odyssey*. Volume ii: Books ix–xvi, Oxford.

Hiltbrunner, O.
    1950 *Wiederholungs-und Motivtechnik bei Aischylos*, Berne.

Hobbes, T.
    1651 *Leviathan, or the Matter, Forme & Power of a Common-Wealth Ecclesiasticall and Civill*, London.

Hoey, T. F.
    1970 'Inversion in the *Antigone*: a note', *Arion* 9, 337–45.

Holt, P.
    1999 '*Polis* and tragedy in the *Antigone*', *Mnemosyne* 52, 658–90.

Hose, M.
    2006 '*Vaticinium post eventum* and the position of the *Supplices* in the Danaid trilogy', in Cairns and Liapis (eds) 2006, 91–8.

Huffman, C.
    1993 *Philolaos of Croton*, Cambridge.
    2008 'The *Pythagorean precepts* of Aristoxenos: crucial evidence for Pythagorean moral philosophy', *CQ* 58, 104–19.

Humphreys, S. C.
    1993 *The Family, Women, and Death: Comparative studies*, 2nd edn, Ann Arbor MI.

Hutchinson, G. O.
    1985 (ed.) *Aeschylus:* Septem contra Thebas, Oxford.
    1999 'Sophocles and time', in Griffin (ed.) 1999, 47–72.

Iakob, D.
    1994 Πινδάρου Πυθιόνικοι, Heraklion.

Jaeger, W.
    1947 *The Theology of the Early Greek Philosophers*, Oxford.

Janko, R.
    1992 (ed.) *The* Iliad: *A commentary* vol. iv, Books 13–16, Cambridge.
    2001 'The Derveni papyrus', *CP* 96, 1–32.

Bibliography

Jebb, R. C.
    1893   (ed.) *Sophocles. The plays and fragments.* Part I: *The* Oedipus Tyrannus, 3rd edn, Cambridge.
    1900a   (ed.) *Sophocles, The plays and fragments.* Part II: *The* Oedipus Coloneus, 3rd edn, Cambridge.
    1900b   (ed.) *Sophocles. The plays and fragments.* Part III: *The* Antigone, 3rd edn, Cambridge.
    2004   (ed.) *Sophocles:* Oedipus Coloneus, = Jebb 1900a, reprinted with a new introduction by R. Rehm, Bristol.

Jennings, V. and Katsaros, A.
    2007   (eds) *The World of Ion of Chios*, Leiden.

Johnston, S. I.
    2008   *Ancient Greek Divination*, Malden MA.

Jordan, B.
    1979   *Servants of the Gods: A study in the religion, history, and literature of fifth-century Athens*, Hypomnemata 55, Göttingen.

Jouanna, J.
    2007   *Sophocle*, Paris.

Judet de la Combe, P.
    2001   *L' Agamemnon d' Eschyle. Commentaire des dialogues*, 2 vols, Lille.

Kahn, C. H.
    1979   *The Art and Thought of Heraclitus*, Cambridge.
    2001   *Pythagoras and the Pythagoreans*, Indianapolis.

Kaimio, M.
    1985   'Theme of victory in Aeschylus' *Oresteia* and *Agamemnon* 314–16', *Arctos* Suppl. 2, 79–97.

Kamerbeek, J. C.
    1948   'Sophocle et Héraclite (quelques observations sur leurs rapports)', in *Studia Varia Carolo Guliemo Vollgraff a discipulis oblata,* Amsterdam, 84–98.
    1978   (ed.) *The Plays of Sophocles.* Part iii: *The* Antigone, Leiden.

Kane, R.
    2005a   *A Contemporary Introduction to Free Will*, Oxford.
    2005b   (ed.) *The Oxford Handbook of Free Will*, Oxford.

Kannicht, R.
    1969   (ed.) *Euripides:* Helena (2 vols), Heidelberg.
    2004   (ed.) *Tragicorum Graecorum Fragmenta*, vol. v, *Euripides*, 2 vols [= *TrGF* 5], Göttingen.

Käppel, L.
    1989   'Das Theater von Epidauros', *JDAI* 194, 83–106.

Kelly, A.
    2009   *Sophocles:* Oedipus at Colonus, London.

Kierkegaard, S.
    1843/1962   *Enten-Eller. Andet Halvbind, Samlede Værker* iii, Copenhagen.
    1987   *Either/Or* ii, ed. and trans. H. V. Hong and E. H. Hong, Princeton.

Kirkwood, G. M.
    1958   *A Study of Sophoclean Drama*, Ithaca NY.
    1969   'Eteocles Oiakostrophos', *Phoenix* 23, 9–25.

1991 'Order and disorder in Sophocles' *Antigone*', *ICS* 16, 101–9.
Kitto, H. D. F.
  1956 *Form and Meaning in Drama: A study of six Greek plays and of Hamlet*, London.
  1966 *Poiesis: Structure and thought*, Berkeley.
Kitzinger, R.
  1993 'What do you know? The end of Oedipus', in Rosen and Farrell (eds) 1993, 539–56.
  2008 *The Choruses of Sophokles'* Antigone *and* Philoktetes*: A dance of words*, Leiden.
Knox, B. M. W.
  1955 'Sophocles' *Oedipus*', in C. Brooks (ed.), *Tragic Themes in Western Literature*, New Haven, 7–29. Reprinted in Knox 1979, 96–111.
  1957 *Oedipus at Thebes: Sophocles' tragic hero and his time*, New Haven CT.
  1964 *The Heroic Temper: Studies in Sophoclean tragedy*, Berkeley and Los Angeles.
  1972 Review of Burnett 1971, *CP* 67, 270–9. Reprinted in Knox 1979, 329–42.
  1977 'The *Medea* of Euripides', *YCS* 25, 193–225. Reprinted in Knox 1979, 295–322 and in E. Segal (ed.) 1983, 272–93, 440–44.
  1979 *Word and Action: Essays on the ancient theatre*, Baltimore.
  1980 'Sophocles *Oedipus Tyrannus* 446: Exit Oedipus?' *GRBS* 21, 321–32.
  1983 'Sophocles and the *polis*' in J. de Romilly (ed.), *Sophocle*, Vandoeuvres-Geneva, 1–37.
Konstan, D. and Rutter, K.
  2003 (eds) *Envy, Spite, and Jealousy: The rivalrous emotions in ancient Greece*, Edinburgh.
Kovacs, D.
  1987 'Treading the circle warily: literary criticism and the text of Euripides', *TAPA* 117, 257–70.
  1993 'Zeus in Euripides' *Medea*', *AJP* 114, 45–70.
  1994 *Euripides:* Cyclops, Alcestis, Medea, Loeb Classical Library 12, Cambridge MA.
  1996 *Euripidea Altera*, Leiden.
  2003 *Euripidea Tertia*, Leiden.
  2009a 'Do we have the end of Sophocles' *Oedipus Tyrannus*?', *JHS* 129, 53–70.
  2009b 'The role of Apollo in *Oedipus Tyrannus*', in Cousland and Hume (eds) 2009, 357–68.
Krause, J.
  1976 ΑΛΛΟΤΕ ΑΛΛΟΣ: *Zum Motiv des Schicksalswechsels in der griechischen Dichtung bis Euripides*, Munich.
Kyriakou, P.
  2006 *A Commentary on Euripides'* Iphigenia in Tauris, Berlin.
Lada-Richards I.
  1999 *Initiating Dionysos*, Oxford.
Lakoff, G.
  1987 *Women, Fire, and Dangerous Things: What categories reveal about the mind*, Chicago.
Lakoff, G. and Johnson, M.
  1980 *Metaphors We Live By*, Chicago.
Lanni, A.
  2006 *Law and Justice in the Courts of Classical Athens*. Cambridge.

Bibliography

Laplace, P. S.
    1902   *A Philosophical Essay on Probabilities*, Eng. trans., New York (Fr. orig. 1814).

Latte, K.
    1968   'Schuld und Sünde in der griechischen Religion', *Kleine Schriften zu Religion, Recht, Literatur und Sprache der Griechen und Römer*, Munich, 3–35 (orig. 1920/1).

Lattimore, R.
    1947   'The first elegy of Solon', *AJP* 68, 161–79.

Lawrence, S. E.
    2007   'Eteocles' moral awareness in Aeschylus' *Seven*', *CW* 100, 335–53.
    2008   'Apollo and his purpose in Sophocles' *Oedipus Tyrannus*', *Studia Humaniora Tartuensia* 9. A. 2 (http://www.ut.ee/klassik/sht/).

Leaf, W.
    1900–2   (ed.) *The* Iliad, 2 vols, 2nd edn, London.

Lee, K. H.
    1976   (ed.) *Euripides:* Troades, Basingstoke.

Lefèvre, E.
    1987   'Die Unfähigkeit, sich zu erkennen: Unzeitgemäße Bemerkungen zu Sophokles' *Oidipus Tyrannos*', *WJbb* 13, 37–57.

Lefkowitz, M. R.
    1989   '"Impiety" and "atheism" in Euripides' dramas', *CQ* 39, 70–82. Reprinted in Mossman (ed.) 2003, 102–21.

Lenz, L.
    1981   'Zu Aischylos' *Septem* ', *Hermes* 109, 415–39.

Lesky, A.
    1961   *Göttliche und menschliche Motivation im homerischen Epos* (SB Heidelberg 1961.4).
    1966   'Decision and responsibility in the tragedy of Aeschylus', *JHS* 86, 78–85.
    2001   'Divine and human causation in Homeric epic', in Cairns (ed.) 2001a, 170–202 (abridged translation of Lesky 1961).

Letters, F. J. H.,
    1953   *The Life and Work of Sophocles*, London.

Leurini, L.
    2000   *Ionis Chii Testimonia et Fragmenta*, 2nd edn, Amsterdam.

Levine, D. B.
    1985   'Symposium and the *polis*', in Figueira and Nagy (eds) 1985, 176–96.

Liapis, V.
    2012   *A Commentary on the* Rhesus *Attributed to Euripides*, Oxford.

Liddel, P.
    2007   *Civic Obligation and Individual Liberty in Ancient Athens*, Oxford.

Lloyd, M.
    1986   'Divine and human action in Euripides' *Ion*', *Antike und Abendland* 32, 33–45.
    1987   'Cleobis and Biton (Herodotus 1.31)', *Hermes* 115, 22–8.
    1992   *The Agon in Euripides*, Oxford.
    2005a   *Sophocles:* Electra, London.

Lloyd-Jones, H.

2005b   (ed.) *Euripides:* Andromache, 2nd edn (1st edn 1994), Warminster.
2007   (ed.) *Aeschylus*, Oxford Readings in Classical Studies, Oxford.

Lloyd-Jones, H.
1957   'Notes on Sophocles' *Antigone*', *CQ* 7, 12–27. Reprinted in Lloyd-Jones 1990, 368–87.
1962   'The guilt of Agamemnon', *CQ* 12, 187–199. Reprinted in Lloyd-Jones 1990, 283–99.
1964   'Sophocles, *Antigone* 1096–7 (and *Philoctetes* 324)', *CR* 14, 129–30. Reprinted in Lloyd-Jones 1990, 388–9.
1971   *The Justice of Zeus*, Berkeley and Los Angeles (2nd edn with unchanged pagination 1983).
1990   *Greek Epic, Lyric, and Tragedy: Academic papers*, Oxford.
1994   (ed.) *Sophocles*, vol. ii: Antigone, The Women of Trachis, Philoctetes, Oedipus at Colonus, Loeb Classical Library 21, Cambridge MA.
2002   'Curses and divine anger in early Greek epic: the Pisander scholion', *CQ* 52, 1–14. Reprinted in Lloyd-Jones 2005, 18–36.
2005   *The Further Academic Papers of Sir Hugh Lloyd-Jones*, Oxford.

Lloyd-Jones, H. and Wilson, N. G.
1990a   (eds) *Sophoclis fabulae*, Oxford.
1990b   *Sophoclea: Studies on the text of Sophocles*, Oxford.

Long, A. A.
1968   *Language and Thought in Sophocles: A study of abstract nouns and poetic technique*, London.

Long, T.
1974   'Τε καί and κοπίς in Sophocles' *Antigone* 602', *RM* 117, 213–14.

Loraux, N.
1986   'La main d'Antigone', *Mètis* 1, 165–96.

Lurje, M.
2004   *Die Suche nach der Schuld. Sophokles'* Oedipus Rex, *Aristoteles'* Poetik *und das Tragödienverständnis der Neuzeit*, Munich.

MacDowell, D. M.
1963   *Athenian Homicide Law in the Age of the Orators*, Manchester.
1990   (ed.) *Demosthenes:* Against Meidias, Oxford.

MacKay, L. A.
1962   'Antigone, Coriolanus, and Hegel', *TAPA* 93, 166–74.

Maehler, H.
1982   (ed.) *Die Lieder des Bakchylides. Erster Teil: die Siegeslieder*, Leiden.

Maitland, J.
1992   'Dynasty and family in the Athenian city state: a view from Attic tragedy', *CQ* 42, 26–40.

Manuwald, B.
1992   'Oidipus und Adrastos: Bemerkungen zur neueren Diskussion um die Schuldfrage in Sophokles' *König Oidipus*', *RM* 135, 1–43.

March, J. R.
1987   *The Creative Poet: Studies on the treatment of myth in Greek poetry*, BICS Suppl. 49, London.

Bibliography

Marcovich, M.
   1967   (ed.) *Heraclitus: Greek text with a short commentary. Editio Maior*, Merida.

Mastronarde, D. J.
   1986   'The optimistic rationalist in Euripides: Theseus, Jocasta, Teiresias', in M. Cropp, E. Fantham, S. E. Scully (eds), *Greek Tragedy and its Legacy: Essays presented to D. J. Conacher*, Calgary, 201–11.
   1988   (ed.) *Euripides:* Phoenissae, Leipzig.
   1994   (ed.) *Euripides:* Phoenissae, Cambridge.
   2002   (ed.) *Euripides:* Medea, Cambridge.
   2005   'The gods', in Gregory (ed.) 2005, 321–32.
   2010   *The Art of Euripides*, Cambridge.

McAuslan, I. & Walcot, P.
   1993   (eds) *Greek Tragedy, Greece & Rome* Studies 2, Oxford.

Meier, C.
   1993   *The Political Art of Greek Tragedy*, Eng. trans. Cambridge (Ger. orig. 1988).

Mendelsohn, D.
   2002   *Gender and the City in Euripides' Political Plays*, Oxford.

Michelini, A. N.
   1987   *Euripides and the Tragic Tradition*, Madison WI.

Mikalson, J. D.
   1991   *Honor thy Gods: Popular religion in Greek tragedy*, Chapel Hill NC.

Miller, F. D., Jr.
   1995   *Nature, Justice, and Rights in Aristotle's* Politics, Oxford.

Minadeo, R. W.
   1985   'Characterization and theme in the *Antigone*', *Arethusa* 18, 133–54.

Minar, E. L.
   1942   *Early Pythagorean Politics*, Baltimore.

Mogyoródi, E.
   1996   'Tragic freedom and fate in Sophocles' *Antigone:* notes on the role of the "ancient evils" in "the tragic"', in Silk (ed.) 1996, 358–76.

Morris, I.
   1992   *Death-Ritual and Social Structure in Classical Antiquity*, Cambridge.

Mossman, J. M.
   2003   (ed.) *Euripides*, Oxford Readings in Classical Studies, Oxford.

Müller, C. W.
   1996   'Die Thebanische Trilogie des Sophokles und ihre Aufführung im Jahre 401: Zur Frühgeschichte der antiken Sophoklesrezeption und der Überlieferung des Texts', *RM* 139, 193–224.

Müller, G.
   1956   'Der homerische Ate-Begriff und Solons Musenelegie', in *Navicula Chiloniensis: Studia philologa Felici Jacoby professori Chiloniensi emerito octogenario oblata*, Leiden.
   1961   'Überlegungen zum Chor der *Antigone*', *Hermes* 89, 398–422.
   1967   (ed.) *Sophokles:* Antigone, Heidelberg.

Musurillo, H.
   1967   *The Light and the Darkness: Studies in the dramatic poetry of Sophocles*, Leiden.

Nagy, G.
   1985   'Theognis and Megara: a poet's vision of his city', in Figueira and Nagy (eds) 1985, 22–81.
   1990   *Pindar's Homer: The lyric possession of an epic past*, Baltimore.

Nesselrath, H. G.
   1992   *Ungeschehenes Geschehen: 'Beinahe-Episoden' im griechischen und römischen Epos von Homer bis zur Spätantike*, Stuttgart.

Neuburg, M.
   1990   'How like a woman: Antigone's "inconsistency"', *CQ* 40, 54–76.
   1993   '*Ate* reconsidered', in Rosen and Farrell (eds) 1993, 491–501.

Noussia-Fantuzzi, M.
   2010   (ed.) *Solon the Athenian, the poetic fragments*, Leiden.

Nussbaum, M. C.
   1986   *The Fragility of Goodness: Luck and ethics in Greek tragedy and philosophy* (2nd edn with unchanged pagination 2001), Cambridge.

O'Brien, M. J.
   1988   'Tantalus in Euripides' *Orestes*', *RM* 131, 30–45.

O'Connor-Visser, E. A. M. E.
   1987   *Aspects of Human Sacrifice in the Tragedies of Euripides*, Amsterdam.

Olson, S. D.
   2002   (ed.) *Aristophanes:* Acharnians, Oxford.

Onians, R. B.
   1954   *The Origins of European Thought about the Body, the Mind, the Soul, the World, Time, and Fate*, 2nd edn, Cambridge.

Ormand, K.
   1999   *Exchange and the Maiden: Marriage in Sophoclean tragedy*, Austin TX.

Ostwald, M.
   1973   'Was there a concept ἄγραφος νόμος in classical Greece?' in E. N. Lee, A. P. D. Mourelatos, and R. M. Rorty (eds), *Exegesis and Argument: Studies in Greek philosophy presented to Gregory Vlastos*, Assen, 70–104.
   1986   *From Popular Sovereignty to the Sovereignty of Law: Law, society, and politics in fifth-century Athens*, Berkeley and Los Angeles.

Otto, W. F.
   1937   'Ursprung der Tragödie. Aischylos', Vortrag vor der Königsberger Gelehrten Gesellschaft, Januar 1937. Repr. in Otto 1962, 162–9.
   1962   *Das Wort der Antike*, ed. K. von Fritz, Berlin.

Oudemans, T. C. W. and Lardinois, A. P. M. H.
   1987   *Tragic Ambiguity: Anthropology, philosophy, and Sophocles'* Antigone, Leiden.

Padel, R.
   1992   *In and Out of the Mind: Greek images of the tragic self*, Princeton.
   1995   *Whom Gods Destroy: Elements of Greek and tragic madness*, Princeton.

Paley, F. A.
   1870   (ed.) *The Tragedies of Aeschylus*, 3rd edn, London.

Papademetriou, J.-T. A.
   1997   *Aesop as an Archetypal Hero*, Athens.

Papadopoulou, T.
   2005   Heracles *and Euripidean Tragedy*, Cambridge.

Bibliography

Parker, R.
- 1983 *Miasma: Pollution and purification in early Greek religion*, Oxford.
- 1996 *Athenian Religion: A history*, Oxford.
- 1997 'Gods cruel and kind: tragic and civic theology', in Pelling (ed.) 1997, 143–60.
- 1999 'Through a glass darkly: Sophocles and the divine', in Griffin (ed.) 1999, 11–30.

Patzer, H.
- 1958 'Die dramatische Handlung der *Sieben gegen Theben*', *HSCP* 63, 97–119.

Pearson, A. C.
- 1917 (ed.) *The Fragments of Sophocles, edited with additional notes from the papers of Sir R. C. Jebb and W. G. Headlam*, 3 vols, Cambridge.
- 1928 'Sophocles' *Antigone*', *CQ* 22, 179–90.

Pelling, C.
- 1997 (ed.) *Greek Tragedy and the Historian*, Oxford.
- 2005 'Pity in Plutarch', in R. H. Sternberg (ed.), *Pity and Power in Ancient Athens*, Cambridge, 277–312.

Pender, E. E.
- 2000 *Images of Persons Unseen: Plato's metaphors for the gods and the soul*, International Plato Studies 11, St Augustin.

Peradotto, J.
- 1992 'The ideological mapping of *Oedipus Tyrannus*', *TAPA* 122, 1–15.

Perlman, S.
- 1964 'Quotations from poetry in Attic orators of the fourth century BC', *AJP* 85, 155–72.

Pink, T.
- 2004 *Free Will: A very short introduction*, Oxford.

Pinker, S.
- 2007 *The Stuff of Thought: Language as a window into human nature*, London.

Podlecki, A. J.
- 1966 'Creon and Herodotus', *TAPA* 97, 359–71.

Pöggeler, O.
- 2004 *Schicksal und Geschichte: Antigone im Spiegel der Deutungen und Gestaltungen seit Hegel und Hölderlin*, Munich.

Pohlenz, M.
- 1954 *Die griechische Tragödie*, 2 vols, 2nd edn, Göttingen.

Porter, J.
- 1994 *Studies in Euripides' Orestes*, Leiden.
- 2009 'The setting of the prologue of Sophocles' *Antigone*', in Cousland and Hume (eds) 2009, 335–43.

Porzig, W.
- 1926 *Die attische Tragödie des Aischylos*, Leipzig.

Powell, A.
- 1990 (ed.) *Euripides, Women, and Sexuality*, London.

Raven, J. E.
- 1948 *Pythagoreans and Eleatics*, Cambridge.

Regenbogen, O.
- 1933 'Bemerkungen zu den *Sieben* des Aischylos', *Hermes* 68, 51–69.

Rehm, R.
- 1994 *Marriage to Death: The conflation of wedding and funeral rituals in Greek tragedy*, Princeton.
- 2003 *Radical Theatre: Greek tragedy and the modern world*, London.
- 2004 '*Oedipus Coloneus*: Introduction', in Jebb 2004, 31–56.

Reinhardt, K.
- 1949 *Aischylos als Regisseur und Theologe*, Berne.
- 1957 'Die Sinneskrise bei Euripides', *Die Neue Rundschau* 68, 615–46. Reprinted in *Tradition und Geist* (Göttingen, 1960), 227–56, and in E.-R. Schwinge (ed.), *Euripides* (Wege der Forschung 89; Darmstadt, 1968), 507–42; Eng. trans. in Mossman (ed.) 2003, 16–46.
- 1961 *Die* Ilias *und ihr Dichter*, Göttingen.
- 1979 *Sophocles*, Eng. trans. H. Harvey and D. Harvey, Oxford (3rd Ger. edn 1947).

Richardson, N. J.
- 1974 (ed.) *The Homeric Hymn to Demeter*, Oxford.

Rickert, G.
- 1989 Hekōn *and* Akōn *in Early Greek Thought*, Atlanta.

Riedweg, C.
- 2005 *Pythagoras: His life, teaching, and influence*, London.

Ritchie, W.
- 1964 *The Authenticity of the* Rhesus *of Euripides*, Cambridge.

Robbins, F. E.
- 1916 'The lot oracle at Delphi', *CP* 11, 278–92.

Robert, C.
- 1915 *Oidipus: Geschichte eines poetischen Stoffs im griechischen Altertum*, 2 vols, Berlin.

Roberts, D. H.
- 1987 'Parting words: final lines in Sophocles and Euripides', *CQ* 37, 51–64.

Robinson, T. M.
- 1987 (ed.) *Heraclitus: Fragments*, *Phoenix* Suppl. 22, Toronto.

Rohdich, H.
- 1968 *Die euripideische Tragödie*, Heidelberg.
- 1980 *Antigone: Beitrag zu einer Theorie des sophokleischen Helden*, Bibliothek der klassischen Altertumswissenschaften, n.F., 2. Reihe, 69, Heidelberg.

Romilly, J. de
- 1971 *La loi dans la pensée grecque des origines à Aristote*, Paris.

Rosen, R. and Farrell, J.
- 1993 (eds) *Nomodeiktes: Greek studies in honour of Martin Ostwald*, Ann Arbor MI.

Rosenfield, K. H.
- 2003 *Antigone – de Sophocle à Hölderlin: la logique du 'rhythme'*, Paris.

Rosenmeyer, T. G.
- 1952 'The wrath of Oedipus', *Phoenix* 6, 92–112.
- 1982 *The Art of Aeschylus*, Berkeley and Los Angeles.
- 1993 'Elusory voices: thoughts about the Sophoclean chorus', in Rosen and Farrell (eds) 1993, 557–71.

Bibliography

Rosivach, V. J.
   1979   'The two worlds of the *Antigone*', *ICS* 4, 16–26.
   1983   'On Creon, Antigone and not burying the dead', *RM* 126, 193–211.
   1987   'Execution by stoning in Athens', *Cl.Ant.* 6, 232–48.

Rösler, W.
   1970   *Reflexe vorsokratischen Denkens bei Aischylos*, Meisenheim am Glan.
   1993   'Die Frage der Echtheit von Sophokles, *Antigone* 904–20 und die politische Funktion der attischen Tragödie', in Sommerstein et al. (eds), 1993, 81–99.

Rousseau, J. J.
   1762   *Du contrat social: ou principes du droit politique*, Amsterdam.

Ryan, A
   1996   'Hobbes' political philosophy', in T. Sorell (ed.), *The Cambridge Companion to Hobbes*, Cambridge, 208–45.

Saïd, S.
   1978   *La faute tragique*, Paris.

Sandin, P.
   2003   *Aeschylus' Supplices: Introduction and commentary on vv. 1–523*, Gothenburg.

Sarkissian, H., Chatterjee, A., De Brigard, F., Knobe, J., Nichols, S., and Sirker, S.
   2010   'Is belief in free will a cultural universal?', *Mind & Language* 25, 346–58.

Schadewaldt, W.
   1961   'Die Wappnung des Eteokles. Zu Aischylos' *Sieben gegen Theben*', in *Eranion* (Festschrift H. Hommel), Tübingen, 105–16.
   1970   'Der *König Oedipus* des Sophokles in neuer Deutung', in *Hellas und Hesperien*, 2 vols, 2nd edn, Zurich and Stuttgart, i. 466–76 (orig. 1956).

Schein, S.
   1975   'Mythical illusion and historical reality in Euripides' *Orestes*', *WS* 9, 49–66.
   1997   'Divinity and moral agency in Sophoclean tragedy', in A. B. Lloyd (ed.), *What is a God? Studies in the nature of Greek divinity*, London and Swansea.

Schmid, W. and Stählin, O.
   1929–34 *Geschichte der griechischen Literatur* (part 1), vols 1–2, Handbuch der Altertumswissenschaft 7. 1–2, Munich.

Schmitt, A.
   1988   'Menschliches Fehlen und tragisches Scheitern: Zur Handlungsmotivation im Sophokleischen *König Ödipus*', *RM* 131, 8–30.
   1990   *Selbständigkeit und Abhängigkeit menschlichen Handelns bei Homer: Hermeneutische Untersuchungen zur Psychologie Homers*, Abh. Mainz 1990.5, Stuttgart.

Schwyzer, E.
   1950   *Griechische Grammatik*, vol. ii, Munich.

Scodel, R.
   1982   '*Hybris* in the second stasimon of the *Oedipus Rex*', *CP* 77, 214–23.
   1984   *Sophocles*, Boston.
   1992   Review of Schmitt 1990, *AJP* 113, 621–24.

Scullion, S.
   2005   '"Saviours of the father's hearth": Olympian and chthonian in the *Oresteia*', in R. Hägg and B. Alroth (eds), *Greek Sacrificial Ritual, Olympian and Chthonian*, Stockholm, 23–36.

Seaford, R.
  1986 'Immortality, salvation, and the elements', *HSCP* 90, 1–26.
  1987 'The tragic wedding', *JHS* 107, 106–30.
  1990 'The imprisonment of women in Greek tragedy', *JHS* 110, 76–90.
  1993 'Dionysus as destroyer of the household: Homer, tragedy, and the polis', in T. H. Carpenter and C. A. Faraone (eds), *Masks of Dionysus*, Ithaca NY, 115–46.
  1994 *Reciprocity and Ritual: Homer and tragedy in the developing city-state*, Oxford.
  1998 'Tragic money', *JHS* 118, 119–39.
  2003 'Aeschylus and the unity of opposites', *JHS* 123, 141–65.
  2004 *Money and the Early Greek Mind*, Cambridge.
  2005 'Mystic light in Aeschylus' *Bassarai*', *CQ* 55, 602–6.
  2012 *Cosmology and the Polis: The social construction of space and time in the tragedies of Aeschylus*, Cambridge.
Searle, J.
  1999 *Mind, Language, and Society: Philosophy in the real world*, London.
Segal, C. P.
  1978 'Sophocles' *Antigone*: the house and the cave', *RCCM* 20, 1171–88.
  1981 *Tragedy and Civilization: An interpretation of Sophocles*, Cambridge MA.
  1986 *Interpreting Greek Tragedy: Myth, poetry, text*, Ithaca NY.
  1995 *Sophocles' Tragic World: Divinity, nature, society*, Cambridge MA.
  2001 Oedipus Tyrannus: *Tragic heroism and the limits of knowledge*, 2nd edn, Oxford.
Segal, E.
  1968 (ed.) *Euripides: A collection of critical essays*, Englewood Cliffs NJ.
  1971 'The two worlds of Euripides' *Helen*', *TAPA* 102, 553–614.
  1983 (ed.) *Oxford Readings in Greek Tragedy*, Oxford.
Seidensticker, B.
  1972 'Beziehungen zwischen den beiden Oedipusdramen des Sophokles', *Hermes* 100, 255–74.
  2003 'The chorus in Greek satyrplay', in E. Csapo and M. C. Miller (eds), *Poetry, Theory, Praxis: The social life of myth, word, and image in ancient Greece*, Oxford.
Seiler, H.
  1954 'Homerische ἀάομαι und ἄτη', in *Sprachgeschichte und Wortbedeutung* (Festschrift A. Debrunner), Berne, 409–17.
  1955 s.v. ἀάω in Snell and Mette (eds) 1955, 9–12.
Sewell-Rutter, N. J.
  2007 *Guilt by Descent: Moral inheritance and decision making in Greek tragedy*, Oxford.
Silk, M. S.
  1985 'Heracles and Greek tragedy', *G&R* 32, 1–22. Reprinted in McAuslan & Walcot (eds) 1993, 116–37.
  1996 (ed.) *Tragedy and the Tragic: Greek theatre and beyond*, Oxford.
Smyth, H. W.
  1956 *Greek Grammar* (revised by G. M. Messing; 1st edn 1920), Cambridge MA.
Snell, B.
  1928 *Aischylos und das Handeln im Drama*, Berlin.

Bibliography

1930 'Das Bewußtsein von eigenen Entscheidungen im frühen Griechentum', *Philologus* 85, 141–58.
1953 *The Discovery of the Mind*, Eng. trans., Cambridge MA.

Snell, B. and Mette, H. J.
1955 (eds) *Lexikon des frühgriechischen Epos. Lieferung 1:* α-ἀεικής, Göttingen.

Solmsen, F.
1937 'The Erinys in Aischylos' *Septem*', *TAPA* 48, 197–211.

Sommer, I.
1998 *Zivile Rechte für Antigone: zu den rechtstheoretischen Implikationen der Theorie von Luce Irigaray*, Baden-Baden.

Sommerstein, A. H.
1978 *Aristophanes:* The Knights, Peace, The Birds, The Assembly Women, Wealth, Harmondsworth.
1980 'Notes on the *Oresteia*', *BICS* 27, 63–75.
1989 (ed.) *Aeschylus:* Eumenides, Cambridge.
2002 'Comic elements in tragic language: the case of Aeschylus' *Oresteia*', in A. Willi (ed.), *The Language of Greek Comedy*, Oxford, 151–68.
2006 (ed.) *Troilus*, in A. H. Sommerstein, D. G. Fitzpatrick and T. H. Talboy, *Sophocles: Selected fragmentary plays*, volume I, Oxford.
2008 (ed.) *Aeschylus,* 3 vols., Loeb Classical Library 145–6, 505, Cambridge MA.
2010a *Aeschylean Tragedy,* 2nd edn, London.
2010b *The Tangled Ways of Zeus and Other Studies in and around Greek Tragedy*, Oxford.
2011a 'Sophocles and the guilt of Oedipus', *CFC:egi* 21, 93–107.
2011b 'Once more the end of Sophocles' *Oedipus Tyrannus*', *JHS* 131, 85–93.

Sommerstein, A. H., Halliwell, S., Henderson, J., and Zimmermann, B.
1993 (eds) *Tragedy, Comedy and the Polis*, Bari.

Sorum, C. E.
1981–2 'The family in Sophocles' *Antigone* and *Electra*', *CW* 75, 201–11.

Sourvinou-Inwood, C.
1988 'Priestess in the text: *Theano Menonos Agrylethen*', *G&R* 35, 29–39.
1989a 'Assumptions and the creation of meaning: reading Sophocles' *Antigone*', *JHS* 109, 134–48.
1989b 'The fourth stasimon of Sophocles' *Antigone*', *BICS* 36, 141–65.
1990 'What is polis religion?', in O. Murray & S. Price (eds), *The Greek City: From Homer to Alexander*, Oxford, 295–322.
1997 'Tragedy and religion: constructs and readings', in Pelling (ed.) 1997, 161–86.

Spira, A.
1960 *Untersuchungen zum Deus ex machina bei Sophokles und Euripides*, Kallmünz.

Steidle, W.
1968 *Studien zum antiken Drama*, Munich.

Steiner, G.
1983 'Variations sur Créon', in J. de Romilly (ed.), *Sophocle*, Vandoeuvres-Geneva, 77–104.
1984 *Antigones: The Antigone myth in western literature, art, and thought*, Oxford.

Stinton, T. C. W.
1975 '*Hamartia* in Aristotle and Greek tragedy', *CQ* 25, 221–54. Reprinted in id., *Collected Papers on Greek Tragedy* (Oxford, 1990), 143–85.

Storey, I. C.
  2008 *Euripides:* Suppliant Women, London.
Swift, L. A.
  2010 *The Hidden Chorus: Echoes of genre in tragic lyric*, Oxford.
Taplin, O.
  1977 *The Stagecraft of Aeschylus*, Oxford.
  1978 *Greek Tragedy in Action*, London.
Thalmann, W. G.
  1978 *Dramatic Art in Aeschylus'* Seven against Thebes, New Haven CT.
Theunissen, M.
  2002 *Pindar: Menschenlos und Wende der Zeit*, Munich.
Thomson, G.
  1996 (ed.) *The Oresteia of Aeschylus*, 2 vols, 2nd edn, Amsterdam and Prague.
Torrance, I.
  2007 *Aeschylus:* Seven against Thebes, London.
Torrance, R. M.
  1965 'Sophocles: some bearings', *HSCP* 69, 269–327.
Trapp, M.
  1996 'Tragedy and the fragility of moral reasoning: response to Foley', in Silk (ed.) 1996, 74–84.
Tuck, R.
  1996 (ed.) *Thomas Hobbes: Leviathan. Revised Student Edition*, Cambridge.
Tyrrell, W. B. and Bennett, L. J.
  1998 *Recapturing Sophocles'* Antigone, Lanham MD.
Ugolini, G.
  1987 'L'Edipo tragico sofocleo e il problema del conoscere', *Philologus* 131, 19–31.
  2000 *Sofocle e Atene: vita politica e attività teatrale nella Grecia classica*, Rome.
Usener, H.
  1903 'Dreiheit', *RM* 58, 1–47, 161–208, 321–62.
Utzinger, C.
  2003 *Periphades Aner: Untersuchungen zum ersten Stasimon der Sophokleischen "Antigone" und zu den antiken Kulturentstehungstheorien*, Hypomnemata 146, Göttingen.
Vellacott, P. H.
  1964 'The Guilt of Oedipus', *G&R* 11, 137–48.
Vernant, J. P.
  1990a 'Intimations of the will in Greek tragedy', in Vernant and Vidal-Naquet 1990, 49–84 (orig. 1972).
  1990b 'Oedipus without the complex', in Vernant and Vidal-Naquet 1990, 85–111 (orig. 1967).
  1990c 'Ambiguity and reversal: on the enigmatic structure of *Oedipus Rex*', in Vernant and Vidal-Naquet 1990, 113–40 (orig. 1970).
Vernant, J.-P. and Vidal-Naquet, P.
  1990 *Myth and Tragedy in Ancient Greece*, Eng. trans., 2nd edn, New York.
Verrall, A. W.
  1887 *The* Seven against Thebes *of Aeschylus*, London.

Bibliography

Versnel, H. S.
   2011   *Coping with the Gods: Wayward readings in Greek theology*, Leiden.

Vian, F.
   1963   *Les origines de Thèbes: Cadmus et les Spartes*, Paris.

Wecklein, N.
   1902   (ed.) *Aischylos:* Sieben gegen Theben, Leipzig.

Wehrli, F.
   1931   *Lathe biōsas: Studien zur ältesten Ethik bei den Griechen*, Berlin.

West, M. L.
   1974   *Studies in Greek Elegy and Iambus*, Berlin.
   1978   (ed.) *Hesiod:* Works and Days, Oxford.
   1979   'The Prometheus trilogy', *JHS* 99, 130–48. Reprinted with a postscript in Lloyd (ed.) 2007, 359–96.
   1987   (ed.) *Euripides:* Orestes, Warminster.
   1990a *Aeschyli tragoediae cum incerti poetae Prometheo*, Stuttgart.
   1990b *Studies in Aeschylus*, Stuttgart.
   1998   *Iambi et Elegi Graeci*, 2nd edn, Oxford.
   1999   'Ancestral curses', in Griffin (ed.) 1999, 31–45.

West, S.
   1999   'Sophocles' *Antigone* and Herodotus book three', in Griffin (ed.) 1999, 109–36.

Whitman, C. H.
   1951   *Sophocles: A study of heroic humanism*, Cambridge MA.

Wilamowitz-Moellendorff, U. von
   1899   'Exkurse zum *Oedipus* des Sophokles', *Hermes* 34, 55–80.
   1914   *Aischylos: Interpretationen*, Berlin.

Wilkins, J.
   1990   'The state and the individual: Euripides' plays of voluntary self-sacrifice', in Powell (ed.) 1990, 177–94.

Willi, A.
   2010   'Register variation', in E. J. Bakker (ed.), *A Companion to the Ancient Greek Language*, Malden MA, 297–310.

Williams, B.
   1993   *Shame and Necessity*, Berkeley and Los Angeles.
   2006   'Tertullian's paradox', in *Philosophy as a Humanistic Discipline*, Princeton, 3–21 (orig. 1955).

Willink, C. W.
   1986   (ed.) *Euripides:* Orestes, Oxford.

Wilson, P. J.
   1996   'Tragic rhetoric: the use of tragedy and the tragic in the fourth century', in Silk (ed.) 1996, 310–31.

Winnington-Ingram, R. P.
   1965   'Tragedy and Greek archaic thought', in M. J. Anderson (ed.), *Classical Drama and its Influence: Essays presented to H. D. F. Kitto*, London, 29–50.
   1979   'Sophoclea', *BICS* 26, 1–12.
   1980   *Sophocles: An interpretation*, Cambridge.
   1983   *Studies in Aeschylus*, Cambridge.

Wolff, C.
- 1968 '*Orestes*', in E. Segal (ed.) 1968, 132–49. Reprinted in E. Segal (ed.) 1983, 340–56.

Wolff, E.
- 1958 'Die Entscheidung des Eteokles in den *Sieben gegen Theben*', *HSCP* 63, 89–95.

Wright, M.
- 2005 *Euripides' Escape-Tragedies: A study of* Helen, Andromeda, *and* Iphigenia among the Taurians, Oxford.

Wyatt, W. F.
- 1982 'Homeric *ate*', *AJP* 103, 247–76.

Yamagata, N.
- 1994 *Homeric Morality*, Leiden.
- 2005 'Disaster revisited: Ate and the Litai in Homer's *Iliad*', in E. J. Stafford and J. E. Herrin (eds), *Personification in the Ancient World*, Aldershot.

Yoshitake, S.
- 1994 'Disgrace, grief and other ills: Herakles' rejection of suicide', *JHS* 114, 135–53.

Yunis, H.
- 1988 *A New Creed: Fundamental religious beliefs in the Athenian polis and Euripidean drama*, Göttingen.
- 2000 'Politics as literature: Demosthenes and the burden of the Athenian past', *Arion* 8, 97–118.

Zeitlin, F. I.
- 1965 'The motive of the corrupted sacrifice in Aeschylus' *Oresteia*', *TAPA* 96, 463–508.
- 1990 'Thebes: theater of self and society in Athenian drama', in J. J. Winkler and F. I. Zeitlin (eds), *Nothing to Do with Dionysos? Athenian drama in its social context*, Princeton, 130–67.

Zellner, H. M.
- 1997 'Antigone and the wife of Intaphrenes', *CW* 90, 315–18.

Zuntz, G.
- 1955 *The Political Plays of Euripides*, Manchester.

SUBJECT INDEX

Aeschylus, Theban trilogy of 40–1
Aesop 193–4
agency xii–xiii, xviii, xxxvii, 3, 11, 29, 71–2, 121–6, 134, 137, 139–43, 145–7, 219
Allan, W. 219
allegory xxiii–xxv, xxix–xxx, 4
alternation xxxiii–xxxv, xxxviii–xl, 104, 149, 152–5, 158–9, 177, 194, 196, 205–26
ambiguity ix, xxvii, 21, 46, 61–2, 85–6
amēchania 205
Anaxagoras 26
anthropomorphism xxxvii, 142–3
Antiphon 184
apatē xii–xiii, xv–xvi, xx, xxii, xxvi, 6–7
apeiron see limit/unlimited
Apollo, role in S. *OT* 128–42, 145, 147, 154, 157–8, 160
'archaic chain' (of wealth, *koros*, *hybris*, and *atē*) xvi, xxvi, xxxi, 152–3
aretē 25, 42, 206, 211
Aristophanes 207
Aristotle xl–xli, 1, 17–18, 22–4, 27, 32, 48, 92–3, 101, 149, 178, 194–5
atasthaliē 154
atē xi–xxxv, 1–15, 31–2, 98, 104, 139, 143, 182, 200, 205

Baltussen, H. 31
Benardete, S. 108
Bloom, A. 81
Budelmann, F. 101
burial xix–xxi, 82, 89–90, 95–7, 101, 106–8, 210
Burian, P. 213, 218
Burnett, A. P. 207, 219

Cairns, D. L. 208, 213
Campbell, L. 43
Catch-22 12
causation 56, 123–5, 137–42, 144, 157
chance *see tychē*
chess 137–8
Chiron 196
chorus, roles and functions of 127, 130–1, 151–3, 156, 175–7
chthonic and Olympian 30, 32–3, 95, 108
cosmology xxxvi–xxxvii, 17–18, 20, 22, 24–8, 30–2, 33
Croesus 2, 139, 193
Cropp, M. 217

curse xv, 10, 39–40, 45–7, 53, 58, 61–4, 66, 69–70, 91, 95, 174–5, 185, 201, 220
(*see also* family, cycles of suffering in)

daimōn xiii, xxxviii, 13, 32, 55, 62, 66, 132–5, 143–5, 148, 152, 193, 196, 202, 220
Dale, A. M. 218–19
Dawe, R. D. xviii, xxiii
Dawson, C. M. 46
decision xxxviii, 22, 39, 44, 50–1, 54–9, 62–3, 65, 67, 69–73, 217
Democritus 2–3
determinism 122–7
deus ex machina 217, 222
dikē, *dikaiosynē see* justice
Dionysus xxviii–xxix, 18, 195, 201–2
divine intervention xii, xiv, xxiii, xxvi, xxviii–xxxiv, xxxvi–xxxvii, xxxix, 3, 5, 11, 119–71 *passim*, 174–8, 186, 207–8, 210, 215, 217, 219, 221–2
Dodds, E. R. 95, 120–7, 134, 138, 147, 159, 178, 205
Doyle, R. E. 8
Draco 183–4
duty 66, 70

elpis see hope
Empedocles xxxvi–xxxvii
envy *see phthonos*
ephemerality xl, 194, 206, 221–2
epinician 156
Erinys, Erinyes xii, xiv–xvi, xxi–xxii, xxiv–xxv, xxviii, xxxviii, 6–9, 22, 30, 32–3, 45, 53, 58, 62–3, 66, 94–5, 143, 220
erōs xxxii, xxxvi–xxxvii, 7–8, 211
ethnicity 20
etymology xii, xvi, xx, xxvi, xxviii–xxix
euboulia xxix–xxx, xxxii
eudaimonia xii, xxiii, xxvi, xxviii, xxx–xxxi, xxxiii–xxxv, xxxvii, xxxviii–xli, 2, 148–9, 152–5, 177, 193–4, 196, 205, 212, 217
(*see also* alternation; *olbos*)
Eustathius xxv
exchange xxii, xxxv–xxxvi
exemplarity xxiv, xl, 9, 104, 148–9, 153–5, 158, 177, 201

family, cycles of suffering in xiv–xv, xxiv, 73, 81, 85–6, 90–5, 103–7, 174, 220–2

Subject Index

fate xxxvii–xxxviii, 61–4, 68–70, 122–8, 134, 139, 141–8, 150–4, 157–8, 176–7, 183, 205–7
fiction 141–2
fortune, mutability of *see* alternation
Fraenkel, E. 7
Fränkel, H. 206, 211, 223
free will 62, 70, 72, 119, 122–8, 134, 136–42, 146–7
Furies *see* Erinys, Erinyes

Garvie, A. F. 9
gender xix, 20, 22–4, 26–7, 83, 102
genealogy of concepts 7–8
Gill, C. xi, 71–2
Goldhill, S. ix
Gomme, A. W. 123–4
Griffith, M. 206
Griffith, R. D. 159
guilt 72–3
    archaic conception of 173–91 *passim*
    inherited *see* family, cycles of suffering in;
    see also curse
Guthrie, W. K. C. 23

Hall, E. ix
hamartia xviii, xxii–xxv, xxxii, 121, 178
happiness *see eudaimonia*
harmonia 21, 24–7, 29, 33
Harris, E. M. 182
health and disease xxii, xxiv–xxv, xxviii–xxix, 3, 25, 28–30, 103, 194, 198–9
Heath, M. F. 90, 208
Hegel, G. W. F. 72
hekōn/akōn antithesis 70, 122, 134–6, 138, 154, 183–4
Heraclitus xxxvii, 17–23, 26–7, 150, 176
Hermes, sphere of influence of 55, 60–1
hero-cult 185–6
hero-worshippers 222 (*see also* pietism)
Herodotus 2, 19, 139, 195, 205, 221
Hobbes, T. 84, 99, 101, 110
Holt, P. 89, 108
Homer
    and Aeschylus 21–2, 43–5, 58–9, 64–6
    and Sophocles xxiii–xxv, 200
    atē in xi–xii, xvii–xviii, xx, xxv, 2–4, 10, 12
    human vulnerability in xxxviii–xxxix, xl–xli, 194
honour *see timē*
hope xii, xiv, xx, xxii–xxiii, xxxi, xl, 206, 221
Hutchinson, G. O. 66
hybris xiii, xvi, xix, xxvi, xxxi, xxxix, 1–2, 4, 6, 28–9, 91–2, 95, 97, 151–2, 154, 156, 158, 176, 213–14

incest 85–6
Ion of Chios 18, 25–6, 30–1

irony xvi, xix, xxi, xxxii–xxxv, 8, 11, 63, 82, 95–6, 101–3, 127, 130–6, 145, 150–1, 156, 176

justice xvii–xviii, xxvii, xxxix, 20, 27–30, 32, 82, 84, 89, 98–9, 152, 175, 183–4, 210
    divine xxviii, xxxiii–xxxiv, xxxix, 7–8, 11, 69, 94–5, 109, 121–2, 126, 145, 147, 149, 152–4, 156–9, 173–9, 186–7, 206, 208, 213–14, 216–17, 220–1

kairos 48, 52, 67
Kamerbeek, J. C. 83–4
Kannicht, R. 218
Kant, I. 66, 71–2
kerdos xxi–xxii, xxv, xxix, xxxi–xxxiii, xxxv, 2, 9, 97
Keres 145
Kierkegaard, S. 69–72
Knox, B. M. W. 83, 222
koros xvi, xxvi, 28–30
kosmos 25–7, 69, 100–1, 159–60
Kovacs, D. 137–8, 150, 210, 216–17
kratos 25–6

Labdacids xiv–xv, xvii, xix, xxxiii, 41, 81–3, 85–6, 90–5, 103–4, 106–7
Laplace's Demon 123, 138
law xiv, xvi–xvii, xix, xxi, xxx, xxxiii, xxxv, xxxvii, 61, 84, 88–91, 95–6, 98–9, 102, 104, 107–10, 125, 131, 147–8, 151–3, 182–4, 187
    Athenian 1, 27–8, 33, 89, 147–8, 183–4
    Cretan 2
Lefèvre, E. 151, 159
Lefkowitz, M. 208
limit/unlimited 23–31
Litai xviii, xxiii–xxv, 3
Lloyd-Jones, H. 94, 159, 207–8
lot, selection by 58–62
Lurje, M. 150, 175

MacKay, L. A. 95
mania 134–5 (*see also* mind, disturbances of)
manteia see prophecy
Manuwald, B. 139
March, J. R. 186
marriage xxxvi, 23, 40, 85, 98, 103, 105–6, 145–7, 181–3, 197, 211, 214
Mastronarde, D. M. 208, 210
mathematics 24, 154 (*see also* number)
measure *see metron*
Mendelsohn, D. 215–16
meson 23–5, 27–8, 30
metaphor xx, xxvi–xxvii, 19, 21–2, 28, 31, 61, 142–6, 154
metoikia 93
metron 28–9

miasma 46, 70, 90, 107, 134, 151, 181–4, 186–7
Midas 193–5, 202
mind, disturbances of xi–xxxv, xxxviii, 3–5, 7, 9–11, 31–2, 47, 49, 65, 70, 93–4, 98, 103–4, 135, 139, 143, 182, 205
modernism 81, 207–8, 220
moira 33, 60, 128, 134–5, 143–5, 151–2 (*see also* fate)
money xxx–xxxii, xxxv, 28, 97
mystery-cult 18, 21

Nietzsche, F. 207
Nixon, R. M. 100
number 17, 23–6, 32

oikos 82–3, 85, 99, 102, 104–7
olbos xxvi, xxxi, xxxiii, 193, 212–14, 220
old age 41–4, 47–9, 53, 65, 193–4, 198–201
omens xxxv, 21, 157
oracles xiii, 11, 40, 58, 63–4, 66–70, 91, 129–31, 133–4, 137, 139, 144–5, 147, 150–3, 156, 174–5, 183, 186 (*see also* prophecy)
opposites xxxvi–xxxvii, 17–38 *passim*, 195
over-determination xxxviii, 56, 69, 136–42, 177, 179, 183
paradox 19, 194, 199
Parker, R. C. T. 221
Peitho/*peithō* 7–8, 26–7
Peradotto, J. J. 141, 160
peras see limit/unlimited
personification xiv, xx, xxiii–xxiv, 7–9, 33, 61, 142–6 (*see also* metaphor)
pessimism xxix, xxxvii, 149, 158, 208, 218
pharmakos 158
philia xxxvii, 85, 95, 98
Philolaus 24–6, 31
phthonos 156–7, 198–9, 217, 221–2
pietism 208, 219, 222
Pinker, S. 125
pity xl, 83, 149–50, 152, 158, 180, 187, 209–10
Plato 1, 17–18, 24–7, 29, 48, 89–90, 107–8, 181, 196, 210
plot xxxvii–xl, 129, 133–4, 147
polis 24, 27–8, 30, 33, 81–4, 87–8, 90–104, 107–9, 199
politics ix, xxix, xxxv–xxxvi, 5, 17, 24, 26–9, 33, 82–5, 87–8, 92–3, 96–103, 109, 206, 210, 215–16, 220
pollution *see miasma*
presocratic philosophy xxxvi
  and Aeschylus 17–38 *passim*
  and Sophocles xxxvi–xxxvii
presumption, human 155, 157–9, 213–14
progressivism x–xi, 142, 173, 178, 187
Prometheus Bound, authenticity of 5, 12
prophecy xxix–xxx, xxxiv–xxxv, 66–7, 69, 127–8, 131–6, 139, 157–8, 186, 209

Protagoras xix
Proteus 196
puns 151
Pythagoras, Pythagoreanism 17–18, 22–33

rationalism xi, xxvii, xxix, 210
Rehm, R. 173
religion
  and morality 151–3, 156
  and the *polis* 109
responsibility xi, xiii–xiv, xxxiii–xxxiv, xxxvii, 62, 70–3, 105–6, 122–7, 140–2, 147, 173–4, 178–87
retaliation 176, 181, 183–5, 187
revenge 17, 20–2, 30–3, 82, 197
ritual 21, 26, 32–3, 82–4, 88, 90, 105, 152, 158, 182
Roberts, D. 216
Rosenmeyer, T. G. ix

sacrifice xxxvi, 21, 33, 39, 105, 145, 157, 181, 211–12, 215
satyr-play 40, 196
scales, image of xxxv–xxxvi, 21–2, 31, 60–1
Schein, S. 221–2
Schlegel, A. W. and K. W. F. 207
Schmitt, A. 71, 151, 158–9
Seaford, R. xxxvi–xxxvii, xlii, 211
Searle, J. 124–5
self-sacrifice 211, 215
Semnai Theai 201
Sewell-Rutter, N. J. 72–3, 174
ship of state, image of xxvii, xxx, xxxv, 93, 104
Silenus 193–6, 201–2
Silk, M. 217
Snell, B. 71–2
Socrates 72, 173, 181, 193, 196, 207
Solon xvii, xxxix, 2, 28–30, 82, 84, 94–5, 193, 199, 205, 207, 214, 216, 218–19, 221
sophists xix, 17, 205, 207
sōtēria xix–xx, xxii, xxx–xxxi, xxxv, 102, 107
Sphinx 42, 90–1, 156, 177
staging 44, 47–62, 133
Stallmach, J. xi
stasis 103
Stoicism 66, 123
storm, imagery of xxvi–xxvii, 200, 220
suicide 86, 103–6, 134, 136, 185, 211, 217
sympathy *see* pity

Taplin, O. 44, 57
Thalmann, W. G. 63–4
Theognis 2, 5, 92, 97, 194–5, 199, 214–15
Theunissen, M. xliii
Thucydides 207
timē 44, 65, 67, 96–7, 152, 156
torch-race 19–20

255

Subject Index

treason 89
tychē xxviii, xxxiii–xxxv, 3, 25–6, 55, 58, 61, 104, 124, 129, 133–4, 138, 145, 156, 207, 209, 212–13
tyranny 29, 82, 84, 88, 96–7, 99, 101, 103, 107–8, 151–2, 176

vase-painting 195
Vernant, J.-P. ix, xxix
vicissitude *see* alternation
violence 147, 176–7 (*see also* revenge)
viper 92
voluntary/involuntary *see hekōn/akōn* antithesis

wealth xii–xiv, xvi, xx–xxi, xxxi, xxxiii, xxxv, 2–3, 7, 17–18, 28–30, 196, 214
Wecklein, N. 50–1

West, M. L. 212, 221
Whitman, C. 173
Wilamowitz-Moellendorff, U. von 50–1
will 71, 124–5
Williams, B. A. O. xi, xliii, 71–2, 184, 207
Winnington-Ingram, R. P. xxxviii
wrestling 31–3

youth xiii, 41–4, 47–9, 65, 194, 196, 198–9
Yunis, H. 87

Zeus
 in Aeschylus 27, 30–3, 60–1
 in E. *Med.* 216–17
 Sōtēr 32–3
Zuntz, G. 213, 215

INDEX LOCORUM

AESCHYLUS
Agamemnon
145	21
156–9	21
163–6	21
167–78	31
222–3	xxviii
312–14	19
355–61	6
381–4	7
636–7	29
643	10
730–1	6
735–6	6
750–2	29
819	xxvi, 6
854	19
1001–3	29–30
1005–13	30
1124	10
1192	7
1268	6
1331	30
1387	32
1431–6	8
1476	32
1487	212
1559–62	20
1566	xiv
1572	32

Choephori
244–5	32
309–13	20
313	10
339	31–2
466–8	xxviii
470	21
578	32
594–8	9
829–30	9
835–6	9
1065–76	32

Epigoni (R)
fr. 55	32

Eumenides
517–37	27–9

696–9	30
736–41	22
758–60	33

Persians
93–100	xiii
97–101	7
724–5	xiii
739–42	xiii
1007	7

[*Prometheus Bound*]
746	12
886	12

Seven against Thebes
1–4	48, 52
8–9	44
10–20	41–2
35	44
69–72	45–6, 53
74–7	45
271–9	48
282–6	55
287	49–50
312–16	6, 10, 11
407–8	50
448	50
472–3	50
505	50
508–11	55, 60
553	50
601	5
621	50
653–7	46–7
672	50
686–8	6, 10, 11
689–91	62
702	65
720–91	10, 95
727–33	61
745–9	63, 91, 188 n. 6
785–91	63
1001	6, 10, 11

Suppliants
24–6	32
104–11	6–7, 10
444	10

257

Index Locorum

ALCAEUS (L–P)
fr. 70. 10–13   5

ANACREON (*PMG*)
395   194, 199

ANAXIMANDER (DK)
A 9   xxxvi

ARCHILOCHUS (W)
128. 4–7   206
130   206

ARISTOPHANES
Clouds
1321–1453   181

Peace
364–6   60
1332–3   85

ARISTOTLE
De Caelo
268a10   24

Eudemus (Gigon)
fr. 65   194, 202 n. 7

Metaphysics
986a   22

Nicomachean Ethics
1100a4–9   xl
1101a6–13   xl

Politics
1253a27–9   93
1287a8–18   101
1302b25–31   101
1453a7–17   178

ARISTOXENUS (Wehrli)
fr. 23   23
fr. 35   29

BACCHYLIDES,
Epinician Odes
5. 50–175   149
5. 155–62   194–5

CERTAMEN HOMERI ET HESIODI
74–9   195

DEMOCRITUS (DK)
B 213   2–3

DEMOSTHENES
8. 34   210
19. 246–7   87

DIODORUS SICULUS
4. 4. 3   195

EMPEDOCLES (DK)
B 17. 24   xxxvi

EURIPIDES
Alcestis
91   12

Andromache
519–22   213

Bacchae
1348   208

Hecuba
342–78   211
1138–44   213

Helen
38–41   219
711–21   218

Heracles
168–9   213

Heraclidae
608–18   212, 222
862–6   212–13
928–40   213
972–80   215, 217

Hippolytus
120   208

Medea
807   217
1415–19   216

Orestes
449–53   222
971–81   220–1

Peleus (Kannicht)
fr. 617a   212

Phoenissae
21–3   188n. 7

[*Rhesus*]
332   218, 221
443–57   221
582–4   221

258

Suppliants
1–11	209
34	209
95–7	209
194–249	209–10
331	209, 218, 221
549–57	209–10
734–9	209
747	209
949	209
1060–3	211

Trojan Women
612–13	214
723	213
884–8	208

HERACLITUS (DK)
B 10	26
B 33	84
B 50	26
B 119	xxxviii, 176

HERODOTUS
1. 30	193
1. 32	2, 221
3. 40–3	217
8. 138. 2	195

HESIOD
Theogony
26	196

Works and Days
230–1	4–5

HOMER
Iliad
1. 117	199
2. 394–7	200
3. 164–5	179, 190 n. 28
4. 365–400	53
5. 891	199
6. 161–99	58
8. 472–6	139
8. 517–28	43–4
9. 47	95
9. 501	xviii, xxiv
9. 504–12	xxiii, xxv
15. 618–22	200
16. 88–96	139
16. 684–91	139–40
17. 446	194
18. 117–21	143–4
19. 87–8	143, 179, 190 n. 28
22. 297–305	65
24. 209–12	143
24. 524–34	149, 153

Odyssey
1. 32–43	xxxviii, 154
18. 130–7	194, 206
20. 67	46

IBYCUS (*PMG/PMGF*)
282a. 8–9	5

ION OF CHIOS (DK)
B 1	25

MENANDER
Dis Exapaton (Sandbach)
fr. 4	194

MIMNERMUS (W)
2. 3–5	198, 199
5. 4–5	194, 199

OVID
Fasti
3. 285–311	196

PHILOLAUS (DK)
B 1	25
B 4	25
B 6	25, 26

PINDAR
fragments (M)
157	195–6

Olympian Odes
1. 55–63	5

Pythian Odes
2. 21–41	4
3. 20–7	4
8. 95–7	149, 194

PLATO
Laws
873a–c	89–90
909b–c	90

Meno
76b	210

Philebus
25d–26c	25, 29

Protagoras
322b	108

Index Locorum

Symposium
216c–e   196

Timaeus
31b–c   24–5

PLUTARCH
Moralia
388ab   23
833a   89
834a   89

Life of Phocion
37. 2   89

SAPPHO (L–P)
fr. 198   8

SEMONIDES (W)
1. 1–7   2–6

SIMONIDES
lyric fragments (*PMG*)
575   8

elegiac fragments (W)
20. 5–8   198–9

SOLON (W)
4c. 3   28
4. 5–6   28
5. 6   28
6   28
13. 25–32   94–5
13. 63–70   xxxix, 205, 214, 218
16   28
37. 9–10   28

SOPHOCLES
Ajax
552–9   199
764–7   156
1185–90   11

Antigone
4   xiv
9–10   85
16   83
17   xiv
18   83
36   90
37–8   85
49–60   xiv–xv, 86
59–60   84
60   83
61–2   102
63   84
67   84
67–8   xvi, 93
73–6   85
79   84
99   xvi, 93
100–5   83
118–19   89
175–7   xix, 93
178–90   87, 93, 98
184–6   xix–xx, xxii, xxx
189–90   xxx
199–202   89, 90, 96
208–11   98
211–14   96
218–22   xxxi, 96
278–9   96, 108
304–14   xx–xxi, xxxi, 97, 103
354–6   xxvii
379–80   xv
381–3   xvi, 93
396   101
423–8   86
460–70   xxxii
471–2   xv–xvi, xxvii, 91–2
480–5   xvi, xxi, 91
485   xv
486–9   95
508–10   102
521   108
531–3   xxi, xxv, 92
561–4   xvi, 93
583–625   xii, xiv–xvi, xix–xx, xxv–xxvi, xxxiii, xxxvii, 93–5, 200
622–5   xiii
658–9   95
660   101
663–7   xvii, 98
666–7   84, 100
668–76   100
677   101
697   92
730   101
734–41   97–9, 102
750–2   103
773   93, 181
793–4   xxxvii
824–32   93
834–7   92
850–2   93
853–6   xvii
856–67   xv, 86
868   93
889   181
890   93
901   101
907   84
925–8   xviii, xxiv

929–30	xxvii	*Oedipus Tyrannus*	
1015	xxii, 103	8	177
1023–7	xxiv	14–21	42–3
1029–30	106	16	155
1039–44	95–6	31–9	156
1056	103	33–4	177
1074–6	xxiv–xxv	40	177
1091–4	xxii	46	177
1096–7	xxviii, 104	80–1	129
1103–4	xxii–xxiii, xxv, xxix–xxx	96–8	129–30
1113–14	xxx, 104, 107	103–11	130
1155–71	xxxiii–xxxv	216–18	155
1158–60	xxxiv, 104	263	145
1175–7	104–5	266	136
1202–4	156	278–81	130
1206–14	xxxv	372–7	127–8, 144, 154
1219–43	103, 106	393–8	156
1257–60	xxiii, 104	441–2	145, 156
1263–4	105	454–6	128
1272–4	xxviii	496	197
1301–5	105–6	498–506	127
1315	105	711–14	174
1319–20	106	711–22	131
1337–8	xxxvii	713	145
1347–53	xxx	724–38	132
		776–7	145
Electra		810–13	176, 178
935–6	11	828–9	132
1298–9	12	845	133
		863	145
Oedipus at Colonus		872	131
84–105	186	873	176
112	196	882–910	131
139	196	883–96	175
258–74	141, 180–1, 185	887	145
394	186	903–10	151
431–44	179	911–23	133, 145
525–6	141, 181–2	977–8	134
545–8	141, 181–2	1076	145
664–5	186	1080–1	134, 145
668–719	201	1184–5	148
960–99	141	1186–92	154
969–77	182–3	1193–6	143, 177
992–6	184	1196–1200	177
997–9	183	1202–4	177
1132–5	182	1213–15	145, 154
1211–23	196–7, 199, 201	1227–31	134, 136
1223–38	197–9, 200, 201	1258–61	132–3
1224–7	193	1283–5	11
1239–48	199–200, 201	1299–1302	134, 144–5
1276–7	201	1311	145
1383–96	185	1327–37	135–6, 177–8
1565–7	186	1391–1408	145–6
1586	201	1414–15	141
1720–1	201	1458	145
		1478–9	166 n. 69
		1524–30	177

261

Index Locorum

Trachiniae
1	196
144–7	198
727–30	185
1264–78	67–8

THEOGNIS
43–52	97
402–6	xii
425–8	194–5
541–2	92
631–2	5
731–42	95

THUCYDIDES
1. 138. 6	89
2. 60. 2–4	88
6. 42	58–9

Tragicorum Graecorum fragmenta adespota
455	xii